Biblical Ethics

Bi

Unders   the culture of death

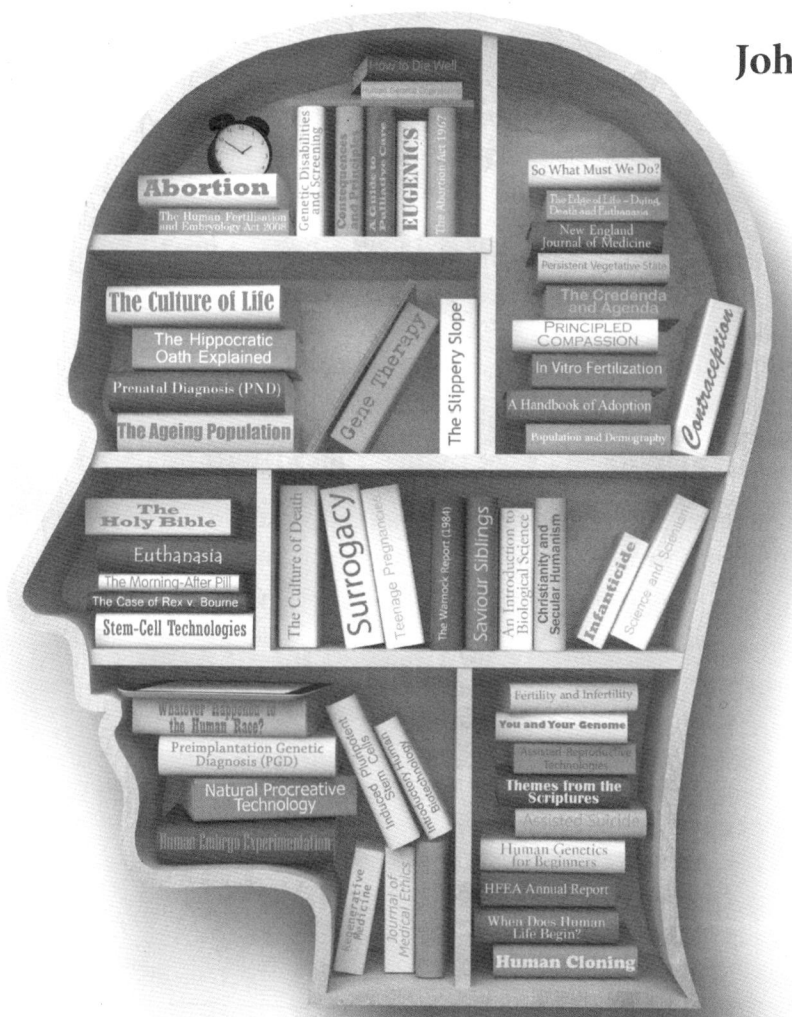

John R Ling

DayOne

Revised & Updated

© Day One Publications 2014

First published as *Responding to the Culture of Death*, 2001.
Revised and updated.

All Scripture quotations are taken from The New International Version.©1973, 1978, 1984, International Bible Society. Published by Hodder and Stoughton.

British Library Cataloguing in Publication Data available

ISBN 978-1-84625-427-7

All rights reserved

No part of this publication may be reproduced, or stored in a retrieval system, or transmitted, in any form or by any means, mechanical, electronic, photocopying, recording or otherwise, without the prior permission of Day One Publications.

Printed by Orchard Press Cheltenham Ltd

For Esther, Rachel, Naomi, Mia,
Tiana, Joshua, Gwen and Caleb

ENDORSEMENTS

Thoroughly biblical, highly readable, concise yet remarkably comprehensive—a heartfelt call for all Christians to engage with bioethics. I hope many will both read it and respond to it.
> **–Dr Trevor Stammers, Programme Director, Bioethics and Medical Law, St Mary's University, London**

This revised and expanded edition of Dr Ling's still concise but broad-ranging book on life issues is excellent. It is important for thinking Christians to keep abreast of the vital ethical issues that it covers so clearly. We give thanks to God for such an informative and challenging book.
> **–Gary Brady, Pastor of Childs Hill Baptist Church, London**

While medical advances have brought innumerable blessings to people in the last fifty years, they have also spawned a dizzying world of questions about life and death. John Ling's *Bioethical Issues* is a welcome help to navigate these dangerous waters, offering a map of current medical options, and the compass of wisdom to discern what is right.
> **–Dr Joel R. Beeke, President of Puritan Reformed Theological Seminary, Grand Rapids, Michigan**

This is a wonderful resource. In the complex and fast-moving arena of medical science, John Ling explains the ethical issues, sets out the biblical principles and points us towards an appropriate response. We honour God by defending and cherishing human life, not only within our own families and church fellowships, but also in our nation as an expression of our love for our neighbours.
> **–Bill James, Pastor of Emmanuel Evangelical Church, Leamington Spa**

CONTENTS

ACKNOWLEDGEMENTS	14
QUOTATIONS	15
HOW I CAME TO RESPOND	18
1. INTRODUCTION	23
1.1 THE ORIGINS OF THE CULTURE OF LIFE	23
1.2 THE ORIGINS OF THE CULTURE OF DEATH	24
1.3 THE CULTURE OF DEATH ON YOUR DOORSTEP	27
1.4 THE TRUE CREDENDA AND AGENDA	29
2. THEMES FROM THE SCRIPTURES	31
2.1 HUMAN LIFE IS UNIQUE AND SPECIAL	32
2.2 HUMAN LIFE BEGINS AT CONCEPTION	36
2.3 HUMAN LIFE REQUIRES STEWARDSHIP	44
2.4 HUMAN LIFE ENDS IN NATURAL DEATH	46
2.5 HUMAN LIFE IS NOT TO BE TAKEN	48
2.6 HUMAN LIFE NEEDS SPECIAL CARE	50
2.7 A LITTLE, BUT IMPORTANT, ADDENDUM	53
2.8 THEMES FROM THE SCRIPTURES: IN CONCLUSION	55
3. SOME OF THE PRIMARY ISSUES	57
3.1 FACTS AND FIGURES, STATISTICS AND DATA	58
3.2 ABORTION	58
3.2.1 ABORTION AND TWO FACTS	59
3.2.2 ABORTION IN PRACTICE	61

Contents

3.2.3 ABORTION AND MORNING-AFTER PILLS — 63

3.2.4 ABORTION UNREGULATED, UNLAWFUL AND UNDERCOVER? — 64

3.2.5 ABORTION AND MENTAL HEALTH — 69

3.2.6 OTHER EFFECTS OF ABORTION — 71

3.2.7 ABORTION AND FOUR RESERVATIONS — 74

3.2.8 ABORTION PERSONALLY — 77

3.2.9 ABORTION IN THE FUTURE — 78

3.2.10 ABORTION: IN CONCLUSION — 81

3.3 IN VITRO FERTILIZATION (IVF) — 82

3.3.1 IVF AND INFERTILITY — 82

3.3.2 IVF AND THE WARNOCK REPORT — 83

3.3.3 IVF IN PRACTICE — 84

3.3.4 IVF AND BIOETHICAL DILEMMAS — 86

3.3.5 IVF AND HEALTH RISKS — 90

3.3.6 IVF AND FATHERHOOD — 92

3.3.7 IVF ALTERNATIVES — 93

3.3.8 IVF REJECTED—WHAT IS LEFT? — 95

3.3.9 IVF IN THE FUTURE — 96

3.3.10 IVF: IN CONCLUSION — 98

3.4 SURROGACY — 100

3.4.1 WHAT IS SURROGACY? — 100

3.4.2 SURROGACY QUESTIONED — 101

3.4.3 SURROGACY ASSESSED — 102

Contents

3.4.4 SURROGACY AND THE WARNOCK REPORT — **103**

3.4.5 MODERN-DAY SURROGACY ARRANGEMENTS — **104**

3.4.6 SURROGACY IN THE FUTURE — **106**

3.4.7 SURROGACY: IN CONCLUSION — **106**

3.5 HUMAN EMBRYO EXPERIMENTATION — **107**

3.5.1 HUMAN EMBRYO EXPERIMENTATION AND THE WARNOCK REPORT — **108**

3.5.2 HUMAN EMBRYO EXPERIMENTATION IN PRACTICE — **110**

3.5.3 HUMAN EMBRYO EXPERIMENTATION IN THE FUTURE — **113**

3.5.4 HUMAN EMBRYO EXPERIMENTATION: IN CONCLUSION — **114**

3.6 HUMAN CLONING — **115**

3.6.1 CLONING TECHNIQUES — **115**

3.6.2 CLONING PURPOSES — **116**

3.6.3. HUMAN CLONING HYPE AND HOAX — **118**

3.6.4 HUMAN CLONING IN THE FUTURE — **119**

3.6.5 HUMAN CLONING: IN CONCLUSION — **119**

3.7 STEM-CELL TECHNOLOGIES — **121**

3.7.1 STEM CELLS AND REGENERATIVE MEDICINE — **121**

3.7.2 STEM CELLS AND BIOETHICS — **122**

3.7.3 STEM-CELL TREATMENTS: A SHORT HISTORY — **122**

3.7.4 INDUCED PLURIPOTENT STEM (IPS) CELLS — **123**

3.7.5 STEM-CELL TREATMENTS, BAD — **125**

3.7.6 STEM-CELL TREATMENTS, GOOD — **126**

Contents

3.7.7 EMBRYONIC STEM-CELL TREATMENTS	127
3.7.8 STEM-CELL TECHNOLOGIES IN THE FUTURE	129
3.7.9 STEM-CELL TECHNOLOGIES: IN CONCLUSION	131
3.8 HUMAN GENETIC ENGINEERING	132
3.8.1 HUMAN GENETICS: THE BASICS	132
3.8.2 HUMAN GENETIC ENGINEERING AND EUGENICS	133
3.8.3 HUMAN GENETIC ENGINEERING AND THE DESIGNER BABY	135
3.8.4 HUMAN GENETIC ENGINEERING IN THE FUTURE	136
3.8.5 HUMAN GENETIC ENGINEERING: IN CONCLUSION	137
3.9 GENETIC DISABILITIES AND SCREENING	139
3.9.1 GENETIC DISABILITIES IN GENERAL	139
3.9.2 GENETIC SCREENING IN GENERAL	141
3.9.3 SCREENING AND PRENATAL DIAGNOSIS (PND)	144
3.9.4 PREIMPLANTATION GENETIC DIAGNOSIS (PGD)	147
3.9.5 LIMITATIONS OF PND AND PGD SCREENING	149
3.9.6 SCREENING FOR SAVIOUR SIBLINGS	151
3.9.7 SO WHAT SHOULD A COUPLE DO?	155
3.9.8 GENETIC DISABILITIES AND SCREENING IN THE FUTURE	156
3.9.9 GENETIC DISABILITIES AND SCREENING: IN CONCLUSION	158
3.10 GENE THERAPY	158
3.10.1 GENE THERAPY: THE BASICS	159
3.10.2 GENE THERAPY IN PRACTICE	160

Contents

3.10.3 GENE THERAPY IN THE FUTURE	162
3.10.4 GENE THERAPY: IN CONCLUSION	162
3.11 INFANTICIDE	**163**
3.11.1 WHAT IS INFANTICIDE?	163
3.11.2 WHAT IS NOT INFANTICIDE?	164
3.11.3 INFANTICIDE: A SHORT HISTORY	164
3.11.4 INFANTICIDE LEGALLY	166
3.11.5 JUSTIFYING INFANTICIDE	166
3.11.6 PRACTISING INFANTICIDE IN THE WEST	168
3.11.7 PRACTISING INFANTICIDE IN THE EAST	170
3.11.8 THE CASE OF JOHN PEARSON	171
3.11.9 INFANTICIDE IN THE FUTURE	173
3.11.10 INFANTICIDE: IN CONCLUSION	173
3.12 EUTHANASIA AND ASSISTED SUICIDE	**174**
3.12.1 WHAT IS EUTHANASIA?	175
3.12.2. UNDERSTANDING SUICIDE	176
3.12.3 SUICIDE IN THE BIBLE	177
3.12.4 EUTHANASIA AROUND THE WORLD	178
3.12.5 EUTHANASIA IN THE NETHERLANDS	180
3.12.6 EUTHANASIA IN OREGON AND BELGIUM	182
3.12.7 EUTHANASIA IN THE UK	184
3.12.8 THE CASE OF ANTHONY BLAND	188
3.12.9 EUTHANASIA AND PALLIATIVE CARE	189

Contents

3.12.10 EUTHANASIA: WHY THE APPARENT CLAMOUR? **191**

3.12.11 EUTHANASIA AND DOCTORS **192**

3.12.12 EUTHANASIA AND LEGAL CRITERIA **194**

3.12.13 EUTHANASIA AND FAMILY BURDENS **195**

3.12.14 FEARS ASSOCIATED WITH DYING AND DEATH **197**

3.12.15 DEATH AND THE BIBLE **199**

3.12.16 EUTHANASIA AND ASSISTED SUICIDE IN THE FUTURE **200**

3.12.17 EUTHANASIA AND ASSISTED SUICIDE: IN CONCLUSION **202**

3.13 THE PRIMARY ISSUES: IN CONCLUSION **203**

4. SOME OF THE SECONDARY ISSUES **205**

4.1 THE NEED FOR ETHICAL INTEGRATION **205**

4.2 A FALSE VIEW OF BIOETHICS **205**

4.3 UNDERSTANDING THE TIMES **206**

4.4 EVERYONE HAS A WORLDVIEW **207**

4.5 SCIENCE AND SCIENTISM **208**

4.6 THE IMPORTANCE OF PRESUPPOSITIONS **209**

4.7 CONSEQUENCES AND PRINCIPLES **210**

4.8 HUMAN VALUE AND WORTH **211**

4.9 THE MEANING OF AUTONOMY **212**

4.10 THE PROBLEM OF RIGHTS **213**

4.11 THE NATURE OF DEPENDENCY **214**

4.12 CHANGING VIEWS OF THE MEDICAL PROFESSION **215**

Contents

4.13 FINANCIAL RESOURCES AND MEDICINE — 216

4.14 THE CHANGING ROLE OF THE LAW — 217

4.15 THE SLIPPERY SLOPE — 217

4.16 SECONDARY ISSUES: IN CONCLUSION — 220

5. WHEN DOES HUMAN LIFE BEGIN? — 221

5.1 THE LAZY SCHOOL — 222

5.2 THE AGNOSTIC SCHOOL — 223

5.3 THE GRADUALIST SCHOOL — 224

    5.3.1 AFTER BIRTH — 226

    5.3.2 AT BIRTH — 227

    5.3.3 VIABILITY — 228

    5.3.4 SOME PHYSIOLOGICAL INDICATOR — 228

    5.3.5 PRIMITIVE STREAK — 230

    5.3.6 IMPLANTATION — 232

5.4 THE CONCEPTION SCHOOL — 234

5.5. WHEN DOES HUMAN LIFE BEGIN? IN CONCLUSION — 236

6. HOW DID WE GET THE ABORTION ACT 1967? — 237

6.1 PRE-1967 ABORTION LAWS — 237

6.2 THE SOCIAL REVOLUTION — 240

6.3 THE ABORTION LAW REFORM ASSOCIATION — 241

6.4 CHILDREN AS A DISASTER — 241

6.5 THE LEVER OF HARD CASES — 242

6.6 THE PRACTICE OF ILLEGAL ABORTION — 242

Contents

6.7 INEQUALITIES IN MEDICAL PRACTICE	**243**
6.8 THE ROLE OF CONTRACEPTION	**243**
6.9 THE CASE OF REX V. BOURNE	**244**
6.10 THE PRO-LIFE AND MEDICAL LOBBIES	**246**
6.11 THE ABORTION ACT 1967	**246**
6.12 THE HUMAN FERTILISATION AND EMBRYOLOGY ACT 1990	**249**
6.13 THE HUMAN FERTILISATION AND EMBRYOLOGY ACT 2008	**251**
6.14 THE US SITUATION	**252**
6.15 HOW DID WE GET THE ABORTION ACT 1967? IN CONCLUSION	**256**
7. WHAT OF THE FUTURE?	**258**
7.1 THE GENERAL OUTLOOK	**259**
7.2 THE PC WORLD	**263**
7.3 SEXUAL BEHAVIOURS	**265**
7.4 GENOMIC MEDICINE	**269**
7.5 POPULATION AND DEMOGRAPHY	**272**
7.6 THE AGEING POPULATION	**275**
7.7 MISCELLANEOUS FUTURES	**276**
7.8 THE PAST GOOD, PRESENT GOOD AND FUTURE GOOD	**277**
7.9 WHAT OF THE FUTURE? IN CONCLUSION	**278**
8. SO WHAT MUST WE DO?	**280**
8.1 RESPONDING IS A HEAD-HEART-HAND AFFAIR	**280**
8.2 WE MUST PRAY	**282**
8.3 WE MUST EDUCATE	**283**

8.4 WE MUST ENGAGE	**288**
8.5 WE MUST CARE	**295**
8.6 WE MUST SUPPORT	**298**
8.7 SO WHAT MUST WE DO? IN CONCLUSION	**299**
9. RESOURCES	**301**
9.1 BOOKS	**301**
9.2 JOURNALS AND MAGAZINES	**302**
9.3 WORLDWIDE WEBSITES	**302**
9.4 FILM LIBRARY	**303**
ENDNOTES	**304**
INDEX	**308**

ACKNOWLEDGEMENTS

As the author, of course, I must take responsibility for the conception of this book, but there are many who have helped me greatly during the time of its gestation and birth.

First, there were those men who informed and shaped my early thinking about bioethical issues. Above all, there were the late Francis Schaeffer and C. Everett Koop, who, with their project *Whatever Happened to the Human Race?* opened my eyes to the issues of abortion, infanticide and euthanasia in the late 1970s. Second, there have been many friends and co-labourers within LIFE, the UK's leading pro-life charity, especially Jack and Nuala Scarisbrick, who have been, and remain, shining examples of people who respond, not only by speaking out against such horrors, but by actually doing something positive to resist and overcome them. Third, there have been those good Christian men and women who, during the 1980s and 1990s, contributed to the success and influence of Evangelicals for LIFE, a former specialist grouping within the LIFE organization. Fourth, there have been my opponents—some ranting feminists, a few thoughtful students and a handful of sceptical Christians—who have made me think harder and longer about these bioethical issues. Fifth, there has been my pastor, Geoff Thomas, who has helped keep me on the narrow road for the last forty years by the means of 2 Timothy 3:16 and personal support. Finally, there is my wife, Wendy, who has been a real helpmeet and encourager in this work; without her, this book would never have been completed.

QUOTATIONS

'... for the *foetus*, though enclosed in the womb of its mother, is already a human being (*homo*), and it is almost a monstrous crime to rob it of the life which it has not yet begun to enjoy. If it seems more horrible to kill a man in his own house than in a field, because a man's house is his place of most secure refuge, it ought surely to be deemed more atrocious to destroy a *foetus* in the womb before it has come to light.'

John Calvin, *Commentaries on the Four Last Books of Moses*, 1563

'One of the surest characteristics of a civilized society is its respect for the sanctity of human life. Indeed, life in all its forms demands our respect, but it is human life in particular whose sanctity we affirm, because it is the life of persons made in the image of God (Genesis 9:6).

'By this criterion our country has for twenty years steadily been slipping back into barbarism. For the abortion statistics are truly horrifying, and the framers of the 1967 Abortion Act never intended, or even anticipated, that it would permit the slaughter of nearly three million unborn children. No, the Act has been seriously—even flagrantly—abused. In consequence, morally sensitive people will not rest until it has been repealed and its provisions tightened. Nor can we come to terms with any legislation which tolerates experimentation on the living human embryo.

'Moreover, the sanctity of human life extends beyond the foetus to the well-being of the mother, of the family and of the child after birth. I am thankful that LIFE cherishes this holistic vision. We are anti-abortion and anti-experimentation because we are pro-life. We need to be consistent in the seeking to protect human life at every stage in its journey from the womb to the tomb.'

John R. W. Stott, *Evangelicals for LIFE* newsletter, 1987

Quotations

'... it is an appalling thought that in the present state of this country and its morals—the whole condition of society—somehow or other we are failing. When we contrast ourselves with what our forefathers did in such times, I think we should put on sackcloth and ashes and feel utterly ashamed of ourselves. We seem to be living in our "cieled houses" and to be ready to believe that everything is all right as long as everything is all right with us. The whole general situation seems to pass by default as far as we are concerned ...

'Now I think that one can justify movements and societies for the purpose of taking action of a social or a semi-political nature. Here you are not in the realm of doctrine but you are confronted by practical circumstances in which certain things need to be done as, for instance, the Clapham Sect with regard to the abolition of slavery. I do not think that there is any difficulty about justifying that.'

Martyn Lloyd-Jones, *Knowing the Times*, 1989

'Anyone who has ever seen a sonogram or has spent even an hour with a textbook on embryology knows that the emotions are not the deciding factor. In order to terminate a pregnancy, you have to still a heartbeat, switch off a developing brain, and, whatever the method, break some bones and rupture some organs.'

Christopher Hitchens, *The Nation*, 1989

'If the Church of Jesus Christ, or indeed the individual Christian, ceases to proclaim God's righteous standards and the inevitable ruin which follows upon disobedience, we are being cruel and unloving to our fellow human beings. They may look at us one day and say: "You *knew*, and you didn't warn us!" We will have been guilty of not blowing the trumpet.'

Raymond Johnston, *Caring and Campaigning*, 1990

'I preach on abortion every year, and I have for about 20 years on Sanctity of Life Sunday. I am "violently" pro-life, meaning it's a sin, and a wicked sin, to kill unborn children.'

'So in conclusion, let us not simply be a passive and apathetic people priding ourselves on our avoidance ethic. Let us live in the power of the grace that called us out of darkness into light and let us turn back to that very dark and dying culture and declare the excellencies of the One who called us, and let us be rich in good deeds, so that people might see the kind of Master we serve and give him glory on the day of visitation.'

John Piper, Alliance Defense Fund Conference
and the Sanctity of Life Sunday sermon, 2000

'If you falter in times of trouble,
   how small is your strength!
Rescue those being led away to death;
   hold back those staggering towards slaughter.
If you say, "But we knew nothing about this,"
   does not he who weighs the heart perceive it?
Does not he who guards your life know it?
      Will he not repay each person according to what he has done?'

Proverbs 24:10–12

HOW I CAME TO RESPOND

Preface to the first edition

When it comes to bioethics, I was a late starter. Somehow or other, the debate surrounding the Abortion Act 1967 passed me by, even though at the time I was a student at that hotbed of radical student politics, Leeds University. I should have known better. Instead, my bioethical wake-up call probably came in 1971, while I was studying at Pennsylvania State University. One Sunday, a preacher at the church I attended held up a copy of *Life* magazine and showed the amazing photographs, taken by Lennart Nilsson, of the developing unborn child. 'Look,' he said. 'See how wonderfully you and I have been formed in the womb. Yet some people want to kill such exquisite life.' It was my introduction to the issue of abortion, though I was largely unmoved.

Yes, I was a late starter, and I was also a late developer. *Mea culpa*. It took almost another ten years before I was again challenged by the subject of abortion. This time it was coupled with the issues of infanticide and euthanasia in the book and films associated with the *Whatever Happened to the Human Race?* project of the late Francis Schaeffer and C. Everett Koop. Now the bioethical penny dropped. Two years later, I became the founding chairman of the Aberystwyth LIFE Group, co-founder of Evangelicals for LIFE and the regional representative for Wales on the Central Committee of the LIFE organization—my life was never to be the same again!

Since that time, I have spoken on many of these bioethical issues at public, church, school, university and women's meetings throughout the UK. I have also addressed similar gatherings in Denmark, Germany, the Netherlands and Latvia. In addition, I have written numerous articles on subjects such as abortion, in vitro fertilization (IVF), genetics, surrogacy and euthanasia for a range of newspapers and magazines, both Christian and secular. I have been invited to broadcast several times on radio and television. I have also been a 'foot soldier' and organized fundraising events, mailshots, leaflet deliveries, petitions and so on. For the last ten years I have taught a course entitled 'Science and Society: Bioethical Issues' for undergraduate students at the University of Wales, Aberystwyth.

These are my pro-life credentials. Yet they are a catalogue of almost

How I came to respond

'too little, too late'. In that respect I am not unlike the majority of other evangelical Christians, but that is no excuse. Almost all of us have been bioethical 'Johnny-come-latelies'. But how could this be? How could an educated family man, who reads newspapers, watches television and has easy access to the best libraries and other information systems throughout the world, be unaware of, and unmoved by, these issues that are directly affecting many of the people around him? I do not know the answer, but I sometimes ask myself the question.

The culture of death

Twenty years ago, when I first responded, it was all so much simpler. By and large, there was then only one issue: abortion. To that continuing horror can now be added the complexities of infanticide, surrogacy, in vitro fertilization, human embryo experimentation, genetic engineering, euthanasia, prenatal screening, eugenics, contraception, gene therapy, infertility, cloning, persistent vegetative state, foetal pain and several others.

This is a sad, sad list of medical endeavour. Over each of these topics hangs the pall, or the smell, of death, because practically all of them can result, directly or indirectly, in the death of human beings. They are examples of a perverse and inhumane medicine—a medicine that has gone wrong. This is a medicine that has its roots in secular humanism, and the fruits it produces are horrible. Indeed, they constitute what I and others have called the 'culture of death', the subtitle of this book. Of course, not all medicine has become so corrupted or tainted. But make no mistake: this culture of death is the very warp and weft of much of modern medicine and it has impacted us all.

The purpose of this book

Negatives can sometimes help define the positives. This book is *not* an academic book. It does not get bogged down with scores of obscure references and tedious footnotes, but that does not mean it is a book for the unthinking. This book is *not* a theoretical book. It does not dissect the minutiae of sterile bioethical ideologies; rather it is a practical workbook. This book is *not* a comprehensive book. It does not encompass every bioethical topic, but it does deal with many of the key issues and some

Preface

crucial statements. Prominent among these are abortion and the statements of the Warnock Report (1984). So this book is a taster of bioethics, a mere primer, yet also a principled manual.

When I have presented any of these bioethical issues to Christian audiences, two particular topics tend to generate the greatest interest. One is exploring what the Bible has to say, and the other is answering the question 'So what can we do?' This primer, above all, rehearses these two topics. Apart from the chapter that surveys 'Some of the primary issues', these topics occupy the two largest chapters of the book. And that is how I always wanted it to be. It is the great Christian interlock—the exposition of Scripture followed by the application of Scripture. I am still convinced, just as I was in the late 1970s, that when a Christian understands, or 'sees', these bioethical issues in the light of Scripture, that all-important question of what we can do will inevitably be asked, and earnestly so.

Therefore the aim of this book is rather simple, and twofold. First, it is to provide Christians with the biblical basis for understanding past, current and future bioethical issues, especially within this area of human medicine. It is for those Christians who, in their heart of hearts, know that they should be against abortion, surrogacy, human embryo experimentation, euthanasia and the like, but are not quite sure why. They have never seriously thought through these issues. If that is your position, this book was certainly written with you in mind. But it is not intended as a primer only for armchair casuistry. Biblical Christianity demands that its doctrines affect our lives, and radically so. This is the book's second aim. It wants you out of your armchair and doing. It wants you to respond. It wants to change how you think, speak and act about these bioethical issues. This is what nowadays we might call 'joined-up Christianity'.

John R. Ling
Aberystwyth
January 2001

Preface to the second edition

As the Prime Minister of the United Kingdom of Great Britain and Northern Ireland Harold Wilson once famously declared, 'A week is a long time in politics.' If that is so, a dozen years is definitely a long, long, long time in bioethics. *Responding to the Culture of Death* was first published in 2001, and bioethical issues have relentlessly marched on during the intervening decade and more. Hence the need for this second edition.

The book now has a new, no-nonsense title. Yet *Bioethical Issues* is still a beginner's book, an entry-level reader, or, as the first edition called itself, a primer. However, every chapter has been extensively revised and expanded, the text has been tweaked and the paragraphs polished—the book is now twice the size of the original. Statistics have been updated. Novel issues, such as stem-cell technologies, human-admixed embryos, saviour siblings, assisted suicide and the Human Fertilisation and Embryology Act 2008 have been included. Questions for personal reflection and group discussion have also been added. In many ways, it is a new book.

But not all has changed. Amid the complex flux of bioethics, three issues have remained resolutely constant. First, the truths of Scripture—the once given—continue as they were, as they are and as they will be (2 Tim. 3:16). Second, the moral condition of men and women—fallen, sinful and lost (Rom. 3:23)—is unchanged, and so we all persist as rebels in desperate need of rescue. Third, the culture of death is still with us—indeed, it is flourishing on our doorsteps—and therefore the call to respond has become ever more urgent.

As a consequence, the twofold aims of the original book roll on. Yet understanding and responding to this culture of death, the very subtitle of this second edition, can be both wearying and wearing. At times it can seem that, in the words of 2 Corinthians 4:8–9, we are hard pressed on every side, perplexed, persecuted and even struck down. The full-orbed Christian life can certainly get tough. But listen: we are not crushed, not in despair, not abandoned and not destroyed. And though I am often alarmed by news, distraught by events and disappointed by the responses of others—particularly of Christians—I still believe that truth will finally win the day. That is gospel comfort. So I do not lose heart and I keep pressing on. Ultimately, it is not about me or you; it is about God's purposes and his glory. For that I am ever thankful.

Preface

During the past decade, since the first edition was published, I have moved up a generation; I now have eight grandchildren, maybe more by the time you read this! My new status of Grandpa has served not only to reinforce how we are all 'fearfully and wonderfully made' (Ps. 139:14), but also to galvanize my resolve to cherish, defend and protect all human life, from fertilization until natural death. So it is to this newborn generation of my family that I dedicate this second edition. May they yet live to see and enjoy the establishment of an enthusiastic culture of life. The realization of that hope depends so much upon how Christians understand and respond to these bioethical issues during the coming years.

So, how about you? Are you 'in' or are you 'out'? And if the latter, why, and on what grounds? With all due respect, you too need a bioethical epiphany. I hope this book helps bring it on.

John R. Ling
Aberystwyth
New Year's Day, 2014

CHAPTER 1

Introduction

1.1 The origins of the culture of life

It is often said that Western human medicine has a long and illustrious history—and that is true. Its origins lie in a fascinating combination of the Greek and pagan Hippocratic Oath, and the Hebraic and religious Judaeo-Christian doctrines. For well over two thousand years, these two grand pillars have underpinned medical ethics and medical practice. Their influence for good can be demonstrated by, for example, the enduring Hippocratic instruction to doctors, commonly summarized as *Primum non nocere* and translated as 'First, do no harm', plus the so-called Christian Golden Rule, spelled out in Matthew 7:12, but also much earlier—and more succinctly—as 'love your neighbour as yourself' (Lev. 19:18; Matt. 22:39). These two great maxims, together with other of the Hippocratic and Judaeo-Christian precepts, provided practitioners of medicine with a powerful restraint—things forbidden—as well as a positive motivation—things encouraged—and it was these stipulations that kept medicine largely safe and wholesome for twenty and more centuries.

Medicine was, from its earliest times, regarded as the healing art. The doctor's duty was to care for, to treat and, if possible, to cure the patient. In short, good medicine was an integral part of a culture of life. Sickness and disease were regarded as medicine's constant enemies, although the inevitability of natural death was well understood and accepted. But unnatural death was something else. Any doctor who caused it was a renegade; deliberately killing patients was never a part of proper Hippocratic–Christian medicine. Indeed, the Hippocratic Oath specifically forbade both euthanasia and abortion: 'I will give no deadly drug to any, though it be asked of me, nor will I counsel such, and especially I will not aid a woman to procure abortion.' Moreover, the Sixth Commandment, 'You shall not murder' (Exod. 20:13), kept a similarly pre-emptive check on those early medical practitioners. Such practices were regarded as bad medicine and therefore anathema to the culture of life.

For two millennia, medicine did, on the whole, uphold this culture of life. The progress of medicine has been spectacular and we have all benefited from its surgery, drugs, vaccinations and so on. The average life expectancy in Britain at the beginning of the twentieth century was a mere forty-five years for men and forty-nine for women; now it stands at seventy-eight and eighty-two, respectively. Today our lives are, in many ways, significantly easier than those of our forebears, primarily because of the application of good medicine. Its culture of life has undeniably brought health and happiness. For this we should be grateful.

1.2 The origins of the culture of death

So we may ask, where did modern medicine go wrong? How did we lose this wonderful culture of life and gain this ugly culture of death?

Medicine's own guiding principles, its own 'ethical benchmarks', its 'core values', demonstrate just how recently it became corrupted. Initially, as we have seen, the Hippocratic Oath took an uncompromising stance against abortion and euthanasia, and insisted that doctors 'First, do no harm'. During the intervening two thousand years, other oaths, or declarations, concerning medical ethics and practice echoed this Hippocratic Oath. For example, the Declaration of Geneva, adopted by the General Assembly of the World Medical Association in 1948, stated, 'I will maintain the utmost respect for human life from the time of conception, even under threat, I will not use my medical knowledge contrary to the laws of humanity.' In the same year, the General Assembly of the United Nations adopted the Universal Declaration of Human Rights, of which Article 3 declared, 'Everyone has the right to life …' These two life-affirming documents were written a mere two generations ago.

But more recent revisions have been much weaker affairs. They have reflected the great shift in society as a whole—and in bioethical issues in particular—away from this culture of life. For example, in 1947, the British Medical Association (BMA) affirmed that the Hippocratic Oath '… enjoins … the duty of caring, the greatest crime being co-operation in the destruction of life by murder, suicide and abortion'.[1] Yet by 1997, that same BMA had produced its draft revision of the Hippocratic Oath,

INTRODUCTION

which stated, 'I recognize the special value of human life but I also know that the prolongation of human life is not the only aim of health care. Where abortion is permitted, I agree that it should take place only within an ethical and legal framework.' Similarly, in 2005, the World Medical Association approved a revision of the Declaration of Geneva, which modestly asserted, 'I will maintain the utmost respect for human life; I will not use my medical knowledge contrary to the laws of humanity, even under threat.' The removal of that vital phrase 'from the time of conception' not only eliminated the implicit anti-abortion stance of the original, but it also simultaneously introduced doubt about the fundamental issue of when human life begins.

Can you see the downgrade? The bulwarks of Hippocratic–Christian medicine had been breached. For two millennia, medicine had maintained a high view of human life. Human life was described by adjectives such as special, unique, sacred, inviolable and non-expendable. Within the last sixty or so years, medicine has adopted a low view of human life. Nowadays, human life can uncontroversially be considered as cheap, insignificant, exploitable, trivial and expendable. This is the culture of death.

These changes, at the very hub of medical ethics and practice, have been alarmingly rapid. Indeed, just about all aspects of our society—be they education, welfare, science, law, economics and so on—have similarly been transformed. In truth, we have become dominated not only by some pallid liberal democracy, but also by an ever-increasingly aggressive secular humanism. This newfangled worldview can be neatly defined in the words of the ancient Greek sophist Protagoras as 'Man is the measure of all things'. Man, and not God, is now the centre of all things. Man, and not God, is now the law-giver and the judge. Ethics are now man-centred and arbitrary rather than God-centred and absolute. Practice is now pragmatic and utilitarian, rather than robust and principled. This is the prevailing mindset of our age—and in medicine it has encouraged the spread of the culture of death.

Now modern medicine operates firmly within this culture of death. For example, although abortion has been practised throughout the ages, it was never regarded as proper medicine; it was unlawful, done in secret, performed by quacks and charlatans. Nowadays, it is generally lawful, widely advertised and openly practised by untold thousands of highly

Chapter 1

qualified doctors worldwide. Abortion now occurs every day, in the hospitals of every health authority and in the private clinics of every city, wherever we live. An estimated 42 million abortions are performed each year throughout the world. This is part of the culture of death.

For the last fifty or so years, our medical services have been developing ever more sophisticated programmes of prenatal screening followed by prenatal diagnosis (PND) to search out the unborn who are disabled. Once detected, they are commonly destroyed before birth. Can you comprehend it—doctors prescribing death as a treatment? This is the modern-day practice of eugenics, and it is part of the culture of death.

When the low-weight and the 'unthrifty' are born, there is an increasing tendency to let them die. Some hospitals, under the guise, for instance, of the Groningen Protocol, make no caring efforts with babies born below a certain weight. Disabled neonates can suffer a similar regimen. After all, we already kill the disabled in utero, so why not kill the disabled newborn, those who have slipped through the PND screening net? This is infanticide, and it is part of the culture of death.

In 1990, the UK Parliament sanctioned the creation and use of human embryos for infertility treatments and for research purposes. As a result, some 250,000 embryos are created in the UK each year and at least 50 per cent of these are deliberately destroyed, 'discarded' or 'allowed to perish'. It has turned into a global pandemic, with unknown millions of human embryos either swiftly trashed or cryogenically stored and routinely destined to die frozen. This is embryo destruction on an industrial scale, and it is part of the culture of death.

Towards the end of the twentieth century, a few countries legalized some restricted forms of euthanasia. The twenty-first century has witnessed a growing number of campaigns seeking to decriminalize euthanasia generally and assisted suicide particularly. So far, these calls have been strongly resisted in the UK and elsewhere. Nevertheless, more jurisdictions are now, legally or covertly, practising euthanasia. Thousands of their most defenceless citizens—the elderly, the sick and the disabled—are being intentionally killed each year. In the UK, some hospital patients have been lawfully denied food and drink, a course of action that, we are assured, is in their 'best interests', even though it leads to their deaths. Greater longevity and its increasing medical costs will do nothing to lessen the calls for such practices. This is euthanasia, and it too is part of the culture of death.

These issues are not just for the practitioners of medicine and scientific research, or for lawyers, politicians or other so-called experts, as if they were matters that belonged only behind closed hospital or laboratory doors, or within courtrooms or the debating chambers of the Establishment. These topics have spilled out of the hospital wards, private clinics, research centres and the corridors of power into our homes, workplaces and churches—they are now on our doorsteps. They have affected and infected us all, both those within and those without the church. That is why we all need to grasp something of these bioethical issues.

1.3 The culture of death on your doorstep

We all live in this culture of death. It is a vindication of the fact that 'The mind of sinful man is death' (Rom. 8:6) and 'all who hate me [the Lord] love death' (Prov. 8:36). How else can you explain why every urbane, prosperous, educated society wilfully puts to death its own offspring, its smallest, its weakest, its oldest and its most vulnerable members? And the collective demand is for even more of the same. Such thoughts and actions have become dominant drivers of our culture. And all this is happening on your very own doorstep.

Are you still unconvinced? Have you yet to be persuaded of the need to think and act bioethically? Let me try another tack. While the statistics that follow are derived from one geographical location, one set of doorsteps—those of the UK—you can easily find the corresponding data for your own doorstep, whether you live in Europe, North America, Australasia or anywhere else. They will not be dissimilar. In other words, we are all in this bioethical catastrophe together.

Pause for a moment. Think. When you consider yourself, your family, your congregation, your neighbours or your work colleagues, what do you 'see' bioethically?

- Do you see infertility? An estimated 1 in 7 couples has problems conceiving. What should such couples do if they want to start a family? Should they accept childlessness, should they adopt, or should they resort to assisted-reproductive technologies (ARTs), like IVF or surrogacy?

Chapter 1

- Do you see teenage pregnancies? During 2011, in England and Wales, 31,051 girls aged under eighteen conceived, though 48.8 per cent of their pregnancies ended in abortion. And among that teenage total were 5,991 girls under sixteen—below the legal age of consent to sexual intercourse.
- Do you see that 1 in every 4 women in the UK has had an abortion? And many of these women will still be suffering psychologically, if not physically. In 2012, 203,419 abortions were performed in England, Wales and Scotland—about 780 every weekday. Since the Abortion Act 1967, the total number of legal abortions carried out here has been well over seven million.
- Do you see men and women with typically late-onset diseases? These include various cancers, Parkinson's and dementias, like Alzheimer's—the last currently affecting around half a million people in the UK. As we live longer, the incidence of these sorts of diseases will rise.
- Do you see those who are suicidal? In 2011, there were 6,045 suicides in the UK—equivalent to one every ninety minutes, with one attempted every five minutes. The suicide rate for men is three times higher than that for women. Those most at risk are middle-aged men.
- Do you see individuals with serious genetic defects, like those for sickle-cell anaemia, muscular dystrophies and Huntington's disease? Everyone carries genes that are potentially hazardous. For example, about 4 per cent of us have the gene for cystic fibrosis. These disorders are not always expressed because they depend upon many other factors, such as with whom we have children, our lifestyles and our environments.
- Do you see people, especially young people, with sexually transmitted infections (STIs)? *Chlamydia trachomatis* is now the most common STI in the West, with almost a quarter of a million new cases reported each year in the UK. Generally, STIs can be easily and effectively treated with antibiotics, but, if left untreated, they can lead to severe long-term health problems, including infertility.
- Do you see that at least 1 in every 4 people will suffer from a mental illness during his or her lifetime? These include various forms of anxiety and mood disorders, dementias and schizophrenia.

- Do you see illegitimate children? The proportion of conceptions outside marriage in the UK reached 47.5 per cent in 2012—the highest-ever figure. It is an indicator of how the structure of traditional marriage-based family life is crumbling. Such disintegration generates its own relational, financial, social, medical and bioethical problems.
- Do you see that 100 per cent of those people currently living around you will die? A total of 499,331 people died in England and Wales during 2012—equivalent to about 1,360 every day. Such occasions bring with them the uncomfortable problems of dying and death, and the coming threat of euthanasia.

These and other bioethical issues—and, more importantly, the people directly affected by them—reside in your neighbourhood, on your doorstep. And someday, and probably sooner than expected, *you* too will almost certainly have to face some life-sized, bioethical crisis and will be required to make some big, life-changing decisions. That is where 'the bioethical rubber hits the road'. How will you cope? How, in the heat of the moment and amid the clamouring voices, will you be able to make the correct assessment and the right choices? In other words, how will you understand and respond? Don't wait—now is the time to get a decent grounding and formulate a rugged and consistent approach to these issues. Don't wait—at the doctor's desk, at the hospital bedside, at the end of the phone is (almost) too late to start. Are you now convinced that you too need a clear-headed, big-hearted, open-handed grasp of these bioethical issues? Then, please, don't wait.

1.4 The true credenda and agenda

So, what must we understand and how should we respond? The Christian answer can be framed within the Bible's twofold pattern, the dual configuration for all Christian living as encountered at Romans 12, Ephesians 2:11 and numerous other such scriptural crossroads.

First, the truths, the doctrines, the statutes and the precepts are presented, as in Romans 1–11 and in the opening thirty-three verses of Ephesians. These are the *credenda*—the things to be believed. Then, second, comes the call to think, to speak, to live those very truths, as in Romans 12–16 or the remaining four and a half chapters of Ephesians. These are the *agenda*— the things to be done. So it is first principles, then action. First, the ethical

Chapter 1

bedrock is gathered and assembled. Second, the practical responses are developed and applied. The order is decisive. The biblical way is, perhaps not surprisingly, the opposite of the world's way. Visit any high-street bookshop and pick up a book on bioethics, and it will almost certainly begin with some hard and tragic personal cases and their attempted resolution (its agenda), and then from these it will seek to develop an all-encompassing set of ethics (its credenda). This is the cart-before-the-horse approach to bioethics and its outcomes are invariably feeble and utilitarian, like so much shifting sand. It provides no sound rock upon which to anchor proper understanding and subsequent responses.

By contrast, the combination of the biblical credenda first, with its agenda second, generates that greatest of all outcomes, *principled compassion*. This does not involve a set of rigid, harsh and uncaring rules or frosty regulations, nor a collection of touchy-feely, mawkish mush or trite instructions. Rather, it is the application of solid, truthful, often costly answers to deep and serious human dilemmas. It is conscientious and comprehensive. As we shall see, it is truly a head-heart-hand affair.

Therefore, to start with, we need to crank up our brains, apply our minds and construct that essential set of foundational truths—our credenda. For the Christian, our credenda are contained in the Bible. We are *sola Scriptura* people: the Word of God is our ultimate authority. That neither excuses us from hard thinking, nor makes everything bioethically simple. But it does create an absolute standard against which to judge the issues and devise answers. It also explains why our conclusions are often at variance with those of non-Christians; the fact is, we do bioethics differently. So, the first stop for the Christian is Scripture. What does it have to say? How can its teaching captivate our intellects and marshal our thinking, then garrison our hearts and stir our emotions, and finally galvanize our agenda and direct our actions? How can the Bible achieve this essential head-heart-hand affair? How can it help us understand and respond to these bioethical issues? Move on to the next page!

CHAPTER 2

Themes from the Scriptures

Welcome to the credenda. The firmest foundation for a proper understanding of, and ultimately responding to, these bioethical issues can be constructed from six major themes from the Scriptures. I like to think of them as the six stout legs that support a sturdy table, or the six hefty planks that constitute a well-built platform. And this biblical platform is unshakeably heavy-duty. It is one upon which you can stand firm and not be shy or apologetic. It is not like the wobbly, do-it-yourself botches produced by secular humanists, with their utilitarian thinking, their uncertain declarations and their arbitrary decisions. Once grasped, these themes from the Scriptures will provide you with not only a sure foundation, but also the basis for profound insight and perceptive judgement of all bioethical issues, whether past, present or future. Structure brings strength. These themes are the substructural fundamentals upon which a true and lasting bioethical superstructure can be safely built. While the issues may change, these themes from the Scriptures remain everlastingly constant and durable. They are forever settled.

Yet beware: it is so easy, often frighteningly easy, for us to adopt the mores, the thought patterns, the values, the Zeitgeist of our sad, unbelieving world. And we can so easily drift along on this tide of secular humanism—like so many dead fish—and offer no critique of its thinking, no resistance to its practices and no real charity to its victims. Yet every Christian is called to stand up for truth and to resist evil (Eph. 6:10–20). Therefore, Christians are often necessarily controversial, contrarian and counter-cultural. Christians should frequently find themselves swimming, or even struggling, against the tide—and that can be difficult, even dangerous. It therefore behoves us to get all the assistance we can. The Bible, as it says of itself, 'is God-breathed and is useful for teaching, rebuking, correcting and training in righteousness, so that the man of God may be thoroughly

Chapter 2

equipped for every good work' (2 Tim. 3:16–17). Or, as Schaeffer and Koop succinctly put it in their book, *Whatever Happened to the Human Race?*, 'God gives the pages, and thus God gives the answers.'[1] Here then is the groundwork and support we need: here are these six themes from the Scriptures. They are presented briefly, certainly not comprehensively, but hopefully comprehensibly. So, let's get thoroughly equipped. To the credenda!

2.1 Human life is unique and special

What better place to start than the first book of the Bible, its first chapter, and even its first verse? The Scriptures begin with that boldest of declarations: God created everything. The finite creation is the work of the infinite Creator. The universe exists and it has meaning and form because it was created by the infinite-personal God. Within those last three words, a mere seven syllables, is the genius of Christianity. Some religions have infinite gods, but these are not personal; other religions have personal gods, but they are not infinite. Only Christianity has a God who is both infinite and personal—limitless yet knowable. And this God's creative attributes can be made clearer by expounding the Hebrew word *bara*, which means 'created'. It occurs at three key points in the unfolding of creation.

First, it occurs in Genesis 1:1. 'In the beginning God created [*bara*] the heavens and the earth.' Here is the unadorned affirmation that God created something out of nothing, that is, *ex nihilo*. This must be one of the most trenchant sentences ever written. It is so uncluttered, yet it is so majestic. Look up into a clear night sky and be amazed. Look down a microscope and be astounded. Watch a sunrise over the mountains or a sunset over the sea and be awestruck. Let your doxology flow! He created it all.

The second time the word *bara* occurs is in Genesis 1:21: 'So God created [*bara*] the great creatures of the sea and every living and moving thing with which the water teems, according to their kinds, and every winged bird according to its kind.' Here and in verse 24, God creates animate beings—the fish of the sea, the birds of the air, the animals of the land.

The third occasion on which the word is used is in Genesis 1:27: 'So God created [*bara*] man in his own image, in the image of God he created [*bara*] him; male and female he created [*bara*] them.' The preceding statement, in verse 26, signifies a notable change. Previously God simply spoke and it was; that is, he commanded creation, by his fiat. Now it becomes 'Let us ...', that is, the Father, Son and Spirit enter into 'consultation' before man and woman are created and endowed with worth, identity and purpose. In addition, the threefold repetition of *bara* in verse 27 adds force. It is as if the Triune God calls out to us, 'Attention! Listen! This is really important!' Genesis 1:27 is about to become our bioethical cornerstone, *sine qua non*, the very heart of the matter. Capture its significance and you touch transcendence.

Here then is the opening chapter of the Bible. The cosmos is fashioned. The Creator's overall assessment of his creation is, '... it was very good' (Gen. 1:31). This is the beginning of the culture of life and, in particular, of human life: it was 'good'—no, it was 'very good'. This inaugural chapter displays a flow; it is an account in three phases: the creation of the inanimate, the creation of conscious life, and the creation of man. So, early in Genesis, and then throughout the rest of the Bible, there is a clear distinction between man—and, of course, in the generic sense, woman too—and all other created forms of life. We are *sui generis*, of our own kind, like no other. The Bible maintains that human life is the pinnacle of God's creative endeavours, or what John Calvin, in his commentary *Genesis*, called, 'the most excellent of all His works'[2] and 'something great and wonderful'.[3]

The Bible therefore insists that men and women are unlike all else. We are never non-man or non-woman. Humans stand out as spectacularly different from all other species. We have personality, language, abstract thinking, moral agency, accountability, creativity, cumulative culture and spirituality; we understand the past, the present and the future; we cooperate with unrelated individuals; we express and suppress the truth; we possess (a lost) righteousness; and much, much more. We are unique and we are special. Why? Because we are made in the image of God, in the likeness of Deity. We all bear the *imago Dei*—now admittedly distorted and tarnished by sin, but not entirely undone. This creational attribute was given to no other. This is the basis of the dignity of all human beings; it is the grounds of our worth. Human beings—men, women and children—are not nothing; our lives are not junk, our identity is not meaningless, and our purpose is not futile. All are intrinsically worthy of the highest respect and protection, as opposed to offhand contempt and negligence. Why? Because

Chapter 2

we—you, me, our neighbours, the tramp in the gutter and the king on his throne, the born and the unborn, the weak and the strong—are all made in the likeness of God. It is a Bible theme established in Genesis 1:27 and explicitly celebrated all the way through to James 3:9. Yes, let us say it again: we are unique and we are special. This is good news for the best of days and for the worst of days. It is breathtaking information.

This astonishing truth can also be captured from other angles. Consider the worth of a human being from, for example, the perspective of the great biblical theme of redemption. Redemption is God's determination, starting in Genesis 3, to bring men and women back to himself, even after they rebelled and resolutely rejected him. Why does he bother? Why does he care? Primarily, because we are made in his image, because we belong to him. That is why he has determined to rescue, regenerate and restore not poppies, parrots or pigs, but only us, only those made in his image, only the bearers of the *imago Dei*. That is a measure of how valuable we are. As the Redeemer once exclaimed, 'How much more valuable is a man than a sheep!' (Matt. 12:12). We all bear this ancient, creational worth—in the sense that Adam was our progenitor—as well as a modern-day, procreational worth—in the sense that we are all participants in the Adamic heritage—both of which are God-given and eternal.

These propositions from Genesis are crucial in understanding who we are, and in assessing our worth, identity and purpose. We are dealing here not only with biological life, but also with biographical life. And these creational doctrines are not addressed to God's people alone. These are truths for all. It makes no difference whether you are a believer or an unbeliever because these words have ramifications for the whole of the human race. If these great biblical truths are ignored, denied or thrown out of the window, what is left? Then what are men and women? We are just 'cogs in a mechanistic universe', or 'products of time and chance in an impersonal world', or 'chemical scum on a moderate-sized planet'. These are the very conclusions of modern man about himself. Read, for example, the works of Jean-Paul Sartre, Jacques Monod, Richard Dawkins or Stephen Hawking, who have been among the leading literary and scientific proponents of this bleak worldview during the last hundred years. Alas, this is also what Generation X, the children of the post-World War II baby boomers, and their children, Generation Y or the Millennials, have been raised on at home, at school and at university.

This is all fascinating stuff, but it is no mere fancy philosophy—it affects us all, deeply. You see, the way we view human life determines how we think about, and act towards, ourselves, and by extension and implication, the rest of the human race too. And this modern thinking, this unbiblical worldview, has produced a low view of human life, in both thought and practice, so that human life is now commonly regarded as unexceptional, insignificant, cheap and disposable. We must say that such a brutal conclusion is logically inescapable, because if you and I are not unique and special, the door is open to any practice, any cruelty. Our society has largely rejected the Bible's high view of man. So why are we surprised that infanticide, pornography, euthanasia, human embryo destruction, abortion, child sex abuse, violence and evil of all kinds are so widespread? We should be shocked by such practices, but not surprised—what else would we expect? Pushed to its ultimate conclusion, such a worldview cannot make the distinction between kicking a chair and kicking a child. After all, they are both only collections of molecules containing mostly carbon, oxygen, hydrogen and nitrogen atoms, plus a little sulphur, phosphorus and so on. This is the low view of human life in thought and deed. It inexorably degenerates into that culture of death.

In total contrast, the Bible's view of man, as made in the image of God, produces a high view of human life. All human life is therefore precious. All human life is therefore inviolable. All human life is therefore to be respected, protected, defended and cherished. This inexorably generates that culture of life. These two opposing worldviews bear totally different fruits: one is good and beautiful; the other is bad and ugly.

We must understand all this with crystal clarity. Man made in the image of God, as the bearer of the *imago Dei*, must be foundational to our thinking. If we get this wrong, everything else that follows will also be wrong. It is like buttoning up a shirt: if one button goes into the wrong buttonhole, everything that follows will be out of kilter. Carrying on is useless, because it will never right itself. The only way forward is to unbutton the lot, go back to button one, and start again. Go back therefore to Genesis 1—it is the bioethical bedrock.

CHAPTER 2

2.2 Human life begins at conception

One of the most persistent and significant questions in bioethical discussions is this: when does human life begin? Indeed, because it is such a central question, the whole of Chapter 5 is devoted to answering it fully. In the meantime, the following abridged answer is provided. Underlying this apparently straightforward and seemingly innocuous question are much more sinister ones, such as: should we destructively experiment on human embryos? When should human life be protected by law? Should we end early human life by abortion? So, the original question twists and turns and is subtly reformulated to become: what is the biological nature of the unborn? What is 'it'? What is its legal and ethical status? Does it have rights? Is it human? Is it 'one of us'?

Some say that an embryo, and for that matter a foetus too, is inhuman, though they concede that somehow it is 'becoming' human. Others maintain that it is only a piece of tissue, or a crude collection of undifferentiated cells. Some consider that it is a 'potential' human being. Others believe that sentience, the ability of the pre-born to interact with their environment, is the defining characteristic of the start of authentic human life. Still others state that viability, when a child can survive outside the womb, is the test of genuine human existence.

These woolly statements fly in the face of truth, both biblical and scientific. But why would supposedly intelligent people ever hold such errant opinions in the first place? It is because they have an ulterior motive. They want to retain the option, and the power, to destroy human embryos, to eliminate unborn children. Their bogus beliefs therefore allow them to evade the reality of their actions. They can therefore say, 'It was never a real baby—it was just a little something and nothing.' This is what the culture of death does—it bends the truth and it encourages people to deceive themselves and others.

One such deceived person was Naomi Wolf, one of the darlings of the US feminist movement who had long been a leading supporter of 'abortion on demand'. She would rally the sisterhood in chanting their slogans, such as, 'A foetus is nothing, a foetus is nothing'. Then in 1994 she became pregnant and, in the midst of morning sickness, she came to the realization that this slogan was a lie and that another one, 'Abortion stops a beating heart', was

Themes from the Scriptures

incontrovertibly true. Her unthinking rhetoric had collapsed in the face of reality—she could escape it no more.[4]

Another prime example of this wayward type of thinking is found in the Warnock Report (1984), which is discussed more fully in later chapters. This report was the most important and influential document on matters concerning early human life to be published during the twentieth century. Even today it remains the touchstone for much of contemporary bioethical thinking. Faced with the big question, it unhelpfully concluded that 'when life or personhood begin … are complex amalgams of factual and moral judgements. Instead of trying to answer these questions directly we have therefore gone straight to the question of how it is right to treat the human embryo'.[5] The authors of the Warnock Report, like many others, preferred to sidestep the question by pretending that it is an unfathomable, philosophical matter. Yet amazingly, having failed to answer the big question and thereby resolve just when human life does begin—and thus define the bioethical and legal status of the human embryo—the Warnock Committee pragmatically moved on to consider how the human embryo should be used for infertility treatment and exploited in scientific research. This is bioethics at its very worst and, of course, it results in more evasion and deception, as well as macabre medicine and science. Yet this type of sloppy, wrong-headed thinking is exactly how we got easy abortion, widespread human embryo destruction, and, in general, the culture of death.

Thankfully, the Scriptures are clearer than much of our society's muddled thinking. But to begin with, two caveats. First, the Bible is not a textbook of embryology or gynaecology. That is not its purpose. Yet, having said that, let us assert that the Bible does contain all that is necessary to guide us in matters of truth, faith and practice; hence, on these bioethical issues, it is not silent. In other words, the Bible is not exhaustive, but it is sufficient—it does not tell us everything, but it does tell us enough. Second, what follows is not an attempt at simplistic 'proof-texting'. The Bible has a unity, and its true meaning and teaching on any particular subject is determined, not on the weakness of an isolated verse or two taken out of context, but on the strength of comparing and contrasting all of its contents, themes and concepts. This is how Christian doctrines are properly constructed. When this exegetical pattern is followed, the effect of citing 'verse after verse' and

Chapter 2

'text upon text' is that of generating a weight, a momentum, an irresistible insistence from the Scriptures. This exercise, when applied to the current question, will constrain us to conclude that the Scriptures teach that human life does indeed begin at conception, fertilization, day one—all synonyms for this most remarkable starting point.

Only a few of the relevant passages of Scripture will be examined here, so you are being short-changed. But as you continue to read the Bible you will see for yourself, again and again, in different verses, at various times, in a variety of places and under diverse circumstances, the same insistent theme: human life begins at conception.

For a start, God's benediction on our first parents, recorded in Genesis 1:28—'Be fruitful and increase in number'—was not rescinded by the Fall. Instead, we see the same injunction repeated three times—in Genesis 8:17; 9:1; 9:7—and then being continually fulfilled throughout the Scriptures. From Eve onwards (Gen. 4:1), conception is regarded as evidence of God's continuing kindness to those who deserve no such thing. And the resulting children are seen as signs of God's grace and favour: 'children [are] a reward from him. Like arrows ... Blessed is the man whose quiver is full of them' (Ps. 127:3-5). But there is much, much more to consider.

Genesis 25:21-26 recounts the early lives of Esau and Jacob. In the womb of Rebekah they were not just two vague non-entities, or assemblies of undifferentiated cellular material, or even 'potential' lives; rather they were already real, pre-born babies with *imago Dei* worth, true identities and legitimate purposes. In addition, we are introduced here to an awesome concept: the foreknowledge of God; he sovereignly knows the end from the beginning. In the foreknowledge of God, these twin brothers, Esau and Jacob, were not even just two babies, but rather they were two future leaders, two nations, two peoples (Gen. 25:23). Here was redemptive history in the making, not on the battlefield or at the temple, but in a woman's womb. The entire lives of these two boys—from day one to death, from womb to tomb—were known to God. My contention here is that human life, physically and personally, begins at conception, but in reality, from God's perspective, he has known all of us long, long before that. Such mysteries of foreknowledge and omniscience are beyond our full comprehension, but we bow to him and to his Word. The finite fails (again) to comprehend the infinite.

This tenet of the foreknowledge of God is repeated in Jeremiah 1:5. Here, God tells Jeremiah, 'Before I formed you in the womb I knew you, before you were born I set you apart; I appointed you as a prophet to the nations.' Yes, God oversaw Jeremiah's postnatal life—as he oversees ours too, which we are now living. Yes, God also knew Jeremiah in his prenatal, pre-born life—and us in ours, too. Yes, Jeremiah had worth, identity and purpose at conception—and so did we. Jeremiah was therefore known by God as man, boy, foetus, embryo and zygote—and even, in the foreknowledge of God, before that, before Jeremiah ever became a physical entity. The fact is, we all have a 'pre-history' in the Creator's mind, but conception is when our earthly, corporeal life started.

In Judges 13:1–7, an angel of God told Samson's mother, 'you are going to conceive and have a son.' She was then instructed, 'Now see to it that you drink no wine or other fermented drink and that you do not eat anything unclean.' Why these restrictions? Because her child-to-be, Samson, was to be a Nazirite, and therefore such drink and food were never to enter his body, not even from across his mother's placenta. Why, then, if the zygotic, embryonic, foetal or pre-born Samson was not Samson proper, was his mother hedged about with such dietary conditions during her pregnancy, and, just to make sure, before she even conceived him? There is only one answer: because what was going to be in Manoah's wife's womb was the actual Samson, tiny but undisguised; it was Samson from conception, Samson from fertilization, Samson from day one.

Psalm 139:13–16 is a paean of praise from King David, as well as a ringing acknowledgement of God's creative involvement with all those made in his image, from day one and throughout, 'All the days ordained for me …' (Ps. 139:16). David too, like us, was known by God from his earliest times. He reinforces this truth in Psalm 51:5: 'Surely I was sinful at birth, sinful from the time my mother conceived me.' Here we have the twofold condition of mankind: sinners by practice *and* sinners by nature. When David was born, he committed sins—he became a sinner by practice, 'from birth'. But before that, as soon as 'my mother conceived me', he was 'sinful'—a sinner by nature. We too cannot help it—it is our very nature: we commit sins because we are 'sinful'. When did we become sinful sinners? As soon as we entered the human race. When did we enter the human race? As soon as our mothers conceived us. QED!

CHAPTER 2

Questions surrounding the beginning of human life are perhaps nowhere more clearly expounded than by the incarnation of the Lord Jesus Christ. It is a cardinal doctrine of Christianity that the second person of the Trinity became a man. 'The Word became flesh and made his dwelling among us' (John 1:14). In Matthew 1:20, Joseph is told that 'what is conceived in her [Mary] is from the Holy Spirit'. Here is the incarnation. The Lord Jesus Christ did not suddenly come down from heaven to appear in that feeding trough in a Bethlehem outbuilding. The incarnation occurred nine months earlier, in Nazareth, when he was conceived in Mary. Nor does the Bible permit us to believe that Deity was somehow poured into Christ's body at a later date, or that this mere man was subsequently promoted to the rank of the Son of God. The plain truth is that Jesus was incarnated at conception. All else is heresy. Charles Wesley was not doctrinally or biologically correct, though perhaps poetically licensed and rhymingly pardoned, when he wrote in his Christmas hymn, 'Our God contracted to a span, incomprehensibly made man'.[6] The Christ was once, just like us, much smaller than a span; in fact, he too was as small as, or even smaller than, the full stop at the end of this sentence. It was God in a womb, incarnated as a zygote. Now that is—but not quite—incomprehensible! He came to share our humanity. He came as 'very God', but also as 'very man'. He was one person with two natures, the divine and the human—the so-called hypostatic union (John 1:1–14; Col. 2:9), as expressed in the Chalcedonian formula of AD 451. He came as a real human being, like us in every way except that he was without sin. Just think how much Christ's condescension and incarnation dignify human life. While there may be no single Bible verse, no scriptural *coup de grâce*, which single-handedly and definitively clinches the conception argument, for me, Matthew 1:20 comes powerfully close. It sends me aquiver. Moreover, as the writer to the Hebrews puts it, 'So Jesus is not ashamed to call them brothers ... he had to be made like his brothers in every way' (Heb. 2:11, 17). That is to say, his physiological development, prenatally and postnatally, from conception onwards, was entirely like ours, 'in every way'. Since his earthly life began when he was conceived in Mary's womb—albeit supernaturally, without human sperm—it is not a great leap of either reason or faith to conclude that you and I also began then—albeit naturally, with human sperm. Through whichever of these routes, it is always conception that marks the common start of all human life. There is no room here for imagining that somehow, at a later date, we became other than what we already were, namely, fully human, or that some essential feature was subsequently and exogenously added on. The Bible knows of no such gradualism. Yes, of course we have developed as the days and years have passed, but that has always been endogenous growth and progression, set in motion on day one. The zygote is complete and human from the onset—full stop.

Doctor Luke records yet another astonishing incident that occurred a few days after Joseph's extraordinary visitation (Luke 1:39–45). Here Elizabeth, six months pregnant with John the Baptist, is visited by the newly pregnant Mary who is carrying the Christ-child as a tiny embryo, the embryonic Immanuel, 'God with us'. What an occasion it is when two happily pregnant women meet! But there is more here, because the unborn John, previously foretold as being full of the Holy Spirit (Luke 1:15), hears Mary's greeting, but above and beyond that, and consonant with his prophetic role, he recognizes that he is in the presence of the incarnate Son of God. And what is his response? To leap for joy! So here are two unborn boys who both demonstrate the deepest spiritual dimensions of what it means to be fully human, to bear the *imago Dei*. There can be no doubt that the lives of John the Baptist and Jesus Christ had not only begun, but were, in fact, in full developmental swing. Conception was their mutual beginning. Meanwhile, Elizabeth, filled with the Holy Spirit, exclaims that Mary is indeed 'the mother of my Lord' (v. 43). Here is post-incarnational, prenatal recognition, and holy jubilance.

In addition to these repeated references to the event of conception, the Bible often calls attention to the event of birth, as indeed we do with announcements, cards, parties and those recurring anniversaries with cakes and candles. Childbirth is an undeniably pivotal occasion, yet Scripture makes no bioethical distinction between the unborn child and the born child. This continuity of prenatal and postnatal life is expressed in the New Testament by Luke's indiscriminate use of the Greek word *brephos* for both; for example, in referring to the unborn John the Baptist (Luke 1:42, 44) and the newborn Christ-child (2:12, 16), as well as to the babies brought to Jesus to be blessed (18:15).

This theme of continuity, of human life as a continuum from conception to natural death, is also found in the Old Testament. For instance, it is

Chapter 2

magnificently expressed in three ways in Psalm 139:13–16. First, King David acknowledges, albeit in the non-scientific language of 1000 BC, God's creational oversight during his earliest days: 'For you created my inmost being; you knit me together in my mother's womb.' This 'you/your' and 'me/my' relationship is a theme recurring in nearly every verse. It is God the Creator ('you') who directs and purposes the beginning of personal, prenatal life ('me'). Second, there is the repetition of the personal and possessive pronouns, 'I/me/my'. They express the continuity of life between the adult David and the just-conceived David, as both the author and the subject of this psalm. Whether in the womb or on the kingly throne, it was always David, never less than David. In other words, once conception has occurred, a new human life is inaugurated, whether it is David's or yours, and the pattern is always the same—zygote to cadaver. Third, there is the particular use of the 'me/you' pronoun couplet. This is a poignant expression of a man ('me') knowing God ('you'), as well as a man ('me') being known by God ('you'); the created and the Creator are in communion. Here is the most profound description of what it means to bear the *imago Dei*. We are never just potential human beings; we are, from conception onwards, God-created, God-known, actual human beings already possessed of God-given worth, identity and purpose—human biology and human biography are beautifully woven together in the divine plan.

These verses from Psalm 139 are a remarkable articulation of God's intimate involvement in the entirety of every individual human life. Each of us is an ongoing work of God. Neither the Bible nor biology knows of any developmental process, stage or event of which it can be said, 'Before this, I was not; now, I am'. To put it another way, there is a demonstrable continuity throughout every human life. Scripture knows of no discontinuity, no discriminatory demarcations, in either prenatal or postnatal life, that forge a disjunction between human and non-human life—and nor should we.

Finally, as any schoolchild who as part of his or her religious education had to read the King James Version of the Bible will tell you, 'The Bible is full of begetting'. This somewhat archaic word describes the key role of the father in procreation: it is by 'fathering' that he passes on his genetic material to the next generation; it is how he achieves posterity, how he puts another branch into his genealogical tree. In one sense, he does nothing else during the next nine months, because the mother is the one involved

THEMES FROM THE SCRIPTURES

with implantation, nutrition, gestation, labour and birth. This emphasis on begetting—as found, for example, in Genesis 5 and Matthew 1—is synonymous with conception. It defines when a man becomes a father and a woman becomes a mother. The Bible repeatedly declares and records it as a most noteworthy event—two adult lives are changed as another one is begun.

Scientifically, what happened at your conception, on day one of your life? It was the fertilization of one ovum, from all of your mother's thousands, by just one sperm, from all of your father's billions. Each of these gametes contained twenty-three chromosomes and when they combined, something wonderful happened. They were no longer just a sperm and an ovum; now they were a new cell, called, perhaps rather unattractively, a zygote. And that zygote contained all that was necessary for the unique individual that was you. Genetically, you were then complete. The only additional requirement you needed then, and indeed have needed ever since then, was nutrition. So conception was the point when biblically and scientifically you started. Fertilization occurred, the post-conception cascade commenced and your life trajectory was launched. It was the beginning of 'I'.

Since your conception, the only changes that have occurred have been in terms of development. The pattern has been this: zygote (1 cell) → morula (16+ cells) → blastocyst (day 6) → embryo → foetus (8+ weeks) → unborn child → newborn child → infant → toddler → youngster → teenager → adult → thirty-something → middle age → pensioner → old age → death. This is the continuum of human life; it is a seamless journey from conception through to natural death. Thus, human life begins not at birth, or at twenty-four weeks, or at eighteen weeks, or when brainwaves or blood are first detectable, or at implantation. The irrefutable fact is that we all began at conception as one cell, as a zygote, and that we spent the first nine or so months of our lives inside our mothers. Hands up if you were never once a zygote!

There is no disagreement here between the truth of the Bible and the truth of science—the one simply reinforces the other; they are the best of friends. The evidence is overwhelming. If you doubt that human life begins at conception, fertilization, day one, then you have a fundamental argument with modern biology and with Scripture. Many of the major doctrines of biblical, historic, orthodox Christianity, including those of the nature of

Chapter 2

man, the foreknowledge of God, the incarnation and redemption, depend upon this propositional truth.

2.3 Human life requires stewardship

No one should ever doubt or deny that God is the most gracious of givers. 'Every good and perfect gift is from above, coming down from the Father' (James 1:17). It is one of God's communicable attributes, his essential character, to give and give. Among the greatest of his gifts is human life: 'he himself gives all men life and breath and everything else' (Acts 17:25). Human life is not a right, a choice, a reward or a punishment—it is a gift.

This gift of earthly life begins with our conception and ends with our death. The Old Testament describes that time span as 'the few days of life God has given' (Eccles. 5:18) and, for some, it can literally be as short as a few days, or perhaps as long as ninety or more years. Whatever its length, all human life is properly understood as a God-given gift.

Furthermore, the Bible uses the motif of the 'gracious gift of life' (1 Peter 3:7), which has significance for at least three reasons. First, a gift reminds us of grace. Our lives are demonstrations of God's grace—his unmerited favour to undeserving men and women. Christians are living, breathing testimonies to God's grace (Rom. 6:23). Second, a gift, especially one as great as life, deserves gratitude from the one to whom it is given towards the Giver (Ps. 139:14)—we are to be 'overflowing with thankfulness' (Col. 2:7). Third, such a gift from God must be valuable, so it deserves to be carefully nurtured and protected (Deut. 30:19).

We are therefore to treasure what God has given us. Simply put, we are to be good stewards of his gifts. Christian stewardship has become a neglected concept. It is too often considered only in connection with topics like money or the environment. But we are also to be good stewards, cautious caretakers, of human life. Such stewardship is to be practised in no fewer than three arenas: me, mine and ours. First and foremost, it means that we are answerable to our Maker for the stewardship of our own lives—me (Rom. 14:12). Second, we are to have a custodial concern, an oversight, for the lives of those within our close circle, our immediate family—mine (1 Tim. 5:8). And third, we are to have a practical interest in the lives and well-being of our neighbours and the wider human family, even the whole human race—ours (Luke 10:30–37).

Learning to be good stewards of our own lives will prevent us from slipping into that ersatz wisdom of modern men and women who reject the idea of 'stewardship' in favour of 'ownership'. 'It's my life, my body; I shall do with it as I please,' is their autonomous cry. But we do not 'own' our lives. By creation, both Christians and non-Christians belong to God (Gen. 1:27; Rom. 4:16). Moreover, by redemption, Christians are told categorically in 1 Corinthians 6:19–20 that 'You are not your own; you were bought at a price'.

This prevailing notion of ownership is dangerous because it encourages people to live lives of unrestraint and self-determination. It encourages the quest for absolute autonomy, frequently resulting in a cruel indifference towards others, especially the vulnerable. It also engenders an insistence upon rights, especially 'my rights'—again, often to the detriment of others. By contrast, stewardship makes people circumspect, mindful of their Owner, careful with what has been entrusted to them. It stirs up the exercise of responsibility towards others, rather than their denigration and that predatory grabbing of what is 'mine'. It seeks a fulfilment of duties and care towards others, rather than selfishly serving self. Above all, good stewardship never involves the intentional return of the gift; grace is never to be shunned. This includes the premature termination of the stewardship; stewardship of our lives is our lifelong privilege. Therefore, intentionally and prematurely ending human lives by euthanasia, infanticide, abortion, embryo destruction, suicide and the like can never be regarded as the marks of good stewardship.

So we are stewards, not owners, of this gift—this marvellous, fragile, unpredictable entity called human life. It is the gift of God for us to enjoy, in times both of ease and of trouble. Even in the most difficult episodes of life, God continually attributes value and meaning to our lives. We, on the other hand, can be so contrary. The required correctives are found in Scripture. When life is tiring and tiresome, and we begin to feel sorry for ourselves, God rebukes us with the reminder that 'my thoughts are not your thoughts, neither are your ways my ways' (Isa. 55:8) and then the open invitation is offered, 'Come to me, all you who are weary and burdened, and I will give you rest' (Matt. 11:28). And when life is hard, almost too hard, and we fear that we are sinking, the Scriptures declare, 'No temptation has seized you except what is common to man. And God is faithful; he will not let you be

Chapter 2

tempted beyond what you can bear. But when you are tempted, he will also provide a way out so that you can stand up under it' (1 Cor. 10:13).

Too often we lose perspective and fail to see the bigger picture. What is our abiding purpose in this life? What is 'our chief end'? Nothing expresses this quite so pithily as the answer to Question 1 of the Westminster Shorter Catechism (1648): 'Man's chief end is to glorify God, and to enjoy him for ever.' Therefore, our little lifespan, our short stewardship, is to be lived out in devotion to, and in service of, God. 'The few days of life God has given' are our probation. We are not staying long; we are soon moving on. The Christian is preparing for an eternal life of peace, fulfilment, joy and rest. Life, now lived in the face of personal and entangling sin (Heb. 12:1) and the global bondage to decay (Rom. 8:21), is awkward and abnormal. We now experience hardship and pain—if not for ourselves, then certainly among our family, neighbours and friends. Christians live in the real and rough world, yet we believe that God is mindful of the weak and their sufferings (Lev. 19:14; Matt. 12:20) and that, despite the seemingly conflicting evidence around us at times, grace and mercy will eventually triumph (1 Cor. 15:54–57), and finally our Saviour will take us to our Father's home (John 14:1–4).

That is the Christian perspective on being a steward of human life. Bearing the *imago Dei* is not a cruel sentence imposed by a remote, austere being, but rather a privileged adventure to be lived out with the 'friend of sinners', day by day, and, not least, during its final days. Therefore, we love life and we are honoured and excited to be granted stewardship of it.

2.4 Human life ends in natural death

This is bioethical plank or leg number four. God is the Creator (Gen. 1:27), the Giver (1 Tim. 6:13) and the Sustainer of human life (Ps. 54:4). But God is also the Taker of human life. Our deaths, as well as our lives, are in this God's hands: 'The LORD brings death and makes alive' (1 Sam. 2:6). How can it be otherwise with a sovereign God?

Such sovereignty at life's end is asserted by the psalmist with words of no more than two syllables: 'when you take away their breath, they die and return to the dust' (Ps. 104:29). Job agrees: 'Naked I came from my mother's womb, and naked I shall depart. The LORD gave and the LORD has taken away; may the name of the LORD be praised' (Job 1:21). The Lord

Themes from the Scriptures

Jesus Christ endorses the very same truth: 'Are not two sparrows sold for a penny? Yet not one of them will fall to the ground apart from the will of your Father ... So don't be afraid; you are worth more than many sparrows' (Matt. 10:29, 31). Thus, your death is in the hands of God, according to his will, by his chosen manner, at his timing, in his selected place. Would you want it any other way?

Therefore, to choose, engineer or bring about death, whether our own or someone else's, without divine sanction, is to usurp God's prerogative. It is to challenge his providence. It is to trespass into his domain. Such a biblical precept sticks in the craw of today's secular humanists. Such talk is an offence against their ardent pursuit of total autonomy. 'My Way' is not just the title of a song popularized by Frank Sinatra; it has become the mantra of modern men and women, especially as they approach death. It includes those depressingly tell-tale, self-sufficient lyrics: 'For what is a man, what has he got? If not himself, then he has naught.' Small wonder that it has become the anthem most frequently requested at funeral services and karaoke bars around the world.

But all this autonomy talk and egocentricity is nothing new. Rebellion, defiance and self-centredness have long been human characteristics. These traits were at the heart of the great question in the Garden of Eden (Gen. 3:11): who is to rule, the Creator or the created, God or man? With man striving to arrogate the role of God and seeking to be in control, it was bound to go wrong. Violence and untimely death were sure to be among its ugly outcomes. And so it was—the first unnatural death, the original killing of one bearing the *imago Dei*, was just around the corner (Gen. 4:8). Cain, the murderer, was the precursor and Abel, the victim, was the prototype. And so it is today. And so it will be tomorrow. Perhaps too often we underestimate the incidence of violence, and the effects of a world constantly inhabited by the violent and awash with violence. Genesis 6:11 was a devastating analysis of the plight of the ancient world: 'Now the earth was corrupt in God's sight and full of violence.' What an indictment; yet who would dare gainsay that this is not also a continuing and accurate assessment of our twenty-first-century world?

Thus, unnatural death entered human history and rapidly flourished. How else can you account for the origin and persistence of the culture of death? Consider, for example, the current drive to legalize euthanasia. This

Chapter 2

is fundamentally yet another reflection of man and woman's longing to be entirely autonomous and to bring about untimely death. They have already obtained the legal permission and the practical means to end human life in vitro (embryo destruction), in utero (abortion) and ex utero (infanticide); now they crave to square the circle to include life in senio (euthanasia, in old age). Such culture-of-death advocates have but one common goal, namely, to own the right to intervene to bring about the premature death of any human being, by any method, at any time, at any place. Historically, those involved in procuring such unnatural deaths have always been the enemies of wholesome, Hippocratic–Christian medicine. Nowadays, the collaborators in this culture of death are far and wide. They flaunt its hideous ethics and perform its dreadful practices here, there and everywhere—and they must be confronted and countered. Unnatural death is a curse.

2.5 Human life is not to be taken

The Cain and Abel narrative (Gen. 4:8–12) demonstrates that human life is precious and sacrosanct. The killing of one made in God's image, namely, Abel, brought down divine anger. 'The LORD said, "What have you done? Listen! Your brother's blood cries out to me from the ground"' (Gen. 4:10). This first taking of a human life, unprecedented murder, was an offence to a holy God.

The killing of animals was acceptable (Gen. 9:3), but human beings were different. The written prohibition against their slaughter was originally set out in Genesis 9:6: 'Whoever sheds the blood of man, by man shall his blood be shed; for in the image of God has God made man.' So what underpins this protective precept? Not a set of complex and specious theological arguments, but rather this one simple fact that we have already seen—we are all made in the image of God; we all bear the *imago Dei*.

The Sixth Commandment (Exod. 20:13; Deut. 5:17) can be applied here too: 'You shall not murder.' That is, the deliberate taking of the life of another human being is unnatural, wrong and sinful. Such an action violates God's righteous law. However, Scripture does not forbid the taking of *all* human life. Though beyond the remit of this book, Scripture does contain limited sanctions in the cases of, for example, capital punishment, self-defence and war. What Scripture does forbid is the taking of *all innocent* human life. The word 'innocent' in this context does not mean 'without sin'

Themes from the Scriptures

but 'without harm'; that is, the embryo, foetus, child or adult has instigated no injustice, caused no offence, committed no crime. This theme, of the culpability of those who take innocent life, is expounded in Isaiah 59:7 and repeated in Romans 3:15: 'Their feet rush into sin; they are swift to shed innocent blood. Their thoughts are evil thoughts; ruin and destruction mark their ways.' It was also part of Judas's confession: '"I have sinned," he said, "for I have betrayed innocent blood"' (Matt. 27:4). Therefore, innocent human beings are absolutely not to be killed deliberately, ever. Consider then how God must view the deliberate and wholesale destruction of such life in what today we call human embryo experimentation, abortion, infanticide, euthanasia and so on.

In former times, even the accidental killing of another human being was followed by a penalty (Num. 35:6): the killer had to flee to a city of refuge. And if a house was to be built with a flat roof, the owner had to surround it with a parapet (Deut. 22:8). Why? So that fellow human beings did not fall off and injure, or even kill, themselves. These were not punitive regulations, but rather expressions of God's caring concern for those bearing the *imago Dei*. He does not want any of us to come to harm; God is altogether pro-life, and we should be too.

This same Fatherly concern to protect his image-bearers is also expressed in Exodus 21:22–25. Some have made a meal of misinterpreting this passage, claiming that it proves that the unborn child is less valuable than the mother and therefore can be subjected to abortion. These verses do no such thing. They teach that if men were fighting and one of them accidentally—that is, with no premeditated intent—struck a pregnant woman, and this induced a premature but safe birth—not a fatal miscarriage—of her child, if neither the mother nor her baby were badly harmed, a fine was to be imposed, the penalty for reckless fighting. The misunderstanding of this passage centres on the use of the Hebrew noun *yeled* and the verb *yatza*. The former commonly refers to 'offspring' or 'child', while the latter means to 'go out' or to 'come forth'. That is, they describe the ordinary birth of a child, as in Genesis 25:26; 38:28–30; Job 3:11; 10:18; Jeremiah 1:5; 20:18. Miscarriage, entailing the death of the child, is indicated in none of these verses. Yet 'miscarriage' has been the mistranslation in, for example, the Revised Standard Version of the Bible, based on the Septuagint. There is a perfectly good Hebrew word for miscarriage—*shakol*, as found in Genesis 31:38; Exodus 23:26; Hosea 9:14—

Chapter 2

but it is not the word used in this Exodus passage. Nevertheless, if either the mother or her child suffered serious injury, or died as a result of the incident, the penalty was 'life for life, eye for eye' and so on—the *lex talionis*, the law of retaliation (Exod. 21:23). In other words, both mother and unborn child were regarded as precious and were to be protected equally under the law. Indeed, the specified penalties imposed for an assault on a pregnant woman and her unborn child were greater than those for any other citizen of Israel whose death was caused accidentally (the perpetrator had only to flee to a city of refuge, Num. 35:6).

God is jealously caring of innocent human life. Its defence and protection is a recurring theme throughout Scripture. To be sure, the unbending commands of the Old Testament were intensified in the New. According to Christ, anyone who simply hates another person is in breach of the Sixth Commandment (Matt. 5:21–22). This same stringent ethic is repeated in Romans 13:10: 'Love does no harm to its neighbour.' Even wishing to hurt my fellow citizen is akin to killing him or her. In other words, the Bible declares a non-negotiable prohibition on the hating and taking of innocent human life, whether it is pre-born or born, young or old. Such bearers of the *imago Dei* are to be defended and protected, not terminated, murdered, slaughtered, squashed, suffocated, overdosed, exterminated, destroyed, or even just plain killed.

2.6 Human life needs special care

We hear so much about abortion for the physically and the mentally disabled, or euthanasia for the sick and senile. And some Christians, though appalled by, for example, easy abortion or creeping euthanasia, are confused and sometimes reticent to condemn these practices, often because of these so-called 'difficult' or 'hard' cases. So how can our thinking be biblically informed here? There are several guidelines to take into account.

To begin with, we need to remember that the sickly unborn girl, the newborn boy with special needs, the Down's syndrome teenager and the senile man are all human—all bearers of the *imago Dei*. Their lives may be difficult, but they are not tragic and death-deserving. We are not to define them by their difference, but by their joint membership with us of the human race. They were made in the image and likeness of God, and they still bear the image and likeness of God. Genesis 1:27 is always our biblical, bioethical ground zero.

But there is more. The conversation between Moses and God recorded in Exodus 4:10–12 included an appropriate rebuke to Moses. God said, 'Who gave man his mouth? Who makes him deaf or mute? Who gives him sight or makes him blind? Is it not I, the Lord?' Here is a mystery of providence. God sovereignly makes some of us markedly disabled. I do not fully understand why, and nor do you. Nevertheless, we are given a little additional insight in John 9:1–3, where Jesus said that a man was blind from birth 'so that the work of God might be displayed in his life'. We should also note from John 9:3 that such handicap was not the direct result of sin, whether of the sufferer or of the parents. These words of the Lord Jesus Christ should dispel those wicked, accusatory old wives' tales that have for too long confused the issue of disability; it is never God wreaking vengeance. Our understanding in this area is perhaps far from clear, yet we must again submit to the teaching of Scripture and learn from its Author.

However, what is patently clear is that God does have a special concern for the welfare of the disabled. Leviticus 19:14 plainly warns, 'Do not curse the deaf or put a stumbling-block in front of the blind, but fear your God. I am the Lord.' And we know that the gentle Messiah would never break a bruised reed, nor would he ever snuff out a smouldering wick (Isa. 42:3; Matt. 12:20). We also understand that it is in the weaknesses of humans that the power of God is displayed and made perfect (1 Cor. 1:26–31; 2 Cor. 12:9).

Yet over and above even these provisional reassurances, there is still the Christian's eternal consolation: these handicaps, these disabilities, are but temporary. Isaiah 35:5–6 tells us that they will disappear on that great Day: 'Then will the eyes of the blind be opened and the ears of the deaf unstopped. Then will the lame leap like a deer, and the mute tongue shout for joy.' And 'He will wipe every tear from their eyes. There will be no more death or mourning or crying or pain, for the old order of things has passed away' (Rev. 21:4). Heaven will make us whole.

Much of our ambivalence about disability, and about those so affected, is rooted in this world's thinking. Far too readily we have adopted the mindset of our age and we have become too cosy living within this culture of death. How many of us draw back when we are about to be hugged

Chapter 2

enthusiastically by a Down's syndrome child? How many of us prefer to bypass a woman with senile dementia? We may excuse our behaviour as polite shyness or perhaps British reserve but, for many of us, it is a shameful reminder that we too can be silent partners in our society's commitment to getting rid of such people. Ground E of the Abortion Act 1967 explicitly sanctions abortion for the unborn handicapped. And at the other end of the age spectrum, the majority of the UK public apparently want some kind of euthanasia legalized for the elderly, sick and disabled. Society's communal wish is clearly for killing rather than caring.

We have been too easily inveigled into thinking that this world is for only 'the big, the bright and the beautiful', the present-day paradigm of perfection. This has become one of the most dreadful and divisive aspects of our society; we tend to think of ourselves as normal people, and we place ourselves in a group over here, and then there are the so-called handicapped, the disabled, the incapacitated and the senile, as a sub-standard lot, whom we consign to a group over there. And Christians can so easily be caught up in this contemporary wave of apartheid. The remedy is axiomatic: those with special needs need special care. In a world so enamoured with the notions of diversity and equality, it is deplorable that we have forgotten to apply these values to all those who, without exception, are made in the image of God. We should be ashamed of ourselves.

Furthermore, ask this question: which of us is *not* disabled? The truth is that we are all physically and mentally handicapped. Few of us have outstanding physical strength, skills or endurance—I doubt if any reader is, or is ever likely to be, an Olympic Games gold medallist. And as we become elderly we become weaker and less agile. All of us really are, or will soon become, physically disabled. Similarly, few have dazzling mental abilities. Can you remember the date of your father's birthday, or, on a Monday morning, the preacher's three sermon points from the day before? Exactly! Many of us forget more than we learn—we really are all mentally disabled. And even if you spurn the idea that you are physically and mentally impaired, the Bible declares that you are handicapped, and hugely so, by sin. Even the best of us has missed the mark, by a long, long way (Rom. 3:23).

Finally, the real antidote to this type of sub-Christian thinking about disability is found in Isaiah 52:14. Here we have a prophetic glimpse of the yet-to-come sufferings of the weak and mutilated Saviour: 'Just as there were many who were appalled at him—his appearance was so disfigured beyond that of any man and his form marred beyond human likeness ...' Here he is, the Saviour of the world, the One whom you probably profess to love, follow and serve. Here he is, hanging on the cross, suffering for our sins, the just dying for the unjust, in order that we might be rescued and brought back to God. So here is the inconvenient question: if you were there at Golgotha, would you have drawn back and turned aside from this physically disabled, mentally anguished man, this handicapped Saviour?

The sum total is this: Christians are mandated to have a special concern and care for the weak, the incapable and the vulnerable. James 1:27 insists that we specifically 'look after orphans and widows in their distress'. But our remit of principled compassion extends to those with disabilities, the unborn, the terminally ill, those who have no voice, those who cannot protect themselves. Indeed, all human life needs special care. It is a broad and daunting responsibility, one that is temptingly easy to shirk.

2.7 A little, but important, addendum

There is something else to add here. It is about those people whom I call the 'morally sensitive'. They include some decidedly non-Christians as well as some unsure Christians, but together these people recognize that something has gone seriously wrong in the world. They are as troubled as anyone by our slide towards a cheap and an ever cheapening view of human life. To them, I am *not* saying that to be authentically pro-life one must first believe the above six Judaeo-Christian doctrines with all one's heart. I have been too long associated with the pro-life movement to know that people of other faiths, and of none, can shame the often feeble responses of professing Bible-believing Christians—those of us who should instinctively know and do better.

Nevertheless, the 'morally sensitive' live by their own sets of alternative ethical foundations and convictions. While they may not recognize or regularize them as such, they are often parallel to the Christian's credenda. For instance, first, they acknowledge that human life is special and unique—they readily admit that we are unquestionably distinct from all other life forms. Some of them call this 'human exceptionalism'. Second, they agree that human life begins at conception—it is blindingly obvious, they say. Third, they maintain that all human life ought to be treasured—and not

Chapter 2

trashed. Fourth, they understand that death should be natural—and never intended or hastened. Fifth, they see that killing innocent humans is wrong—and must be forbidden. Sixth, they gladly accept that vulnerable people need special care—and they often strive to provide just that. Others among the 'morally sensitive' regard these bioethical issues as a matter of human rights; the right to life, they say, is the most basic of all rights. They invoke international treaties, such as the European Convention on Human Rights, of which Article 2 states, 'Everyone's right to life shall be protected by law.' For some, it is a civic duty to protect the weak and helpless—defending and speaking up for those who are unable to do so themselves. And for others, it is a question of good medicine—it is simply rotten medical practice for health professionals to kill any of their patients.

So what is the origin of this commendable 'morally sensitive' thinking and responding? The Christian calls it common grace—God's universal goodness to all men and women, both believers and unbelievers (Ps. 145:9; Matt. 5:45b; Luke 6:35b). It is an indelible mark of bearing the *imago Dei*. Only we human beings are moral agents. It is only human beings who seek to formulate moral codes and establish laws and customs using their God-given faculties. Though the Christian maintains that all of us have sinned, all of us are still capable of wonderful deeds of human kindness, spectacular heroism, as well as simple, common decency. In truth, none of us is as morally or actively bad as we could be. Why? Because God continues to exert a curb on the destructive power of our evil thoughts and violent exploits. For example, we retain a conscience that reminds us of the difference between right and wrong; though often suppressed, it is still evident because it is 'written on [our] hearts' (Rom. 2:15). Thus, some men and women are particularly virtuous, noble and entirely pro-life; these folk are among the 'morally sensitive'. Moreover, the beliefs and deeds of such people often stem from an earlier grace when God and his Word were honoured within their families or communities. Theirs are therefore typically copied convictions and behaviours, learned during better days.

So, does the Christian even need to bother to construct biblical credenda? Oh yes, yes, yes! The ethical and practical stance of the 'morally sensitive' is essentially man-made; it is a derived conduct without any specifically coherent framework. It is often the endorsement of that attractive Christian morality, but detached from the essential spurs of Christian faith and divine energy. It is reminiscent of the Enlightenment's doomed attempt at Christian virtue without embracing Christian truth—a wanting the fruits without the roots. By contrast, the Christian's stance is unashamedly transcendent in origin and spiritually energized in action; it is primarily received, intensely personal, all-pervasive as a lifestyle, and all-embracing as a worldview. Christian, never be satisfied with second-best. For Christians, with the Scriptures in their hands and the love of Christ in their hearts, it is the biblical credenda—the truths to be believed—plus the biblical agenda—the truths to be lived—that become compelling and powerful, and which then lead to the exercise of principled compassion.

However, none of these privileges entitles Bible-believing Christians to claim even the slightest hint of superiority, or to practise any form of pietistic isolationism; quite the opposite. Evangelical Christians should be humbled by the example of the 'morally sensitive' and therefore be all the more earnest to make amends for our years of sloth. Nor are there any grounds here for compromising gospel truth; that is never to be the issue at stake. Nor is there any excuse to shun bioethical engagement with co-belligerents of any stripe; we are all in this culture of death together.

2.8 Themes from the Scriptures: in conclusion

To return to these six great themes from the Scriptures, they constitute the Christian's bioethical credenda—the things to be believed. They are the legs that together buttress the most sturdy bioethical table, the planks that structure the most robust bioethical platform. They provide us with the basis for tackling all bioethical issues. They possess a superb internal consistency as well as a challenging external summons to press on. Grasping them will make us better men and women, better citizens and better Christians. Grasping them will lead us to right understanding and eventually to right responding. So, next, what are these controversial bioethical issues that constitute the culture of death and which we first need to understand?

QUESTIONS FOR PERSONAL REFLECTION AND GROUP DISCUSSION

1. *Are these six themes of Scripture's bioethical platform sufficient? Is anything lacking?*

2. *For you, what does it mean to be a bearer of the* imago Dei?

Chapter 2

3. *What aspects of the credenda are you unclear about? How do you intend to resolve them?*

4. *Why does the Christian view of human life depart from that generally held by society?*

5. *How can the Christian begin to appeal to others to adopt a more pro-life perspective?*

6. *Are there limits—and if so, what are they—to bioethical co-belligerency?*

7. *Is your church bioethically aware? If not, what correctives are needed?*

CHAPTER 3

Some of the primary issues

Thankfully, when it comes to bioethical issues, very few Christians are called to become top-notch experts, such as professors of moral philosophy or media pundits. But that does not excuse the rest of us from attaining a decent understanding of the culture of death. If you want a realistic, minimum aim, then you should be able to talk sensibly about these issues over a cup of coffee (or tea, or even hot chocolate) with your son, a workmate, your neighbour, your cousin or ....

These issues are emotive. At times they generate more heat than light. I know—I was there when the pro-abortionists tried to wrench the doors off Birmingham Town Hall during a packed pro-life rally in the 1980s. I have been harassed by screaming pro-choice feminists at meetings of university debating societies, and I have received hate mail from abortion-rights campaigners. Happily, the days of such extreme pro-choice sentiment and violence have largely passed in the UK. But does this present-day apparent tranquillity not indicate the extent to which the culture of death has become subtly embedded in our society and normalized in our brains? Have we become dulled and muted to its reality? Are we sleepwalking into some terrible normality? Do we think that there is no longer any tribulation out there? Come on people—wake up!

What we must recognize is this: if we are to speak winsomely and with any authority, we must get prepared. We need to learn to communicate coolly. We need to know some facts and figures. We also need to be able to refute some popular arguments and myths. Therefore, the following pages supply some background to eleven diverse, current and primary bioethical issues. This information is general in its nature; it is not derived just from the Scriptures, because we must also strive to communicate with those outside, as well as with those inside, the Christian community. This information is also purposely limited because it is intended as a launch pad to help get you started. Once started, you will begin to grow in knowledge and, hopefully,

CHAPTER 3

wisdom. Believe me, your second conversation, discussion, letter, article, broadcast, interview, lecture or debate on any of these primary issues will be much better than your first.

3.1 Facts and figures, statistics and data

This is perhaps a good place for a little excursion into that land of pitfalls universally known as statistics. Six words of warning. First, be ready: this book is riddled with statistics. They are essential. By what other means can you grasp the numerical dimensions of a particular issue? Second, be inquisitive: seek out the relevant facts and figures for your own location, country, state, town, doorstep. Enlist the Internet as your statistical sidekick, but please use only bona fide sites. Third, be careful: it is easy to misinterpret and misrepresent data, and the media and others often do. Fourth, be aware: understand, for example, the difference between the two types of figures most usually quoted. There are 'totals', as in 'The total number of eggs consumed by people in the UK during 2012 was 11,470 million'. And there are 'rates', as in 'The annual rate of UK egg consumption was therefore 180 per person'. Both figures tell the same story, but from different perspectives. Here is a hint: a rate is always 'per' something, including 'per cent'. Fifth, be realistic: all published data are dated; even the most recently collected, collated and circulated figures are 'out of date', usually by at least a year or two, but they are still valid and enlightening. Sixth, be an Anglophile: the statistics in this book are mainly home-grown, derived from the UK. Herein lies an extra level of potential confusion caused by the quirky history of 'this scepter'd isle' (as it is called in Shakespeare's *King Richard II*, Act 2, scene 1). The UK is composed of Great Britain and Northern Ireland. Great Britain is composed of England, Wales and Scotland. Various published figures refer to these different countries. Yes, it is easy to get confused, but I have done my best to keep everything clear.

3.2 Abortion

Francis Schaeffer and C. Everett Koop wrote in their magnificent book *Whatever Happened to the Human Race?*, 'Of all the subjects relating to the erosion of the sanctity of human life, abortion is the keystone. It is the first and crucial issue that has been overwhelming in changing attitudes toward the value of life in general.'[1] These authors were spot on then and,

SOME OF THE PRIMARY ISSUES

more than three decades later, they still are. Unless, and until, you have worked out your stance on abortion, you will not settle much else in the realm of bioethical issues. So, as they say, let's start with the low-hanging fruit.

3.2.1 ABORTION AND TWO FACTS

We can start by grasping two sets of irrefutable facts—nobody doubts or disagrees with these. First, the numbers. These are the official statistics for England and Wales, published by the Department of Health. Historically, legalized abortion started here on 27 April 1968—six months after the Abortion Act 1967 had received the Royal Assent—so the first full-year's total relates to 1969 and amounted to 54,819. This was equivalent to a rate of 5.3 abortions per 1,000 women between fifteen and forty-four years old, the age range generally assumed to be their reproductive years. Abortion numbers rose inexorably to around 180,000 by the late 1980s and then, for the last twenty or so years, they have more or less plateaued in the region of 190,000, having breached the egregious 200,000 boundary three times between 2006 and 2008.

That is the historic overview. Now consider the contemporary picture. During 2012, the total number of abortions performed in England and Wales, on residents plus non-residents, was 190,972, or equal to a rate of 16.5 per 1,000 women aged fifteen to forty-four. The 1967 Act does not extend to Northern Ireland—abortion remains largely illegal there. However, in Scotland, the total figure for 2012 was 12,447. In other words, the grand total for Great Britain was well in excess of 200,000; to be precise, it was 203,419. This is similar to the entire population of cities like England's York, Wales's Swansea or Scotland's Aberdeen. It also means that almost 4,000 abortions occur in Great Britain every week. That is approximately 780 every weekday—every Monday, every Tuesday, every Wednesday ... Can you believe that? Sometimes I have to do the arithmetic again, just to check that huge daily figure. It is equivalent to about twenty-five classrooms, or fifteen coachloads, of children each day. If such a blazing catastrophe or appalling road accident killing that number of children were to occur, think of the shock, the graphic newspaper headlines and the constant TV news bulletins. Yet 780 daily abortions evoke none of these. And remember, we are not talking about faraway places, like Nairobi, Moscow or Shanghai.

Chapter 3

This is happening in Great Britain, where you may live and work, and go to hospital and church; in truth, it is on your doorstep.

Nowadays, 1 out of every 5 pregnancies in England and Wales ends in abortion. And an estimated 1 in 4 women in England and Wales will have had an abortion by the time she is forty-five years old. Think about that as you push your shopping trolley around your local supermarket. Since the implementation of the Abortion Act 1967, the total number of abortions performed in England and Wales, from 1968 to 2012, has been over 7 million; to be exact, it is 7,470,251. Some 10 per cent of our population is missing.

Maybe you do not live in the UK. Abortion still occurs on your doorstep, in your neighbourhood, on your home soil—it is a worldwide practice. For example, about 1.1 million abortions occur in the USA each year, 0.5 million in Japan, an estimated 11 million in India and 13 million in China. The global total is now reckoned to be approximately 42 million every year. This equates to a worldwide rate of 28 abortions per 1,000 women aged fifteen to forty-four. Just pause, sit back and try to absorb something of the enormity of abortion. These data are official, staggering and condemnatory.

The second set of irrefutable facts relates to what is aborted. The 'favourite' time for abortion is under ten weeks' gestation: 77 per cent of abortions in England and Wales during 2012 occurred within this developmental period. Such an unborn child would fit snugly into the palm of your hand; she has eyes, fingernails and fingerprints; she moves, she swallows, she digests, she sucks her thumb. Blood has been coursing through her body for several weeks—her rudimentary heart began to beat on about day 21. We have been told that this is just a vague collection of cells, or a little piece of poorly defined tissue. What tosh! We have been duped.

Most abortions in the UK are lawful up to twenty-four weeks. Have you ever seen a child of that age? Such an early-bird daughter was recently born to friends of mine; it would be unthinkable to ever contemplate harming, let alone killing, her. Though babies of this age struggle, most of them survive and thrive. What a topsy-turvy world of medical ethics we live in; doctors and nurses can be fighting to preserve the life of such a premature child in the intensive care unit, while down the corridor, in the same hospital, their

Some of the primary issues

colleagues can be deftly destroying an unborn child of a similar age. And if some form of handicap is suspected, not necessarily proved, then there is no time limit: abortion is lawful up to birth—yes, up to forty weeks. In the UK we probably have the most savage abortion law in the whole world; we have been officially aborting just about the longest (since 1968), the latest (up to birth) and the laxest (easy access). Grammatically, these three little words may be adjectival superlatives, but, when they are linked to the termination of the unborn, they become bioethically most pitiable.

3.2.2 ABORTION IN PRACTICE

Abortion continues to be a serious criminal offence in almost all countries around the world. Yet in most of these countries, under particular circumstances, it is now legally permissible. Abortion in the UK remains a crime under Sections 58 and 59 of the Offences Against the Person Act 1861. However, it was decriminalized by the notorious Abortion Act of 1967. This did not legalize abortion unreservedly. It did not grant a right to abortion. It did not provide 'abortion on demand'. Instead, the Act conferred on doctors a defence against illegality, permitting them to terminate pregnancies providing certain conditions were satisfied. The events surrounding the implementation of the 1967 Act are of such importance and consequence that the whole of Chapter 6 is given over to their description. The Act's main provisions, printed on just four sides of Her Majesty's Stationery Office paper, still stubbornly stand after more than four decades. It is a grisly statute that looms up, like some unsightly national monument, to remind us of our malice towards the unborn. Despite numerous attempts at repair and reform it has remained fundamentally intact. Only Section 37 of the Human Fertilisation and Embryology Act 1990 has inserted some minor amendments. The death decree lives on.

Abortions in the UK must now be justified under one or more of seven reasons, or 'statutory grounds', designated A to G. A few facts relating to these grounds will help nuance our perception of the abortion enterprise. As has always been the case, the vast majority of abortions, including 97.3 per cent of the 190,972 in England and Wales during 2012, are carried out under ground C alone. This states that an abortion can be permitted if 'the pregnancy has not exceeded its twenty-fourth week and ... the continuance of the pregnancy would involve risk, greater than if the pregnancy were

Chapter 3

terminated, of injury to the physical or mental health of the pregnant woman'. This is the infamous 'social clause', which can be interpreted to be as long as it is wide, and can include serious cases as well as the frivolous, such as, 'I can't have a baby now, I've just booked my holiday to Greece.' Ground E ('there is a substantial risk that if the child were born it would suffer from such physical or mental abnormalities as to be seriously handicapped') accounted, perhaps surprisingly, for a little under 1.5 per cent of the total in 2012. Ground D ('risk ... of injury to the physical or mental health of any existing children of the family') was invoked for 1.1 per cent of abortions. Ground B ('to prevent grave permanent injury to the physical or mental health of the pregnant woman') continued as a minor justification, cited in fewer than 0.07 per cent of cases. Ground A ('risk to the life to the pregnant woman') is the classic mother v. child scenario, but nowadays, because of advances in obstetrics and gynaecology, such abortions are most uncommon and formed 0.03 per cent of the total. Grounds F and G, which relate to circumstances 'in an emergency' ('to save the life of the pregnant woman' or 'to prevent grave permanent injury to the physical or mental health of the pregnant woman'), are so rarely appealed to these days that their numbers are often no longer recorded, though in 2012 they did amount to 1. These data are further discussed in Section 6.12.

There are several methods by which abortions are procured. They depend primarily upon the developmental age of the unborn child and can be either surgical (53 per cent of the total for 2012) or medical (47 per cent). The main surgical methods are vacuum aspiration (47 per cent of the total, and typically used for pregnancies up to fifteen weeks' gestation) or dilatation and evacuation (D&E, 5 per cent of the total, and used for pregnancies greater than fifteen weeks). There is one principal early medical abortion (EMA) method used to terminate pregnancies up to nine weeks. It proceeds in two stages. First, the abortifacient drug, mifepristone, also known as RU-486, is taken to kill the unborn child. It is then followed, twenty-four to forty-eight hours later, by a second drug, misoprostol, which causes the uterus to contract to expel the dead embryo or foetus. Currently, both drugs must be administered under medical supervision at an approved clinic or hospital.

In 2012, 97 per cent of all abortions for residents in England and Wales were publicly funded by the National Health Service (NHS); 35 per cent were performed in NHS hospitals and 62 per cent were contracted out to independent abortion clinics. The remaining 3 per cent were privately funded. Abortion is now big business. UK government figures show that the cost to the taxpayer in 2010 was £118 million, of which £75 million was paid to the independent clinics. Fees for private clients start at about £650 for a surgical abortion before fourteen weeks, performed under local anaesthetic, and rise to about £1,800 at twenty weeks with a general anaesthetic.

3.2.3 ABORTION AND MORNING-AFTER PILLS

Morning-after pills (MAPs) are frequently described as emergency hormonal 'contraception' (EHC). This is a disingenuous misnomer because MAPs can act *after* fertilization, post-conception. Genuine contraception—the separation of sperm and ovum—means that fertilization is prevented and conception cannot occur. This is the plain meaning of the word from its Latin roots, *contra* (against) and *concipere* (to conceive). Therefore, contraception must, by definition, work *before* fertilization can take place, that is, pre-conceptionally.

Since the introduction of MAPs during the 1980s, their availability has increased rapidly so that they can now be obtained over the counter at pharmacies or online. The commonest brand in the UK is known as Levonelle One Step, and in the USA as Plan B One-Step. The active ingredient in both is the progestogen hormone, levonorgestrel. The manufacturers state that their products are most effective in preventing a woman getting pregnant if they are taken up to seventy-two hours after unprotected sexual intercourse or contraceptive failure. In 2009, yet another type of MAP, marketed as ellaOne in the UK, and as ella in the USA, became available. It contains ulipristal acetate, a selective progesterone receptor modulator, and is claimed to be effective for up to 120 hours.

These MAPs have three modes of action. First, they can have an anti-ovulatory effect, preventing or delaying the production of ova. Second, they can impede the movement of sperm and ova, so they are less likely to come into contact. Third, they can alter the lining of the womb, the endometrium, to prevent any embryo present from implanting. This last post-conception, anti-implantation action inevitably causes the embryo to

Chapter 3

die and therefore constitutes a very early abortion. Hence, MAPs can act as abortifacients.

How many abortions these MAPs initiate is unknown because nobody knows exactly how many MAPs are prescribed, sold or taken, or how often their abortifacient action is triggered. In the UK during 2010, 1 in 5 women aged between eighteen and thirty-five obtained the MAP; that is equivalent to about two million doses nationwide. If just 10 per cent of these acted to abort an early embryo, that would be equal to the entire annual total of UK surgical plus early medical abortions (EMAs). Any such MAP-induced abortions are, of course, not recorded in official government statistics.

3.2.4 ABORTION UNREGULATED, UNLAWFUL AND UNDERCOVER?

It is beyond cavil that a law as bioethically controversial and divisive (and deadly) as the Abortion Act 1967 should be regulated with the utmost administrative rigour and by insistence upon scrupulous compliance. After all, removing and discarding a human embryo or foetus is a serious matter. You might therefore assume that after more than forty years of operating, the stipulations of the Act would now be tightly controlled—but think again. There is growing concern, both inside and outside Parliament, about a distinctly cavalier attitude towards the practice and management of UK abortions. Is the law being stretched, bent or even broken?

For example, contrary to popular belief, the 1967 Act certainly does not permit 'abortion on demand'. Yet if a woman asks for an abortion, her wish is evidently granted; every year, at least 190,000 women in the UK receive such apparently undemanding authorization. One can only wonder: how often do doctors refuse a woman's request? Ever? Presumably, the original sponsors of the Act thought that doctors should, and would—even routinely—say, 'No'.

Nor was abortion foreseen as a method of contraception. Nowadays, all forms of regular contraception are readily accessible—getting pregnant has never been so easy to avoid. Yet thousands of sexually active women either do not use, or misuse, contraceptives and wait until they become pregnant before they decide against having a baby. The numbers having repeat abortions are rising markedly—over a third (36.7 per cent) of women in England and Wales undergoing abortion in 2012 had previously had one or more terminations. Again, one can only wonder: has abortion become an

SOME OF THE PRIMARY ISSUES

alternative, doctor-approved method of birth control? This was never the intention of the 1967 Act.

Or consider 'selective reduction', the practice of terminating a life by injecting potassium chloride into the heart of an unborn twin or triplet, as a consequence mainly of multiple pregnancies caused by 'overzealous' IVF. It is a procedure never envisaged by the architects of the Abortion Act 1967. Yet, in the UK during 2012, a total of ninety-seven unborn children were 'selectively reduced' because their mothers wanted to give birth not to none, but to fewer children. Is that valid grounds for termination? Abortion hard on the heels of IVF is a grotesque type of mixed medicine—deliberate human creation closely followed by deliberate human destruction.

Or think about sex-selective abortion. This has long been widespread in China and India, but investigations during 2012 uncovered evidence of the practice in the UK, offered by doctors willing to falsify the required regulatory paperwork. These gender-based abortions are performed because the unborn child is of the 'wrong' sex—the parents want a different child, usually a boy. Such terminations are outside the provisions of the 1967 Act and are therefore strictly illegal in the UK.

Other examples of noncompliance exist. For instance, the 1967 Act permits an abortion, according to its rubric, only 'if two registered medical practitioners are of the opinion, formed in good faith', that it would meet the terms of the Act. However, this originally protective arrangement, a safeguard against incorrect assessments by doctors and too hasty decisions by women, is now generally regarded as little more than a rubber-stamping exercise of the abortion authorization form HSA1. After all, how often do two doctors ever see, let alone carefully interview and examine, the abortion-requesting woman to enable them to come to their mutually agreed verdict 'in good faith'? Nobody seems to know. In January 2014, the government announced that during 2012, only 46 per cent of women who had abortions under ground C were recorded as being seen by one or more of the certifying doctors. But a few days later, the government admitted that this figure was incorrect and impossible to specify accurately. Furthermore, some doctors and clinics have been caught flouting these regulations by pre-signing the required documentation. Others are known to have returned the abortion notification form HAS4 to the Chief Medical

Chapter 3

Officer, as required by the Act, but only partially completed. These are breaches of the law.

These examples of disregard, even contempt, for the 1967 Act are dismissed by some pro-abortionists as minor lapses under the administrative demands of an outdated statute. For them, even the modest restrictions of the 1967 Act are too rigid. Despite the Act's liberal nature and scope, pro-abortion campaigners have repeatedly sought to undermine its legal boundaries and to extend its reach. Their continuing challenges have called for the revocation of the two-doctor signature rule, the introduction of no-questions-asked abortion, the administration of early medical abortion (EMA) medication at home without medical supervision, and the Act's introduction into Northern Ireland. All such attempts have so far failed. For some, disdain for the Act and its prohibitions continues.

Then there is the fundamental issue of consent. All medical procedures require the informed consent of the patient. Abortion is not without recognized hazards, both mental and physical. To explain these fully, pre-abortion information, offered by independent advisers, would be a sensible arrangement to ensure that at least the spirit of the Act is being followed. But attempts to decouple the counselling of pregnant women from the providers of abortion—who may have a vested interest, financial and otherwise, in the outcomes—have been strongly resisted. Likewise, the idea of a cooling-off period—a day or two for women to reconsider their options—has been vigorously opposed by abortion providers. These are hardly radical proposals—they have already been implemented in, for example, Germany and some US states. What is so wrong with giving women proper choice and ensuring fully informed consent? Sadly, those five little words, 'If only I had known', have become a haunting motto for too many women who have undergone abortions unaware of the risks, and now wish they had not. Pregnant women deserve a better deal.

Despite these anomalies in abortion practice, it has always been assumed that the official abortion figures, collected and released by the UK government, are accurate. Indeed, in Section 3.2.1 above I wrote that 'nobody doubts or disagrees with these'. Was my confidence misplaced? Consider one apparent statistical discrepancy. The National Down Syndrome Cytogenetic Register (NDSCR) collects data from all the clinical cytogenetic laboratories in England and Wales. It reported that in 2010,

SOME OF THE PRIMARY ISSUES

1,188 unborn children were prenatally diagnosed with Down's syndrome and that 942 of them were aborted. However, the official government figures, published by the Department of Health, record that in 2010, only 482 abortions were performed for Down's syndrome, under ground E. Why the 50-per-cent disparity? Are the Department's figures wrong? Are doctors neglecting to report, or fabricating their form-filling, deliberately or negligently, and therefore illegally? Is this discrepancy indicative of an even greater failure to record and publish the numbers of abortions performed for reasons other than ground E? Is the annual total of some 190,000 abortions in England and Wales an underestimate? Something, it seems, is not right.

Now go to the dark, outer limits of the 1967 Act. The ethics and practice of eugenic and late abortions are especially gruesome and, for many people, they rightly cause deep bioethical anxiety. What is their extent? After resisting disclosure for six years, the UK's Department of Health had to be ordered by the High Court to reveal the relevant information. Between 2002 and 2010, a total of 17,983 abortions were performed in England and Wales under ground E—that is, for reasons of disability; 1,189 of them were performed after twenty-four weeks. These facts prompt at least seven additional concerns. First, if abortions are legal, withholding their details from the public is surely counter to governmental transparency. Second, what does abortion for suspected disability, under ground E, say to those already born disabled? Is it 'What a pity, you slipped through the screening and prenatal diagnosis (PND) scheme'? Third, we have lexically engineered these people. When we abort them, they are the 'handicapped' (the very word used in the 1967 Act), but when they survive we call them the 'disabled' and provide them with benign assistance. Fourth, since these ground-E abortions depend upon 'substantial risk' of handicap, rather than proven handicap, some 'normal' unborn children will have been erroneously aborted because of 'false-positive' PND test results. Fifth, among the medical conditions used to justify these abortions are cleft lip and palate, Down's syndrome and spina bifida. While some of these disorders can be serious, most are not incompatible with life outside the womb and none of those affected deserves the death penalty. Several are readily treatable— for example, surgery for cleft palate can be remarkably successful. Sixth, the incidence of late abortions persists. Figures for 2012 alone show that

Chapter 3

there were 2,860 performed at more than twenty weeks, with 160 at over twenty-four weeks, including 28 at thirty-two weeks and over. These are particularly horrid—some such children are not only 'capable of being born alive', but also of surviving. Seventh, eugenic abortions, and, above all, late eugenic abortions, say something unsavoury about us: collectively, we have a nasty streak.

Finally, should ground-E abortions even be performed? Consider two aspects. First, what is their legal basis? The 1967 Act declares it to be 'that there is a substantial risk that if the child were born it would suffer from such physical or mental abnormalities as to be seriously handicapped'. Although the criteria of 'substantial' and 'seriously' are not defined, they are known, in practice, to be subjectively and liberally interpreted. Furthermore, it is impossible to predict the degree of handicap that any disability will produce, despite the Act's requirement to do so. Much will depend upon the responses of the disabled child, the parents and the medical staff. Recall the astonishing feats of disabled athletes in past Paralympic Games. Then consider the fact that, for example, many Down's adults are cheerily contented and gainfully employed. The very existence of ground-E abortions acts as a disincentive to strive for such medical, athletic and social accomplishments. Second, the indication of any suspected abnormalities carries the entitlement to abort up to full term, forty weeks. On the other hand, an unborn child with no such disability can be aborted only up to twenty-four weeks. Is this not discriminatory? It seems to fly in the face of the Equality Act 2010, which prohibits anyone treating another less favourably because of his or her disability. The 1967 and 2010 Acts appear to be at loggerheads. The disability community rightly calls for the removal of all discrimination—but the 1967 Act seemingly perpetuates it. These matters surrounding eugenic abortion warrant debate and resolution.

It is evident that Parliament, the Department of Health and the police must be more proactive and vigilant. Evidence suggests that the Abortion Act 1967 is not being correctly enforced or adequately monitored. Moreover, the Care Quality Commission (CQC), the NHS watchdog in England, which oversees the legal compliance of abortion services, patently has work to do. Any abortion performed outside the provisions of the 1967 Act is illegal under the Offences Against the Person Act 1861. Offenders could be subject to lifetime imprisonment, and those who knowingly falsify information, such as abortion-authorization documents and numerical returns, could be prosecuted under the Perjury Act 1911. Abortionists, like the rest of us, must obey the law, or face the consequences.

3.2.5 ABORTION AND MENTAL HEALTH

Abortion and its subsequent effects on women's mental health have been contentious issues for decades. Abortionists have consistently underplayed, denied and even ignored the existence of any adverse psychological sequelae. They say that post-abortion syndrome (PAS) is a myth. They say that any negative outcomes experienced by a woman who has had an abortion are due to other factors, such as a pre-existing psychiatric illness, lack of friendly support or too great an emotional connection with her foetus, rather than the abortion as such. But that is not the pro-life case. The pro-life claim is that abortion is rarely the sole cause of mental health problems, but rather it is an increased risk, a trigger, an aggravating factor for many women. Pregnancy-crisis counsellors can certainly tell countless stories of women's ensuing grief, regret, guilt, substance abuse, heartbreak and pain following an abortion. Here is the nexus where cold research and warm narrative clash: psychological analysis can be too objectively detached, whereas anecdotal evidence can be too subjectively attached. As a consequence, evident symptoms, which may not become apparent for several years, do not always fit neatly into the diagnostic 'tick boxes' of particular mental disorders, so that these women have often been dismissed as mentally healthy. Hence the commonly held medical conclusion: no link exists between abortion and adverse mental health.

But pay attention! An emerging corpus of peer-reviewed research from around the world, especially from New Zealand and the USA, including even some published by pro-choice investigators, is demonstrating that women are indeed more likely to suffer from a variety of mental health problems—including anxiety, depression and suicidal behaviours—subsequent to abortion, compared with those whose pregnancies go to term. To date, the largest review of the subject, a meta-analysis of twenty-two previous studies involving 877,181 participants, found that 'Women who had undergone an abortion experienced an 81% increased risk of mental health problems, and nearly 10% of the incidence of mental health problems was shown to be attributable to abortion'.[2] PAS really is out there, unless you decide to turn

CHAPTER 3

a blind, pro-choice eye to it. Curiously, some abortion clinics have begun to offer post-abortion counselling—a rather odd provision for a repudiated condition. On the other hand, how many women would want to return to their abuser for help? The proper, remedial measure for future public policy is simple: every woman seeking an abortion should be warned of the increased risks to her mental health, and those who suffer such sequelae should be provided with appropriate support. Informed consent and appropriate care—are they too much to ask for?

Notwithstanding the pros and cons surrounding these heated and ongoing controversies, consider this novel thesis. As already noted, most abortions (97.3 per cent of the 2012 total) in England and Wales are performed under ground C, the so-called 'social clause', which sanctions abortion for reasons of increased 'risk ... of injury to the physical or mental health of the pregnant woman'. The Department of Health, commenting on its own 2012 statistics, explained that 'The vast majority (99.94%) of ground C-only terminations were reported as being performed because of a risk to the woman's mental health'. In other words, the 'physical' health risk is hardly ever cited as grounds for abortion; during 2012, it was used just 108 times.

Then in November 2011, the Royal College of Obstetricians and Gynaecologists published its updated guideline, *The Care of Women Requesting Induced Abortion*, and stated, 'Women with an unintended pregnancy should be informed that the evidence suggests that they are no more or less likely to suffer adverse psychological sequelae whether they have an abortion or continue with the pregnancy and have the baby.'[3] And in December 2011, the National Collaborating Centre for Mental Health at the Royal College of Psychiatrists published a large-scale review of the relevant literature, entitled *Induced Abortion and Mental Health*. It stated that 'The rates of mental health problems for women with an unwanted pregnancy were the same whether they had an abortion or gave birth'.[4] Together, these two high-ranking publications declared categorically that the continuation of a pregnancy does *not* involve risk of injury to the mental health of the pregnant woman greater than if the pregnancy were terminated. This is a bioethical thunderbolt. Seemingly, 99.94 per cent of the abortions for residents of England and Wales performed under ground C for mental health reasons—that is, at least 97 per cent of all legal abortions, now numbering over 185,000 each year—are outside the provisions of the Act and are therefore illegal. Has a coach and horses been driven through the Abortion Act 1967, year after year? This thesis needs testing in the courts.

3.2.6 OTHER EFFECTS OF ABORTION

Over and above all these facts and figures, accusations and speculations, arguments and counter-arguments, there remains the elephant in the room. Can you see it? Never forget it: every abortion—legal or illegal, coerced or voluntary, early or late, surgical or medical—ends the existence of a real, live human being. Never forget him, her and them.

We all live in societies that put to death our young and even claim that there is some virtue in doing so. We are told that abortion is carried out for the good of the mother, the sake of the child, or both. Our taxes and our votes support it. And if we say and do nothing, our heads, hearts and hands condone such malevolent public policies. We have been too easily seduced by the *argumentum ad populum* fallacy: abortion must be OK because lots of people say it is OK.

Yet abortion has had profound and deleterious effects upon individuals, families, societies and our very civilization. For instance, abortion has confounded the unique role of women in the bearing and caring of children. We have asked women to be gentle and compassionate, yet abortion changes these expectations. Their peers, doctors, husbands and boyfriends tell women that abortion is 'for them', but in reality abortion is 'against them'. Abortion has damaged many women physically and mentally. Though abortion procedures are well practised, haemorrhage, sepsis and physical damage to the reproductive tract and other organs are still reported, especially among young, physiologically immature girls. As already discussed, the adverse mental health issues, often grouped under the umbrella of PAS, are becoming more widely recognized, though grudgingly by some, as serious medical conditions. Abortion can indeed inflict devastation upon women.

In addition, evidence for an association between abortion and breast cancer—the so-called ABC link—from both Western and more recently Eastern countries is mounting. For example, a meta-analysis, published in 2013, of thirty-six studies covering fourteen provinces in China concluded

Chapter 3

that one abortion increased the risk of breast cancer by 44 per cent, two abortions by 76 per cent and three abortions by 89 per cent.[5] As the generation of women first exposed to legalized abortion grows older, this ABC connection may become more evident. There is also increasing confirmation of a positive association between induced abortions and subsequent births occurring prematurely, with their often serious health complications and high related medical costs. Though abortion may not be the primary cause of these adverse effects, it appears to be a significant risk factor. And though the risks may be relatively small, the large numbers of abortions performed each year mean that the outcomes must be regarded as numerically and medically important. Then again, repeat abortions might be expected to increase the incidence and intensity of these poor outcomes. If so, the bad news is that in 2012, 36.7 per cent of women in England and Wales undergoing abortion had previously had one or more terminations. But even the mention of these contraindications is abhorrent to the abortion industry; most of its practitioners and supporters strenuously deride the existence of any such adverse links. Yet for how much longer can they deny the actualities and aftermaths of abortion? The overall message remains sad and uncomplicated: no woman gets away from abortion scot-free.

Families are affected too. Abortion has distorted that centre of safety, nurture and love in every society as it is right there, in the home, that abortion is often decided upon. Family members are time and again the victims and the propagators of the abortion conspiracy, namely, that 'abortion is safe and simple', while for many it brings guilt, remorse and long-term grief. Men are also affected. Abortion has abrogated their traditional role as protectors of women and children. Abortion, proposed and intended, renders the unborn child effectively fatherless, defenceless and exposed to peril. In addition, it has subverted that most deep and complex of relationships between a parent and a child: abortion abruptly ends this. Abortion can create an immediate void in the parents' lives. There is not only embryonic or foetal loss, there is a real loss for real parents: a man and a woman have irrevocably become a father and a mother, and for some, even though their dead child was unfelt and unseen, abortion can become a major death experience.

Abortion never occurs in a relationship vacuum; abortion can be the cause and the result of failed relationships. For example, it is estimated that

Some of the primary issues

between 40 and 50 per cent of couples break up following an abortion, with a collapse of intimacy and trust often the primary causes. In addition, some pregnant women undergo abortion in the hope of 'hanging on' to their man, a strategy that frequently fails. All of this has produced a new deceitfulness and selfishness, because abortion 'for the sake of the child' is really for the sake of the mother and father. Moreover, it has caused uncertainty in the minds of some born children—if my parents aborted my sibling, did they ever really want me? It has frustrated the hopes and roles of grandparents. It has helped promote promiscuity and undermine marriage by 'covering up' pregnancies arising from fornication and adultery. So we may well ask, when did abortion ever produce or strengthen personal and family relationships? Abortion does not solve problems; it typically exchanges one set for another.

The advent of easy access to abortion has, in part, been the cause of a huge decline in the number of child adoptions. In 1968, the year legalized abortion started in the UK, there were 27,000 adoptions in England and Wales. In 2012, there were just 5,206. Adoption, with its biblical precedents—such as 2 Samuel 9; Galatians 4:4–7; and Ephesians 1:5—used to be the route by which many infertile couples raised a family. For many, it has become a virtual cul-de-sac: for each adoption completed in 2012, thirty-six children were wasted by abortion. Can that be a sensible outcome?

Easy abortion has seared the conscience of much of the medical profession—and that of the public too. Abortion has wrecked the historic foundations of medical ethics and practice, namely, the Hippocratic Oath and the Judaeo-Christian doctrines. How can the Hippocratic dictum, 'First, do no harm', be reconciled with the practice of abortion? How can the edict of Matthew 22:39, 'Love your [unborn] neighbour as yourself', be fulfilled by killing him or her? The doctor has become a medical schizophrenic, a life preserver but also a life taker. And nowadays, because abortion has become such a routine part of obstetrics and gynaecology training and practice, many Christian and 'morally sensitive' doctors and nurses—among the best we have—will be deterred, even excluded, from making careers in these areas of medicine. Abortion has undermined the profession's illustrious history.

But the effects of abortion have gone even wider; we have all been affected. For example, abortion has hardened our attitude and blunted

Chapter 3

our compassion towards the weak. The 'search and destroy' approach of prenatal screening and diagnosis (PND), which usually results in the abortion of the unborn disabled, has fostered ambivalence in our society towards the born disabled. It has thus eased the way for the next logical development in the culture of death, infanticide. If killing up to birth is legal, why not up to birth plus a day or two? Furthermore, it has fostered an indifference to say, Third World devastation and famine. How can our response to such deprivations ever be adequate while we have such a cheap view of human life at home? Clearly, the unborn child is not the only victim of abortion. Abortion is bad, bad, bad.

3.2.7 ABORTION AND FOUR RESERVATIONS

At a distance, abortion can seem to be a fairly simple bioethical issue, but face to face it can be a monster. A few people want more abortions; most people want fewer. But how many want none? Abortion generates personal and societal schism. So Mary Smith and Tom Brown both say, 'Yes, I think abortion is wrong, but ...' Ah, the indulgent, non-judgemental 'but'. Twenty-first-century men and women can too easily assume that displays of moderation and tolerance are the hallmarks of intellectual integrity and emotional maturity. As a consequence, ours is an age uncomfortable with absolutes and dogmas. The children of postmodernism no longer seek truth in terms of objective absolutes; relativism rules their reasoning. But Christians are not unfamiliar with absolutes—we weave words such as almighty, infallible, pure, inerrant, omniscient and perfect into our everyday language. And how can the one true God be absolutely other than 'a spirit, infinite, eternal, and unchangeable, in his being, wisdom, power, holiness, justice, goodness and truth'?[6] Or think of the Ten Commandments—no wriggle room there. Christians live and breathe absolutes. So why do some shy away from taking an unconditional, wholehearted, 100-per-cent pro-life stance on bioethical issues? What are their uncertainties? Their doubts and fears should never be lightly dismissed—they can be weighty and encumbering—but, by the same token, they must never be exploited in order to evade commitment and avoid duty. Their reservations are epitomized by four 'hard case' questions. These need answering.

Number one: what about disability? Consider four propositions. First, the practices of abortion, infanticide, embryo destruction and euthanasia performed on the grounds of handicap are confronted throughout this book. Read Section 2.6 again. Second, at different times, different groups within society have been regarded as inferior. Once it was slaves, peasants and women; now it is the disabled. They have been declared subordinate, substandard and therefore disposable. That most fundamental of human rights, the right to life, has increasingly been denied them. That gift of bearing the *imago Dei* has been illicitly withdrawn. On what basis? Because they are unwanted, unloved, costly, unproductive and surplus to requirements? Third, that list of adjectives is an indictment of any society aspiring to be civilized. It should be inimical to the Christian. Fourth, does the Bible support such an odious worldview? No, of course not. Instead, quite the opposite is found throughout its pages: wicked people are condemned, good people are praised, and the poor and disabled are helped and restored. So do not make the disabled your 'hard case' to justify a less than unreserved opposition to the culture of death, and in particular to abortion.

Number two: what about rape? Again, four propositions. First, rape is a dreadful, dreadful crime; whether committed by a stranger, a colleague or a family member, it is to be abhorred, wholly and utterly. It is violent and destructive. Figures released in 2013 estimate that around 85,000 women in England and Wales are now raped each year. Such an attack may leave a woman physically injured, but she will without doubt be emotionally damaged. Second, mercifully, rape rarely leads to pregnancy. The woman may be in the non-fertile phase of her menstrual cycle, using contraception, too young or too old to conceive, or sterile. Sexual intercourse may have been incomplete, or the rapist may be infertile. Third, she may become pregnant, so what then? What would an abortion solve? It will not take away the ordeal or the memory of the rape; to agree to an abortion, a second violent attack upon her, will not unmake it. Of course, she never wanted a baby by this man, under these circumstances; but the unborn child is guiltless, and causing his or her death, making him or her a second victim, is no solution to the woman's immediate or future situation. Moreover, the baby is genetically half hers and possibly the only child she will ever have. Such women require skilled help—emotional and practical assistance for months, perhaps even years. During pregnancy women can, and do, change their feelings and their choices. They need time to think and consider their options, not be briskly hurried off to the nearest abortion clinic. With positive support, some raped

Chapter 3

and pregnant women do come to love their children and keep them, while others will put them up for adoption. Fourth, none of this is straightforward or easy. While abortion will never make the rape go away, it can make matters far worse. To choose birth rather than death is to bring something good out of what was initially a deeply unwanted pregnancy. It is the loving, courageous, strong response. Yes, rape is a 'hard case', but does it really justify killing the innocent, unborn child? Let the child live and bring joy and healing either to the mother or to the adoptive parents.

Number three: what about the backstreet? A return to 'backstreet' abortion, with its images of old crones, coat hangers, hot baths and bottles of gin, is still used to abuse those who wish to limit abortion and repeal its legal provisions. Such an argument is spurious, again for at least four reasons. First, for abortion to become illegal again it will have to be accompanied by a change in the hearts and minds of the general population; the prerequisite will be a more pro-life society, which would then genuinely welcome such pro-life legislation. Second, any return to the backstreet, though criminal, would be technically safer now. After all, there are thousands of doctors out there who, through frequent practice, have become very skilled in abortion procedures—a few 'bent' ones would keep the backstreet mostly sterile and secure. Third, 'easy, legal abortion' created a new clientele among women who would previously never have contemplated abortion while it remained illegal. The unthinking response of many people, post-1967, has been, 'If it's legal, it must be OK'. On the other hand, a future society, educated and captivated by a culture of life, would have little cause or call for abortion. The backstreet would be nigh-on deserted. Fourth, there has been a recent rise in the numbers of early medical abortions (EMA) using readily available abortifacients, such as RU-486, as well as emergency 'contraception', like the copper intra-uterine device (IUD, or the 'coil') and morning-after pills (MAPs); these would lessen any demand for backstreet abortions of a surgical nature. While abortion may never disappear, the bad old backstreet, whatever its previous extent and danger, will never reappear.

Number four: is abortion ever justified? The simple answer is 'No'. Consider three facets. First, under what circumstances would you justify killing an adult human being? Would it be war, self-defence or even capital punishment? None of these conditions applies to the non-aggressive, non-violent, innocent, unborn child. What has he or she done to deserve death? Second, there is one type of medically justifiable, bioethically sound exception. An example is that of a woman with an ectopic tubal pregnancy, where the unborn child is growing in a Fallopian tube rather than in the uterus. The pregnancy cannot continue there; the death of the unborn child is inevitable. Most cases are resolved by spontaneous regression, which requires no intervention; otherwise doctors will act to remove an already dead embryo. If the pregnancy continues, there will be an increasing risk of rupture and severe haemorrhaging, and so surgery may become necessary to save the mother's life—yet the death of her unborn child is both unavoidable and unintentional. In this instance, it is *only* the mother's life which can be saved—the unborn child is too young to survive, and relocation to the uterus is medically impossible. Or think about the classic mother v. child example of a pregnant woman who has advanced cancer of the uterus. Her proposed radiotherapy and chemotherapy will kill her unborn child, but, if untreated, the cancer will kill her. If she dies, they both die. The family and the medical team are faced with an inescapable dilemma: there are two patients, yet both cannot live. Thankfully, this sort of catch-22 crisis is becoming more uncommon, because if the unborn child can be coaxed to viability, say, at twenty-eight or thirty weeks, he or she can be delivered by Caesarean section and the mother's cancer treatment can be started immediately, perhaps saving both lives. Third, over the years I have collected newspaper reports of this sort of predicament. In about half, the mother decided to sacrifice her life for the sake of her unborn child; in the remainder, the child was 'aborted'. But this is *not* abortion in the sense of the 1967 Act. There was no intention to kill. This was good medicine, which allowed one patient to live rather than both die. Such a medical intervention, an 'indirect abortion', is bioethically light years away from those millions performed deliberately, avoidably and often solely for personal convenience.

So, have your 'hard case' reservations been answered or just exposed again? Some clear thinking and a conscious disentangling from the Zeitgeist can be surprisingly helpful in coming to truthful and robust conclusions. Yes, abortion does raise difficult cases and rare medical crises, but they must be honestly faced and settled.

3.2.8 ABORTION PERSONALLY

Quite a few people reading these pages will have been caught up in abortion, whether directly or indirectly. Some will have had an abortion, and maybe

Chapter 3

more than one. Others will have encouraged, or even pressurized, a daughter, girlfriend, sister, wife, colleague or stranger to have an abortion. If so, the stark truth cannot be dodged—you have done wrong. The Bible says you have sinned. But all is not lost—far from it. There is forgiveness for your actions and freedom from your guilt. The God of the Bible is a pardoning God. 'If we confess our sins, he is faithful and just and will forgive us our sins and purify us from all unrighteousness' (1 John 1:9). If you have been up close and personal with abortion, you need to have dealings with God. Go to the Lord Jesus Christ and seek, and find, grace, mercy and forgiveness. There is rescue and recovery from abortion.

3.2.9 ABORTION IN THE FUTURE

For the foreseeable future, abortion will persist as the most divisive of bioethical issues. This cruel practice will still be with us in, say, 2020—indeed, it will never, ever, go away entirely. The annual number of abortions recorded in England and Wales will probably remain static at around 200,000—this figure has changed little over the last decade. Similarly, the annual rate will hover around 17 abortions per 1,000 women aged fifteen to forty-four years old. Our eight millionth abortion will occur sometime during 2015—it will be a most solemn milestone.

One reason for this apparent statistical status quo is the greater use of morning-after pills (MAPs) with their abortifacient action. Their growing popularity—an estimated two million doses were supplied to UK women during 2010—masks the true number of abortions occurring because these self-administered, MAP-induced, very early abortions are not recorded in official statistics. Hence, the likelihood is that the 200,000 total of doctor-administered abortions, as published by the Department of Health, will remain unvarying; maybe it will even decrease slightly. MAPs obviously represent a lucrative market for both manufacturers and retailers—for example, sales of Plan B in the USA reached $88 million for the year ending May 2012—so new products and wider distribution patterns can be expected. How long will it be before 'legislative creep' allows them to be on sale on supermarket shelves and dished out, free of charge, in schools?

Another discernable trend is the rise of medical, as opposed to surgical, abortions. These early medical abortions (EMAs) started with the 1991 licensing approval of RU-486 and by 2001 they accounted for 13 per cent of all abortions in England and Wales; by 2012, that figure had climbed to 47 per cent. RU-486 must currently be administered during the first nine weeks of a pregnancy under supervision at a registered medical facility, such as a hospital, doctor's surgery or clinic. These stipulations have already been challenged, unsuccessfully, in the courts. If, and when, these current regulations are revoked, women will be able to take the EMA drugs at home and abort there too. But think about the implications. Taken in private, women would lack the physical and emotional support and information they deserve. There would be no way of monitoring their safety. Problems associated with heavy bleeding are not uncommon, and any incomplete or failed EMAs, which currently account for 2 to 3 per cent, would require the additional trauma of surgical terminations. If EMA has been portrayed as a quick and easy two-step process, women will be ill-prepared for what may follow. Going through the procedure alone, at home, could be a frightening time, particularly for younger women and girls. Home should be a place of warmth and security, not the location for an abortion with potentially nasty complications or memories of a lonely medical ordeal. In addition, women would have to cope with the disposal of a dead embryo or foetus, which for many could be a harrowing experience with possible psychological sequelae.

Analyses of recent abortion statistics for England and Wales suggest two other future trends. First, the numbers of repeat abortions are continuing to rise. As stated above, over a third of those (36.7 per cent, or 67,956 women) undergoing an abortion during 2012 had had one or more previously; ten years ago, that figure was 31 per cent. The fact that 153 of these women had had six or more abortions is almost beyond comprehension. It seems that increasing numbers of women are using abortion as a method of birth control; such repeat abortions are costing the NHS around £1 million each week. The second trend relates specifically to women in the thirty to thirty-four age group. They too are having more and more abortions—a total of 30,353 during 2012, an 8.5 per cent increase over the previous two years—but with a 47 per cent repeat rate, they are the fastest-growing group of abortion repeaters. Why is this? No doubt several reasons exist. Certainly, mounting financial pressures and opportunities on career ladders have caused many of these women to delay childbirth and family life; they continue to work to pay the mortgage and chase job promotions while their

Chapter 3

biological clocks continue to tick. For them, having a child in their thirties is ill-timed; abortion is their solution. Some, sadly, believe they can catch up later in life with the help of IVF; too few have calculated its failure rate, especially for older women. This chattels v. child trend is a sorry development of our times. It looks set to continue.

Every commercial enterprise knows that marketing is the key to gaining and maintaining future business. From April 2012, private abortion clinics were, for the first time, allowed to advertise on UK television and radio to promote their 'post-conception advice services' (PCAS)—what a euphemism! So, along with beer and car advertisements, those for abortion may now be beamed right into your sitting room, without your permission or request, but at your expense. In 2010, UK taxpayers contributed a massive £75 million to these private abortion clinics. Only they can afford such high-end advertising; pro-life pregnancy crisis groups can hardly afford Yellow Pages. This forthright use of commercial media represents another step in the trivialization of human life. Is the termination of a pregnancy really in the same category as product retail? Where next? On buses, sports stadiums, street hoardings, unsolicited emails, church noticeboards?

As already explained, abortion is currently the most common medical procedure that takes place without proper, fully informed consent—not that the primary patient, the unborn child, is capable of giving such permission. It is the woman who is frequently denied full information about the risks of physical and mental health sequelae. The evidence is amassing and it surely cannot be too long before the medical establishment, and particularly the abortion industry, must admit to at least some of abortion's adverse indications. In the future, the dissemination of those warnings should cause pregnant women to think at least twice before considering or consenting to abortion.

Meanwhile, the immediate future does not look bright. We are stuck in this abortion quagmire, with its deep social, economic, physical, medical and ideological roots. The long-term remedy lies mainly with pro-life education, especially of the next generation. But these youngsters do not need the sort of value-free sex education currently given in most schools. If it is, allegedly, unrealistic to teach abstinence—the only sure route to avoiding teenage pregnancy and teenage abortion—parents and churches are faced with an even greater responsibility and challenge. Some measure

Some of the primary issues

of the uphill nature of this educational task is expressed by this question: what reason has a girl or a woman to say 'No' nowadays? Unintended pregnancy's quick fix is still abortion, freely available on the NHS and readily performed by abortion clinics. The dénouement: the woman's problem solved, the boyfriend absolved, colleagues consoled, the private clinic rewarded, the NHS unburdened, society relieved. It looks like a win-win situation for everyone—except that deep down, we know it to be not so. The future need is for that deep-seated truth to be spoken and spread. Eventually it will be heard.

3.2.10 ABORTION: IN CONCLUSION

Schaeffer and Koop were entirely right: 'Of all the subjects relating to the erosion of the sanctity of human life, abortion is the keystone.' Abortion is always corrosive. History teaches us that when any society regards, and therefore begins to treat, human life as a cheap and disposable commodity, the outcome is always bad. Our world has persisted in putting to death its unborn offspring, those who are among our most precious legacies. The full cost of such a public policy has yet to be calculated, let alone paid.

The sheer scale and callousness of abortion is hard to grasp. After all these years, I still redo the arithmetic and I still shudder when I survey this inane enterprise. It has become the silent holocaust. Legalized abortion was never meant to be like this. Back in 1966, when the Medical Termination of Pregnancy Bill was going through the UK Parliament, abortion was envisaged as something for the poor, overworked woman struggling with three or four children, living in squalor with a useless, drunken husband. It was truly regarded as a final option, a last resort. Today, most abortions are for young, single women in good health, in decent housing, with a regular income and carrying healthy unborn children.

Have you ever seen the products of a typical abortion? I am not in favour of placarding giant images of them through town centres or at shopping malls. But discreet pictures of the tiny severed hands, the torn feet, and the crushed body and head are horrifying because they are the dismembered parts of 'one of us'. It is petite carnage. The pieces are human pieces and therefore they (should) grieve us. Just what are we doing? How could we ever have let this madness start? How could we have let it continue for over forty years? And some in the UK want to make it even worse; for

CHAPTER 3

them, 200,000 abortions each year are not enough. Similarly, for others throughout the rest of the world, 42 million abortions each year are still too few.

Shame on us all! If you have not shed tears over the practice and aftermath of this issue, you have not yet understood abortion.

3.3 In vitro fertilization (IVF)

In vitro fertilization (IVF) is the most familiar of the assisted-reproductive technologies (ARTs), which include other procedures such as artificial insemination and surrogacy. IVF came to the attention of the general public with the birth just before midnight on Tuesday, 25 July 1978 of Louise Joy Brown, the world's first 'test-tube' baby, at the Oldham and District Hospital in Greater Manchester. Since then, IVF treatment has escalated so that currently almost 2 per cent of all births in the UK are IVF babies. What is more, there are now at least five million children worldwide who have begun life in this unnatural way.

3.3.1 IVF AND INFERTILITY

Much of the impetus behind the development of ARTs, and particularly IVF, has been for the treatment of infertility. Infertility problems, difficulties in conceiving, are not uncommon and are generally estimated to affect 1 in 7 couples. A third of these cases are caused by problems in women, a third in men, and the remainder are unexplained. Such conditions are usually associated with either damaged or blocked Fallopian tubes, ovulatory problems or endometriosis in women, and poor quality or a low count of sperm in men. But there are many, many other minor causes, such as drug and alcohol abuse, smoking, obesity, stress, poor nutrition, previous abortions, increasing age, polluted environments and sexually transmitted infections (STIs). Among the last is the surprisingly, even frighteningly, widespread *Chlamydia trachomatis*, which is now reckoned to infect as many as 1 in 10 sexually active young women. It tends to be asymptomatic, so most are unaware that they are infected, but it can cause pelvic inflammatory disease (PID), which can lead to infertility. There is a mountain of future infertility problems quietly amassing out there.

Nevertheless, to keep a true perspective on this topic, it should be remembered that 84 per cent of couples who have regular sexual

SOME OF THE PRIMARY ISSUES

intercourse, say two or three times per week, without contraception, will achieve a pregnancy within a year. And about 92 per cent of such couples will conceive within two years. In addition, for some couples, a few simple lifestyle changes, such as eating healthily and exercising frequently, can increase the likelihood of conception.

While there is no doubt that infertility can cause deep psychological distress in some people—as recorded in several biblical narratives, including those of Sarai in Genesis 16 and Rachel in Genesis 30—few would argue that every couple has the right or entitlement to children. Such a notion is indeed foreign to the Bible's worldview, which maintains that God is sovereign in both infertility (1 Sam. 1:5) and fertility (Luke 1:36–37).

3.3.2 IVF AND THE WARNOCK REPORT

In the early 1980s, it became clear that the fast-moving innovations of the ARTs were outstripping our bioethical, legal and social thinking. Technology was not only making children, it was also remaking parenthood. It used to be received wisdom that every baby had one mother and one father. That was no longer necessarily so. A baby could have as many as five parents— two fathers and three mothers. For example, in a surrogacy arrangement coupled with IVF, there might be the commissioning father and mother (an infertile couple), the genetic parents (a gamete-donating man and woman) and the biological mother (a surrogate). The whole ART enterprise was becoming uncontrollably complex, and, in some cases, definitely absurd. To counter this, the then Conservative government set up, in July 1982, a Committee of Inquiry into Human Fertilisation and Embryology, chaired by Dame (now Baroness) Mary Warnock. The Committee's terms of reference were 'To consider recent and potential developments in medicine and science related to human fertilisation and embryology; to consider what policies and safeguards should be applied, including consideration of the social, ethical and legal implications of these developments; and to make recommendations'. The landmark Warnock Report was published two years later, in July 1984.

The Warnock Report addressed the UK situation, but it was also a global forerunner: the world was watching and waiting for clear bioethical statements and practical guidance with regard to these novel technologies. However, the Report turned out to be a dog's breakfast. Its thinking was

Chapter 3

in too many places muddled and shallow, and it often avoided the major issues, or simply fudged them. For instance, it eschewed basic questions like 'When does human life begin?' and 'What is the moral status of the human embryo?' The Warnock Report thus became one of the most influential examples of unprincipled, utilitarian thinking of the twentieth century, yet its bioethical reach has extended comprehensively and internationally into the twenty-first century. Indeed, I would judge the Warnock Report to be the most formidable bioethical document of the past forty years; it has changed almost everything human.

Basically, the Report recommended that IVF treatment should be generally available, regardless of whose gametes were involved, with no restriction on the supply, use, sale or purchase of ova, sperm or embryos, and no restriction on ova donation, sperm freezing or the production of multiple 'spare' embryos. Also, the Report recommended that human embryos be specifically created for research—as opposed to treatment—but that such embryos should not be transferred to a woman; moreover, they should not be kept alive for more than fourteen days. Nearly all of these recommendations were incorporated into the Human Fertilisation and Embryology Act 1990. The following year, the Human Fertilisation and Embryology Authority (HFEA) was established as the statutory licensing body with a remit to regulate fertility treatments using human ova and sperm, as well as treatment and research involving human embryos. Over the years, the HFEA has proved to be little more than a quango of 'poachers-turned-gamekeepers', because its membership has consisted predominantly of IVF practitioners and human-embryo experimenters, or at least, supporters of such. There has never been a single staunchly pro-life voice on any of its numerous committees. In fact, I applied to join during the initial trawl for members, but I never even received a reply!

3.3.3 IVF IN PRACTICE

The essential features of all IVF treatments include the collection of an ovum, which is checked; if it appears to be satisfactory, sperm is mixed with it in a glass (Latin *vitrum*, hence *in vitro* fertilization) dish and the contents are incubated at 37°C for three or more days. If fertilization occurs, which is not inevitable, the three-day-old 'cleavage stage' or five-day-old 'blastocyst stage' embryo is again examined before being transferred (note,

SOME OF THE PRIMARY ISSUES

not 'implanted', as many journalists and broadcasters still erroneously insist) to the woman's uterus via a catheter through her cervix. Here, implantation, which again is not inevitable, may occur.

There have been several variations on this basic IVF theme. For example, GIFT (gamete intra-fallopian transfer) mixes ovum and sperm together before transferring them to the Fallopian tubes with the idea that conception will be facilitated in its 'natural' environment. During the 1990s, micromanipulation procedures were introduced, including subzonal insemination (SUZI), whereby a single sperm is partially inserted into an ovum. These two methods have now been largely superseded by ICSI (intracytoplasmic sperm injection), which is chiefly employed in cases of male infertility, where sperm, because of perhaps poor morphology and/or motility, is unable to penetrate the outer layer, the zona pellucida, of the ovum. ICSI overcomes this inability by artificially injecting one sperm directly into the cytoplasm of the ovum; the picture of the narrow catheter penetrating the bulbous ovum frequently accompanies IVF-related news items on TV. Its increasing popularity means that ICSI is currently used in about 53 per cent of all IVF treatments in the UK.

Besides distinguishing between these basic methods, comprehending the entire range of IVF procedures and their associated statistics is complicated by the use of gametes and embryos, which can be fresh or frozen, own or donated. Furthermore, IVF treatments can involve heterosexual or same-sex partners, as well as women categorized by defined age groups. Consequently, the vast mass of statistical information published by the HFEA can be dense, even opaque. I have had to make several inquiries under the Freedom of Information Act 2000 to clarify some of it. To their credit, the personnel at the HFEA have always been obligingly helpful.

From its lowly and tentative beginnings in the 1970s, the fertility industry is now big business. There are currently some seventy-four clinics in the UK providing various fertility treatments. They deliver the majority of IVF cycles, 60 per cent of which are privately funded, with 40 per cent paid for by the NHS. In 2010, they generated an estimated £500 million in the UK, while the 450 fertility facilities in the USA received fees of approximately $4 billion. These days, most countries around the world have specialist clinics that offer treatments ranging from simple artificial insemination to full IVF, while some even undertake surrogacy.

Chapter 3

To achieve a better understanding of IVF, consider the following UK statistics published by the HFEA. First, a warning: these data are a snapshot and are therefore not entirely straightforward because, for example, women undergoing successful treatments towards the end of any recorded twelve-month period will not give birth until the following year. And women may also create embryos but then store them for their own future use, perhaps a year or so later, or donate them to others. So sometimes the numbers do not appear to tally. Nevertheless, they do give a valuable insight into the nature and extent of IVF practice. In a twelve-month period spanning 2010–2011, a total of 48,147 women underwent 61,726 IVF treatment cycles. Over 200,000 embryos were created, but only 89,648 were transferred. Outcomes for women using their own fresh ova were 14,225 'live birth events', producing 17,041 'take-home' babies. Obviously, during that year, several women underwent more than one treatment cycle, which frequently involved transferring more than one embryo. The multiple-birth rate was 19.8 per cent (compared with 1.6 per cent among naturally conceived babies) or, put another way, about a third of all IVF babies were either twin or triplet siblings. The overall success rate of IVF, calculated by the HFEA as 'live birth events' per 100 treatment cycles, was 24.5 per cent; conversely, it had a 75.5 per cent failure rate.

3.3.4 IVF AND BIOETHICAL DILEMMAS

This may all seem wonderful: bouncing babies for at least some infertile couples. But there are bioethical difficulties, dilemmas, even nightmares, associated with IVF. Take, for example, the bizarre reality of grandmothers giving birth to their own grandchildren. What about post-menopausal women having babies? What about posthumous fatherhood? What about babies having more than two parents? What about same-sex parents? Such unnatural affairs are nowadays not unknown consequences of IVF. The idea of the child with two mixed-sex parents, conceived naturally with their own gametes, born to them and nurtured by them, can seem so twentieth century.

OK, those are examples from the wacky end of IVF. So what about mainstream IVF for the ordinary infertile man and woman? How can that be so wrong, when it seems so right? That question has too seldom been asked. For a start, some consider that the whole of IVF is artificial and that

SOME OF THE PRIMARY ISSUES

this technological 'making' of children is morally unacceptable. Children as laboratory products is an uneasy concept. It must certainly be conceded that the process of IVF is very different from normative parenthood, where a child is the result of life expressed in the procreative act of married union, and therefore has much to do with deep human integrity and profound human relationships, as opposed to the manipulation of gametes in a drab laboratory environment overseen by white-coated technicians. Simply put, IVF separates the procreative and the unitive aspects of human sexuality. Such honestly held convictions of IVF disapproval are supported by strong bioethical, theological and sociological reasoning, but the Warnock Report virtually ignored them all.

Perhaps more people would find the basic protocol of IVF, as described above, to be acceptable for the relief of infertility of a married couple when, say, the woman has blocked Fallopian tubes or the man produces insufficiently motile sperm. But this 'one-for-one' embryo production and transfer routinely occurs in *no* IVF clinic in the UK. The success rates of all IVF procedures have always been terribly poor; Louise Brown was attempt number 104. Even now, after more than thirty-five years of IVF, the chance of a 'take-home' baby from one treatment cycle is typically less than 25 per cent, and realistically for some couples it is less than 10 per cent.

To increase the probability of success, IVF clinics superovulate women, that is, they treat each woman with a regimen of fertility drugs, such as Clomid, so that she produces as many as ten or even twenty ova, instead of the normal one each month. The 'best' of these ova are then mixed with sperm so that multiple—perhaps five or more—human embryos are produced. These are subsequently scrutinized and the 'best' embryos are transferred to the woman's womb. Since 2004, the HFEA's policy guideline has been that for women under the age of forty, no more than two embryos should be transferred; for women over forty, the maximum is three. This raises another of IVF's inherent problems: scrutiny, assessment, selection and transfer of only the 'best'. This is essentially quality control of human beings. As a consequence, embryos are discarded because there are too many, or because, for some other reason, they are deemed unfit or unwanted. After all, what doctor would dare transfer less than seemingly 'perfect' human embryos into a woman's womb? IVF is constantly dogged by these sinister eugenic overtones and undercurrents.

Chapter 3

Which brings us to the tragic heart, the bioethical core, of the matter: supernumerary embryos. It is these dual procedures, namely, the creation and the transfer of multiple embryos, that give rise to the two severest bioethical and medical dilemmas associated with IVF. They lead, first, to the unavoidable accumulation of excess, surplus, 'spare' embryos and, second, to the establishment of multiple pregnancies—this latter issue is discussed below in Section 3.3.5. Amid the pressured pursuit to achieve pregnancies, these practices of 'making' and 'moving' multiple embryos may seem logical, though bioethically and medically perilous. Yet the resolution of this predicament, at least for the greater part, has always been in the hands of the IVF practitioners. Simple: create fewer and transfer fewer. Instead, doctors have, on the face of it, been too enamoured with their clinics' success ratings to give thought to any bioethical misgivings or even to their patients' health.

And there is more. There are now unknown thousands of frozen embryos destined for destruction because their standard, maximum storage period of ten years is about to end. Many of these will be 'orphans'. Why? Because the IVF clinics have lost contact with the parents, labels have dropped off the embryo storage vessels, or records have been misplaced, lost or not updated so that some of the embryos' parents, who have divorced, died or simply moved house, cannot now be traced. It has turned into a double disaster—bioethical and administrative.

Never think of IVF as uncomplicated. There are the many additional 'costs'. These can be financial costs—not inconsiderable at between £4,000 and £5,000 per treatment cycle in the UK. And there can be psychological costs—typically characterized by the stress of the IVF treadmill with its gruelling schedule of frequent injections, blood tests and monitorings for the woman. And there can be relationship costs—tensions between the infertile couple, especially when a third-party gamete donor is involved. And there can be disappointment costs—because of IVF's overall failure rate of approximately 75 per cent.

These are not fictional issues. On the day I am writing this, *The Times* reports the story of an ordinary thirty-nine-year-old woman, Justine Bold, who wanted to be a mother. Her attempts meant that she had undergone 'a laparoscopy, three IVF cycles, steroids and anti-coagulants, hormone treatments and, most devastating of all, losing a baby soon after becoming

SOME OF THE PRIMARY ISSUES

pregnant. Having spent £30,000, she is now resigned to the fact that she will never have a baby.[7] It is a story repeated in clinics up and down the country'. These are not my words, but they express my fears.

Finally, and again, there is this insuperable core problem of IVF's 'spare' embryos. What happens to them? They have one of three fates: they may be stored at −196°C, be experimented upon or be thrown away. Ponder these HFEA data that relate to the year 2010 (they are slightly different from those recorded in Section 3.3.3, which refer to a twelve-month period spanning 2010–2011). During 2010, UK fertility clinics created 234,701 human embryos. Another 31,103 embryos were moved from previous frozen storage and thawed. That means there was a total of 265,804 embryos 'in use'. What happened to them? Only 84,721 (31.9 per cent of the total) were transferred to women. Another 49,364 (18.6 per cent) were frozen and stored. Just 57 (< 0.1 per cent) were donated to other women. A further 4,372 (1.6 per cent) were donated to research. But 127,944 embryos—the greatest single proportion (48.1 per cent)—were, to use the HFEA's euphemism, 'discarded'. Because all embryos used in research must be destroyed within fourteen days, the sum of the last two figures represents the total annual destruction, that is, 132,316 embryos, or 49.7 per cent of the total 'in use'. Note, this is the minimum number destroyed because many additional embryos will die, or will already have died, in frozen storage. In other words, the grim fact emerges: IVF destroys (at least) half of the embryos it creates.

Think about this with an informed bioethical mindset. IVF procedures in the UK destroy substantially more than 100,000 human embryos each year, whereas abortion procedures destroy some 200,000 unborn children. Is abortion twice as bad as IVF, or is IVF only half as bad as abortion? Or think about it this way. The HFEA calculates the IVF success rate as 'live birth events' per 100 treatment cycles; that figure in 2010 was 24.1 per cent. But of the 265,804 embryos 'in use', only 16,045 survived to become 'take-home' babies. Therefore an arguably better performance indicator would be the number of children born per hundred embryos created. When this is calculated, the success rate plummets to a measly 6 per cent. Or put another way, 19 out of every 20 human embryos created by IVF are destroyed by IVF. It is hard to square all this destruction with the Warnock Report's statement that 'we were agreed that the embryo of the human

Chapter 3

species ought to have a special status' and its subsequent recommendation 'that the embryo of the human species should be afforded some protection in law'.[8] Status and protection—where are they?

Now ask another of those fundamental questions: is this any way to treat living, human embryos? At least three aspects need to be considered. First, is this 'spare' embryo human? There is really no doubt here. Can the fruit of human gametes be anything other than human? The embryo in question cannot be that of a dog, a donkey or any other non-human. Second, is this human embryo alive? The Warnock Report states, 'At fertilisation the egg and sperm unite to become a single cell.'[9] It then explains how this zygote divides 'into first two, then four, then eight ... by a process called cleavage ...' and diversifies rapidly and spontaneously, so that 'the subsequent developmental processes follow one another in a systematic and structured order, leading in turn through cleavage, to the morula, the blastocyst ...'[10] If the embryo were not alive, this would be inexplicable; this very growth is diagnostic of the fact that the embryo is alive. Third, is this living human embryo 'one of us', a human being? As already noted in Chapter 2, the Warnock Report prevaricates at this most important question, stating that, 'when life or personhood begin ... are complex amalgams of factual and moral judgements'.[11] Oh yes, how the simple can become so complex. Warnock failed this crucial test. But we already know the answer, do we not? The bioethical downside of Warnock's indecision is that human embryos, with no decided moral status, are deemed legally and bioethically fit for anything—or nothing.

3.3.5 IVF AND HEALTH RISKS

IVF is never risk free. For a start, superovulation, as an integral component of all mainstream IVF, can be hazardous. In a third of women it can cause mild ovarian hyperstimulation syndrome (OHSS), with 5 per cent suffering from what are classified as moderate or severe forms; in a very few women it has proved fatal. In an attempt to minimize these risks, some clinics use a technique called in vitro maturation (IVM) to collect immature ova and mature them in the laboratory for a day or two prior to fertilization. But because IVM uses less or no hormonal stimulation, fewer ova can be harvested and their degree of maturation can be insufficient, rendering them 'not fit for purpose'. Then again, superovulation can also produce poor quality ova, which often fail to fertilize, as well as a uterine environment that can be hormonally unfavourable for embryo implantation. Some clinics circumvent this latter problem by freezing the embryos and transferring them a menstrual cycle or two later, when the woman's hormonal balance is more physiologically normal.

And here it comes again: that other bioethical core issue of IVF—multiple pregnancy. This is seriously serious. In fact, it is now acknowledged by practitioners and regulators around the world to be IVF's single greatest health hazard for both unborn children and their mothers. For children, multiple pregnancy is associated with prematurity, low birth weights, long-term neurological disorders (cerebral palsy, for example, is six times higher than among singletons), stillbirths (approximately four times higher) and neonatal deaths (seven times higher). In addition, multiple-baby-carrying mothers are more prone to miscarry, haemorrhage and suffer from, for example, high blood pressure, pre-eclampsia and gestational diabetes. These risks have sometimes been minimized by that unspeakable practice of 'selective reduction', whereby one or more siblings are destroyed by piercing their hearts in utero, as discussed in Section 3.2.4.

Other health risks exist, too. It has been reported that IVF pregnancies have a greater probability of becoming ectopic. Moreover, it is now reckoned that IVF infants are 32 per cent more likely to have birth defects than children conceived naturally. IVF children, especially it seems among those conceived by ICSI, have elevated risks of developing genetic disorders, such as retinoblastoma, Angelman or Beckwith–Wiedemann syndromes, heart valve defects, cleft lips and palates, plus digestive system abnormalities. In addition, there have been warnings that the incidence of hypertension, cancers, obesity and related diabetes may rise significantly in IVF children as they reach their fifties and beyond.

Can these problems be explained? The hazards associated with multiple pregnancies, whether the result of natural or IVF conception, are well documented and understood. However, the reasons for the increased health risks linked solely to IVF are less clear. They may be caused by pre-existing genetic defects among the infertile parents—after all, they were unable to conceive naturally, so maybe their gametes were somehow already impaired. Then again, it may be that IVF embryos are subjected to chemical and physical damage caused by the laboratory protocols of drug stimulation, incubation media composition, culture conditions, freezing and thawing, and other manipulation procedures. The causes are disputed, but the effects are not.

While the sub-standard ethics of IVF persist, its basic practice is undergoing a major procedural change. Clinical evidence is proving—somewhat counter-intuitively—that less means more. While women who choose to have two embryos transferred are more likely to become pregnant, those who opt for an elective single-embryo transfer (known as an eSET) improve their chances of delivering a full-term, healthy baby almost fivefold. In the near future, the eSET option is likely to become the 'default position' for IVF, at least in the UK. In addition, the HFEA already requires that all clinics have a 'multiple birth minimization strategy' in place. Gone will be the bad old days of IVF sextuplets and so forth. But here is the fundamental bioethical caveat: let no one imagine that eSET, transferring just one embryo, will solve the 'spare' embryo crisis; it will most emphatically not. Supernumerary, multiple embryos will still be created for eSET-type IVF; it is just that fewer will be transferred. The leftover 'spares' will still accumulate, still be abused and still be destroyed.

3.3.6 IVF AND FATHERHOOD

It is an irrefutable fact of life that each of us has a father and a mother. Nowadays, they can be just social, genetic, biological or legal parents—but yes, we are (still, just about) family. In other words, nitty-gritty biology and the Bible tell us that ever since the post-Adamic generation, we have all been the products of sperm plus ova. Furthermore, the God-ordained structure of a family is father-mother-child—it is a neat and wholesome threesome. Yet the abnormal nature of IVF has challenged this. Whereas sperm and ova are still required, this historic, conventional family configuration can now be defied. Lesbian couples and single women can use IVF without the need for a father—they need only a sperm donor. But proper fatherhood transcends the mere genetic; it demands a social, psychological role. Of course, some fathers are absent, absconding or awful—their intentional shortcomings are never to be excused—but IVF has the power to demean, even deny, proper fatherhood. Put another way, a man can be the father *of* a child without being the father *to* that child. This retrograde arrangement has become known as 'part-time fatherhood' or 'fatherhood lite'.

This practice of creating 'patchwork families' is deeply flawed. Even the authors of the Warnock Report recognized this: 'we believe that as a general rule it is better for children to be born into a two-parent family, with both father and mother.'[12] The admirable phrase 'the need for a father' was inserted into the Human Fertilisation and Embryology Act 1990 to ensure that this issue of child welfare was considered prior to all IVF treatments. However, proponents of the Human Fertilisation and Embryology Bill (2008) wanted this basic stipulation replaced by the sociological piffle 'the need for supportive parenting'. Eventually, when the Bill came to the House of Commons and after its members had bickered for three hours over this assault on the natural order, so-called 'equality' won the day. Now, according to the Human Fertilisation and Embryology Act 2008, any and every grown-up can be 'a supportive parent'.

This episode highlights a fundamental weakness of law. Laws can never define, even less produce, what we (almost) all want, namely, good parents. But that is no reason to stop aspiring to the ideal. Why should legislating for the mediocre or worse become the norm? The erasing of 'fathers' from the statute book has sent out a dangerous message. It will confirm in the minds of many reluctant fathers that their roles are unimportant, that parental obligations are for losers, that they can be less bothered about 'sowing their wild oats' and that any government agency will only half-heartedly pursue them to provide financial support for their children. That is dreadful news for children and mothers, as well as for fathers. How can the deliberate creation of 'fatherless children' ever be a good idea?

3.3.7 IVF ALTERNATIVES

Mainstream, conventional, traditional IVF has proved to be a bioethical catastrophe. It is therefore disheartening to learn of both Christian and 'morally sensitive' infertile couples considering, or even using, it. Some have argued that modified, bioethically less-objectionable IVF procedures exist. Are they right? Consider three lines of their reasoning.

First, a few clinics offer what is known as natural-cycle IVF, which involves collecting and fertilizing the one ovum produced each month and then transferring, if successfully produced in vitro, that one and only created embryo. Initially, this may seem an attractive proposition—no fertility drugs, no hormones, no excess ova, no spare embryos. But its success rate

Chapter 3

is far, far lower than those of mainstream, hormonally stimulated, multi-embryo IVF procedures. During 2010, according to HFEA data, only thirteen 'take-home' babies were born after 141 women underwent 194 natural-cycle IVF treatment cycles.

Second, there is the relatively new technique of ovum freezing, also known as oocyte cryopreservation or egg vitrification. This has been used by women patients prior to undergoing cancer treatments; chemotherapy and/or radiotherapy can cause temporary or permanent damage to their ovaries. It has also been used by go-getting, career-oriented women and others who wish to delay childbirth by attempting to beat their biological clocks, a practice more scornfully referred to as 'keeping their eggs fresh in the freezer'. It employs fertility drugs, so although there are multiple ova, there are not necessarily any multiple 'spare' embryos—until, of course, any ensuing mainstream IVF procedures create some. And then all the usual IVF dilemmas kick in. So it is not a bioethically satisfactory solution. Again, 'take-home' babies are rare—UK successes have been in single figures. Although these two IVF modifications exist, their poor success rates have deterred most clinics from ever considering, let alone offering, them.

Third, there is 'embryo adoption', as pioneered in 1997 by the US Christian-based non-profit agency Snowflakes. The idea behind its Frozen Embryo Adoption Program is, according to its website, to allow 'spare' IVF embryos to 'realize their ultimate purpose—life'.[13] So an infertile married couple can adopt another man and woman's 'spare' frozen embryos—sometimes referred to as 'frosties'—and have them transferred to the adopting wife at an IVF clinic. It may seem altruistic and a partial solution to the surfeit of IVF embryos, but think of the drawbacks. Such adoption challenges the nature of marriage and its role in procreation, as all IVF does. In addition, it is different, legally and psychologically, from traditional child adoption because the recipient mother is also the gestational mother. To date, after sixteen years in business, just over 3,000 adopted Snowflake embryos have been thawed, and about 340 babies have been born. That is hardly a dent in the estimated 600,000 frozen embryos stored throughout the USA. And the financial cost—$12,000 to $16,000 per adoption—makes it an even less attractive proposition.

Moreover, there is an additional predicament to consider with all three of these examples. Entering any IVF clinic, for any kind of treatment, is

SOME OF THE PRIMARY ISSUES

at least planting a firm foothold on the bandwagon of mainstream IVF, a sort of hitching a ride, which entails at least a physical, if not a bioethical, complicity. And following the almost inevitable failure of any of these three non-standard IVF procedures, the pressures, both personal and clinical, to climb fully aboard that IVF wagon must be presumed to be more than strong. The uncomplicated conclusion remains: all IVF is best avoided.

3.3.8 IVF REJECTED—WHAT IS LEFT?

So what should infertile couples do? Pastorally, they need wise, informed counsel, not unthinking conveyance onto the IVF treadmill or bandwagon. Initially, there are some simple low-tech procedures to try. Everyone should recognize that self-inflicted factors, such as alcohol and other drug abuse, STIs and smoking, to name just a few, need to be addressed. Lifestyle changes, like regular exercise and decent nutrition, will help some couples; keeping fit is always beneficial for the body, before, during and after pregnancy. In addition, self-knowledge measures, such as ovulation-cycle awareness and stress recognition, can be valuable. The positive effects and the de-stressing outcomes of a two-week holiday in places as exotically dissimilar as Cardigan Bay or Copacabana Beach have proved to be fascinatingly, if only anecdotally, successful in establishing pregnancies.

Then there are the more complex low-tech procedures. Some couples may want to consider medical investigations and interventions, perhaps low-level drug stimulation of the ovaries, treatment for endometriosis, or even surgery for blocked or damaged Fallopian tubes. Artificial insemination by husband (AIH) may also be deemed appropriate for a married man and woman where the former, perhaps because of physical limitations or medical reasons, cannot naturally inseminate his wife. But when these bioethically unobjectionable therapies fail or are unsuitable, what is left? Rejecting all forms of IVF and other ARTs, such as surrogacy and artificial insemination by donor (AID), because they both bring a third party into a marriage along with at least technical adultery, couples have two long-standing, and bioethically better, options: they may be able to adopt born children, or they may become reconciled to being childless. As already noted, both courses of action are accompanied by biblical precedent and principled compassion.

Yet there is now a third option, known as Natural Procreative Technology (NPT). Its principal aim is to determine and then, if feasible, treat the

CHAPTER 3

underlying causes of a couple's infertility, enabling them to conceive naturally. NPT is not able to overcome all causes of infertility, such as premature ovarian failure or a complete absence of sperm. Nevertheless, for hundreds of couples it has been successful with results as good as, or better than, those claimed by most IVF clinics. A scientific, peer-reviewed assessment, published in 2008, concluded that 'NPT provided by trained general practitioners had live birth rates comparable to cohort studies of more invasive treatments, including ART'.[14] Moreover, NPT has none of the bioethical baggage of IVF: it is pro-woman, pro-man and pro-child, with no 'spare' embryos, no donor sperm or ova, no gamete or embryo freezing and no deliberate destruction of human life. It is also minimally invasive and relatively low cost. Its pro-life credentials are attractive and its success rate is impressive. Its future looks bright. NPT is available worldwide. In the UK, further details can be found at www.lifefertilitycare.co.uk.

All of these approaches are judged to be bioethically sound—anything to avoid those aggressive, invasive, dangerous, expensive ART methods, such as IVF and surrogacy.

3.3.9 IVF IN THE FUTURE

Both infertility and the ARTs are here to stay. Our post-Warnock world has opened Pandora's box of bioethical novelties and its dangerous contents have escaped. Infertility and reproductive tinkering have now become well-established features both of the human condition and of modern medicine. Infertility will continue to be a pressing problem for many—currently, an estimated 3.5 million people in the UK. One cannot but wonder at the paradox as some 50,000 women each year in the UK submit themselves to IVF while another 200,000 submit themselves to abortion. Could more not meet halfway? This maelstrom of babies 'wanted' and 'unwanted' is simply staggering. Faster, less bureaucratic fostering and adoption would help; both these family-affirming measures should be in future political manifestos, as well as in the present minds of many. Have you and yours ever considered fostering and adoption? Perhaps you should.

The debates over the nature of infertility—whether it is a medical condition, whether it is a variation of normal, whether it is often self-induced, whether everyone has the right to children, whether the world needs more babies, and so on—will continue. Likewise, the arguments about IVF—whether is an excessive therapy, whether such costly hi-tech procedures can be justified, whether they are medically safe, and whether the recommended three free treatment cycles for eligible women should be funded by the UK taxpayer in a cash-strapped, over-burdened NHS—will not go away. Amid these wranglings, the National Institute for Health and Clinical (now Care) Excellence (NICE) issued new guidelines in 2013 for England and Wales which recommended not only earlier interventions with NHS-funded IVF, but also an increase in the upper age limit for treatment, from thirty-nine to forty-two. It sparked yet another partisan clash in the battle between increasing treatment access and decreasing finance. The point is that IVF has now generally achieved the status of normal medicine and its advocates will in future be fighting for more clients and more funding.

Yet hi-tech IVF and other ART procedures will never be the panacea for all of the estimated 1 in 7 infertile couples. So let us think outside the box for a moment and take a bioethical flight of fancy into the future. If IVF, and ARTs in general, currently have only a limited application, could they not be used in an entirely different arena, a new market, a fresh outlet—namely, the spawning of children for the fecund, the fertile? Think about it—others already have. Ordinary reproductive sexual intercourse could then become a twentieth-century remnant. Think about the future three-pronged benefits of control, convenience and cost-effectiveness that large-scale IVF could bring. First, the control will allow prospective parents, governments and employers to manage breeding and thereby optimize productivity at work, and thus attain and maintain fiscal stability, even prosperity, for themselves and their nations. Think IVF—a citizen's duty! Second, the convenience will come from the coordination of working rotas, IVF treatment cycles, IVF doctors' time and hospital facilities. Think IVF—resource efficiency! And third, cost-effectiveness will be achieved by linking IVF to preimplantation genetic diagnosis (PGD) and the production of only healthy, sex-selected embryos for more delighted consumers. Think IVF—combat disability! The upshot will be fit babies of the right sex, with the characteristics we want, when we want them. How smart is that? And there will be fewer strings attached because State-funded surrogates and crèches will do more of the hard work of child bearing and rearing for us. Then we will be much freer to pursue our careers and our pastimes. Ah, at last, that modern goal of more 'me-time'. Maybe. Maybe not.

Chapter 3

The closing years of the twentieth century recorded some preposterous cases of ARTs and parenthood. This century will undoubtedly achieve similar, but probably even more extreme, examples. Try picking some future 'winners' of your own. Here are four of mine. First, how about castrating all pre-pubescent boys, freezing their gamete-producing cells, and letting them reproduce by IVF at a later date, at the behest of the State? That would solve the teenage pregnancy crisis. But one snag is that intact older men would then impregnate teenage girls. So, better still, now that we have the technology to freeze and thaw ova successfully, why not remove and freeze all ova from teenage girls and return them only if and when breeding is allowed? Second, what about a lesbian couple—Jean and Ovida—who, rather than using donated sperm, use somatic cell nuclear transfer (SCNT), the reproductive cloning technique, to transfer Jean's genetic material to one of Ovida's denucleated ova? A little laboratory tweaking will ensure fertilization. If Ovida carries the baby, who must be a girl because she is derived from Jean's genes, the child would have no father, but two mothers—Ovida, the surrogate, biological and legal mother, and Jean, the genetic mother. Third is the male parallel, that is, two men, Roy and Troy, having a baby without a proper mother. Cloning procedures could introduce the nucleus from Roy's sperm into a denucleated donor ovum to produce a 'male egg'. This could be fertilized with sperm from Troy using standard IVF techniques, then the embryo could be transferred to a surrogate, and bingo—a baby with two fathers but no real genetic mother. Fourth, what about using a 'spare' embryo left over from IVF, harvesting some of the embryonic stem cells, reprogramming them to create ova- and sperm-producing cells and using these to fertilize each other, and then transferring the resulting embryo to a surrogate? The genetic mother would then also be the genetic father—one non-adult person as both parents. You think these possibilities are crazy? Well, you should understand that some scientists have already discussed the feasibility of these and other similarly hideous scenarios. The required technologies are here right now, or just around the corner. Could this be the future of human IVF and parenthood?

3.3.10 IVF: IN CONCLUSION

To conclude, what has IVF achieved? Of course, it has produced some lovely babies. But they must not be exploited as cute pawns to disguise the

Some of the primary issues

introduction of medical treatments where 'the end justifies the means'—that old Machiavellian phrase, so beloved of today's utilitarian thinkers, movers and shakers, and those IVF practitioners.

Much of IVF's harm is directly attributable to the conclusions of the Warnock Report. It sanctioned and encouraged this 'inside-out' science—the formerly strictly 'inside' human embryo could latterly be relocated 'outside'. Now it could be used and abused. As a result, countless thousands upon thousands of embryos in the UK, and millions around the world, have been knowingly wiped out. IVF has been a modern scientific venture of irrecoverable loss. Human embryos once enjoyed respect, protection, wonder and status. Now those attributes are gone—and so easily and so rapidly too, with barely an opposing voice, and all within a generation. The human embryo should never be regarded as a product, object, artefact or mere thing.

IVF began as a treatment for married couples who, for various reasons, were unable to have their own biological children. It was odd and abnormal, but small scale. Now it is a huge, booming, multinational industry. Now married and unmarried people, same-sex couples, and single men and women are using it either directly or indirectly to get progeny. And it has inaugurated other subsidiary, bioethically dubious businesses—there is now brisk, worldwide dealing in womb renting, eugenic testing, sex selection, gamete trading, and lots more, either over-the-counter, at the clinic or online. Procreation is fast becoming the new retail activity, like any other commercial enterprise. It is yet another example of the misuse of sex and money—two of the greatest controllers of human behaviour, and two of the greatest causes of human downfall.

IVF has thus produced a view of human life that is pretty cold, if not chilling, where human ova, sperm and embryos are little more than laboratory materials, and where human sexuality is simply a biological phenomenon. It is a prescription for a clinical, dehumanized world where there is not much awe, little reverence and virtually no dignity. In short, IVF has further encouraged the trivialization of human life, sanctioned and accomplished the destruction of human embryos on an immeasurable, industrial scale, and thus hastened the spread of the culture of death. All IVF is best avoided.

CHAPTER 3

3.4 Surrogacy

In terms of the culture of death, surrogacy is perhaps less than first rank. At least, it seems a less barbarous practice since there is no primary intention to kill another human being. Nevertheless, it can be as complex bioethically, medically, psychologically, financially and certainly legally as any of the other assisted-reproductive technologies (ARTs). As a preliminary warning, beware: prosecutors, payments and parenthood do not usually mix easily, or happily.

3.4.1 WHAT IS SURROGACY?

This is a good question. The Warnock Report gives this definition: 'Surrogacy is the practice whereby one woman carries a child for another with the intention that the child should be handed over after birth.'[15]

There are two major variations on this theme. First, in the most common type, known as traditional, partial or straight surrogacy, the husband is fertile but his wife is unable to sustain a pregnancy, perhaps because of illness or irreparably damaged Fallopian tubes, or because she has had a hysterectomy. Or maybe she is one of the new class of professional or celebrity women who is simply too busy to go through a nine-month pregnancy herself. The surrogate woman, who may be hired, a friend or even a family member, is then inseminated, artificially or naturally, with the husband's sperm. The surrogate, because she is using her own ova, is the biological, genetic and legal mother of the child. Second, there is also full, gestational or 'host IVF' surrogacy, where embryos are created by IVF using gametes either from the commissioning parents or from sperm and ova donated by others. Resulting embryos are then transferred to the surrogate, who, because she does not provide any ova, has no genetic relationship to the child, but she is still the biological and, by birth, the legal mother.

Of course, the mix-and-match permutations of modern-day procreative roles mean that surrogacy can be employed by couples whether married or unmarried, whether heterosexual or homosexual, as well as by single men or women to create two-parent, single-parent or same-sex 'families'. As Warnock rightly concluded, 'There are thus many possible combinations of persons who are relevant to the child's conception, birth and early environment.'[16]

3.4.2 SURROGACY QUESTIONED

Surrogacy provokes some hefty questions. There are at least three surrounding topics on which to brood (pun intended). First, we need to ask, and answer, some of those fundamentals, such as: who are we? Are we simply cogs in a mechanistic universe? Is it right and proper to breed regardless of whose gametes are used? Does every woman (and/or man) have the right to a child? These, and other related questions, have been addressed in the preceding pages. The Bible-believing Christian and the 'morally sensitive' will give very different answers from those of the surrogacy advocate.

Second, unfashionable as it may be in some quarters, we cannot ignore the marriage covenant, that grand creational ordinance which has structured our societies and put us into families (Gen. 2:24; Ps. 68:6). It was given for our good. If proof were ever needed of the almighty upheaval in societal norms this century, it may be found here: marriage in England and Wales is no longer defined as 'the union of one man and one woman'. On 17 July 2013, the Marriage (Same Sex Couples) Act 2013 received the Royal Assent. Whatever next—State-sanctioned polygamy? But it is the pure and simple, one-man–one-woman marriage that has founded families from the beginning of recorded history. Every human society has its roots in naturally created and traditionally structured family life. Only an obtuse few would argue that strong family life is not beneficial for a society; even past and present UK governments would disagree with such an asinine proposition. Furthermore, the physical, procreative relationship is reserved for within the marriage covenant only (Matt. 19:4-6; Heb. 13:4), and the intrusion of any third party—surrogates, and sometimes ova and sperm donors—subverts this.

Third, children should be regarded as a precious inheritance, as gifts from God (Gen. 17:16; Ps. 127:3). The traditional biblical, and therefore the best, pattern is that children are conceived, born and nurtured within the conventional family unit. As already noted, even the authors of the Warnock Report acknowledged this: 'we believe that as a general rule it is better for children to be born into a two-parent family, with both father and mother.'[17] Deliberately creating 'patchwork families' is never a good idea.

Chapter 3

3.4.3 SURROGACY ASSESSED

So how does surrogacy measure up? It often begins with an act of adultery. Some may argue that artificial insemination is only minor or technical adultery—how easily situation ethics can trump Bible principles. One of the earliest surrogate motherhood pacts was between Sarai, Abram and Hagar (Gen. 16). This has been cited as a biblical justification for this old practice. It is no such thing! Verse 2 of that chapter shows the frustrated Sarai seeking to overcome her infertility by using Hagar as a surrogate. It initially looked like a sensible, friendly arrangement, but what followed was tension, separation and broken relationships among all the parties concerned (Gen. 21:8–11), particularly the women (Gen. 16:4–6). To make a long story short, it was a disaster.

If such an early surrogacy agreement was problematic, its modern-day counterparts are not without dilemmas too. There have been a sufficient number of freakish cases and human-relationship minefields linked to surrogacy to cause even its most ardent fans to think again. Some cases are so outlandish that I have, from time to time, challenged others to sit around the dinner table and construct the most preposterous surrogacy scenario they could think of; they have never come close to reality.

Let me illustrate this with a notorious case from the late 1990s, that of Claire Austin, a single mother in England. Take a deep breath. She already had two daughters of her own, plus three from previous surrogate arrangements, one of which ended in abortion. But she wanted to try being a surrogate mother just one more time. The commissioning couple were an Italian man and a Portuguese woman living in France. The sperm was obtained from a fifty-year-old American via a Danish sperm bank. The insemination procedure was carried out in Athens by a Greek doctor. Twins were conceived. At twenty-one weeks of the pregnancy, the commissioning couple wanted to discover the twins' sex. When told that they were both girls, they admitted that they wanted boys and asked Claire Austin to abort them. She refused and sought other commissioning parents over the Internet. Eventually, she was successful and the twins, Danielle and Emma, went to live with a lesbian couple and their Puerto Rican nanny in Hollywood. Claire Austin and that couple, Tracey Stern and Julia Salazar, argued over medical bills and subsequently fell out. She then declared, 'Down with the cult of surrogacy!' Then she said, 'Never again ... well, unless for a friend!'[18] See what I mean? Is that not weird? Is not this sorry tale the catastrophic actuality of 'babies as commodities' and freewheeling procreation?

Surrogacy enthusiasts respond to such censure by citing evidence purporting to show that most parents using surrogates possess exceptional levels of love and parenting skills and that their families are generally closer and better adjusted than those with naturally conceived children. Perhaps that is true. But such psychological studies, typically conducted when the children are young—often less than one year old—can hardly be regarded as definitive; only time will tell. Anyway, 'happiness' appraisals are hardly the issue at stake here.

Surrogacy brings other tangled bioethical questions to the table. For example, if a married couple can hire a surrogate mother, should an unmarried couple, a single woman or a single man also be able to? What about surrogacy for a lesbian, transsexual or gay couple? Should a surrogate be allowed to, or can she be made to, have an abortion? Should a surrogate child be permitted to know his or her genetic and biological parents? Can the child inherit their property? Supporters of surrogacy may well argue that 'surrogacy is the ultimate gift of one woman to another', but the momentum of twenty-first-century surrogacy has either smartly swept most of these untidy bioethical questions under the carpet or celebrated them as the epitome of an equality-and-diversity ideology.

3.4.4 SURROGACY AND THE WARNOCK REPORT

So what did the Warnock Committee think of surrogacy? Tellingly, it did not mention love, deep affection or emotion in Chapter 8 of its Report, or, for that matter, anywhere else. Nor did it discuss the nature of surrogacy, or its effect on adult/parent-and-child relationships, though these are known to be powder-keg matters. Instead, while saying 'Yes' to virtually everything within its remit, the Warnock Report wanted surrogacy agencies outlawed and all surrogacy arrangements made illegal—though two Committee members were more accepting of the practice and wrote their own Expression of Dissent.[19] Nevertheless, the Report announced, 'we are all agreed that surrogacy for convenience alone ... is totally ethically unacceptable'.[20] Why such strong words? Is it not strange that, in the midst of so much permissiveness and uncertainty in the Warnock Report, it could

CHAPTER 3

suddenly become so prohibitive and assertive? Apparently, the members of the Committee were worried about money. If money changed hands, they thought there must be some monkey business going on. The Committee was concerned about 'the danger of exploitation of one human being by another'.[21] Note, it was only the use of *adults*—not the *child*—by other adults that was considered to be unacceptable. Moreover, the Committee declared, 'That people should treat others as a means to their own ends, however desirable the consequences, must always be liable to moral objection.'[22]

We may, for once, agree with the Warnock Report. But should we not go further? Should we view surrogacy not only as the commissioning mother wanting a child, but also as the surrogate mother—and in law, she is the legal mother—*not* wanting her child? She has deliberately embarked on a pregnancy with the clear intention that she will abandon her baby. The birth of any child is surrounded by a spectrum of emotions, perhaps none stronger than that of the mother's love for the child she has carried and delivered. The surrogate knowingly sets out to ignore these natural instincts. Furthermore, can a commissioning mother develop this maternal love without the psychological and physical springs of this bonding, namely, pregnancy and childbirth? Surrogacy is not like adoption. The great difference is that adoption seeks to enhance the love for, and security of, the child. Surrogacy has the long-term, premeditated intention of just the opposite. It should be shunned.

3.4.5 MODERN-DAY SURROGACY ARRANGEMENTS

While surrogacy in the UK is not illegal, commercial surrogacy was banned by the Surrogacy Arrangements Act 1985 and surrogacy arrangements were made legally unenforceable by the Human Fertilisation and Embryology Act 1990. Though it is still illegal to advertise for surrogate mothers or commissioning parents, a few not-for-profit surrogacy agencies have sprung up to forge the necessary connections. It is estimated that between 50 and 100 babies are born to surrogate mothers in the UK each year; nobody really knows because no official records are kept and some surrogacy arrangements stay purposefully secret.

The 1985 Act did, however, allow 'reasonable expenses' to be paid to the surrogate, including items like clothing, travel expenses and loss of earnings, which by 2010 apparently averaged £15,000. Surrogates are loath to admit that money is their motivation. They prefer to say that altruism is their spur—though this has become widely known as 'the nod-wink rule'. In addition, the 1985 Act stated that the child would not automatically belong to the commissioning parents because no prior agreements could be legally binding on either party. However, commissioning parents can now make a parental order—a fast-track adoption procedure—six weeks after the child's birth to transfer legal parenthood from the surrogate mother to the commissioning parents, whether the child is born in the UK or abroad.

Such originally stringent legal stipulations have predictably become more relaxed—it is that 'mission creep' or slippery slope which is built into every bioethical issue. For example, in 2010, a High Court judge allowed a British couple to keep a child even though they paid in excess of 'reasonable expenses' to their American surrogate. In effect, surrogacy-for-profit was endorsed. Again, commercial surrogacy arrangements made abroad, though illegal in Britain, have now been approved by British courts. For instance, in 2010, a British couple went to Ukraine and contacted a willing surrogate, who produced a baby for them. According to Ukrainian law, the baby's parents were the British couple; according to British law, the Ukrainian woman and her husband were the parents. The baby was thus rendered stateless and parentless, but in 2011, the British couple were awarded parenthood by the High Court, in the 'best interests' of the child's welfare. Essentially, British law had capitulated in what was, admittedly, an intractable predicament. However, taken together, these judgements have given the green, or, at least, the amber, light to buying surrogate children overseas.

By contrast, in other parts of the world, like India and Ukraine, surrogacy is not only entirely lawful, but it is also a large-scale business, with legally binding contracts made before the births. In 2002, the practice was legalized in India and that country has now become the world centre for 'surrogacy tourism', or what is more politely known as 'outsourced pregnancy'. The sector is largely unregulated; the Indian government has long promised tighter legal restrictions, but apart from some minor rules introduced in 2013, it has repeatedly dithered and decided nothing of substance. In the interim, the costs there, reckoned to be approximately £18,000 for the complete package, have remained about a third of those in the Western

Chapter 3

world, with surrogacy estimated to be worth £1.5 billion annually to the Indian economy. The surrogate mothers may be paid as much as ten times their normal income—a life-changing sum—but there are well-founded reports of coercion by husbands, as well as of corruption and exploitation by unscrupulous middlemen.

Meanwhile, whenever and wherever surrogacy is sought, all would-be commissioning parents are again and again advised to contact a good local lawyer before embarking on any such arrangements. Apparently, a learned counsel is essential to unpick and sort out the contractual, financial, legal and immigration hazards. Such words of foreboding should frighten off all but the most obsessive intending parents, or IPs, as they are known in the trade.

3.4.6 SURROGACY IN THE FUTURE

How times have changed since the Warnock Report gave surrogacy, especially any involving financial gain, the thumbs down. At that time, surrogacy, whether commercial or informal, was a rather clandestine affair. More recently, it has become truly voguish, particularly among so-called celebrities. First, there was Sarah Jessica Parker, then Elton John, then Nicole Kidman. In all three cases the surrogates were American and significant amounts of money changed hands. It has all been so admired by the popular media. Have these surrogacy transactions set up a new bioethical tipping-point? Are we now on the verge of life imitating art, reproductive culture following popular culture? Are the procreational whims of a few international entertainers now encouraging a worldwide fashion for surrogacy? In California, perhaps not surprisingly, the total package—highly professional, highly expensive, with glossy pictures of pretty, well-groomed, well-educated, aspiring surrogates—has become West Coast humdrum. At times, the near future can look so unsightly.

3.4.7 SURROGACY: IN CONCLUSION

Does surrogacy dehumanize women? Does it exploit vulnerable women? Is it womb-renting and baby-selling? Does it demean children as trade items, objects to buy and sell? Yes, yes, yes and yes.

Many regard surrogacy as dehumanizing because it treats a woman in her most intimate and unique physiological role of a mother as merely a paid, or unpaid, nine-month incubator, who will then hand over her child.

She becomes a reproductive appliance. Surrogacy is then little different from renting out her sexual-reproductive organs, as in prostitution. She is exploited physically and emotionally. Surrogacy deliberately breaks the deep relationship between birth mother and baby, with money usually the accepted salve for a wounded heart and a troubled conscience. Moreover, it is frequently the poor who are cajoled into selling their generative potential because surrogacy tends to be one class exploiting another; it is nearly always the hard-up student or domestic worker who bears the child for the wealthy architect or accountant, rather than the other way round. While it is entirely right and proper to pay for goods and services, childbearing should never become part of such trading deals.

Whereas it may not be on the main line of the culture of death, surrogacy has the capacity to derail the well-being of both the individual and society. It can weaken marriage, upset the traditional structure of the family, distort the mother–baby relationship, disconnect conception, childbearing and nurture, commodify children, break the genetic bonds of parenthood, encourage third-party liaisons, distort historic legal presumptions, challenge God's creational design, wreck … OK, that's enough; stay well away from surrogacy.

3.5 Human embryo experimentation

IVF and the other assisted-reproductive technologies (ARTs) are not the only practices that use, abuse and destroy human embryos. Human embryo experimentation is also part of the culture of death. This too is a bioethically complex and unfailingly fatal undertaking, for two reasons. First, it is seldom, if ever, performed for the good of the patients, and certainly never with their informed consent. Second, by law, all such embryos must be destroyed within fourteen days. Furthermore, this research is inextricably linked to IVF because most of the required raw material, the experimental subjects, are the 'spare' embryos left over from IVF treatments. A secondary supply also exists since the Human Fertilisation and Embryology Act 1990 approved the creation of embryos solely for experimental purposes—but in 2011, this source accounted for only seventy-four embryos, compared with over 4,900 'spares' obtained from IVF.

The human embryo as 'raw material' is a troubling concept—intuitively, we feel that something is wrong. Essentially, it was the development of IVF

Chapter 3

as a treatment that bequeathed the human embryo to research scientists for experimentation. What had previously been internal, IVF made external—it was the realization of a novel 'inside-out' science. We could now see it, study it, manipulate it, analyse it, store it, even create it, and finally destroy it. This unprecedented access to the human embryo has not only revolutionized the ARTs, it has also ushered in this wholly destructive discipline of human embryo experimentation.

3.5.1 Human Embryo Experimentation and the Warnock Report

In 1984, the Warnock Report noted that 'many people feel an instinctive opposition to [human embryo] research which they see as tampering with the creation of human life. There is widely felt concern at the possibility of unscrupulous scientists meddling with the process of reproduction in order to create hybrids, or to indulge theories of selective breeding and eugenic selection'.[23]

In defiance of its own acknowledgement of such widespread public disquiet, the Warnock Report unaccountably recommended the use of human embryos in experimental research. This was all the more remarkable because seven of its sixteen Committee members also opposed such experimentation in some form or other, and the Report includes their two Expressions of Dissent.[24] Nevertheless, the main Report produced two arguments in favour of the practice.

The first argument concerned the status of the embryo: 'A human embryo cannot be thought of as a person, or even a potential person. It is simply a collection of cells which, unless it implants in a human uterine environment, has no potential for development.'[25] The Report continues, 'There is no reason therefore to accord these cells any protected status.'[26] Therefore, Warnock recommended 'that research on human *in vitro* embryos ... should be permitted'.[27] These brash statements require further scrutiny. First, Warnock's attempts to define the moral worth of the human embryo are breathtakingly feeble—they are unconvincing and ineffectual. Herein lies Warnock's supreme failure. Undefined human embryos are unregarded and undefended human embryos—little somethings and nothings. Second, Warnock's language lacks precision. For example, 'potential' is a dangerous word—it can lead to serious understatement. A human embryo is not merely a 'potential person'—it is already a real, actual one. See Section 5.3 for a

SOME OF THE PRIMARY ISSUES

discussion of the prejudicial usage of the word 'person'. Again, 'embryo' is not a trivial term—it denotes one stage of genuine, authentic human life, akin to 'foetus', 'teenager' or 'adult'. We all once experienced life as embryos, foetuses, teenagers ... Third, an adult can also be described as 'simply a collection of cells'. This may be just about the ultimate in scientific reductionism, but it does contain a certain truth. Fourth, an embryo does have the 'potential' for development, but not the 'opportunity' if it is not transferred to a woman's womb; the Report muddled these two words. Warnock was granted the unique time and place to define the status of the human embryo—and it failed.

The second of Warnock's arguments in favour of embryo experimentation is connected with respect and protection. The Report states, 'We found that the more generally held position, however, is that though the human embryo is entitled to some added measure of respect beyond that accorded to other animal subjects, that respect cannot be absolute ...'[28] Hence, human embryos can be used as laboratory material. Instead of offering a well-thought-out, rigorously argued case, the Warnock Report opted for 'the more generally held position'. But since when has the 'generally held position' been the measure of what is right and proper? I know, and I think you do too.

So, according to the Warnock Report, the human embryo is a 'sort of' human being, worthy of some respect and protection. This is all uneasy stuff. Back in the mid-1980s, the world was watching and waiting for some definitive answers to these big questions, but instead of delivering the goods, the Warnock Report preferred to dodge, duck and deflect. Sadly, since its publication, the Report has continued to shape the bioethical thinking of the next generation and to provide many of the quasi-arguments to justify medical science's ethics and practices concerning experimenting with human embryos. The Warnock Report served only to quicken the culture of death.

Having controversially recommended the use of human embryos for research, the Warnock Committee was then faced with deciding just how long such embryos could legally be kept alive. As the Report put it, 'some precise decision must be taken in order to allay public anxiety'.[29] However, the Report had already confirmed that 'biologically there is no one single identifiable stage in the development of the embryo beyond which the

Chapter 3

in vitro embryo should not be kept alive'.[30] The Committee had indeed painted itself into a bioethical corner. Warnock tried to rescue itself by settling for fourteen days. How irrational was that? Undoubtedly mindful of the absurd arbitrariness of this time limit, the Committee attempted to construct an argument that at about day fourteen of embryonic development, the primitive streak appears and, that, contrary to its previous assertion, this somehow does signify an 'identifiable stage in the development of the embryo'. The nature and significance of the primitive streak are further discussed below in Section 5.3.5. Despite this reprehensible misuse of reason and biological knowledge, Warnock's fourteen-day rule became, via the Human Fertilisation and Embryology Act 1990, the law of the land. Utterly amazing!

3.5.2 HUMAN EMBRYO EXPERIMENTATION IN PRACTICE

For too many people—and some overexcitable sectors of the tabloid press—the spectre of human embryo experimentation conjures up thoughts of playing God, fears of Frankenstein or visions of mad scientists and barmy dictators. Such sentiments are quite irrational, and they do nothing to advance public understanding of the issues. Nevertheless, there is one aspect of human embryo experimentation that has all the trappings of such science fiction and science fact: cloning. Human cloning is a topic of such weight and threat that it warrants extended coverage. It is considered separately in Section 3.6 below.

The champions of all other types of human embryo experimentation have always insisted that such research is essential for three main reasons: to increase the success rate of IVF, to provide treatments for genetic diseases, and to improve contraceptive methods. After more than two decades, human embryo experimentation has actually achieved very little. In truth, it is not needed. First, there are other ways of, for example, treating many types of infertility without resorting to IVF and destructively experimenting with human embryos; some have already been explained in Section 3.3.8. Second, the development of new treatments and cures for genetic disorders and other serious diseases by, for example, adult stem-cell technologies and somatic gene therapy do not require the use of human embryos as experimental material, as discussed in Sections 3.7 and 3.10 below. Third, research into better methods of contraception—as opposed to abortifacient methods—is

SOME OF THE PRIMARY ISSUES

properly directed at sperm and ova, not human embryos. Anyway, most so-called 'contraceptive failures' are associated not with ineffective current methods, but rather with simple misuse by men and women. Some of these alternatives to human embryo experimentation may be less glitzy and less newsworthy, but they are, for sure, less bioethically offensive.

Ever since human embryos were deprived of legal protection, at least during their first fourteen days of life, scientists have been destroying them with vigour and creativity. Blame, if you like, those scientists for their lack of bioethical insight and backbone, but also acknowledge that it was the general public and their parliamentary representatives who originally granted them the go-ahead to follow their biological dreams. The intellectual impulse to unravel the mysteries and mechanisms of the earliest days of human life is compelling, whether for purely academic pursuit or to search for medical applications; yes indeed, the thirst for that elusive breakthrough with its attendant kudos and power, and perhaps even a Nobel prize, can prove to be quite unquenchable. Let us be entirely clear here. Scientific endeavours and medical research are undeniably a societal good, but only when they are conducted within a robust, principled, ethical framework. Whenever they become destructive of human life, as in embryo experimentation, they can no longer be classed as good.

And to keep science good, it needs to be regulated and restrained by tough, prohibitive laws. Yet every bioethical topic, from abortion to zygote, is continually targeted by those who wish to breach established legal boundaries; some call this progressive liberalization. The field of human embryo experimentation is no exception. Consider, for example, genetically altered human embryos. The creation of these entities was specifically banned by the Human Fertilisation and Embryology Act 1990. Unremitting pressure, mainly from an elite scientific lobby, to repeal that ban continued until the Human Fertilisation and Embryology Act 2008 finally gave way and permitted their production and experimental use. Bioethically, this was the opening of a very different door to unknown, and maybe unwanted, events and situations. It was also a dangerous door—one that still remains ajar—because once any experimental procedure is granted legal authorization, it is rarely rescinded; on the contrary, it is habitually extended by 'mission creep'. Yet, so far, this over-hyped biological enterprise has achieved virtually nothing. Take two cases in point.

Chapter 3

First, in 2006, there was the ballyhoo that greeted the proposal to create the human-admixed embryo, a cytoplasmic hybrid embryo produced when a denucleated ovum from an animal is 'fertilized' by human genetic material via the cloning procedure known as somatic cell nuclear transfer (SCNT), a subject discussed in Section 3.6 below. There is something inherently distasteful about mixing genetic material from animals with that from human beings, even if the animal's contribution is only 0.1 per cent of the total DNA. A biblical case against such experimentation can be made from the early chapters of Genesis, from the 'Do not mate different kinds of animals' of Leviticus 19:19, and from the Bible's high and inviolable view of human life. Yet in 2008, the Human Fertilisation and Embryology Authority (HFEA) approved licences for the production of these human–animal hybrids using cows' ova and human nuclei. This research was said to be essential for two reasons. First, since human ova were in short supply, animal ova could circumvent this scarcity. Second, these hybrids, or at least the extraction of their ostensibly 'indispensable' embryonic stem cells, would aid the discovery of cures for serious diseases; the big three, Parkinson's, Alzheimer's and diabetes, were invariably mentioned. Both of these arguments were fallacious because other, and better, source materials and treatments were already available, such as the increasingly effective use of adult stem-cell therapies, plus the then recently discovered induced pluripotent stem (iPS) cells. Human-admixed embryos are both unethical and unnecessary. Indeed, this once 'vital' project of human embryo experimentation has now been all but abandoned. Even so, the precedent set by its official licensing means that time-honoured bioethical and legal boundaries have been breached, for ever. Did someone mention slippery slopes …?

Second, in 2011, there was the call to approve another novel and controversial technique of human embryo experimentation, known colloquially as 'three-parent' IVF. This might enable parents-to-be with particular inherited disorders, namely, mitochondrial diseases, to avoid passing them on to their would-be children. These diseases affect about 1 in every 200 births each year; some are symptomless, some are serious, a few are fatal. Mitochondria are found in every cell of the human body and contain a very small amount of DNA compared with that found in the cell's nucleus. This mitochondrial DNA is inherited exclusively from the mother, through the mitochondria present in the cytoplasm of her ova, so it will be present, not in the nucleus of any zygotes, but in their cytoplasm. Using IVF to create day-one embryos or zygotes, followed by a method called pronuclear transfer (PNT), it may be possible to extract the nucleus from an unhealthy, disease-affected zygote and transplant it into a second, healthy donor zygote from which the nuclear DNA has previously been removed. The resulting zygote would therefore contain nuclear DNA derived from the mother and father, but also mitochondrial DNA from the maternal donor, the 'third parent'. This 'new', and in theory, healthy early embryo could then be transferred to the putative mother using standard IVF techniques. An analogous method called maternal spindle transfer (MST) would extract and transfer nuclear DNA from human ova rather than from human embryos. Already, in preliminary trials of PNT, dozens of human embryos have been created and destroyed. Moreover, there are concerns about the social consequences of establishing children with three genetic parents. And, since this is a form of germline gene therapy—in a word, eugenic—genetic changes will be heritable and automatically passed on to future generations. This would assail another long-established scientific and bioethical frontier, which, for good reasons, has never previously been crossed. The procedure is currently experimental and remains banned for treatment purposes by the Human Fertilisation and Embryology Act 2008. But will 'three-parent' IVF, though of unknown efficacy and safety, eventually be granted the therapeutic go-ahead? Will another bioethical Rubicon be crossed? Did someone mention slippery slopes again …?

3.5.3 HUMAN EMBRYO EXPERIMENTATION IN THE FUTURE

As long as human embryos are available—and IVF generates them daily by the thousand—they will be the likely 'fodder' for destructive experimentation. Of course, the minor experimental fiddling with embryos at the edges of established treatment technologies, like IVF and PGD (preimplantation genetic diagnosis), will continue, but this is not the type of hard-core science under discussion here. This more basic, boundary-pushing embryo experimentation has, in the past, been distinguished by its extraordinary lack of scientific moment. It is therefore difficult to foresee any specific focus for its future. Even the use of human embryos for so-called therapeutic cloning and the production of embryonic stem cells—

CHAPTER 3

the one-time little darlings of chief scientists and leading politicians—has got stuck in a non-functional rut and been overtaken by other and better technologies, as described in Section 3.7 below. Nevertheless, who can doubt that a few inventive academics will not dream up some novel schemes for which human embryos will again be deemed 'essential'? After all, a few years ago, whoever could have predicted the creation of those unnatural oddities known as human-admixed embryos? And will there be calls for the fourteen-day rule to be extended? And will current rulings prohibiting eugenic, germline experimentation be torn up? Or will human embryo experimentation simply come to nothing?

3.5.4 HUMAN EMBRYO EXPERIMENTATION: IN CONCLUSION

The recommendations from the Warnock Report concerning human embryo experimentation[31] and their subsequent incorporation into the Human Fertilisation and Embryology Acts 1990 and 2008 have produced a trail of embryo destruction and nothing of much benefit in return. The cost, the loss and the harm have far outweighed any gain.

This casual destruction of early human life has induced a new kind of bioethical blindness. Bioethically, we have become less sensitive and more hard-hearted. Does such a forthright statement need some supporting evidence? Here it is, largely unrecognized and untold, but still irrefutably true. Our consenting to human embryo experimentation has resulted in three innovative and outlandish outcomes. First, we have publicly accepted that human beings can be the subject of research and experimentation that is not for their own benefit and is without their informed consent. This is a major departure from traditional medical ethics and practice. Second, we have established a new crime, that of keeping a human being alive after fourteen days, the upper limit for embryo research proposed by the Warnock Report and now enforced by statute. For the first time, it is a crime *not* to kill a fellow human being. Third, we have created a new race of human beings. They are created in laboratories, they never leave laboratories, and they are killed in laboratories. Is this not just about the last word in exploitation and manipulation of human life? Are we not suffering from advanced bioethical myopia, tunnel vision and numerous blind spots? Every human embryo needs respect and protection. Human embryo experimentation—who needs that?

3.6 Human cloning

The one bioethical issue always guaranteed to grab the media headlines is another offshoot of embryo experimentation: cloning. The general public has a fascination with it, especially human cloning, and not just the sort found in science-fiction books and films. On 25 February 1998, the *Daily Mirror* carried this headline: 'Plans to Clone Elvis Presley from His Toenail'. A group called ACE (Americans for Cloning Elvis) had gathered 3,000-plus signatures on a petition urging the extraction of Elvis's DNA from one of his toenails—apparently collected from a hotel waste bin by an ardent fan—to produce his double. In a poll the following year, Mother Teresa of Calcutta was voted the most popular choice for cloning, closely followed by Michelle Pfeiffer. So much for popularism!

However, the more serious aspects of cloning came to the world's attention on 5 July 1996, when, in a shed just outside Edinburgh, a mother gave birth to a 6.6 kg offspring. It was a snow-white Finn-Dorset lamb called 6LL3, more commonly known as Dolly.

3.6.1 CLONING TECHNIQUES

Cloning is technically complex but bioethically straightforward. There are two techniques. First, there is embryo splitting. This can occur naturally in the womb and produces monozygotic, or identical, twins, even triplets. It can also be induced artificially in the laboratory. Thus, individual cells can be removed by microsurgery from an early human embryo, say, from a sixteen-cell morula. These cells could then be cultured, stimulated to divide, and eventually they could result in identical embryos, or clones.

Second, there is somatic cell nuclear transfer (SCNT), sometimes still referred to as cell nuclear replacement (CNR). There is no natural equivalent to this. The nucleus, which contains the genetic material, is first removed from a somatic, or body, cell, perhaps a skin or a liver cell, taken from the animal to be cloned. This nucleus is then transferred to a donated ovum from the same species, which is denucleated, that is, from which the nucleus has previously been excised. The 'new' ovum is then cultured and electrically stimulated by a process called electroporation, which causes the cell to divide as if it were a naturally fertilized zygote. Because sperm is not needed in SCNT, the technique could signal the end of men in human reproduction. But that is another issue!

CHAPTER 3

SCNT is not new; it has been used since the 1950s to, for example, clone frogs from tadpole cells. However, what was significant about Dolly was that she was the first mammal to be cloned by SCNT using an adult cell from another animal, namely, an udder cell from a six-year-old sheep. Even so, the technique was far from efficient because Professor Ian Wilmut and his team at the Roslin Institute prepared 277 reconstructed sheep embryos, but only thirteen survived; of these, which were transferred to surrogate ovine wombs, only one, Dolly, went to term. Additional attempts by others using SCNT to clone mammals, from little mice to large cows, have often resulted in offspring with compromised health issues and developmental abnormalities. In her later years, Dolly suffered from a progressive lung disease and severe arthritis and was put down on St Valentine's Day 2003. She was stuffed and is now on display in the Connect Gallery at the National Museum of Scotland in Edinburgh. Controversy still surrounds her mortality. Some believe it was premature because she was genetically derived from a six-year-old animal, which may have hastened Dolly's ageing processes of both telomere shortening and accumulated DNA damage. Put simply, maybe she was old before her time.

3.6.2 CLONING PURPOSES

There are two purposes for cloning, and specifically human cloning. And it makes no difference whether the requisite embryos are obtained from embryo splitting, SCNT, as 'spare' embryos from IVF treatments, or produced in the laboratory exclusively for research purposes.

First, there is therapeutic cloning. The single cell of a newly fertilized ovum, namely, a zygote, as well as the cells of every rapidly developing early embryo, have a most amazing capacity—they all have, according to the word used in the Warnock Report,[32] 'totipotential'. That is, these cells, known as stem cells, have the ability to multiply and to develop into any of the 200 or so different types of cells required for the human body. Perhaps they will become cells of heart, skin, lungs, bones, pancreas or fingernails. Therapeutic cloning would exploit this natural property of stem cells. For example, cells, say skin cells, taken from a human patient, would be cloned by SCNT to produce human embryos. These embryos' stem cells would then be harvested and tweaked to produce other types of cells, perhaps nerve cells, or to regenerate spare tissues, perhaps cardiac muscles, or even to build bodily parts, perhaps hip joints. So, the much-heralded motive behind therapeutic cloning is that the embryonic stem cells produced could be used to replace a patient's diseased or damaged cells and thus conquer disorders like Alzheimer's, Parkinson's and diabetes. Such therapeutic cloning means that the cells, the tissues, or the organs produced would be histocompatible, that is, there would be no problems of tissue rejection because they would be genetically identical to the patient's originals. That may all sound exciting, but hold on—not so fast. The indisputably great bioethical downside, the cause of intercontinental bioethical anger and angst, is that the harvesting of embryonic stem cells always destroys the human embryo.

Since the 'success' of the ovine Dolly, researchers have repeatedly tried to clone human embryos to produce lines of embryonic stem cells that could be used either for research or for treatment. It has proved to be a more-than-difficult assignment. One problem is the lack of the key resource, human ova—hundreds, thousands would be needed. While human sperm are plentiful and accessible, ova are scarce and inaccessible. Another problem is that while some researchers have successfully created cloned embryos of several mammalian species, the human sort stop dividing before the all-important blastocyst stage of 70–100 cells that is necessary before stem-cell harvesting can begin. By late 2011, some determined scientists had managed to reprogramme human ova and produce a few lines of human embryonic stem cells but, because of the methodology used, the cells contained an extra set of chromosomes—so these abnormal stem cells neither matched those of the donating patients, nor were of any therapeutic use. Human biology can certainly be different and subtle. When it comes to cloning, men are plainly not mice. It seems that human therapeutic cloning is just not working. But why even bother to try? The very existence of adult stem cells and induced pluripotent stem (iPS) cells is more than sufficient, as demonstrated in Section 3.7 below.

Second, there is reproductive cloning. Today, this is widely used for farm animals such as sheep, pigs and cows. One fear is that it may be used tomorrow for humans. The Human Reproductive Cloning Act 2001 rendered reproductive cloning in the UK illegal: 'A person who places in a woman a human embryo which has been created otherwise than by fertilisation is guilty of an offence.' Instinctively, we know that reproductive cloning is

Chapter 3

wrong. Nevertheless, the required embryos could still be prepared legally in several places, including the UK, and then transported to a country where reproductive cloning is not illegal. Already people have expressed interest in such technology for several, typically selfish, reasons. Copying themselves, they say, would obviate the ageing process and ensure their own 'immortality'. It has also been proposed for families who may wish to replace a dead loved one, or for bereaved parents who long to replace a 'lost' child, or for infertile couples who want children using at least some of their own genetic material.

In 2000, the Donaldson Committee Report recommended to the UK Parliament that reproductive cloning should be banned, but that therapeutic cloning should be allowed. The latter was discussed almost exclusively as if cloned human embryos were the only source of the much-celebrated, highly desirable stem cells. The possibility of using the alternative of adult stem cells was largely ignored. Such a blinkered approach to promoting progress in science and medicine was, and still is, inexcusable. The following year, Parliament approved an extension to the Human Fertilisation and Embryology Act 1990, namely, the Human Fertilisation and Embryology (Research Purposes) Regulations 2001, which sanctioned the use of human embryos for research into therapeutic cloning. Thus the UK became the first country in Europe to permit such human cloning.

3.6.3. HUMAN CLONING HYPE AND HOAX

So far, we have seen a variety of animals reproductively cloned and born—sheep, mice, cattle, goats, rabbits, cats, pigs, mules, dogs and more. But never have we witnessed a reproductively cloned human baby. However, this 'golden jackpot' has been claimed several times by an array of crackpots, such as the cultic Raelians and medical mavericks like Severino Antinori and Panayiotis Zavos. But they have never delivered the goods: they have turned out to be no more than publicity-hungry mountebanks. They are easily dismissed.

A more disturbing case of human cloning hype and hoax was that of Woo Suk Hwang. In 2004, and again in 2005, he claimed in that prestigious US journal, *Science*, to have cloned human embryos by SCNT and extracted several patient-specific embryonic stem-cell lines from them. The media circus went wild—patients with diabetes, Alzheimer's and Parkinson's would soon be cured, the lame would walk and the deaf would hear. Hwang was feted as a genius and a national hero; the South Korean government even issued a postage stamp in his honour, depicting a paralysed patient leaping out of a wheelchair. Then in 2005, the truth began to seep out. Minor irregularities in his studies were cited. Female colleagues had been illicitly paid for their ova used in his experiments, and the published photographs of the reputed stem cells were not originals. A month later, one of Hwang's research team claimed that many of the stem-cell lines were fakes. The media pack descended again, but this time it was decidedly hostile. Further investigations were launched and finally, just before Christmas 2005, Hwang came clean. He confessed his fraud and resigned from his university post. The golden boy of human cloning was declared to be a liar and a cheat.

The whole fiasco threw up some serious questions. Is the peer-review publication system, upon which scientific progress largely depends, sufficiently rigorous? If so, how could academic experts have been so readily deceived? Had the press, and gullible others, been hoodwinked by the hype of the embryonic stem-cell lobby? How could scientific objectivity be so easily trounced by passion and politics? Would the successes of treatments using non-embryonic stem cells now get a fairer hearing? Scientific truth, integrity and transparency had taken a hard hit—and so had human therapeutic cloning.

3.6.4 HUMAN CLONING IN THE FUTURE

Here is the key question: why would anyone even bother with human cloning in the future? Therapeutic cloning is on the way out—it has been superseded by adult stem- and iPS-cell technologies—and reproductive cloning is just plain terrifying. But though the latter is currently banned in most countries, in the future maybe it … By now you should know how to complete such sentences.

3.6.5 HUMAN CLONING: IN CONCLUSION

You may well agree that all human cloning should be banned. But just for a moment, try this little diversion of creative reasoning. Contrary to public opinion, it may be argued that therapeutic cloning is actually bioethically worse than reproductive cloning. At least in the latter, the embryo lives on. In the former, the cloned embryo is destroyed for the therapeutic benefit of

Chapter 3

others. Therefore, therapeutic cloning contradicts a fundamental principle of medical research, as the Declaration of Helsinki (2008, revised) affirms: 'In medical research involving human subjects, the well-being of the individual research subject must take precedence over all other interests.' So are you now bewildered or bemused? OK, the diversion is over. None of this sophistry validates any human cloning. It should always be forbidden. Indeed, in 2005, the United Nations Declaration on Human Cloning called on member states 'to adopt all measures necessary to prohibit all forms of human cloning inasmuch as they are incompatible with human dignity and the protection of human life'. In other words, ban the lot.

All talk of human cloning should make us nervous. Our primary objection must be that it results in the exploitation and the wilful destruction of human embryos. It represents an assault on the unique nature of human beings and their interrelationships. Moreover, it is only the purpose that distinguishes therapeutic from reproductive cloning—the former may continue legally for up to fourteen days on the researcher's laboratory bench in the UK, the latter up to nine months in the womb of a surrogate mother somewhere else. Any experimentation associated with either procedure will continue to destroy human embryos. It is always wrong to use any human life as a means to an end—it is that culture of death again.

All support for human cloning must be challenged. Its ethics tend to be totally utilitarian and utterly self-serving. They are part of the scientific imperative 'We have the technology, so why not use it?' The pro-cloning lobby has tried to steal the moral high ground by explicitly rejecting the reproductive variety. 'It's abhorrent,' they say. Indeed, they have gone even further: they now pretend to reject all human cloning because they have lexically engineered therapeutic cloning to be known only as SCNT. Thus, the dreaded C-word has been sidestepped and the general public can be unknowingly insulated from the fact that SCNT can be the starting point for either type of cloning. Furthermore, the pro-cloners have accused those who are opposed to therapeutic cloning of depriving people with debilitating diseases of possible cures. What sniping nonsense.

The fact is, we do not want, or even need, human cloning. Reproductive cloning is repellent. And the perceived benefits of therapeutic cloning can be achieved without this wholesale destruction of human embryos—better ways have been found. Instead, we should welcome non-embryonic,

SOME OF THE PRIMARY ISSUES

adult and induced pluripotent stem-cell technologies. They are a novel and revolutionary approach to medicine, yet they are also bioethically uncontroversial. We are not anti-science, anti-research, anti-medicine or anti-progress. But we do insist that science and medicine are practised firmly rooted within a culture of life. Read on: some good news—at last—is coming next.

3.7 Stem-cell technologies

Now this topic is—and I use the word advisedly—awesome. Stem-cell technologies are just about the hottest of 'hot-button' issues in contemporary medicine, yet stem cells have been around (almost) for ever. Think about it. New human life begins with a one-celled zygote, then the process of cell division, or cell cleavage, rapidly produces two, four, eight, sixteen, thirty-two, sixty-four cells, (almost) ad infinitum. These cells of the early embryo are called stem cells and they are totipotent or pluripotent, that is, they have the capacity to become, by the process of cell differentiation, any of the approximately 200 types of cells that constitute the complexities of the adult body, as already noted in Section 3.6.2 above. In other words, these unspecialized embryonic stem cells are destined to develop into the specialized cells of muscles, brain, eyes, teeth, liver, kneecaps and so forth. Moreover, in mature adult tissues, for instance, in bone marrow and the intestines, stem cells still exist and function as an internal repair system for the body. That is, they naturally and regularly divide to replace worn out or damaged tissues throughout a person's life. This is basic human biology. It is truly astonishing and awe-inspiring.

3.7.1 STEM CELLS AND REGENERATIVE MEDICINE

The question therefore arises: could this totipotent/pluripotent property of embryonic stem cells be exploited to regenerate and replace our diseased and worn-out cells, tissues and organs? The question is pressing because life expectancy has increased so dramatically—in 1900 in the UK, it was about forty-five years, whereas a century later, by 2000, it had reached around eighty. We are not only living longer, but we are contracting illnesses and dying of causes different from those of our forebears. They were stricken by and died mainly from infectious diseases such as scarlet fever, polio and tuberculosis. We are more likely to suffer and die from

Chapter 3

chronic degenerative and genetic diseases such as cancers, dementias and cardiovascular problems. So, could embryonic stem cells be manipulated to produce, for example, neurons to rejuvenate the brain of the woman with Alzheimer's disease, or cardiac muscle cells for the man who has undergone a heart attack? Such prospects are part of the exciting new discipline called regenerative medicine—and stem-cell technologies are at its very centre.

3.7.2 STEM CELLS AND BIOETHICS

But, and this is a dire 'but', such would-be treatments precipitate a bioethical crisis because, as previously explained in Section 3.6.2 above, the harvesting of embryonic stem cells results in the unavoidable destruction of the human embryo. But, and this is a splendid 'but', there are sources of stem cells other than human embryos. Stem cells exist in bone marrow, umbilical cord blood, milk teeth, eyes, adipose tissue—seemingly in almost every human physiological location—and they are relatively plentiful and easily collected. Therefore, stem-cell technologies and treatments derived from these non-embryonic, or what are commonly called 'adult', stem cells are part of a praiseworthy, wholesome medicine—and the culture of life.

Accordingly, stem-cell technologies have sparked off a bioethical battle, a stem-cell war—it has been embryonic v. non-embryonic. James Thomson, who, in 1998 at the University of Wisconsin, became the first scientist to isolate stem cells from human embryos, astutely recognized the existence of this bioethical conflict zone when he declared, 'If human embryonic stem cell research does not make you at least a little bit uncomfortable, you have not thought about it enough.'[33]

3.7.3 STEM-CELL TREATMENTS: A SHORT HISTORY

It was in the early 1960s that James Till and Ernest McCulloch of Toronto University originally demonstrated the existence of adult stem cells in the bone marrow of mice and described their unique ability for self-renewal and self-replication. And it was in the 1990s that James Thomson and his colleagues derived the first stem-cell lines from human embryos. So our knowledge of stem cells, both adult and embryonic, is not especially recent.

Nor is the therapeutic use of adult stem cells particularly new; it has been practised for decades. In 1956, E. Donnall Thomas began successfully

SOME OF THE PRIMARY ISSUES

treating men and women who were suffering with leukaemias and other cancers of the blood by initially destroying their diseased bone marrow with near-lethal doses of radiation and chemotherapy and then providing them with transplants of healthy bone marrow derived from donors. It was adult stem cells, the haematopoietic stem cells of the donor bone marrow, that re-established a patient's production of healthy blood cells. At that time, a leukaemia diagnosis was virtually a death sentence. Nowadays, this adult stem-cell therapy has become routine and, as a result, tens of thousands of leukaemia patients have been enabled to lead normal, productive lives.

But that is all so last century. In the twenty-first century, stem cells are the biological buzz, the cause for a medical huzza, and they have created their own vast and novel categories. A website search of 'stem-cell technology' in late 2011 produced twelve million hits, while by late 2013 that number had zoomed up to sixty-four million and included stem-cell research, treatments, courses, dedicated journals, even world summits and lots more.

3.7.4 INDUCED PLURIPOTENT STEM (IPS) CELLS

Question: all stem cells are either adult or embryonic, right? No, wrong. In 2006, a biological bombshell exploded. Shinya Yamanaka of Kyoto University discovered how to induce ordinary, adult somatic cells (not adult *stem* cells) to revert to an embryo-like state. He cultured skin cells from adult mice and exposed them to just four genes, namely, Oct4, Sox2, Kfl4 and c-Myc, which coded for specific proteins, known as transcription factors. These in turn triggered the production of other genes that 'undifferentiated' the adult murine skin cells. Yamanaka called these new entities 'induced pluripotent stem cells' (iPS cells). His method of iPS-cell production was, to say the least, surprising, even staggering, yet Yamanaka claimed, 'It's easy. There's no trick, no magic.'[34] This 'reprogramming' or 'deprogramming' has been likened to winding back the clock, taking adult cells back to their embryonic precursors from which they originated—the very reverse of the process of cell differentiation. Previously, this was thought to be an irreversible pathway, that is, the biological traffic went only one way from embryo to adult; we now know differently. The race was on and the bandwagon was rolling—could the same reprogramming occur with human somatic cells? In November 2007, two research groups,

Chapter 3

led separately by Thomson and Yamanaka, simultaneously reported just that: the generation of iPS cells from human adult fibroblasts, skin cells.

It is hard to overstate the medical and bioethical implications of such reprogramming. In a nutshell, iPS cells are stem cells that can be made from an individual's own somatic cells without the need for ova, cloning, or the subsequent destruction of an embryo. What is more, they appear to have most, if not all, of the biological properties of embryonic stem cells. And because iPS cells are 'patient-specific', they are genetically matched to, and therefore would not be rejected by, the patient, who would therefore not need any immunosuppressive drugs if these cells were used in any regenerative treatments. Yamanaka's revolutionary work has been rightly recognized and rewarded by his winning the 2012 Nobel Prize in Physiology or Medicine. Intriguingly, he explained that the motivation behind his work came after he had looked down a microscope while visiting a friend's IVF clinic: 'When I saw the embryo, I suddenly realized there was such a small difference between it and my daughters. I thought, we can't keep destroying embryos for our research. There must be another way.'[35] And so he set about searching for 'another way' and ended up producing iPS cells.

The production of iPS cells was—and still is—game-changing news. Indeed, it was sufficiently ground-breaking for some scientists, including Ian Wilmut, the creator of Dolly the cloned sheep, to abandon therapeutic cloning (SCNT) and their embryonic stem-cell research and instead concentrate their future efforts on iPS cells. Ian Wilmut affirmed that 'This approach [the use of iPS cells] represents the future for stem cell research' and 'I have no doubt that in the long term, direct reprogramming will be more productive'.[36] Similarly, James Thomson, commenting on the stem-cell bioethical war, stated that 'Human ES [embryonic stem] cells created this remarkable controversy, and iPS cells, while it's not completely over, are sort of the beginning of the end for that controversy';[37] in 2007 he claimed that 'A decade from now, this [the adult v. embryonic stem-cell controversy] will be just a funny historical footnote'.[38]

Growing numbers within the scientific community, as well as from the general public, now consider the production and use of embryonic stem cells to be both overhyped and unneeded. From a bioethical point of view, we should rejoice. But we are not there yet. Proper, dependable therapies using iPS cells are still several years away—formidable hurdles remain. Work, such as the translation from animal to human models, safety tests and human clinical trials, must first be completed. Yamanaka-type procedures involve retroviruses, which, as shown in some gene-therapy trials, can activate oncogenes, which can cause cancers. Yet already, methods have been developed which use fewer or even no such vectors. Another of the key topics that is still far from understood is that of directed differentiation, that is: how do these reprogrammed stem cells become and remain, say, neurons only, or cardiac muscle cells only? And then, how can this process be regulated efficiently and with precision within the body? Until these pieces of the biological jigsaw are understood and controlled, there will be no widespread iPS cell cures for human diseases. Even so, laboratories worldwide are reporting positive advances in these areas almost weekly. Indeed, in 2013, details of the world's first human clinical trial using iPS cells were announced in Japan. It will seek to repair retinas damaged by severe age-related macular degeneration (AMD). That country has also begun to create the world's first extensive iPS-cell bank. Keeping up with iPS-cell progress is demanding, but exciting.

3.7.5 STEM-CELL TREATMENTS, BAD

Whereas human treatments using iPS cells are for the imminent future, non-embryonic, adult stem-cell treatments are happening here and now. While rigorously tested therapies remain relatively few and far between, many small-scale trials are reported to be 'successful'. In 2010, there were estimated to be over 200 clinics worldwide—including more than 100 in China alone—offering often unproven stem-cell treatments for scores of disorders, from Alzheimer's disease to wound healing. But just as 'dead flies give perfume a bad smell' (Eccles. 10:1), so, sadly, there are quacks and charlatans selling 'treatments' to desperate patients who have largely exhausted mainstream medical care. Practitioners at these 'clinics' claim that their treatments are safe and effective. But they typically base those assertions on little more than patient testimonials and hyped media accounts; they lack independent, scientific verification. Few offer evidence from controlled clinical studies, or from rigorous follow-up of their own patients.

One such unscrupulous doctor was Robert Trossel, who ran clinics in Rotterdam and in Wimpole Street, London. He charged vulnerable multiple sclerosis patients thousands of pounds for pointless and unjustifiable

Chapter 3

treatments. He injected patients with stem cells never intended for human use that contained material from bovine brain and spinal cord and thereby exposed them to the risk of developing vCJD. In September 2010, he was duly struck off the medical register by the UK's General Medical Council.[39] Beware of fakes and fraudsters.

In addition, beware of words. Stem-cell technologies are riddled with lexical engineering. For instance, a human zygote or embryo is frequently described, and thereby purposefully devalued, as merely a 'fertilized egg'. The blanket statement that 'religious people are against stem-cell research' mischievously conflates embryonic and adult stem-cell technologies and so misrepresents the truth. Then there is the example of ReNeuron, a British biotechnology company developing stem-cell therapies for disabled stroke patients. Its lead product, the CTX cell line, was advertised by the company as being 'derived from non-embryonic human tissue'. Indeed, that is true and it may therefore sound bioethically acceptable. However, the fact is that it was derived in 2003 from the cortex region of the brain of an aborted foetus.[40] Don't be fooled by fancy words.

3.7.6 STEM-CELL TREATMENTS, GOOD

Despite all this doubt, deceit and quackery, there are some well-documented and well-controlled clinical studies with meticulous follow-up of patients using adult stem-cell treatments. Two diverse, but equally astonishing, examples prove the point.

In 2008, *The Lancet* reported the first full transplant of a human organ grown from adult stem cells.[41] It was carried out at the Hospital Clinic of Barcelona on Claudia Castillo, a thirty-year-old mother of two. Her windpipe had been severely damaged as a result of tuberculosis. Researchers harvested a portion of trachea from a donor and stripped off the cells that could cause an adverse immune reaction, leaving a three-dimensional trunk of cartilage. This bio-scaffold was then 'seeded' with stem cells taken from the bone marrow of Ms Castillo's hip, and this new section of trachea was grown in the laboratory over four days. It was then transplanted into the left main bronchus of the patient. Because the stem cells were harvested from the patient's own bone marrow it was not necessary to give her anti-rejection, immunosuppressive drugs. Before the surgery, Ms Castillo struggled to climb a flight of stairs. After the operation, she began to lead a normal life—apparently, she has even been known to go out dancing! This adult stem-cell and surgical procedure was a medical milestone. By 2013, after five years of follow-up, the medical team pronounced the procedure to be 'safe and promising'.

In 2010, a paper in the *New England Journal of Medicine* by Graziella Pellegrini and colleagues reported results from the long-term treatment of one type of blindness using non-embryonic, adult stem cells.[42] The human eyeball is covered by the cornea, and a clear cornea is essential for good eyesight. There is a narrow zone between the cornea and the conjunctiva, known as the limbus; it is the source of corneal epithelial stem cells, which can self-replicate in order to replenish and repair the cornea. If the limbus is destroyed by, for example, ocular burns or infections, this will halt renewal of the cornea and lead to its vascularization, chronic inflammation, scarring and, ultimately, corneal opacity and loss of sight. Conventional treatment is a corneal transplant from a genetically non-identical donor. Not only are suitable donors in short supply, but this treatment is typically short lived. Pellegrini and her co-workers obtained limbal stem cells from the healthy eye of each of 112 patients who had suffered partial or complete loss of vision in one eye due to chemical or thermal burns. These stem cells were cultured and then transplanted onto the patients' other eye, the damaged eye. Procedurally, it was that simple. After an extensive monitoring period of up to ten years, these authors reported that 'Permanent restoration of a transparent, renewing corneal epithelium was attained in 76.6% of eyes', leading to restored or improved vision. This represents a long-term study of a real group of people who have had their lives radically enriched by an adult stem-cell treatment. Nevertheless, it should be noted that not all the patients were cured, the numbers treated were fairly small, the treatment remains largely experimental, and it is not suitable for all kinds of blindness; even so, it is still immensely impressive. I, for one, am amazed by these results.

3.7.7 EMBRYONIC STEM-CELL TREATMENTS

Compare the above two case studies, and a growing number of other peer-reviewed examples of clinical treatments using adult stem cells, with those using embryonic stem cells. Where are they? The truth is that they are just about non-existent. According to the website www.stemcellresearch.org, the score for successful stem-cell research treatments, up to 2010,

Chapter 3

was 73 adult v. 0 embryonic. Technically, and bioethically, the latter have crashed.

It was not until January 2009, after several false starts because of safety fears, that the US Food and Drug Administration (FDA) gave the Geron Corporation, a Californian-based biopharmaceutical company, clearance for the world's first clinical trial of an embryonic stem-cell-based treatment with human patients. In October 2010, the so-called phrase 1 trial—regarded as a proof-of-concept test—began with four patients suffering from spinal-cord injuries. Its primary purpose was to assess the safety of Geron's oligodendocyte progenitor cells, known as GRNOPC1, which had been derived from human embryonic stem cells. The first-year assessment results were eagerly anticipated—the world was waiting. Then on 14 November 2011, Geron abruptly announced that it was abandoning the trial. Geron blamed the decision on 'capital scarcity and uncertain economic conditions'.[43] Others claimed that the trial was both poorly designed and over-ambitious; spinal-cord injuries were judged to be too complex and affect too few people, and so returns, both curative and economic, might take up to ten years. Still others cited the recently imposed ban on the patenting of human embryo products by the European Court of Justice as a setback to anticipated financial profits. Geron had previously announced, 'To date, GRNOPC1 has been well tolerated with no serious adverse events.' But maybe GRNOPC1 was simply not working; if so, continuing the trial would be futile. Or worse, had some negative side effects occurred subsequently or, perhaps more likely, would they occur if the trial continued? Maybe a proliferation of cysts or an onset of various cancers was imminent. Such disorders have been commonly reported in animal trials using embryonic stem cells. Indeed, these were the reasons for much of the FDA's prolonged delay in approving Geron's trial with human patients in the first place. We may never know the truth. But much of the hype surrounding putative cures by using embryonic stem cells suddenly evaporated.

Then in July 2011, another Californian biotechnology company, Advanced Cell Technology (ACT), began two other clinical trials using embryonic stem cells. The first was aimed at Stargardt's macular dystrophy (SMD). This is an incurable form of macular degeneration which can cause blindness, generally in young people aged between ten and twenty years old,

SOME OF THE PRIMARY ISSUES

by attacking the central part of the retina—the macula—and progressively causing impaired vision. The second trial was intended for a common cause of blindness in the elderly, namely, dry age-related macular degeneration (dry AMD). Both ACT trials used retinal pigment epithelial (RPE) cells derived from human embryonic stem cells. Then came news of the first embryonic stem-cell trial to be conducted in Europe. In September 2011, the UK's Medicines and Healthcare Products Regulatory Agency (MHRA) approved the trial as a joint venture between ACT and Moorfields Eye Hospital in London. The proposed initial treatment, a phase 1 trial, was carried out on twelve patients suffering from SMD. Each patient's eye was injected with between 50,000 and 200,000 replacement RPE cells, known as the ACT product, MA09-hRPE, derived from human embryos. Some commentators tried to deflect the truth that the product's source required the obligatory destruction of human embryos by using timeworn comments, such as 'The stem cell line was created in the United States several years ago using a donated embryo of just a few cells, smaller than a pinhead'.[44] How altruistic of the donor, and how very, very tiny was that embryo. Yes, yes—we've heard all this lexical engineering before. In early 2013, reporting on all three trials, ACT announced 'that investigators ... have observed evidence of engraftment of the transplanted human embryonic stem cell (hESC)-derived retinal pigment epithelial (RPE) cells and visual acuity gain in patients treated ...'[45] More detailed results are awaited.

3.7.8 STEM-CELL TECHNOLOGIES IN THE FUTURE

Some bioethical issues, such as abortion and infanticide, are well established and their futures appear to be somewhat static. Not so with stem cells—they are largely unexplored and their futures are dynamic. During the next decade, stem-cell technologies will be everywhere, cut-price and therapeutically effective. At least four future trends are evident. First, there will be a phasing out of using stem cells derived from human embryos. A few human trials will have shown them to be too complex, too unsafe, too costly and too ineffective. Already the world's first such trial has been abandoned. And all that hope—and hype—of stem-cell cures from those horrid human–animal hybrids, known as human-admixed embryos, will be long forgotten. Such technologies will become obsolete. Second, there will be more adult stem-cell treatments, better controlled, researched and reported. History is on their

Chapter 3

side: adult stem-cell technologies have proven to be successful for decades in the form of bone-marrow transplants, and more recently as therapies for dozens of eye, heart, spinal cord, muscle and numerous other disorders. This is not to ignore future technical problems in their production, stability and suchlike. Third, induced pluripotent stem (iPS) cells, while already being used for drug testing and disease modelling, will become the additional therapeutic favourite of the decade; their methods of production will become even simpler and cheaper. And when they are shown to be safe for the treatment of some human diseases, that will be a major leap forward for regenerative medicine. However, the customary difficulties of donor consent, funding, establishing disease-treatment priorities and so on, will arise, but again, any severe bioethical dilemmas seem unlikely. Having said that, in 2012, Japanese researchers reported the production of primordial germ cells (PGCs), which can develop into both ova and sperm, from mouse iPS cells.[46] These were then used reproductively, via IVF and surrogacy, to produce live, fertile mice. Could such techniques be used to create gametes for generating new human life in the future? It raises the dread spectre of reproductive cloning. Such a project would defile the benevolent nature of current iPS-cell technologies. Tough proscriptive laws are required, now. Fourth, adult stem and iPS cells will be used not just for cellular renewal, but also for tissue and organ fabrication, thus reducing the need for the complex, and often inadequate, procedures of organ donation and transplantation. Already this innovative technique of adult stem-cell tracheal transplantation, as described in Section 3.6.7 above, has been extended with the use of artificial tracheas, with *in situ* stem-cell seeding, even with a child patient. It will be many years before complex solid organs, such as kidneys and hearts, are constructed for human transplantation, but in 2013, a stem-cell engineered kidney was transplanted and shown to function in a rat. That must bring some hope to the 51,000 patients currently on kidney dialysis in the UK.

These are four whopping predictions in a field of vast and exciting unpredictability. Who knows? An advance as radical as the production of iPS cells may be discovered tomorrow, or even today. Just as this book is about to go to press, another biological bombshell has been announced. Japanese researchers have shown that simply 'shocking' blood cells by lowering the pH of their environment, to between pH 5.4 and 5.8 for less than thirty minutes, can trigger their transformation into stem cells. These have been awkwardly named 'stimulus-triggered acquisition of pluripotency' cells, or STAP cells. This new method seems to be faster, cheaper and possibly safer than other cell-reprogramming technologies, including iPS-cell production. Haruko Obokata and her colleagues were 'really surprised' by their potentially ground-breaking discovery. So far, the method has used only mouse cells, but experiments with human cells are under way.[47] In the meantime, expect good news of serious stem-cell reprogramming developments, plus their applications in human clinical trials.

3.7.9 STEM-CELL TECHNOLOGIES: IN CONCLUSION

Whatever their future successes or failures, the bioethical take-home message is this: stem-cell technologies, as part of regenerative medicine, are here to stay. However, the production of stem cells from human embryos remains both unethical and unnecessary: unethical, because it destroys human embryos; unnecessary, because stem cells are available from diverse, alternative and uncontroversial sources, namely, adult stem and iPS cells. Moreover, the simplicity, elegance and economics of producing such cells should end all talk and practice of human embryo destruction. But perhaps not entirely, or even immediately so, because some experimenters will insist that they still need to trash human embryos. Many loathe the idea that a human embryo can have any moral status other than that of 'biological raw material'.

What should be our overall response to these stem-cell technologies? It should be sevenfold. First, we should be amazed—stand back and be overwhelmed that we are so 'fearfully and wonderfully made'. Second, regenerative medicine is the next great advance in medical science and we will all benefit. It must, and will, change both our thinking and our lives. Third, the existence and use of non-embryonic, adult stem cells means that, at last, pro-life people have something positive to say—proper science is on our side, and in a few years the general population will agree with us too. Now that is a scoop—we must capitalize on such good news. Human embryos deserve protection; destroying them is prodigal and in vain. And we need to tell the world that it has misunderstood the bioethics and supported the wrong science behind that forlorn enterprise. Fourth, we should create a pro-life pincer movement. If human embryos are not to be destroyed and born children are not to be destroyed, then what about that bioethical heartland of in utero, unborn children? They deserve protection

Chapter 3

too. Fifth, we should be putting our money where our mouth is. We should be financially backing those charities that promote non-embryonic stem-cell research. Perhaps we need an Institute of Ethical Medicine, where good ethics and practice will value and cherish all human life. Sixth, whenever you encounter stem-cell technologies, always ask the one key question: what is the source of these stem cells—are they adult, iPS or embryonic? Seventh, never again say that human biology is dull and boring!

3.8 Human genetic engineering

Human genetic engineering rests upon three pieces of remarkable research spanning over 150 years of scientific endeavour. In about 1860, Augustinian monk Gregor Mendel reported something of the mechanisms of genetic inheritance after crossbreeding thousands of pea plants in his monastery garden. In 1953, James Watson and Francis Crick described, in a two-page article in *Nature*, the three-dimensional structure of the double helix of deoxyribonucleic acid (DNA), the carrier of the genetic code. Then, in 2000, a huge team of international scientists working on the Human Genome Project 'cracked' this human genetic code, that is, they sequenced the 3.3 billion (3.3×10^9) chemical 'letters' of our DNA. These are three of the most wondrous feats of genetics—we should never overlook their significance.

3.8.1 HUMAN GENETICS: THE BASICS

Every one of the estimated 100 trillion—that is, 10^{14} or 100,000,000,000,000—somatic (body) cells in the adult human body holds the human genetic code, contained in about two metres of ultra-thin, super-coiled DNA. Therefore, every human adult has about 2×10^{11} or 200,000 million, kilometres of the stuff, enough to wrap around the earth (with a circumference of 4×10^4 or 40,000 kilometres) some 5×10^6 or 5 million times. Amazed and impressed? So am I.

Let's get personal. Each of your somatic cells possesses your unique human genome in forty-six chromosomes, which collectively contain between 20,000 and 25,000 protein-coding genes. Each gene is basically a short segment of DNA located somewhere along the two metres of chromosomal DNA. The biological significance of a gene is that it specifies, or codes for, the synthesis of a particular protein. The significance of a protein is twofold. First, it can be a structural 'building block' of the body, as a major component of muscles,

SOME OF THE PRIMARY ISSUES

organs, blood, hair and so on. Or, second, it can be a metabolic 'controller' of the body, in the form of an enzyme or a hormone. Therefore, to a large extent, our genes determine who we are, at least in the physical sense. Brown eyes, 1.82 metres tall, mousy hair, size nine-and-a-half feet, medium athletic build, with a metopic suture (look it up!)—well, that is partly who I am, as a result of my own distinctive genetic code.

Our DNA contains our genetic code as a series of just four nucleotide bases—adenine, thymine, guanine and cytosine, known in shorthand by the letters A, T, G and C. These are arranged in pairs on the double helix of DNA as AT, TA, GC or CG. There are about 3,300 million of these base pairs in the human genome, and the Human Genome Project has resolved the particular order, the sequence, of this enormous genetic alphabet—it is a technological marvel. When King David wrote in Psalm 139:14, 'I am fearfully and wonderfully made; your works are wonderful', he did not know the half of it.

So, in 2000, there were the results from the Human Genome Project, which sequenced human DNA and located these all-important protein-coding regions. But because these accounted for less than 2 per cent of the whole genome, the rest was thought to be 'junk' DNA. Then, in 2012, came the results from the ENCODE (the *EN*Cyclopedia *Of DNA* Elements) Project, a worldwide $200 million consortium consisting of thirty-two research groups and more than 440 scientists, which attempted the next step: to characterize the functional elements in the human genome. Its striking conclusion: much of this 'junk' has a definite purpose; in fact, more than 80 per cent of human DNA is now recognized to have at least one biochemical function, or what is known as an epigenetic feature. This includes some four million regulatory regions, or 'switches', that can turn genes off and on to control their expression. All this is just the beginning of an almost unimaginable, unfathomable genetic complexity. The next decade of genomic research is set to reveal further mysteries of human biology, a greater knowledge of human diseases and the development of new medical treatments. It is enough to flabbergast us.

3.8.2 HUMAN GENETIC ENGINEERING AND EUGENICS

Now that we understand more and more about the mechanisms of inheritance, plus chromosomal composition and function, we are beginning

Chapter 3

to alter and control some genes with considerable precision. Much of the drive behind this human genetic engineering has come from the hope of curing genetic diseases (see Section 3.9).

At the outset, we need to appreciate the true meaning of the following three commonly used words: treatment, cure and prevention. They might appear to be synonyms, but that is not so in medical jargon. It is true that aspirin, for example, can be taken as a short-term treatment both to cure and prevent a transient headache, but we are talking here about long-term, serious, genetic illnesses. Hence, a treatment is regarded as an ongoing process of medication—such as everyday insulin injections for a diabetic patient. A cure means that a particular disease suffered by a patient is eliminated, never to return—as with the outcome of a bone-marrow transplant for a leukaemia patient. Prevention is a proactive intervention to ensure that a disease never arises; polio vaccination is a good example for a non-genetic disease. Phenylketonuria testing of newborns is a prevention strategy for a genetic disease; although it does not prevent the onset of the disease, it does signal the need for treatment. Many genetic diseases can be treated, a few can be cured, but prevention has been subjected to lexical engineering and given an ominous bioethical twist. Nowadays, the prevention of several genetic diseases is achieved by destroying not the disease, but the patient. An example would be the unborn child with Down's syndrome, who is detected by prenatal diagnosis (PND) and then aborted; the genetic disease, we are told, is thus 'prevented'. This scenario represents one of the recurring features within the culture of death—killing rather than caring. But with that medical mindset of destruction, how will proper treatments or cures ever be devised and applied? This type of medicine is nothing other than modern-day eugenics.

Eugenics has long contaminated medicine. It has been like a menacing plague, causing bioethical fever and moral delirium among its misguided supporters. The eugenics movement was started in an organized way by Francis Galton, who, interestingly, was Charles Darwin's younger half-cousin. In 1883, Galton first coined the word 'eugenics' (from the Greek *eu*, well, and *genes*, born) to mean the improvement of the human species by means of genetic engineering. This included negative eugenics, the elimination of undesirable genetic traits, as well as positive eugenics, the enhancement of what were deemed to be desirable genetic qualities.

SOME OF THE PRIMARY ISSUES

In 1908, Galton formed the Eugenics Society in London to investigate human heredity and to carry out social-action programmes. Altruism may have motivated some of its members, but race, class and privilege were the concerns of others; superiority and inferiority, and racial and ethnic prejudice were on their agendas. Eugenic thinking and its practice have often forged a link with nationalism. Hitler and the Nazis carried eugenics to its cruel extreme with sterilization programmes that championed Aryan elitism, the non-voluntary euthanasia plan for disabled children and eventually the Final Solution of the Holocaust.

For many years, the early eugenicists propagated an astonishingly simple error. They believed, for example, that mental handicap could be eliminated if they segregated or sterilized affected people, that is, if they stopped them from reproducing. But such a practice is confuted by the Hardy–Weinberg principle,[48] which not only demonstrated the practical ineffectiveness of their eugenic schemes, but also brought about the collapse of their sinister ideals.

Nevertheless, eugenicists still abound today, but the science behind their genetic engineering is not as shoddy as that of their predecessors; they are less naïve and its practice is more disguised. Eugenic motives are rife among some of the new assisted-reproductive technologies (ARTs) as well as some commonly accepted medical practices, such as prenatal screening and diagnosis (PND), a procedure that Nature described as 'eugenics of a mild sort'.[49]

3.8.3 HUMAN GENETIC ENGINEERING AND THE DESIGNER BABY

This 'eugenics of a mild sort' is further discussed in Section 3.9 below. In the meantime, consider the terminus of human genetic engineering: the designer baby. Once dismissed as science fiction, today it is on the cusp of non-fiction. Perhaps it was foreseeable. The fusion of techniques derived from human embryo experimentation, genetic engineering, ARTs and genetic screening was heading only one way—baby designing. Of course, the term 'designer baby' is a journalistic misnomer. It is as foolish as insisting that only an excessively expensive jacket or a pair of swanky socks is 'designer clothing'. All clothing has been designed by someone—maybe well, perhaps badly.

In that sense, every baby has been designed. God is the great Designer. We

Chapter 3

all bear a little tag, 'Made by God', though some prefer the more classical, Italianate label, *'Imago Dei'*. He originated all things and he now directs all things. To this end, God has directed our genetic make-up; as the God of history, he oversaw our ancestors, our family tree, our biological parents and therefore our unique DNA. Yet here is that antinomy of the sovereignty of God and the responsibility of man. He designs, and we also design. He superintends our lives, circumstances, opportunities, times and places; but he also made us significant, free and intentional (Gen. 1:27; 2:16, 20). We therefore have worth, identity and purpose (see Sections 2.1 and 2.2). We are not pre-programmed automata, so we may exercise responsibility and we may make choices every day, big and small. And we certainly decide with whom we procreate; in this very real way we genetically pick and choose our future offspring—and so we become procreative co-designers with God.

We also design postnatally, because once our children are born, we choose and direct, to a large extent, their values, food, schools, discipline and so on. That all sounds sensible and responsible. But what about the possibility of some prenatal, extra-procreative designing? Could we not actively design our children to fit our 'wants', rather than passively accepting them 'as they come'? What about a little genetic rearranging, some wilful eugenic interfering? The very mention of the E-word should cause our hearts to faint and our brains to recall its appalling history. We should flee the very thought.

3.8.4 HUMAN GENETIC ENGINEERING IN THE FUTURE

Yet can anyone doubt that we are moving relentlessly towards some kind of popularly understood 'designer baby'? In our imagination and in our literature, the idea of the designer baby has prompted horror and happiness in roughly equal measures among the general public. Among some scientists and doctors, it persists as a prized goal. They already have the three prerequisites—genetic knowledge, technological capability and sub-standard bioethical principles—so that now they can, albeit it minimally, design a baby. Currently, it is done negatively and clumsily: every year, the combination of prenatal diagnosis (PND) and abortion eliminate thousands of those who are judged to be badly designed—the disabled and the genetically inadequate. And already here, or just around

Some of the Primary Issues

the corner, are techniques for doing it positively, like genetic enhancement, by the selection of gametes from the sporty, the smart and the stunning (caveat emptor: these qualities are rarely found within the same donor) linked to IVF and surrogacy, or by germline gene therapy. Thereafter, the 'designer' road broadens out and leads on to manipulating the human mind, intelligence, memory, personality and so forth. Some are already predicting, while others are busily beavering away towards actualizing, a post-human, transhumanist future.

Is any of this desirable? Does it not ineluctably drive us to regard human life as a selectable commodity and human individuals as merely adjustable devices? Where will it lead? Having a baby is one thing, but getting the right sort of baby, the kind you really want—that will be the real deal. Healthy babies, of the right sex, at the time of your choice, with the physical and emotional characteristics you desire—he will be tall, athletic, artistic, highly intelligent, musical and, of course, handsome, probably with blond hair—how ingenious will that be? It will meet the consumer's demand for product choice—parents as the satisfied customers and their baby as the chosen, high-end product. Some view this prospect as far-fetched. Yet when the Zeitgeist is dominated by a belief in the power of an all-knowing, all-providing scientism, this type of exploitation of biological capability needs no justification. We have the technology, so why not use it? If technology can make better mousetraps, why not better babies? But take heed: any sort of commodification or objectification of children is beset with peril. These avant-garde proposals for the grand designer baby are best seen not as a desirable target, but as a final warning.

3.8.5 HUMAN GENETIC ENGINEERING: IN CONCLUSION

Harnessing human genetics to human medicine is a powerful engineering project. It has the promise and potential for good—if only modern-day genetic engineering could be practised within a culture-of-life framework. Historically, its record has mostly been for ill. Its past associations with crass discrimination and eugenic pogroms, its current malevolent alliance with screening procedures like PGD and PND followed by embryonic and foetal destruction, and its future connection with that impending urge to create designer babies, display themes of mainly bad medicine. The minor

Chapter 3

successes of somatic gene therapy, as discussed in Section 3.10 below, just about save it from universal censure.

But genetics and genetic engineering are not everything. Some believe that all genetic engineering is a threat to our humanness. Some harbour a fear that certain people will manipulate our genes and thus control our behaviour. These fears, unlike many others that have been raised in this book, are largely unfounded. They presuppose that our genes determine entirely who we are and how we behave. But that, even if it were true, would mean, like all deterministic theories, that we would no longer be responsible for what we thought and did. Our limp excuse for sins, criminal activities and antisocial behaviours would then be, 'My genes made me do it.' This cannot be correct. Indeed, if it were true, it would run counter to the rugged insistence of the Bible's teaching that each human being is a free moral agent, responsible before God for his or her own actions, thoughts, affections and intentions (Rom. 3:19; 8:5–8; Eph. 2:3; 4:17–19).

Furthermore, it cannot be true because we already know that our environment—commonly called 'nurture'—in addition to our genes—'nature'—plays a considerable part in our identity, that is, who we are and how we behave. The beginnings of nurture, the genesis of the earliest times of human development from conception onwards, are quite different for each individual. This is why clones, though possessing identical biological 'natures' or genomes, would not be identical people—hence, monozygotic twins are not indistinguishable. Even in the same womb, such human clones experience different micro-environments, and the complexities of their brain cell arrangements, like ours, are wholly unpredictable. Therefore, we really are all different—each person, though made in the image and likeness of God, is unique, just as identical twins are, or even as laboratory-produced, eugenically manipulated human clones would be.

Yet we are still more than mere products of our genetics plus our environment, of our 'nature' plus 'nurture'. Even if we could fully describe a child's genes plus his or her environment, we would never be able to predict the progress and outcomes of that child's life. To describe a person completely we must add what Baroness Warnock called in her 1998 book, *An Intelligent Person's Guide to Ethics*, 'human imagination',[50] or, more fully and precisely in the terminology of the Bible, the 'soul', or the often interchangeable word 'spirit'.

Some of the primary issues

Human genetic engineering will never make a child more patient. Nor will it make a man more generous or a woman more compassionate. Only God can bring about such permanent good in us. Why? Because God does not merely alter our genes or our environment, but rather he transforms our souls, our spirits (2 Cor. 5:17; 1 Thes. 5:23).

3.9 Genetic disabilities and screening

There is perhaps no issue in the whole sphere of bioethics that engenders so much anxiety and ambivalence as that of disability, both mental and physical. Such sentiments are seemingly ubiquitous. In one sense, we are all blameless because one of medicine's principal purposes is to relieve suffering. If you have ever broken a bone, had a bacterial infection or suffered from 101 other maladies, you applaud such good, healing medicine—it has ameliorated your suffering. And the genetically disabled also suffer, so surely medicine should come to their aid too, should it not? Of course, in many ways it does. But in some ways it does not—sometimes it actually wants to destroy them, especially when they are young. In that sense, we are all blameworthy because we have let medicine escape from its wholesome Hippocratic–Christian moorings so that it no longer brings only relief; medicine can now bring death. If you have ever doubted the existence of the culture of death, doubt no more. Our world has adopted a warped view of disabilities and a spiteful opinion of the disabled.

3.9.1 Genetic disabilities in general

Think disabilities—think long and wide. They can be referred to, often pejoratively, as disorders, abnormalities, deformities, diseases, deficiencies, defects and handicaps. They can be minor, like colour blindness, or major, like a stroke. They can be non-genetic, as in cerebral palsy, or genetic, as in sickle-cell anaemia. They can arise from conception, like Edward's syndrome, or be late-onset, like lung cancer. They can be temporary, such as Bell's palsy, or permanent, such as tetraplegia. And there are numerous other defining characteristics and examples—the disability spectrum is indeed long and wide.

But it is those disabilities towards the major and permanent end of the spectrum that are of concern here. High on that list are those with a genetic basis. Genetic disorders are caused by an alteration in an individual's

Chapter 3

DNA. Perhaps one or more genes are missing, repeated or in the wrong order; technically, these are known respectively as deletions, duplications or translocations. Such disorders may be either inherited, from one or both parents—as in the case of cystic fibrosis—or acquired, such as various cancers triggered, for example, by exposure to toxic chemicals. In addition, genetic disorders may be classified as single-gene (cystic fibrosis), multiple-gene (breast cancers) or chromosomal (Down's syndrome) defects. I know, my brain aches too! But even these attempts at basic categorization are too simplistic and are defied by all sorts of exceptions. For instance, Down's syndrome is not one unified disorder—it comes in three types, known as trisomy 21 (which occurs in 94 per cent of those affected), translocation (4 per cent) and mosaicism (2 per cent). In addition, these defects do not occur universally across the human race. Some have an ethnic prevalence, such as Tay-Sachs disease among Ashkenazi Jews, or sickle-cell anaemia among US citizens of African-American descent. Some have an age-related prevalence, like Alzheimer's disease and macular degeneration of the eyes, and some are sex-related, as in Duchenne muscular dystrophy and Turner's syndrome, or prostate and ovarian cancers. And so on. In truth, modern medical genetics is a labyrinthine discipline and far beyond the remit of this little book and the immediate needs of its readers, so, at this juncture, enough is enough—its Gordian knot is hereby cut.

Currently, there are at least 4,000 recognized genetic disorders caused by single-gene defects, and that figure, together with an indeterminately huge number caused by multiple genes, is rising as new ones are identified. Some are relatively common, like cystic fibrosis, but others are exceedingly uncommon, affecting only a very few people worldwide. Some are trivial, with no life-limiting impact; some are debilitating to varying degrees; and some are fatal, even before birth. Some are manifest prenatally, and some become evident only later in life. Estimates suggest that fewer than 1 per cent of UK babies are born with some genetically determined abnormality. During 2011, there were 909,109 conceptions and 723,913 live births in England and Wales, so perhaps as many as 6,000 affected babies were born, including about 700 with Down's syndrome, 300 with cystic fibrosis and 100 with Duchenne muscular dystrophy. There is a subtle, but vital, difference here between the numbers of those detected and those born with a particular disorder—any disparities may be due to non-testing, but also to natural death in utero, miscarriage and, obviously, 'prevention' by abortion.

3.9.2 GENETIC SCREENING IN GENERAL

Screening is a general medical procedure, the basis of which can be either non-genetic, such as periodic dental check-ups, eye tests and blood-pressure monitoring, or genetic. Genetic screening has a threefold rationale. First, it aims to identify a genetic disorder before the onset of debilitating symptoms and so promote early treatment to alleviate suffering. Second, it is used to identify unaffected carriers of defective genes and alert them to the risks of producing affected children. Third, it is employed to detect embryos and foetuses already affected by a genetic disease.

The purposes and benefits of non-genetic screening are obvious and they have led to the creation of their own niche professions, such as dentistry and optometry, in order to cope with basic screening and treatment of large numbers of people for just a few disorders, such as caries and astigmatism. Genetic screening is different. Screening whole populations for thousands of genetic disorders would obviously be an impossible, unnecessary and unwarranted undertaking. So genetic screening has tended to concentrate on a small number of disorders and on particular groupings, such as families with members already affected. More widespread or mass genetic screening does occur for a few specific conditions, such as breast and bowel cancer, and, of course, is conducted with unborn children by way of a familiar part of antenatal care, otherwise known as prenatal screening and prenatal diagnosis (PND), which are specifically discussed in Section 3.9.3 below.

Genetic screening can be a can of worms. One of the earliest screening programmes was for sickle-cell anaemia in the USA during the 1970s. It went disastrously wrong and resulted in discrimination and unfair employment dismissals because of inaccuracies in the analytical techniques used. There were too many 'false negatives' and 'false positives'; in the former, test results failed to detect people with sickle-cell anaemia, and in the latter, people were told they had the disease when they were in the clear.

But genetic screening need not be all bad. For example, if screening could tell us the genetic diseases to which we were prone and which we were likely to develop in later life, we could adapt our lifestyles. 'Predisposition' is the buzzword. If you were predisposed to, say, cardiovascular disease,

Chapter 3

then you could devise a personalized life-plan, a 'do this, don't do that' strategy—take exercise, avoid hypertension, stop eating pies—and thus possibly avoid some of the disease's associated risks. On the other hand, genetic screening can have a huge downside. Our employers would want us screened to ensure that we were not likely to leave them in the lurch by frequent sickness absenteeism, by taking early retirement on medical health grounds, or even by dying prematurely. Our insurance and mortgage companies would also like to know the diseases to which we were predisposed to make sure they would not be financially jeopardized. Furthermore, the results of genetic screening could influence whom we marry: are the happy couple genetically compatible? Becoming pregnant and giving birth could become additionally controlled if screening of both parents and their offspring became more accessible and wide-ranging, or even compulsory.

Many of today's mass screening methods, for, say, cervical or breast cancer in women, rely on microscopic or x-ray examinations for visually detecting abnormalities in cells and tissues rather than direct testing of any genetic components. These current methods are complex, somewhat unreliable and, according to some authorities, of doubtful utility. Similar shortcomings exist for men with, for example, prostate cancer screening, which measures a blood component, prostate specific antigen (PSA), raised levels of which may only be indicative, rather than proof, of any existing trouble. Moreover, for some people, the proposed treatments on offer—drugs, hormones, mastectomy, prostatectomy—are considered to be worse than the diseases. Others prefer not to know if they already have a particular disease or even a predisposition to it—information either way would, they say, blight their remaining years. Others trust that they will die *with* the disease in question rather than *from* it. Counter to such ostrich-like postures is the fact that early detection can often lead to early treatment with the prospect of a better outcome. Nevertheless, for some people, screening, with its intrinsic uncertainties, simply causes alarm and worry, and so they decline to be tested.

Though current screening schemes may be flawed, the hope is that tomorrow's genetically based methods will be more precise because they will focus on evaluating the direct cause—the faulty gene—instead of an effect, such as a cellular or blood-borne abnormality. For example, in 2013 it was announced that a simple saliva screening test, based on detecting genetic variants for breast and prostate cancers, would be available in doctors' surgeries within five years. It would cheaply, accurately and rapidly pinpoint those at high risk of developing these diseases and thus obviate the need for the repeated, and less accurate, non-genetically based mass screening methods currently employed. Perhaps such tests will eventually become more akin to the convenience of pregnancy testing: pop along to the chemist, buy the kit and simply test your own blood, urine or saliva in the comfort of your own home, with the result provided in minutes. What you then do about a positive test result, without ready access to personal genetic counselling, is another matter.

But we are not there yet. It was not so long ago that such relatively straightforward and specific genetic testing was predicted to become the method of choice for the screening of genetically simple diseases, namely, those caused by a single faulty gene, such as Huntington's disease, severe combined immunodeficiency (SCID) or the more common cystic fibrosis. But reality has proved to be more complex. Now even the single gene for cystic fibrosis, called CFTR, is known to have several hundred mutations and therefore can cause many forms of the disease with quite different symptoms and severities. If each mutation requires its own specific genetic test, which mutation do you screen for? Making the situation yet more complex is the fact that most genetic diseases, like the various types of breast and colon cancer, are not single-gene but multifactorial disorders caused by the interaction of several genes. Other genetic disorders relate to whole chromosomes, like Down's syndrome, which is caused by the presence of an additional, third, chromosome 21. We know very, very little about such byzantine complexities. And even the current, best-available genetic testing will often indicate little more than a predisposition to a particular disease; it will not necessarily confirm that the carrier will ever develop the disorder, and if so, to what extent or intensity it might present. In fact, we are all carriers of several gene defects—about 1 in every 25 people is a carrier of the cystic fibrosis gene—but nearly all of us, including our children, will never express these particular diseases for various reasons, including our spouse's genetic make-up, as well as factors such as lifestyle, environment and diet. In other words, genetic screening is not the same as genetic diagnosis: one scans large groups of people, the other attempts to

Chapter 3

pinpoint affected individuals, but even then skilful judgement is required to interpret the true meaning of positive or negative results. Most genetic testing for most genetic disorders is still in its formative years.

3.9.3 SCREENING AND PRENATAL DIAGNOSIS (PND)

For thousands of years, pregnant women knew virtually nothing about their unborn children. These unknowns included the number, sex, size, familial resemblance, well-being, date of birth and so on—they were all part of the mystery and excitement of childbearing. Nevertheless, it has always been common knowledge that an unforeseen few babies would be born with physical or mental disorders. Some societies—notable among them the ancient Jews and the early Christians—welcomed and cared for these disabled newborns, while others subjected them to infanticide. Then along came twentieth-century medical technology to screen and identify in utero those who were thought to be handicapped.

Thus, prenatal screening coupled with prenatal diagnosis (PND) began. Currently, local healthcare providers' policies vary in the type and timing of such antenatal care offered to pregnant women. It should also be noted that all such investigations are optional—it is the woman's choice to accept or refuse. Typically, the first prenatal, or antenatal, appointment occurs at between ten and thirteen weeks' gestation. And herein lies a little etymological confusion about pregnancy progression. 'Gestation' is ordinarily calculated as an unborn child's 'real age'—that is, counting from conception/fertilization/day one—plus two weeks, because doctors traditionally measure the length of a pregnancy from the first day of the mother's last menstrual period (LMP). Conception typically occurs about eleven to twenty-one days after the first day of the last period. So, in medical parlance, a gestational age of nine weeks means the unborn child has a 'real age' of about seven weeks. Interestingly, today's ultra-smart, digital pregnancy-testing kits display how many weeks it is since the woman actually conceived, that is, they use 'real age'.

The first prenatal appointment is used to discuss the general health of the mother—weight, blood pressure, diet and so on—and the progress of the pregnancy, and it usually includes an ultrasound scan (often known as a dating scan) and a blood test. The aim is to confirm gestational age, rule in or out twins (or triplets!), and measure the nuchal translucency (NT) thickness and pregnancy-associated plasma protein-A (PAPP-A) concentrations in the blood for indications of Down's syndrome. The second appointment, at about eighteen to twenty weeks, normally involves another ultrasound scan (a so-called anomaly scan) and further blood tests to measure alpha fetoprotein (AFP), human chorionic gonadotrophin (hCG), unconjugated oestriol (μE_3) and inhibin-A concentrations. These are used to assess any increased likelihood that the unborn child has either Down's syndrome or spina bifida. None of these tests is definitive, so if the results are positive, indicating a higher probability of such disorders, follow-up diagnostic tests will be advised.

There are two such prenatal diagnosis (PND) tests that have been routinely offered to women to detect abnormalities in their unborn children. First, launched in the 1960s, there is amniocentesis. This involves sampling the mother's amniotic fluid from about fifteen to twenty weeks' gestation. Because this fluid contains some of the developing foetus's shed body cells, it can be tested for chromosomal disorders, such as Down's and Edward's syndromes, neural-tube defects, like spina bifida, and genetic disorders, including Duchenne muscular dystrophy and sickle-cell anaemia. Second, since its establishment during the 1980s there is chorionic villus sampling (CVS). This requires, at between ten and thirteen weeks' gestation, a biopsy of the finger-like tissues of the placenta, the chorionic villi. Since their genetic code is identical to that of the foetus, they too can be analysed for several genetic disorders, but excluding non-genetic conditions such as spina bifida.

PND is generally justified on three grounds. First, it can help gauge the feasibility of any required medical interventions, perhaps prenatal or postnatal surgery. Second, it can assist parents to prepare for their babies, especially those to be born with a disability. Third, it can give parents the option to abort. In reality, the last is the most frequent outcome from a positive test result. For example, during 2010 in England and Wales, of the 1,188 pregnancies prenatally diagnosed with Down's syndrome, 942 were terminated—an abortion rate of almost 80 per cent. These figures are not at variance with the 700 or so Down's syndrome babies born in the UK each year because some test results will have been false negatives, and some mothers who subsequently gave birth to Down's children will have declined any testing for the disorder.

CHAPTER 3

PND may sound simple, safe and specific, but, like most medical screening, it is actually none of these. For example, complications can arise from both amniocentesis and CVS because a mother or her child can be physically injured by the sampling needle or by the introduction of bacterial infections. There is also a 0.5 to 2.0 per cent risk that these invasive procedures will cause a miscarriage. Furthermore, the results can be inaccurate—there will always be 'false negatives' and 'false positives'. And neither test will indicate the degree of severity of any detected disorder. Lastly, because PND searches for only a limited number of genetic diseases, it cannot guarantee a so-called 'healthy' baby.

Prenatal appointments, with their incessant sampling and testing, form-filling and note-taking, can be somewhat mundane. Then, one day, a gobsmacking event occurs. It is time for the ultrasound scan. OK, the gel may be chilly, but the views are so engaging, even breathtaking. What a fascinating window! What parents have not become emotional at seeing their 'little bump' wriggling and that tiny heart tick-tick-ticking away? It's our baby! Yes indeed, scans can be surprisingly educational. And, of course, it is a comfort to know that the unborn child is growing properly and that the placenta is looking good, and perhaps to discover whether to paint the nursery blue or pink. But ultrasound scans are not just for fun; measurements are being made—rump to crown, spine to nape thickness—to assess nuchal translucency, just in case Down's syndrome is present; and if that, or any other foetal disorder, is suspected, more tests will follow, and then …?

This is the real problem with screening and PND—their *raison d'être* is to find unborn children with anomalies and, if such are detected and deemed sufficiently serious, the usual chain of events ends with abortion. PND is primarily a 'search and destroy' exercise. Medical screening is ethical when some form of care and effective treatment is available. Diagnosis without treatment can be cruel medicine. Alas, screening and proper treatment are frequently divorced; in the PND context, 'treatment' can be lexically engineered to mean 'abortion'. Yet proper ways of screening and treating genetic diseases do exist. A good example is the neonatal screening for phenylketonuria (PKU): the Guthrie test, perhaps better known as the 'heel prick' blood test. Untreated PKU leads to progressive brain damage and severe learning difficulties, but, when detected sufficiently early, PKU is easily treated by dietary management. Similarly, those detected with a deficiency of the enzyme lactase can be given modified diets restricted in lactose. Those lacking other gene products can be supplied with what they need, so that, for example, people suffering from certain types of diabetes are given insulin, and those with haemophilia A are given factor VIII. Such combinations of screening and treatment make good bioethical sense and the benefits to the newborn and their parents, as well as to all affected children and adults, are obvious. But the aim of PND can be quite different. It can be part of what might be called *médecine sauvage*, where the recommended 'treatment' is to kill the patients, to terminate the affected. PND can be a pitiless subdivision of the culture of death.

3.9.4 PREIMPLANTATION GENETIC DIAGNOSIS (PGD)

The advent of IVF presented another, even earlier, opportunity to detect the unborn disabled. Instead of waiting weeks, even months, before antenatal screening and PND testing of foetuses, early embryos with genetic defects can now be weeded out by preimplantation genetic diagnosis (PGD). This technique was developed in the mid-1980s particularly for parents themselves suffering from a genetic disease, or with a family history of such a disability, to avoid passing it on to their children. PGD begins with conventional IVF. After about three days, one cell is removed from the typically eight-cell IVF embryo. That cell is analysed for specific alterations in its DNA sequence. If all is clear, the remaining seven-cell embryo is transferred to the mother's womb. If some defect is found, the entire embryo is discarded. PGD was never intended to be curative medicine; it has always been a 'find and squash' procedure, part of the overall 'search and destroy' mission, yet another subdivision of the culture of death.

When did PGD start and, more importantly, where will it end? The first child to be born, free from cystic fibrosis, following PGD, was reported in 1992. With its powerful eugenic potential, PGD has remained highly controversial. After a public consultation in 1993, the UK's Human Fertilisation and Embryology Authority (HFEA) rejected the use of PGD for sex selection for social reasons—probably for fear of gender selection by parents for 'family balancing' (such as, for example, to secure a daughter for a family already with three sons), or for other cultural or economic purposes (usually a preferred son and heir)—but allowed it for medical

Chapter 3

reasons, to screen out embryos with 'life-threatening' sex-linked genetic disorders, such as Duchenne muscular dystrophy and haemophilia. But PGD did not stop there; every bioethical issue has a slope which can be incessantly slippery.

During 2006, the HFEA expanded the number of conditions for which embryos could be PGD-screened and for which those found to be either affected or carriers—namely, those with the 'wrong' type of genes—could be destroyed. PGD was already being allowed for a few disorders, such as cystic fibrosis or those which could develop in childhood, such as cancers like retinoblastoma and familial adenomatous polyposis. Both of these cancers have what the HFEA calls 'high penetrance', meaning that children born with these 'susceptibility' gene mutations have a high, perhaps 90 per cent, probability of developing the disease. However, symptoms of these disorders usually occur neither prenatally nor even neonatally, but later in childhood, teenage or adult life. Moreover, many of these 'high penetrance' conditions can be successfully treated and their sufferers can lead estimable, though perhaps shortened, lives. The point is this: the use of PGD can mean that such people are never even allowed to be born.

In May 2006, then, the HFEA went one step further. It approved PGD for some 'lower penetrance' conditions, such as those linked to inherited breast and ovarian cancers associated with mutated BRCA-1 and BRCA-2 genes. Women who carry a faulty BRCA-1 gene have a lifetime risk of about 80 per cent of developing breast cancer and 40 per cent of ovarian cancer. Those with a faulty BRCA-2 gene have a similar risk for breast cancer but less for ovarian cancer. The detection of these 'late-onset' disease genes in embryos raises an additional set of bioethical concerns. For example, not all carriers will develop the disease; perhaps only half will. Moreover, detected carriers can lead normal, healthy lives and some can even adopt lifestyles to avoid the particular disease. At one avoidance extreme, some women carrying a faulty BRCA-1 gene have undergone mastectomy to prevent any risk of developing breast cancer. In 2009, the first UK baby screened by PGD to ensure that she was free from the faulty BRCA-1 gene was born. This was new, uncharted bioethical territory. PGD may have prevented one girl from getting breast cancer when she grows up, but what about those other female embryos—her sisters—who were discarded during the IVF–PGD process? They might have been free from the effects of the rogue gene too and therefore could have grown up to be cancer-free women. And others of them who might have contracted breast cancer in adulthood could perhaps have been treated by existing, or future, therapies. PGD is always surrounded by such life-denying negativity.

Finally, there is a curious cultural caprice to this topic of genetic screening. Contrary to the wishes of virtually all other prospective parents, some, if offered IVF–PGD, would deliberately select embryos with a faulty gene in order to produce an 'unhealthy' baby, a disabled child. The often-quoted example is that of a couple, both with achondroplasia, who would choose and transfer only those embryos that would guarantee that their child would also have achondroplasia, to fit in with their dwarf lifestyle. In a similar, real-life case, a US lesbian couple, Sharon Duchesneau and Candace McCullough, caused a rumpus in 2002 when they chose insemination by a deaf sperm donor in the hope of conceiving a non-hearing child to share their deaf culture; they regarded deafness not as a disability, but as a positive cultural attribute. Their plan worked partially because the conceived and born boy, Gauvin McCullough, is partially hearing.[51] These are rather odd examples of creating the designer baby—with a difference. Maybe in the near future, PGD could guarantee that these couples' unusual, even perhaps perverse, wishes come true.

So how widespread is PGD? At the present time, it is employed relatively rarely, but its use is increasing, year on year. In 2010, a total of only 311 women in England and Wales underwent 383 cycles of IVF–PGD. The HFEA reported that as a result, 135 'take-home' babies were born, but the numbers of affected embryos destroyed were not published. Whatever its extent, PGD is destined to remain bioethically negative and eugenically troublesome.

3.9.5 LIMITATIONS OF PND AND PGD SCREENING

Here is another relevant question: would a more widespread, even compulsory, use of hi-tech screening reduce the numbers born with disabilities? The question is relevant because although screening and PND, in the form of amniocentesis and chorionic villus sampling (CVS), have been used for many years, the incidence of babies born with gene defects has remained largely unchanged. For instance, in England and Wales during 1990, there were 739 babies born with Down's syndrome, whereas in 2010 the figure was still 715. Part of this apparently static twenty-year trend will be due to an increase in the total number of births (706,140 in 1990 and

Chapter 3

723,165 in 2010) and also to more women becoming mothers later in life (9,717 aged forty and over in 1990 and 27,731 in 2010), with their greater risk of conceiving Down's babies. But could hi-tech methods significantly lessen the numbers born? Probably not, for four reasons.

First, there are currently over 700,000 children born in England and Wales each year. Would all their parents be likely to relinquish sexual intercourse for the lacklustre procedures of the IVF and PGD clinics? No. Second, would the already overburdened and underfunded National Health Service ever cope with such mass IVF and embryo screening? No. Third, would a more widespread use of PGD coupled with IVF help? No. These procedures are far too sophisticated and costly. Currently, IVF–PGD is granted to only a few hundred women each year. Fourth, would the selection of couples at heightened risk decrease the incidence of these genetic defects? Probably not. It is well known that the incidence of Down's syndrome increases with maternal age. So why not screen and diagnose those at increased risk, say, the over-thirty-five-year-old pregnant women? In fact, that is current PND policy. About 140,000 women in this age group give birth each year in England and Wales. A more coercive screening strategy of PND linked to abortion would prevent some additional Down's babies being born, but pro-life and other 'morally sensitive' mothers would still refuse to be tested, and anyway, a third of all such Down's children are diagnosed in mothers under thirty-five years of age.

Or consider Duchenne muscular dystrophy. The gene for this disorder is female-carried, but the clinical condition affects only male offspring. A carrier female has a 1 in 2 risk of producing an affected son and the same risk of producing a carrier daughter. Comprehensive PND screening of all the women relatives of already affected boys would identify carriers and they could be offered IVF plus PGD to identify affected and carrier embryos; these could then be destroyed. But even this would not eradicate Duchenne, because about 30 per cent of cases occur by spontaneous mutation in utero.

The prospect of such intense screening raises additional bioethical problems. Consider the complexities of screening for cystic fibrosis, as already raised in Section 3.9.2 above. Something like 85 per cent of cases are caused by one of four commonly occurring genetic mutations. Therefore, using the current genetic tests, we can say to women, 'Yes, you are a carrier', or 'No, you are not', but there is a group of 15 per cent surrounded by uncertainty, and it is an appalling predicament for them. Or what about the woman who is told, as a result of genetic screening, that there is a 20 per cent possibility that her child will suffer from schizophrenia—perhaps, maybe, sometime? What anxieties would be hers? Could she cope? Would it be fair? Is this a sensible and compassionate approach to human medicine? Screening plus treatment is good medicine; screening plus doubt is poor medicine; screening plus destruction is bad medicine.

3.9.6 SCREENING FOR SAVIOUR SIBLINGS

So far, only methods for detecting and terminating the lives of *unborn* disabled children—embryos and foetuses—have been described. What can be done about *born* disabled children? Such genetically handicapped newborns, toddlers and schoolchildren are somewhat trickier patients. Of course, infanticide is an illegal possibility. But for a few twenty-first-century parents and their children, another, more modern treatment method has been devised. It involves the creation of 'saviour siblings'. Initially, it may appear to be a bioethically acceptable, therapeutic type of medicine. However, its underlying premise is not primarily about treating or curing diseases in born children; it is about ending the very lives of those specifically created by IVF if they—the embryonic and the foetal saviour siblings—are found to be disease-infected and tissue-mismatched. Once detected and selected, they are destroyed because they do not fit the requisite biological specifications. It is the old eugenic tactic dressed up in new clothes. This sort of destructive thinking is light years away from the ethics and practice of Hippocratic–Christian medicine.

There are several potentially fatal genetic diseases, especially certain anaemias in children, which can be treated by a donor bone-marrow transplant. If the donated tissue, containing the all-important stem cells, is compatible with the patient's, the end result can be a proper, permanent cure. So far, all good. But the required tissue match can be elusive. The most suitable donors are typically the patient's siblings—1 in 4 brothers or sisters is likely to have the necessary tissue type. Families with lots of children obviously increase the probability of discovering such a match. An alternative strategy is for parents to have additional children in the hope that a matching child will be conceived. Still all good.

Chapter 3

The introduction of IVF and PGD has refined this basic approach. Now, not good. In 1989, PGD was first used to screen IVF embryos for families suffering with X-linked genetic disorders: whenever male embryos were detected, they were simply thrown away. It was, and still is, a controversial procedure with immense eugenic implications. Despite such bioethical drawbacks, PGD began to be used in conjunction with human leukocyte antigen (HLA) tissue typing, or what has now become known as preimplantation tissue typing (PTT). This ensures that the selected embryo is histocompatible with the recipient—otherwise the patient's immune system will reject the 'new' donated tissue—and therefore, once born, will more likely be a suitable tissue donor for saving the life of the diseased sibling.

Thus, the concept of the 'saviour sibling' was formulated. The proposed treatment would involve a transfusion of stem cells, derived not from an unrelated donor's bone marrow, but from the newborn saviour sibling's umbilical cord or other source of stem cells. The first reported trial of this therapy occurred in the USA in 2000, when Adam Nash was born, disease-free and with a tissue type that matched his six-year-old sister, Molly. Their parents were both carriers of inherited Fanconi anaemia, and Molly was a sufferer of this rare, but often fatal, condition. Adam's birth involved the creation of thirty IVF embryos, twenty-four of which were confirmed by PGD to be Fanconi-free and five of which were confirmed by PTT to be tissue compatible. The last in a series of four IVF embryo-transfer procedures was successful. Six weeks after Adam was born, his sister received a transfusion of stem cells harvested from his umbilical cord. It worked—Molly lives on.[52]

Forget for a moment the technological feat; think of the bioethical issues. First, is it right to create made-to-measure 'designer' children? Should not every child be wanted for him- or herself alone? Second, is this not unadorned utilitarianism and human commodification—children conceived and born for specific purposes, to meet the needs of others? Is it not children as medical products? Third, how many human embryos will the IVF procedures alone waste? Fourth, how many additional human embryos will the PGD selection processes waste? Fifth, if the newborn has the incorrect tissue type, will this saviour sibling be regarded as a failure, the wrong sort of baby? Sixth, all human donations, whether blood, bone marrow or whatever, require a donor's informed consent, but how can a newborn give this? It is others who decide the saviour sibling's utility. Seventh, if an additional stem-cell donation is required at a later date, can the saviour sibling refuse?

Such questions initially appeared to weigh heavily on the HFEA as it considered requests to license this sort of treatment in the UK. But, as so often happens, bioethical qualms can seem trivial when compared with the emotional appeals of parents, especially those with disabled children—who can refuse a heart-rending request? And so emotive petitioning trumped ethical principles, and the HFEA surrendered. What follows is the cheerless chronicle of saviour siblings, UK-style. It is a salutary reminder that arbitrary decisions, based on a utilitarian framework of bioethics, produce poor and unsettled outcomes. The HFEA proved itself, again, to be a watchdog with no teeth, a quango with no bite—a real paper tiger.

In 2000, a son, Zain, was born to Raj and Shahana Hashmi. He suffered from β-thalassaemia major, a rare and potentially fatal blood disorder for which he received regular blood transfusions and an intensive drugs regimen. What he needed was a bone-marrow transplant, but no suitably matched donor could be found—none of Zain's three elder siblings or close family members was compatible. The Hashmis' next naturally conceived son had non-compatible tissue. Prenatal diagnosis (PND) showed that another unborn child had the thalassaemia and was subsequently aborted. The Hashmis decided to try for a saviour sibling. Their fertility clinic therefore approached the HFEA to obtain a licence for saviour-sibling PGD and tissue typing. In February 2002, that licence was granted.[53] Twenty-four IVF embryos were created, but none was a match and some were carriers of the disease. In a second attempt, fifteen embryos were created with two exact matches. One of these two embryos stopped developing before transfer, and the other failed to develop after transfer to Mrs Hashmi's womb. Meanwhile, the procedure was challenged in the courts on the grounds that the HFEA had no authority to approve PGD and tissue typing. In December 2002, the High Court ruled that the procedures were indeed unlawful on the basis that they must only be used in the 'best interests' of the IVF-saviour-sibling child to be born, not those of the disabled born child. In April 2003, this judgement was overturned by the Court of Appeal. Later that month, a final appeal to the House of Lords failed when it upheld

Chapter 3

the Court of Appeal's decision. The Hashmis tried again, but in 2004, after a number of unsuccessful attempts, they abandoned any further IVF–PGD treatment cycles.

Also in 2000, Charlie was born to Michelle and Jayson Whitaker. He too suffered from a severe form of anaemia, Diamond–Blackfan anaemia (DBA), and also needed a suitable donor. In 2001, his sister, Emily, was conceived naturally, but she was not tissue compatible. In 2002, the Whitaker's application to the HFEA for a saviour-sibling licence was refused on the grounds that DBA is not primarily an inherited genetic condition and so no specific analytical method was available to test for its presence. Therefore, the screening process would be of no direct benefit to any selected embryos; it would be solely to ensure a tissue match with Charlie. This differed from the Hashmis' case, where PGD testing was required to make certain that any selected embryos were not affected by the inherited genetic disorder, namely, β-thalassaemia major. In 2002, the Whitakers sought treatment in Chicago. There, IVF resulted in nine embryos, three were selected by PGD and tissue typing as matches, and the 'best' two were transferred to Michelle Whitaker. In June 2003, Jamie was born, the UK's first saviour sibling. A year or so later, in July 2004, Charlie was given a successful transfusion of stem cells from Jamie's umbilical cord blood, which had been harvested and stored soon after his birth.

Also in 2004, largely as a result of the Whitaker case, the HFEA reviewed and expanded its policy to include authorization of PGD for tissue typing. As a consequence, in September 2004, the HFEA duly granted Joe and Julie Fletcher permission to have an IVF–PGD tissue-matched baby to help treat Joshua, their son, who suffered from DBA. In mid-2005, the Fletchers had a daughter, Jodie, the first saviour sibling to be conceived and born in the UK, though it was not until 2010 that Joshua received a bone-marrow transplant from his saviour-sibling sister.

These procedures remain controversial and prone to failure. Yet in 2006, the HFEA allowed Charlie and Catherine Mariethoz to produce and tissue type their embryos in the UK to achieve a match for their daughter Charlotte, another sufferer from DBA.[54] By mid-2009, the Mariethozes had completed eight attempts at IVF–PGD at £12–14,000 a time, but with no success. Meanwhile, the HFEA cagily announced that 'each patient's case is approved separately, based on its own merits'. That sounded like pragmatism, as well as a prelude to widening the guidelines to admit more selection and more destruction of more embryos with more disabilities. And guess what ...

Of course, compassion is required for all families with such seriously ill, disabled children. Thankfully, only very small numbers are involved, and these dilemmas should become even fewer in the future. Why? First, because, as time goes by, larger and more comprehensive tissue-donor registers will be compiled, so that tracking down suitable bone-marrow or umbilical-cord donors will become easier. And second, because advances in stem-cell technologies will provide additional banks of stored, compatible, transplantable stem cells.

3.9.7 SO WHAT SHOULD A COUPLE DO?

Couples who are genetically disabled themselves, or come from families with serious genetic conditions, face tough decisions when they consider having children. They need to ask, and answer, some sobering questions. Are we both affected or both carriers? Should we not have a child? Should we adopt? Should we use donor gametes? What about IVF and PGD? Should we proceed with natural conception and hope for the best? If pregnant, should we then undertake prenatal screening and any subsequent PND tests? If so, and they are positive, what then? If we decide to proceed with a pregnancy, what are the risks of that child being either affected or a carrier? If the child is disabled, will we have the resources—financial, emotional, spiritual and so on—to cope?

Of course, many of these questions should also be asked by every couple of reproductive age, not just by those known to be at high risk of bearing a child with genetic disorders. In short, what are a husband and wife's attitudes towards handicap and the prospect of having a child of their own with significant physical or mental disabilities, or both?

Every couple contemplating pregnancy should come to it grown-up and open-eyed. Bearing and nurturing a 'normal' child is a complex, challenging, life-changing endeavour, but for parents of a child with special needs, the demands are extra-special. This may sound like a case for voluntary infertility—no, No, NO! Rather, it is a call to be astute and wise and to settle the extent of your eugenic tendencies before you ever begin procreating.

Chapter 3

3.9.8 GENETIC DISABILITIES AND SCREENING IN THE FUTURE

Our understanding of human genetics and its medical applications is expanding exponentially. Certainly, ever more elaborate techniques are detecting ever more genetic disorders for an ever increasing clientele. Will there soon be any genetic attribute that cannot be screened for and diagnosed? Is all this good, bad or indifferent?

Newer techniques, such as preimplantation genetic haplotyping (PGH) and karyomapping for the unborn, plus comparative genomic hybridization (CGH), microarray chip technology and fluorescence *in situ* hybridization (FISH)—come on, keep up!—for the rest of us, have begun to revolutionize this search for rogue genes. For example, karyomapping can screen for thousands, perhaps for the entire complement, of approximately 15,000 known disorders and other genetic characteristics, simultaneously and rapidly. But what will be the outcome of any positive results, say, among the unborn? Will they be used to prepare parents for their upcoming special-needs child? Will they lead to the founding of new, specialized charities and clinics? Will they drive research to devise new treatments and cures? No, no, no. It will be the same old eugenic solution—more embryo destruction and more abortions for those who are judged to be the genetically inferior.

Meanwhile, for the less sophisticated and the more financially hard-up, there are now do-it-yourself genetic testing kits available in local pharmacies or online. Already popular for establishing paternity, these assorted tests claim to assess an individual's risk of developing various illnesses, such as diabetes, coeliac disease or prostate problems. A somewhat different kind of retail product is represented by the Counsyl Universal Genetic Test, which allows pre-conceptual screening of would-be parents to establish whether they are carriers of over a hundred genetic disorders, such as cystic fibrosis, Tay-Sachs disease and sickle-cell anaemia, which might be passed on to their future offspring. It seems so undemanding—buy your kit, sample your saliva, mail it to the manufacturer and read your results online within three weeks. However, that particular company's tag line is somewhat frightening, if not plainly eugenic: 'We believe that genetic testing is a human right, not a luxury.'[55] Hmm.

Using genetic screening to predict the probability of suffering from a particular disease is one thing, but what is the point of such knowledge if no treatment is available? Moreover, it is debatable whether the widespread

Some of the primary issues

screening of mostly symptom-free people for diseases such as breast or bladder cancers is likely to reduce contingent deaths, whereas the risk of false-positive results and the ensuing unnecessary surgery with its high costs and anxiety, or drug treatments with nasty side effects, are demonstrable drawbacks to such practices. Indiscriminate screening can be like stirring up a hornet's nest.

This raises yet another key question: who should decide the extent to which screening technology can be used within a population? Should it be Parliament, public consensus, healthcare professionals, the individual or an unelected elite, like the HFEA? During 2006, the regulatory expansion of PGD by the HFEA highlighted a particularly cynical element in its decision-making process. At the time, the HFEA was in the middle of a public consultation which included the issues surrounding PGD. But then, out of the blue, it decided to ignore any public opinion and widen the scope of PGD anyway. That step was both pragmatic and unprincipled. The head of the HFEA felt able to declare, 'This is not about opening the door to wholesale genetic testing.' Yet in 2004, the HFEA published a list of forty-two genetic conditions that IVF–PGD clinics were allowed to screen for; by 2012, that list had grown to 205. You may draw your own conclusions about the setting of firm boundaries on the road ahead and whether or not this really is about 'wholesale genetic testing'.

The likely ubiquity of future screening could also mean that producing children will become more technologically controlled—and much less fun. Wannabe parents will have their genomes checked for genetic compatibility. Embryos, conceived of course by IVF, will be subjected to the rigours of quality control by PGD. And just to make sure that the children meet all the requirements of their parents, and of society, they will be prenatally re-screened. Those who do not make the genetic grade will surely be disposed of, destroyed, dispensed with, discarded—choose your own trope. If you thought that eugenics was some out-of-date practice, think again; it is here to stay for a long time yet. All this will presage the true coming of age of the designer baby, the baby as a Grade A, selectively screened, genetically approved commodity. *Au secours!* Whatever will the world of human reproduction be like for my grandchildren?

Currently, it is very, very few people—only those undergoing IVF—who can exploit PGD, though considerably more—the coterie of pregnant

Chapter 3

women—who can use PND. But what about the rest of us, the rank-and-file masses? When will genetic screening impinge on us? Events suggest it could be pretty soon. It was only in 2000 that the Human Genome Project published the first draft sequence of human DNA. That took thirteen years of international collaboration and cost an estimated $3 billion. By 2013, you could have your genome commercially sequenced in less than a day, for less than $1,000. Within the next decade, all of us will probably have undergone some new type of genetic screening and testing. How long will it be before we are all carrying our genomic data secreted in a microchip on a credit card in our back pocket or handbag?

3.9.9 GENETIC DISABILITIES AND SCREENING: IN CONCLUSION

Big bioethical questions and grave misgivings, no matter how theoretically serious they appear to be in the cool environment of the home, office or church, can rapidly evaporate in the climate of the white-hot or, at least, body-heat biotechnology of the hospital or clinic. Often it is the worried, 'morally sensitive' amateurs pitted against the rushed, assertive professionals. The tentative 'should we?' can so easily be overridden by the assured 'surely we must'. Likewise, in the public arena, serious bioethical doubts about IVF, PGD, PND, and so on, can appear so trifling and doctrinaire compared with the heartfelt pleas from childless couples, disabled parents or those with handicapped children. The appliance of bad science—creating, screening, selecting and destroying—can appear so enticing, yet always so eugenic. Beware: you have now been warned.

3.10 Gene therapy

Rather than powering these schemes of smart detection and brutal destruction, could not genetic screening and some genetic engineering be employed more constructively? Why not something new and positive instead of that old and negative formula? In the early 1990s, some medical scientists had that very dream. It was called gene therapy, a cure for genetic disabilities. It was hailed as the cure-all for human ills, the magic bullet for killer diseases, the universal medical potion. Its pioneer, W. French Anderson of the University of Southern California School of Medicine, believed some of that hype too: 'We thought it would immediately translate

SOME OF THE PRIMARY ISSUES

into cures.' Oh dear; how the great therapeutic dream soon plummeted into the toxic nightmare. But as the twenty-first century has rolled on, gene therapy's hope springs eternal. It is beginning to turn into a (mostly) good story.

3.10.1 GENE THERAPY: THE BASICS

Gene therapy appears beguilingly simple. It involves inserting a good gene into cells that carry a bad gene—easy to say, so much harder to do. Basically, there are two types. First, there is germline gene therapy, which inserts healthy genes into unhealthy sperm, ova, gamete-producing cells or early embryos. Its effects would be heritable; therefore it is potentially eugenic, and is currently banned in the UK and in most other countries. Second, there is somatic gene therapy, which inserts healthy genes into unhealthy somatic, or body, cells, such as those of the liver or skin. This is not heritable and little different from transplants, like those of bone marrow, which are already widely accepted as ethical and frequently performed throughout the world.

The basic protocol of somatic gene therapy is that the faulty gene responsible for the disorder must first be identified, then its non-faulty form is isolated, grown in large numbers, and finally transplanted into the patient. So far, the most successful strategies use viruses as the carriers, or vectors, to transplant or bring a particular DNA sequence, the healthy gene, into the defective somatic cells. But there are huge technical problems associated with packaging the good gene's DNA, targeting the right cells, retaining genetic stability, ensuring correct biochemical function, maintaining biological efficiency and so on.

In general, we need not fear somatic gene therapy when it is properly controlled—bioethically, it is an unobjectionable procedure. After all, what is the difference between providing, say, injectable insulin for a diabetic man and tweaking the DNA of his pancreas so that it begins again to synthesize that hormone? Both approaches reside within the ambit of proper medicine and good treatment. However, serious questions lie in wait. When does 'treatment' become 'enhancement', and vice versa? For instance, is it acceptable to increase a girl's resistance to a particular infectious disease, once only and permanently, by a little somatic gene therapy, rather than condemning her to a lifetime of conventional pill-taking, with its probable

Chapter 3

adverse side effects? Is your answer 'Yes'? Then what about inserting genes to improve her physical or mental characteristics? We already expend time, energy and money on encouraging our children to improve their sporting prowess and educational attainment—why not go the whole hog and do it genetically? Now what is your answer? Taking the argument to another level, why not insert a bat's sonar gene to help that girl 'see' in the dark? And your answer now? OK, that's enough silly talk for the moment. But will that seem such a hare-brained proposal in, say, 2030? We have this dreadful ability to turn the bioethically good, be it sex, drugs or somatic gene therapy, into the bioethically bad. Notice has been served.

3.10.2 GENE THERAPY IN PRACTICE

The first approved clinical trial of somatic gene therapy started in the USA in September 1990. The target disease was severe combined immunodeficiency (SCID). Sufferers have an impaired immune system, which sometimes forces them to live in sterile, plastic bubbles to protect themselves against possibly fatal bacterial or viral infections—hence their nickname 'bubble babies'. SCID exists in several forms. One is caused by a defective gene that fails to code for a particular protein, the enzyme called adenosine deaminase (ADA). So these SCID patients are ADA-deficient. One such sufferer was Ashanti DeSilva. She was having frequent injections of PEG-ADA, a synthetic form of the enzyme, but its beneficial effects were decreasing with time. She needed a bone-marrow transplant, but no matching donors were forthcoming. So, at the age of four, she became a gene-therapy patient. Blood samples were taken from her, and from these her faulty T-lymphocytes—the cells with a key role in maintaining the body's immune system—were isolated, grown in a laboratory, and incubated with a retroviral vector containing the normal, healthy ADA gene. Then these genetically engineered T-cells were infused back into her bloodstream. As a result, this therapeutic procedure was confirmed to be safe and her condition improved, though she has needed repeated treatments because the gene-corrected T-cells die naturally. And because she has continued with the enzyme replacement injections, there are still questions concerning the degree of effectiveness of her particular gene therapy. Perhaps it was never going to be a cure, but it undoubtedly was a watershed in genetic-based medicine.

SOME OF THE PRIMARY ISSUES

Since that time, results from numerous small-scale trials have been published, but gene therapy continues to be a largely experimental treatment, still in a protracted infancy. Any reports of progress have been overshadowed by some stunning disasters. In 1999, Jesse Gelsinger, a US teenager with ornithine transcarbamylase (OTC) deficiency—a metabolic disorder of the urea cycle—was a participant in a small gene-therapy trial. After his liver was infused with an adenoviral vector carrying the corrective gene, he suffered a severe reaction, multiple organ failure, and tragically died. The subsequent investigation showed that, in its eagerness for success, his medical team had recklessly overstepped its own safety guidelines. The world of gene therapy was shaken and halted, albeit temporarily.

Before long, calamity struck again. From 1999, another SCID trial was being conducted at the Necker Hospital for Sick Children in Paris. Five of this trial's children developed a leukaemia-like disease, and one died. The cause was the retroviral vector used to insert the healthy gene into the bone-marrow cells—it had activated an oncogene, a cancer-causing gene. Though these cancers were treatable, their onset caused scientific consternation and public condemnation, resulting in the suspension of these French and similar trials in the USA.

By 2002, the news was looking somewhat brighter. Rhys Evans became the first UK child to undergo gene therapy at London's Great Ormond Street Hospital. He was an eighteen-month-old boy, seriously ill and on a ventilator. His was the common X-linked SCID, the boy-only form, known as SCID-X1, which prevents the production of an immune system protein, interleukin-2. He needed a bone-marrow transplant, but again no suitable donor could be found; so instead of giving him someone else's immune system, it was decided to attempt to correct his own via gene therapy. A modified, and now safer, retroviral vector was used to introduce the healthy gene into stem cells isolated from his bone marrow. The engineered cells were then put back into Rhys. It was a triumph. He suffered no adverse effects, his T-cell numbers increased, and they worked properly.

By 2012, as many as twenty children with SCID-X1 had been treated in clinical trials in London and Paris. Some of these treatments had commenced up to ten years previously and eighteen patients were still alive; in seventeen of them, the immunodeficiency had been corrected. In addition, other research teams, in other places, have reported that gene

Chapter 3

therapy, for a growing number of SCID patients, has been either partially or fully successful.

3.10.3 GENE THERAPY IN THE FUTURE

Despite its earlier rough and tough history, efficacious gene therapy is coming. Now, after twenty and more years of anxious effort, lessons have been learned, techniques honed and more circumspect approaches adopted. There has been a decade of hushed achievement, and now gene therapy is back in the news—this time quietly, with hope, but without the hype. Around the world, large-scale trials, involving hundreds of volunteers, are underway for illnesses as diverse as Leber's congenital amaurosis, adrenoleukodystrophy and Parkinson's disease.

However, it is also now clear that gene therapy, even with its vast positive potential, will not provide many magic bullets; the majority of human genetic disorders are far too complex. Trying to tackle and correct them with current gene-therapy methods would be foolhardy. Today's gene-therapy procedures are too specialized, too labour-intensive and too expensive. Future gene therapy will have a major impact only when vectors, which carry the altered genes, are developed that can be, for example, safely injected into patients, in the way that some diabetics now use insulin. Only then will an ever-growing range of diseases be treatable, but it will still be for hundreds of patients, maybe thousands, rather than millions.

3.10.4 GENE THERAPY: IN CONCLUSION

Gene therapy is a winning combination of genetic screening and genetic engineering. Detection of disabilities to be followed by their treatment or cure is a rugged principle and practice of proper medicine. It is the antithesis of the 'search and destroy' strategies of PGD, PND and so on.

Somatic gene therapy is therefore commonly, if not universally, judged to be a part of good medicine, that culture of life. If you generally approve of bone-marrow transplants and a little light genetic engineering, this branch of medicine will cause you little or no bioethical unrest. However, germline gene therapy is quite another issue—primarily, a eugenic issue. But even that has its advocates. They argue that it would be beneficial to allow 'corrected' disease-causing genes to be passed on to future generations. The counter-arguments are that its long-term effects would be unpredictable, it would deny subsequent offspring the right to unmodified DNA, and it would hold enormous scope for eugenic abuse. Though it is currently banned in most countries, including the UK, never say never. Could the tentative approval of 'three-parent' IVF experiments in the UK during 2011, as described in Section 3.5.2, be the start of a germline slippery slope? Everyone knows that the ethics and practice of all bioethical issues have that ingrained habit of slipping and sliding. So, whenever you hear about gene therapy, always ask the basic question: is it somatic or germline?

3.11 Infanticide

Infanticide is the go-between issue, flanked by abortion and euthanasia. Numerically, it may be relatively uncommon, but its ethics and practice are no less explicable or defendable. The fact that it is seldom encountered is no reason for it to be discounted. Infanticide represents a major link in the bioethical chain within the culture of death. First, infanticide is the philosophical link, justifying yet another form of killing young, innocent human life—the newborn instead of the unborn. Second, it is the locational link, killing in a different physical environment—outside, instead of inside, the womb. Third, it is the temporal link running from abortion to euthanasia; it sits between the very young and the old. Infanticide exists as an ugly shackle in the culture of death's human chain. It is bioethically fraught.

3.11.1 WHAT IS INFANTICIDE?

Infanticide is deliberately ending the life of a newborn child either at, or soon after, birth. Some call it neonaticide, filicide or, more officially, neonatal euthanasia—or even the modishly oxymoronic 'after-birth abortion'. It may be accomplished by an act of commission, that is, by direct action, such as one of the parents smothering the child with a pillow or a doctor poisoning the child with a huge overdose of drugs. Or it may be accomplished by an act of omission, such as simple neglect, or the refusal to provide food and fluids, so that the child starves and dehydrates to death. The actual means make little difference—either way, a defenceless, newborn child is killed. The lives of all newborns are protected by law; therefore, their killing constitutes a crime of infanticide, murder or manslaughter.

Chapter 3

3.11.2 WHAT IS NOT INFANTICIDE?

The targets of infanticide are often, but not always, severely disabled newborns. There is a distinction to be drawn here between non-fatal and fatal disabilities. Children born with non-fatal conditions, like Down's syndrome or spina bifida, will, with normal care, food, perhaps some routine surgery and other treatments, survive and flourish. On the other hand, a fatal disability means that the newborn's condition is so grievous that there is no possibility of survival, and he or she will die naturally within a short time, possibly just a few hours after birth. Examples would be extreme prematurity, anencephaly and most cases of Edward's syndrome—conditions that are incompatible with life and untreatable. Such disorders are without hope. That does not imply that the baby's life is useless or without meaning—such a life, though short, can have a disproportionately enduring impact for good.

An anencephalic daughter, Anastasia Joy, was recently born to friends of mine. When first advised of the diagnosis, her mother told the doctors, 'We need to stop talking about "resolving matters" because I need pregnancy care.' After their baby was born early and naturally, her mother wrote, 'She lived for a spellbindingly beautiful eighty minutes. We had her baptized and showered her with love and affection and feel blessed that she was, and is, a part of our family. I am stronger for having had my daughter, not weaker. I am more fulfilled as a mother, not less fulfilled. I am grateful that I held her alive, not angry that she is gone.'[56]

The dying child must be treated with respect, made comfortable, fed and provided with treatment or medication, if required—this is proper palliative care, good medicine. No drug must be given to hasten his or her death, but there may come a time to withhold treatment. After all, the child is fast dying and it would not be good medicine either to 'strive officiously' or to employ extraordinary measures merely to prolong his or her life, or, conversely, to extend his or her dying. Such actions would be futile and burdensome—the baby is terminally ill and death is imminent. And when the child has died, his or her body is to be treated with reverence. A very young child has died, but this is *not* infanticide. This child's death was unavoidable; it was no one's intention.

3.11.3 INFANTICIDE: A SHORT HISTORY

Infanticide, just like abortion and euthanasia, has a long and miserable history. It has been practised widely, in many societies, over thousands of years, especially for reasons of disability, but also as a method of sex selection, limitation of family size, concealment of illicit pregnancies and tyrannous oppression.

It is the slaughter of the innocents. For example, it was used specifically against baby boys by despotic rulers, from Pharaoh to Herod, to wreak vengeance upon the people of God (Exod. 1; Matt. 2:16–18). But it was more generally performed, mainly by means of exposure, by the Greeks and then the Romans. Yet it was never the custom of the ancient Jews. They lived under the creational obligations of Genesis 1:28: 'God blessed them and said to them, "Be fruitful and increase in number; fill the earth and subdue it."' For them, the conception and birth of children were deemed to be blessings from God, signs of Jehovah's grace and favour: 'Sons are a heritage from the LORD, children a reward from him. Like arrows ... Blessed is the man whose quiver is full of them' (Ps. 127:3–5).

Besides such general precepts, God's people of the Old Testament were firmly, repeatedly and specifically barred from participating in the infanticidal practices of their pagan neighbours: 'Do not give any of your children to be sacrificed to Molech, for you must not profane the name of your God. I am the LORD' (Lev. 18:21; 20:1–5). Again, during the time of Isaiah, the prophet spoke against those who 'sacrifice [their] children in the ravines and under the overhanging crags' (Isa. 57:5). Thus, for centuries, the people of God behaved quite differently from their heathen compatriots—they were holy and separate, and for them, infanticide was an abomination.

The coming of New Testament Christianity continued these Hebraic prohibitions of infanticide. Nothing was annulled. Indeed, most ethical imperatives of the Old Testament were not just maintained in the New Testament; they were considerably strengthened. And so it was that the first-century Roman historian Tacitus could record that God's chosen people 'provide for the increase of their numbers. It is a crime among them to kill any newly-born infant'.[57]

As already explained in Chapter 1, it was these Judaeo-Christian doctrines, in tandem with the Hippocratic Oath, that fashioned the foundations of the ethics and practice of ancient medicine. But it was the arrival of New Testament Christianity that purged the Graeco-Roman world of infanticide. In AD 318, Constantine, the first Christian emperor, issued a decree declaring that the slaying of a child of any age by the father was a crime. By the

Chapter 3

end of the fourth century, infanticide had become a crime punishable by death. For the next fifteen hundred years or so, infanticide was regarded as a serious offence by nearly all societies, particularly among those whose ethical mindset and legal system had been shaped by Christianity.

3.11.4 INFANTICIDE LEGALLY

More recently in England and Wales, infanticide has existed as a separate statutory crime—the Infanticide Act 1922 made it a non-capital offence, and the Infanticide Act 1938 defined 'newborn' as up to the age of twelve months. These Acts were designed to demonstrate a degree of compassion towards a mother who kills her child while 'the balance of her mind was disturbed by reason of her not having fully recovered from the effect of giving birth to the child or by reason of the effect of lactation'. It is an idiosyncrasy of English law that infanticide can be committed only by a woman—in fact, only by a mother upon her own child. Fathers and all others, though they can carry out the same deed, would be guilty, not of infanticide, but of murder or manslaughter. These days, such prosecutions are infrequent, convictions are few, and sentences are more lenient. Of the forty-nine UK women convicted of infanticide between 1989 and 2000, only two were sent to prison; the rest were given probation, supervision or hospital orders.

3.11.5 JUSTIFYING INFANTICIDE

How can infanticide ever be justified? As noted in Section 2.2, it is significant that the Bible makes no bioethical distinction between the unborn and the born child. This recognition of developmental continuity is expressed by the use of the same Greek word, *brephos*, for both, as, for example, in Luke 1:42, 44; 2:12; 18:15. Abortionists may be able to salve their consciences and justify their actions by kidding themselves that the unborn child is not 'one of us' because he or she is unseen, untouched and unheard. But what about the born child? What arguments can they, together with their paediatric colleagues, now marshal to continue fooling themselves and excusing their infanticidal activity while in the presence of a visible, tangible, bawling or whimpering baby? Now they are faced with an individual who is unquestionably 'one of us'.

Nearly everyone finds the practice of infanticide morally repugnant, on a par with killing an adult, if a so-called 'normal' child is killed. However, the reaction can be quite different when the child is mentally or physically disabled, especially when severely so. The unborn child who is disabled has long been an especial target of abortionists. We employ hi-tech screening and prenatal diagnostic (PND) methods, including amniocentesis and chorionic villus sampling, to detect handicapped children in utero, and when detected, they are mostly aborted. At the other end of the age spectrum, euthanasia is being increasingly requested and, in some legislatures, practised for the disabled elderly, the sick and the vulnerable. Such killings are regularly rationalized on the grounds that these people are unwanted, incompetent and costly—pretty much the same reasons given for endorsing abortion. These are also the same arguments used to justify acts of infanticide. The thinking, the ethics and the practice behind the big three issues are the same. Here is the bioethical monolith of abortion-infanticide-euthanasia; it is the grand unified theory of the culture of death.

What is more, infanticide is the bioethically consistent response of our age. Whereas the Abortion Act 1967 permitted an unborn child to be aborted up to twenty-eight weeks under ground 4—namely, where there is 'a substantial risk that if the child were born ... it would be seriously handicapped'—the Human Fertilisation and Embryology Act 1990 amended this to ground E to contain 'no time limit'. So now, if handicap is suspected—note, not necessarily proven—the abortion can be performed right up to the time of birth. If this is the law of the land *before* birth, why not extend it by a few minutes or hours until *after* birth? What morally significant arguments can be raised against infanticide in a society that can already lawfully kill its unborn children of forty weeks' gestation? Put another way, if late abortion is legal, why not early infanticide? It is a good question. The cruel logic is surely unassailable.

Infanticide has long had a stalwart supporters' club, with a few particularly celebrated members. Some have argued that the newborn child is not really 'one of us' until as late as one year after birth. Astonishingly, the two Nobel prizewinners James Watson and Francis Crick, who discovered the structure of DNA, have espoused this general proposition (see Section 5.3.1). They have proposed that every newborn should be tested for certain physical and genetic attributes after birth—and if the baby fails, any right to life is forfeited. This is alarming stuff from the elite of the biological sciences. But moral philosophers can be just as scary. For

CHAPTER 3

instance, the ethicist Jonathan Glover justified infanticide in his influential book *Causing Death and Saving Lives*[58] by arguing that 'new-born babies have no conception of death and so cannot have any preference for life over death'.[59] Although such a statement is irrational twaddle, its impulse is manifestly dangerous.

Two other famous backers of infanticide are the bioethicists Helga Kuhse and Peter Singer. In their notoriously shocking book *Should the Baby Live?*,[60] they presented their case for a twenty-eight-day period after a child's birth during which treatment could be legally withheld. Throughout this period, the child could be clinically assessed by an independent review panel, eerily reminiscent of the Nazi child euthanasia committees of the 1930s, before the verdict of life or death is pronounced. These authors recommended the latter course when the child's 'life will … be one of unredeemed misery'.[61] That is a remarkably poignant phrase, yet it could readily be applied to millions and millions of this world's people in a general sense, as well as within a specifically Christian theological context. Are Kuhse and Singer seriously suggesting that deprivation and unhappiness should be used as a criterion to justify the early killing of such victims? Then who among our newborn children is safe?

As you would expect, infanticide also has its twenty-first-century advocates. For example, in 2012, the *Journal of Medical Ethics* published an article online entitled 'After-Birth Abortion: Why Should the Baby Live?' by Alberto Giubilini and Francesca Minerva.[62] They contended that the killing of newborn infants should be permitted on the same grounds currently used to sanction abortion. After all, they insisted, 'both fetuses and newborns do not have the same moral status as actual persons'. They therefore concluded that 'what we call "after-birth abortion" (killing a newborn) should be permissible in all the cases where abortion is, including cases where the newborn is not disabled'. It is a breathtakingly absurd proposal. And although none of their outlandish thinking is new, it is still loathsome.

3.11.6 PRACTISING INFANTICIDE IN THE WEST

Infanticide is not simply the whim of a few Nobel laureates or some big-shot moral philosophers, or the practice of some faraway, uncivilized tribes—it actually occurs on our doorsteps, in our local, cutting-edge hospitals and clinics, carried out by skilled medical professionals. Their rationale: death seems to be in the 'best interests' of the child. Advances in medical technology have enabled newborn babies who would formerly have died to be kept alive and given the necessary preliminary help to live long lives. But in some such cases, parents and doctors have quietly decided not to treat these neonates. These conversations are usually carried on behind closed hospital doors, and few had ever been privy to such infanticidal decision-making discussions until 1973, when two doctors went public in the *New England Journal of Medicine*.[63] Raymond S. Duff and A. G. M. Campbell described how, while working over a two-year period at the Newborn Special Care Unit of Yale University School of Medicine, a total of 299 babies had died there. Of these, forty-three had been deliberately 'allowed to die' after negotiations between doctors and parents. These babies often had Down's syndrome with duodenal atresia—intestinal obstructions—but rather than being operated on to relieve such difficulties, they were starved to death. Even so, Duff and Campbell argued that such non-treatment was justified for these neonates because their 'prognosis for meaningful life was extremely poor or hopeless'. That is a highly loaded subjective assessment, given that many of these newborns were not suffering from 'conditions that are incompatible with life', as discussed in Section 3.11.2 above.

This unofficial kind of 'non-treatment' has since been formalized in many hospitals worldwide. One of the first and most renowned examples is the Groningen Protocol. This is a set of guidelines devised in 2002 and published in 2005 by the Department of Paediatrics at the University Medical Center Groningen in the Netherlands.[64] It outlines criteria by which doctors may act to terminate the lives of severely ill infants, including those with 'a hopeless prognosis who experience what parents and medical experts deem to be unbearable suffering'. Of course, as already mentioned, some children are born with fatal, life-incompatible conditions; they will inevitably die. But a protocol that normalizes death as a medically approved outcome and thereby encourages infanticidal thinking is an enemy of good medicine. Perhaps none of this should be surprising in the Netherlands, a country where voluntary euthanasia for those over twelve years old was legalized in 2001. And how many infanticides take place there? The professional estimate is between fifteen and twenty each year, but the Dutch recognize that its incidence, like that of its adult euthanasia, is undoubtedly under-

Chapter 3

reported. How many cases occur in the UK? Some reckon it to be twenty per year, while others say it must be three times that. The truth is that nobody knows. No parent or doctor is going to volunteer 'infanticide' as the cause of any neonatal death.

Such barbarism in the medical profession can never be right. This is not about neonates with incurable conditions, incompatible with life, with no possibility of survival. This is about directives, resources and bad bioethics. If we cannot cure, then we should care, not abandon the newborn to the sluice room to die, or inject him or her with a lethal cocktail of drugs. However much one may sympathize with the difficulties, present and future, facing the doctors and the parents, there is no escaping the fact that when their intentions are to kill these newborn children, they are wrong; that can never be acceptable behaviour or practice.

3.11.7 PRACTISING INFANTICIDE IN THE EAST

Infanticide is not just a Western practice; it is global, and therefore it has an Eastern counterpart. The one-child policy of China, started in 1979, is well known. The government there has insisted on abortions for those who break the rules. But when a pregnancy is detected too late, infanticide has been the Chinese solution. One such horrifying example, reported in the Western media during 2000, involved officials in Hubei province drowning a healthy baby in a paddy field in front of the 'offending' parents.[65] This was one instance among a total of how many tens, hundreds or thousands? Who knows? In India, gender-driven, female infanticide remains widespread, especially in rural areas. This practice of gendercide has been rampant among, for example, the Kallar caste in Southern India. In one survey of 640 families, 51 per cent admitted to killing a baby girl during the week after her birth. Estimates of India's so-called 'missing girls and women'—the combined total killed by abortion and infanticide—range from twenty-five to fifty million. How many of these were caused by infanticide is unknown and unknowable, but it was definitely some, and certainly too many.

Think about infanticide not just bioethically, practically or numerically, but demographically. The sex ratio at birth (SRB) in every human population is naturally about 105 males to 100 females. In some Chinese provinces, from Henan in the north to Hainan in the south, this ratio has become 130 to 100. In India, the ratio in Punjab, Delhi and Gujarat is 125 to 100. These

SOME OF THE PRIMARY ISSUES

skewed figures are the result of a combination of sex-selective abortion and infanticide. A 2011 report stated that within the next two decades there will be a 10 to 20 per cent excess of young men in parts of these two countris.[66] This is not just the playing out of some political or cultural drama; there will be serious societal implications. For instance, because of the scarcity of women, a significant percentage of these men will never be able to marry and have children. Already in China, 94 per cent of unmarried people aged between twenty-eight and forty-nine are men. The fear is that their inability to find wives may result in increased psychological disorders, violence and criminal activities, such as kidnap, trafficking and rape. We have always been told that the practice of abortion and infanticide would solve social problems, not create them—yes, that is yet another falsehood from the culture of death.

3.11.8 THE CASE OF JOHN PEARSON

No discussion of modern-day Western infanticide would be complete without reference to its most prominent case to come before the UK courts in recent times: that of John Pearson. It was a contentious affair over thirty years ago, but even today it is still contested in bioethical, medical and legal circles. You do not have to be a moral philosopher, doctor or lawyer to understand, and to be appalled by, this heart-rending and scandalous story.

Briefly, the facts are these.[67] On Saturday, 28 June 1980, in Derby City Hospital, Molly Pearson gave birth to a son, John. He was found to have Down's syndrome and, for that reason, he was resolutely rejected by his parents—his mother is alleged to have said to her husband, 'I don't want it, Duck.' Consultant paediatrician Dr Leonard Arthur was called and four hours after the birth, he prescribed treatment for the newborn child by writing on the hospital notes, 'Parents do not wish it to survive. Nursing care only.' This latter was to be a regimen that included no food, but regular doses of an analgesic called DF118, or dihydrocodeine.

Baby Pearson was put in a side ward and died, three days later, in the arms of Margaret Slater, a nurse and herself the mother of a brain-damaged child. The police were called in to investigate and Dr Arthur was charged with John Pearson's murder. The trial at Leicester Crown Court began on 13 October 1981 before Mr Justice Farquharson. After two days of legal

CHAPTER 3

submissions, the charge was reduced from murder to attempted murder. The eighteen-day trial ended with Dr Arthur being found not guilty.

Several aspects of the case are cause for grave concern. During the trial, fears and prejudices leaked out. For example, defence counsel described a Down's syndrome baby as 'a time-bomb' of infections and defects. The judge misrepresented Down's syndrome babies by describing 'the stigmata they bear', their 'lolling tongues' and 'oriental appearance'. He concluded that such people were faced with 'the most appalling handicap'. Such descriptions were not only immaterial to the case, they were also disgraceful comments, offensive to sufferers of Down's syndrome in particular and to disabled people in general.

The 'nursing care only' prescribed for John Pearson was also misrepresented. This strategy denied the child the very thing he needed, namely, milk. He did not need analgesics. Yet the judge considered water and large doses of DF118 to be 'feeds'. The court heard that John Pearson had heart, lung and brain defects. These medical conditions rendered DF118 especially dangerous and inappropriate because the drug suppresses lung and other functions. The manufacturers of DF118 did not recommend its use for children under four years of age and advised that it should be taken *with* food. This baby boy wanted to breathe and eat, yet the healthcare team denied him both. If infections were present, what John Pearson needed were antibiotics. Instead, he was provided only with huge doses of an analgesic, which was finally given at a concentration equal to twice that which would be sufficient to kill an adult. The expert pathologist in court maintained that DF118 was the cause of death—John Pearson died from bronchopneumonia and lung stasis due to poisoning by DF118.

Perhaps because of the medical confusion and legal misdirection, Dr Arthur was acquitted. Nevertheless, the case sent shockwaves through the neonatal wards of UK hospitals, and paediatricians began to practise a more defensive medicine. Charities recommended counselling for parents of disabled newborns to counter the idea that all such children are doomed to a mindless and unrewarding life. But the case of John Pearson also said something blunt about our attitude towards disabled children: it whispered that we are content for some deliberately to be left to die.

Infanticide is always a savage crime. We have no idea how widespread it is—we can probably only underestimate its numbers. The fact that it occurs at all, and sometimes in our best hospitals, says much about the declining state of medical ethics and practice. John Pearson's death diminishes us all; we are less than satisfactory, less than protective, less than caring towards our most vulnerable children. Infanticide will always mock us.

3.11.9 INFANTICIDE IN THE FUTURE

This cruel cousin of abortion and euthanasia will be a constant feature of the coming years. It will occur probably at the same rate, whatever that is—unknown because, as a rule, it takes place secretly behind closed doors. Behind hospital doors is where the 'morally sensitive' nurses can be so disgusted by what they see and hear that they inform the police. Behind house doors is where other infanticidal incidents occur. In some of these cases, the bad news becomes public, and a few of them eventually come before the courts; for others, perhaps the majority, silence and cover-up reign.

For infanticide in other countries, particularly in the East, the future looks appalling. And in the West? Why might infanticide increase here? The Groningen Protocol, the 'active ending of life of infants'—already lawful and acceptable in the Netherlands—is likely to slither across geographical and ethical borders, just as the practice of Dutch adult euthanasia has done. In addition, the pull towards the designer baby, and the simultaneous push against the disabled baby, will make the latter even less acceptable and thus more vulnerable. And other factors will advance infanticidal possibilities—more stressed mothers, more domestic violence, more drug-abusing parents, fewer stable family relationships, fewer dependable fathers and fewer social workers. As a consequence, could the infanticidal crime and its perpetrators come to be regarded as less blameworthy, less irresponsible and therefore more tolerable and tolerated? Could it happen? Could it *not* happen?

3.11.10 INFANTICIDE: IN CONCLUSION

Although infanticide occupies the middle ground between abortion and euthanasia, it is no less horrid than either, and bioethically it is never a middling sort of issue. Nor does trying to lexically engineer its name—and several have tried—diminish its cruelty. To ignore the newborns' cries, to disregard their cravings for milk, to overlook their longings for

Chapter 3

human touch and comfort, and then deliberately to kill them, is almost beyond belief; such actions require a special class of culpable person. These neonates may be normal or disabled, they may be male or female, they may be wanted or unwanted, but they are never deserving of death so soon after their born lives have begun.

Where are the voices raised against infanticide? Has a generation of unbridled abortion and skulking euthanasia rendered us numb and dumb towards infanticide? Why, in diversity-minded and equality-conscious Britain and elsewhere, are the disabled so readily rejected and discarded by parents, doctors and society? Why is there not a worldwide outcry at such practices? Why is the UK's Department for International Development not calling for censure, boycott and embargo of the grossly offending Eastern countries? Why are we sending food aid to those who are prepared to kill 50 per cent of the intended child recipients? How is it that the world's feminists are not up in arms at the mass slaughter of the next generation of the sisterhood? What have you and I done to recognize and to halt this horror?

3.12 Euthanasia and assisted suicide

Euthanasia is probably the most exigent bioethical issue of the twenty-first century. This is reflected in the length of this section—it is long because to understand and to respond to this convoluted issue in the coming days, you need to be armed with an assortment of relevant information.

Some have considered euthanasia to be like the last in a row of three upended dominoes—once the other two have fallen, the third will unavoidably follow suit and topple over. They have reasoned that once a society has accepted the practices of abortion (domino one) and infanticide (domino two), why not domino three, euthanasia? After all, if we already legally abort our unborn and commit infanticide on our newborns because they are unwanted, imperfect or inconvenient, why not euthanize the elderly, the terminally ill and the sick? Intellectually, we may dispassionately acknowledge this domino theory to be the logical sequence in an ever-encroaching culture of death, but emotionally, we should be nothing but alarmed at the prospect.

Yet euthanasia is about dying well. Yes, it is true. In the Middle Ages, the terminally ill were issued with booklets describing the *Ars Moriendi*— the art of dying well—to guide them through their last days and hours.

Some of the primary issues

You see, once upon a time, 'euthanasia' (from the Greek *eu*, well, and *thanatos*, death) was a splendid word, something we could all aspire to: a good and happy death. Then it was hijacked, chiefly by the Victorians, and twisted and turned into something ugly. Now it is associated with hovering doctors, pain, dehumanization, autonomy, patients' rights, living wills, bad decisions and so on. It has become a most unwelcome member of the culture of death.

3.12.1 WHAT IS EUTHANASIA?

Modern euthanasia has its roots firmly planted in the utilitarian worldview of human life. A 'life not worthy to be lived' is its benchmark. A lack of 'productivity' and 'usefulness' are its touchstones. 'Patient autonomy' is its yardstick. 'Compassion' is its falsehood. It is always a shabby affair. In many cases, it is nothing other than medically assisted suicide: it is asking someone else, usually a doctor, to do the dirty work. How can that ever be called 'death with dignity'?

As already noted, lexical engineering is endemic among bioethical issues. Euthanasia is no exception. Once it was blatantly called 'mercy killing', which everyone could plainly understand. Then it became 'the right to die', then 'death with dignity', then 'assisted suicide', and now it has been transmogrified to 'assisted dying'. Do not be fooled; lexical engineering precedes social engineering. Attempting to take the sting out of an action by befogging its definition is a tried and tested strategy within the culture of death. In 2005, even the explicitly named Voluntary Euthanasia Society changed its title to the vacuous Dignity in Dying. There will be no such verbal jiggery-pokery here. What follows is the unvarnished truth, and it makes for joyless reading.

Euthanasia is usually divided into three main categories. First, there is voluntary euthanasia, that is, killing *with* the patient's request. Typically, the lethal drugs are administered by a medical professional. When a doctor is involved, perhaps in prescribing, supplying or handing over the drugs (the dividing line between illegal and legal 'assisting' is unswervingly ambiguous), but the patient him- or herself takes the fatal draught, it is known as doctor- or physician-assisted suicide, DAS or PAS. Second, there is non-voluntary euthanasia, that is, killing *without* an explicit request because the patient is usually incompetent, meaning that he or she is perhaps comatose, senile or

Chapter 3

newborn. It rests on the proposition that it is in a person's 'best interests' to be dead. Third, there is involuntary euthanasia, that is, killing a patient *against* his or her wishes. It is overriding the express will of a person. It is the strong overruling the weak. One of its 'best' examples is the early Nazi euthanasia programme, which eventually led to the Holocaust.

Some like to make a bioethical distinction between 'active' and 'passive' euthanasia. The former is described as an act of commission, where the patient is 'caused to die' by force, a lethal injection or an overdose. On the other hand, 'passive' euthanasia means that the patient is 'allowed to die' by an act of omission, such as the withdrawal of food and fluids, or life support. This 'passive' method is regarded, by some, to be bioethically preferable, a somehow nicer, more benevolent course of action. However, the distinction is false. In the final analysis, the key is intention. If it is the intention of the medical staff to hasten death, to shorten and eventually end the life of the patient, the means make no difference—there may be some practical differences, but bioethically there is none. Both are euthanasia.

3.12.2. UNDERSTANDING SUICIDE

In recent years, pro-euthanasia campaigners have concentrated their efforts on promoting assisted suicide—helping someone to take his or her own life. This may initially appear to be a more compassionate, less serious variety of euthanasia, but make no mistake: for many of these activists, assisted suicide is merely their short-term lever to achieving their long-term goal of legalizing full-blown euthanasia.

For that reason, the first issue to grasp is suicide. Have we been too harsh towards the victims of suicide in the past? Historically, in the UK, their estates went to the Crown, they were refused a proper graveyard burial and so on. This changed with the passing of the Suicide Act 1961. It decriminalized suicide, but it retained punishment for those who assisted. Section 2.1 states, 'A person who aids, abets, counsels or procures the suicide of another, or an attempt by another to commit suicide, shall be liable on conviction on indictment to imprisonment for a term not exceeding fourteen years.' The Act represented a new public tolerance towards suicide and was designed to show sympathy towards the victim rather than approval or ennoblement of the deed. And that is how suicide is now generally perceived—neither entirely unacceptable, nor ever wholly welcome. The Act certainly did not create a right to suicide; in fact, it sought strongly to discourage suicide, which is why 'assisters' are liable to punishment.

There is still no psychological or social theory that is sufficient to explain suicide. However, we do now understand that the majority of those who commit suicide are mentally or physically ill, though often temporarily so. Nevertheless, the suicide does demonstrate a selfish disregard for those left in the aftermath. The exploit is an irreversible declaration that friends and relatives were inadequate.

Suicide can be a sensitive and awkward topic. I am well aware that you may have had a loved one, family or friend who has committed suicide—as I have had myself—and memories may still be painful and consciences tender. The above introduction may appear to be unduly austere and unhelpful. If so, I regret it. Nevertheless, I am duty-bound to explain such issues as clearly as I am able; the truth cannot be served by veiling it. Moreover, there are important pastoral aspects to suicide. Would the Lamb of God, the gentle Jesus, have nothing to say to his people suffering from suicidal feelings, or from the repercussions of a suicide, in order to bring them hope and consolation? This is not the place to rehearse those many and various comforts; they have been presented in my book *The Edge of Life: Dying, Death and Euthanasia*.[68]

3.12.3 SUICIDE IN THE BIBLE

Suicide can be defined as self-murder. The Sixth Commandment, 'You shall not murder' (Exod. 20:13), forbids us from taking the life of any innocent who bears the *imago Dei*, including ourselves. Suicide is a personal assault against the sovereignty of God in all the affairs of human life. Those who commit suicide declare that they have a sovereign rule over their lives and a sovereign reign over their deaths—neither of which is true. Our lives belong to God. He oversaw our conception, he gave us our first breath, he has sustained us and he alone has the entitlement to take it. Reread Section 2.4. Those who commit suicide make themselves the arbiters in a matter not entrusted to them. God alone is the judge; it is his prerogative both to announce life and to pronounce death. 'There is no god besides me. I put to death and I bring to life' (Deut. 32:39). 'The Lord gave and the Lord has taken away; may the name of the Lord be praised' (Job 1:21). As a result of both creation and redemption, we are to live and die according to the perfect will and plan of God. Defy him, and you sin.

Chapter 3

The actual word 'suicide' does not appear in the Bible, but it is not silent on the subject. It contains at least six examples—all of men. The first was Samson, who pulled the temple upon himself (Judg. 16:30). Then the unfaithful Saul and his armour-bearer fell on their swords (1 Sam. 31:4–5). The other three were Ahithophel the conspirator, who hanged himself (2 Sam. 17:23); King Zimri the sinful plotter, who set fire to himself (1 Kings 16:18–19); and Judas Iscariot—the only New Testament example—the betrayer, who hanged himself (Matt. 27:5). Their ends were tragic and none of them, with the exception of Samson, was approved by God. Hebrews 11:32, 39 include Samson among the heroes of the faith. His death should therefore be seen not as a suicide, but rather as an example of heroic self-sacrifice. The other five were corrupt and cowardly men; their lives, and their deaths, are recorded in the Bible as a warning to the rest of us. Suicide is an unnatural death—it is part of the culture of death.

3.12.4 EUTHANASIA AROUND THE WORLD

Ours is a world uncertain about, unprepared for and unnerved by dying and death. Yet several jurisdictions have already legalized some categories of euthanasia. For instance, the Netherlands and Luxembourg permit voluntary euthanasia as well as assisted suicide. Belgium allows voluntary euthanasia, while Switzerland sanctions assisted suicide. The US states of Oregon, Washington and Vermont also endorse assisted suicide. Vagueness and indecision persist in other places. Thus a few countries, such as Colombia, India and Japan, uphold ambiguous laws and clinical practices, while some simply 'turn a blind eye'. Meanwhile, a handful of governments, including those of Montana, France and Canada, are currently stuck in protracted deadlock over the issues of legalization.

By contrast—and this fact comes as a surprise to many—there is strong, worldwide disapproval of euthanasia and assisted suicide. There is a long list of legislatures that have already rejected one or the other. It may make for tedious reading, but it does make a forceful point, namely, that most of the world is not willing to go down the euthanasia drain. Here is the evidence from the last four years. In January 2010, a New Hampshire assisted-suicide bill was defeated by 242 votes to 113. In April 2010, a Canadian euthanasia bill was defeated by 228 to 59. In

November 2010, a South Australian euthanasia bill was defeated by 12 to 9. In December 2010, the Scottish Parliament rejected the End of Life Assistance (Scotland) Bill by 85 to 16. In January 2011, the Israeli Knesset assisted-suicide bill was defeated by 48 to 16. In January 2011, a French euthanasia bill was defeated by 170 to 142. In February 2011, a Hawaiian assisted-suicide bill was defeated unanimously. In March 2011, an Idaho Senate anti-assisted-suicide bill was passed by 31 to 2. In July 2011, an Italian Lower House anti-euthanasia bill was passed by 278 to 205. In September 2011, a Bulgarian euthanasia bill was defeated by 59 to 13. In November 2012, the people of Massachusetts voted against a proposed assisted-suicide law by 51 per cent to 49 per cent. In May 2013, a New South Wales euthanasia bill was defeated by 23 to 13. In May 2013, a Maine assisted-suicide bill was defeated by 94 to 43. In October 2013, a Tasmanian assisted-suicide bill was defeated by 13 to 11.

This list will continue to grow. Let no one think that worldwide legalization of euthanasia is inevitable. But, by the same token, do not drop into some sleepy optimism that it will never be mooted, on your watch, on your doorstep.

As far as Europe is concerned, those determined to end their lives by assisted suicide have often made their final destination the Dignitas 'clinic'—a most inappropriate term for this non-healing facility, which, in truth, is a thanatorium—just outside Zurich. Some have dubbed these visits 'swisside'. During the decade 2002 and 2012, a total of 217 Britons travelled there on one-way tickets. This represents a rate of about twenty people per year. This low figure needs to be set in context against the approximate 500,000 natural deaths that occur in the UK each year. In other words, the publicity created by the few deaths at Dignitas—though granted, those who assisted were overt lawbreakers and bioethical offenders—is out of all proportion to the national death rate. Indeed, since it opened its doors in 1998, the Dignitas organization and operation has remained quite small. In 2011, it assisted a total of 160 people, mainly residents of Germany, to kill themselves. Nevertheless, the government of Switzerland, and an increasing number of its residents, is disturbed by this development in 'suicide tourism' and its tarnishing effect upon the Swiss reputation for all things bright and beautiful, including those army knives, yummy chocolates and ritzy watches.

Chapter 3

3.12.5 EUTHANASIA IN THE NETHERLANDS

The Netherlands is often considered to be the 'home of euthanasia'. The practice has long been officially prohibited but informally tolerated. It was decriminalized during the 1980s and then legalized by its Termination of Life on Request and Assisted Suicide (Review Procedures) Act 2001. Consider some Dutch facts and figures—they are quite unnerving. In January 1990, the Dutch government appointed a commission, headed by the then Attorney General, Professor Jan Remmelink, to examine end-of-life decisions in the Netherlands. In September 1991, the Remmelink Report was published. It reviewed 26,350 cases in which doctors had acted, or not acted, either 'partly with the purpose of shortening life' or with the 'explicit purpose of shortening life' throughout the Netherlands during the previous year. It reported 2,300 cases of voluntary euthanasia plus 400 cases of assisted suicide. However, because the Dutch hold a peculiarly narrow definition of euthanasia, whereby only the voluntary and active varieties are counted, these figures are gross underestimates. When the incidents of non-voluntary and passive killings are included, the real figure becomes 10,558. That is to say, just over 8 per cent of all Dutch deaths during 1990 were as the result of euthanasia. Furthermore, 5,450 of these euthanized patients (52 per cent of the total) had been killed *without* their explicit request, namely, as a result of non-voluntary euthanasia. The take-home message is simple: once a government permits voluntary euthanasia, non-voluntary euthanasia will always follow. This is the point: the legal criteria and safeguards can never be drafted sufficiently tightly to halt abuse. It is that dreaded 'slippery slope' again—that wretched, recurring feature of modern bioethics. To mix metaphors, open the door just a little, for just the few, and soon the multitude will force it wide open. As time goes by, the legal and medical criteria, which once seemed so precise and restrictive, will inexorably become fuzzy and flexible. It always happens, as sure as night follows day. Recall, for example, the legalization of abortion in the UK and its unanticipated escalation, within four decades, to 200,000 terminations each year.

Contemporary Dutch euthanasia statistics offer no greater comfort—they are increasing year on year. During 2011, the officially notified total was 3,695 cases, an 18 per cent increase on the previous year and double the 2006 total. Of these, 3,446 were classed as euthanasia, 196 as assisted suicide and 53 as a combination of the two. According to these figures, euthanasia and assisted suicide accounted for only 2.8 per cent of all Dutch deaths. But proper bioethical and accurate numerical analyses of these data are thwarted by several factors. For a start, there is this restricted Dutch definition of euthanasia. The occurrence of non-voluntary euthanasia, though technically a criminal offence, is recognized, tolerated, rarely prosecuted and not recorded. Passive euthanasia killings are similarly not counted. Moreover, the legal regulations governing euthanasia are knowingly and frequently flouted. It is estimated that approximately a quarter of cases are never registered—is it realistic to expect doctors to report their own possible criminal activities? Furthermore, the growing medical practices of what are euphemistically known as 'intensified alleviation of symptoms' and 'continuous deep sedation' both conspire to mask the precise picture; official Dutch statistics continue to be gross underestimates. Some commentators suspect that if all the intentional life-shortening procedures were taken into account, the real euthanasia figure would be as high as 12.3 per cent of all Dutch deaths. It seems that euthanasia in the Netherlands is currently out of control—medically, bioethically and bureaucratically.

But that is not all. Let no one run away with the idea that the Netherlands is the place to find 'death with dignity'. A Dutch euthanasia will not necessarily be 'a good and happy death'. Research published in the *New England Journal of Medicine* by Johanna Groenewoud and colleagues reviewed clinical problems in 649 cases of euthanasia.[69] It showed that almost a quarter (23 per cent) were botched. These patients had to endure numerous complications, like coming in and out of induced coma, prolonged waiting for death, vomiting and fits. Instead of just 'assisting', 18 per cent of doctors had to act decisively to kill their patients. And they call that 'death with dignity'? I think not!

A decade and more after euthanasia was legalized, what is now happening in the Netherlands? Is the policy settled? Are safeguards now in place and proving to be effective? Are the eligibility criteria explicit and adhered to? Are the Dutch citizens feeling comfortable and protected? What do you think? In 2011, the Dutch doctors' national federation, Koninklijke Nederlandsche Maatschappij tot bevordering der Geneeskunst (KNMG), published a position paper entitled *The Role of the Physician in the Voluntary Termination of Life*.[70] This sixty-one-page document

Chapter 3

rehearsed some rather bland, if not hypocritical, statements, such as, 'The KNMG continues to regard euthanasia and assisted suicide as a last resort measure'. But its pages also contained some disturbing proposals. If its recommendations were implemented, Dutch doctors would be allowed to direct their patients to books and Internet sites containing information about methods of euthanasia. Doctors who have conscientious objections would be obliged to give sympathetic advice and refer patients to pro-euthanasia colleagues. And here is the daunting substance of the document: it recommended that the 2001 Act's eligibility criteria for euthanasia of 'unbearable and lasting suffering' should be extended to include mental and psychological disorders, such as 'loss of function, loneliness and loss of autonomy'. Moreover, it stated that the concept of suffering should be broadened to include 'complications such as disorders affecting vision, hearing and mobility, falls, confinement to bed, fatigue, exhaustion and loss of fitness'. You may well ask, who over sixty-five years of age would be exempt? The document also recognized that currently more than 1 million Dutch elderly are affected by such 'multimorbidity', and that by 2021 that number will have risen to 1.5 million—almost 9 per cent of the total population of the Netherlands. All these people would thus become eligible for euthanasia if the KNMG's suggestions were enacted. Yet even these sweeping proposals will not satisfy the demands of Dutch pro-euthanasia campaigning groups, such as Uit Vrije Wil (By Free Choice). It wants euthanasia to be available for anyone over seventy years old—those who have 'completed their lives'—without any reference to the patient's state of health. And during 2012, for the extra convenience of its citizens, mobile euthanasia units were introduced across the Netherlands to make free-of-charge house-calls, a sort of 'euthanasia on wheels'. Moreover, all prospective clients will be given a choice: they can opt for either a deadly injection or a life-ending drink. Growing old in Holland has never been so grave.

3.12.6 EUTHANASIA IN OREGON AND BELGIUM

The point is this: legalizing euthanasia creates a mindset that generates an appetite for more and more and more. The evidence of increasing numbers from, for example, Oregon, where its Death with Dignity Act was passed

SOME OF THE PRIMARY ISSUES

in 1997, and from Belgium, where its Euthanasia Act was ratified in 2002, is indisputable.

In Oregon, the incidence of physician-assisted suicide has risen every year since its legalization—in 2012, it was nearly five times that of 1998 (seventy-seven v. sixteen cases). While these numbers may seem small, they are significantly greater than the twenty or so Britons who currently go to Switzerland each year to die. The law in Oregon is held in high regard by euthanasia advocates in the UK. However, if its death rate were applied to the UK, it would result in over 1,100 deaths each year. And there are other concerns about the Oregon law. It has no audit system, so possible abuses are never investigated; it relies on honest reporting by doctors. Of the Oregonians who have committed assisted suicide, 1 in 6 suffered from clinical depression which was undiagnosed and untreated. It is reported that cancer patients have been offered assisted suicide rather than oncology treatments. Also, 'doctor shopping' occurs—that is, the practice of finding a willing medical assister. One such doctor issued ten lethal drug prescriptions in just one year. The argument is that only about 66 per cent of those granted a supply of lethal drugs eventually use them. In other words, people find their possession and ready access comforting. Is this really any different from doctors handing out loaded pistols? Can that ever be called good medicine? The Oregon law may be attractive to some; to others, it looks ugly.

The Belgian situation is exceptionally dire. Here there are increasing numbers and also an alarmingly widening scope. Officially reported cases of euthanasia have increased sixfold in ten years, from 235 in 2003 to 1,432 in 2012. However, in some parts of the country it is reckoned that half of cases are not reported and a third are involuntary, yet nobody has been prosecuted. A decade ago, Belgians believed that their new law would uphold proper safeguards and ensure strict compliance. Now, euthanasia has been linked directly to organ harvesting (so-called organ-donation euthanasia, ODE), joint euthanasia for elderly couples, euthanasia after a botched sex-change operation, double euthanasia for deaf twins because of their fear of failing eyesight, and euthanasia for a sexually abused anorexic woman. Euthanasia for psychological suffering among the non-terminally ill has become de rigueur. And that is not all. At the end of 2013, the Belgian Senate voted, by a massive margin of 50 to 17, to approve euthanasia for

Chapter 3

children—a measure expected to be legalized in 2014. Also in the near future, those Belgians with dementia are likely to become eligible candidates. And what about the unhappy—are they next?

Where will it all end? Your guess is as good as mine, but I suspect that we will both be shockingly wrong. Whenever assisted suicide is legalized, it inculcates a change in attitude within a society. It, like abortion did in the 1960s, creates a new clientele. It makes assisted dying appear to be a civilized way out for people, especially among the weak and vulnerable and those fearful of being a burden.

3.12.7 EUTHANASIA IN THE UK

In the UK, the pro-euthanasia lobby is active, well organized, backed by several 'celebrities', funded by a few millionaires and mainly channelled through Dignity in Dying, the organization formerly known as the Voluntary Euthanasia Society. Its primary strategy has been to challenge, in a piecemeal manner, what it regards as its Big Bad Bogeyman, the Suicide Act 1961.

The Suicide Act 1961 has a clear, twofold purpose. It punishes those who act criminally, and it protects the vulnerable—that is what good law should always do. Furthermore, it provides some discretion for prosecutors and judges in the most severe cases. The Act has rightly been described as having 'a stern face and a kind heart'. Nevertheless, several men and women have continued to contest it. In particular, Lord Joel Joffe apparently has a long-standing ambition to amend this statute. First, in 2003, he sponsored his House of Lord's Patient (Assisted Dying) Bill, followed in 2004 and 2005 by revised versions modelled on the Oregon Death with Dignity Act 1997, which he much admires. Despite all these measures being lost, he persisted in 2006 with yet another attempt, his Assisted Dying for the Terminally-Ill (ADTI) Bill. I sat through all 7.5 hours of the debate in the Lords. One of the most memorable speeches came from a man with whom, bioethically, I agree on very little, Lord Robert Winston. He was worried about his ninety-three-year-old mother. Why? Because in her pre-dementia state, sometimes she was lucid and sometimes she was 'elsewhere'. On one occasion, she had said to him, 'I have really reached the end'; then, a little while later, she was enjoying life again. Recognizing that it is impossible, even presumptuous, to try to predict a person's future outlook on life, Lord

Winston could see that any vulnerable person, including his own mother, might so easily fit any proposed criteria or jump over the safeguard barriers of this, or any other, euthanasia or assisted-suicide bill. He was entirely right. The Bill was resoundingly defeated by 148 to 100.

Another player in the House of Lords has been Lord Charlie Falconer, the former Lord Chancellor. In 2009, he tried to slip an amendment into the Coroners and Justice Bill to allow Britons to accompany those travelling to Dignitas, the assisted-suicide 'clinic' in Switzerland, to die, without fear of prosecution. It failed. Then in 2011, he joined forces with Lord Joffe to head the Commission on Assisted Dying. This may have sounded like a grandiose official inquiry, but it was a bogus assembly, stuffed with pro-euthanasia advocates, funded by their rich supporters, pretending to be a rigorous and truth-seeking committee, but with the decided intent of making assisted suicide appear decent and honourable, as well as legally feasible. Its 400-page Report, published in January 2012, concluded, true to form, 'That the Commission finds that the choice of assisted dying could safely be offered to people who are suffering at the end of life and likely to die within twelve months, provided that they satisfy the eligibility criteria.' No surprises there. The Report failed on numerous counts. For example, the forecasting of a person's death usually involves considerable speculation; doctors frequently get it wrong days or weeks, if not twelve months, in advance. And everyone knows that so-called 'eligibility criteria' and 'safeguards' can never be written on a piece of paper in a sufficiently comprehensive manner to protect the weak and vulnerable. Such 'safeguards' tend to protect doctors rather than patients. Legislatures around the world have tried and failed to draft such stipulations. This pre-prejudiced Report is now gathering dust on a thousand library shelves, but its suicidal philosophy lives on.

One of the main challenges to the Suicide Act 1961 has been that of Debbie Purdy.[71] In 1995, she was diagnosed with primary progressive multiple sclerosis. She thinks she wants to kill herself, but not just yet. However, she recognizes that because of her illness she may need some assistance, either to attempt suicide herself, or to travel to the Dignitas 'clinic' with the help of her husband. Herein lies her problem: the Suicide Act 1961, with its maximum penalty of fourteen years' imprisonment for assisters. In the hope of obtaining immunity from prosecution for her husband, she began a legal challenge to the Act. In 2008, she was granted a judicial

CHAPTER 3

review, but her challenge failed. The two High Court judges maintained that any change to the law must be the task of Parliament, not the courts. However, she was given leave to appeal to the House of Lords. This she did. On 30 July 2009, the Law Lords instructed the then Director of Public Prosecutions (DPP), Keir Starmer, to produce guidance clarifying under what circumstances prosecutions would, or would not, follow for those involved in acts of assisting suicide. At that time, ninety-two Britons had gone abroad to end their lives by assisted suicide, and all those who had 'assisted' had been investigated by the police. Some had been charged, but none had proceeded to court.

The DPP duly published the mandated interim guidelines, a public consultation period ensued, and a final document, *Policy for Prosecutors in Respect of Cases of Encouraging or Assisting Suicide*, was released on 25 February 2010.[72] This consisted of sixteen 'public interest factors' likely to favour a prosecution, and six factors against taking any legal action. Keir Starmer stated, 'The policy does not change the law on assisted suicide. It does not open the door for euthanasia. It does not override the will of Parliament.' As a result, assisted suicide remains illegal—the Debbie Purdy case did not change the 1961 Act. Every suspected assisted suicide will still be investigated. No one will be guaranteed immunity from prosecution. However, the new policy did state that, for example, a prosecution where 'the suspect was wholly motivated by compassion' is less likely to proceed than, say, where a doctor or other healthcare professional is involved. All this conveys a subtle message: it tells people in advance that, if certain conditions are met, assisting in suicide can be legally acceptable—that is, you are not likely to be prosecuted. That is a move in the wrong direction.

Soon after the publication of the DPP's policy, the British Medical Association (BMA) issued guidance to doctors facing such requests from patients. It said,

> The BMA advises doctors to avoid all actions that might be interpreted as assisting, facilitating or encouraging a suicide attempt. This means that doctors should not: advise patients on what constitutes a fatal dose; advise patients on anti-emetics in relation to a planned overdose; suggest the option of suicide abroad; write medical reports specifically to facilitate assisted suicide abroad; nor facilitate any other aspects of planning a suicide.[73]

Though these current legal policies and medical opinions are to be welcomed as firm and clear, they will not be the last word on assisted suicide in the UK. The battle goes on.

In 2012, a very different battle line was drawn. Tony Nicklinson was a fifty-eight-year-old who had suffered a massive stroke in 2005, which left him with locked-in syndrome; he was not terminally ill, he was paralysed, but his mind was undimmed. After several years in this condition, unable to commit suicide by himself, he wanted to be killed by a doctor. So he went to court seeking a common law defence of 'necessity', meaning that the doctor would not be charged with murder because it was necessary for him to act to end his patient's suffering. In other words, Tony Nicklinson was asking not for assisted suicide, but for outright euthanasia. He was therefore challenging the law on murder with its mandatory sentence of life imprisonment for anyone convicted. This was even a step too far for the Dignity in Dying organization, which distanced itself from the case. On 16 August 2012, Tony Nicklinson finally lost his High Court legal bid. He was reported to be 'crestfallen, totally devastated and very frightened'. He subsequently refused food and fluids, and died of pneumonia on 22 August. His wife, Jane, vowed to continue her husband's 'right-to-die' campaign and she was granted permission to appeal the Court's decision.

Meanwhile, another man, known only as Martin, who suffered a stroke in 2008 that left him also with locked-in syndrome so that he is virtually unable to speak or move, challenged the DPP's 2010 policy on assisted suicide. Martin wants prosecution exemption for professionals, such as doctors and lawyers, who might assist in arranging for him to go to Dignitas. He too lost his case on 16 August 2012. The High Court's decision on both cases was unanimous: 'it would be wrong for the court to depart from the long-established position that voluntary euthanasia is murder.'

In April 2013, Jane Nicklinson's legal action was joined by Paul Lamb, a fifty-eight-year-old quadriplegic, who also wants to be killed by a doctor. He is almost completely paralysed as a result of a road accident in 1990, he suffers constant pain and has described his life as 'tedious, monotonous and pointless'. But he, like Martin, is not terminally ill. He was granted permission to bring a Nicklinson–Martin–Lamb 'right-to-die' case before the Court of Appeal on the dual grounds of 'necessity'—a law may be broken as a matter of overwhelming urgency—and Article 8 of the European Convention on Human Rights—the right to private and

Chapter 3

family life. On 31 July 2013, the Nicklinson–Lamb portion was dismissed by the Court of Appeal, but Martin's case was upheld. The three judges maintained that the ban on assisted suicide created by the Suicide Act 1961 was a 'proportionate interference' with their rights under Article 8. And the judges reiterated that it was for Parliament, not the courts, to change the law. However, with regard to Martin's appeal, they instructed the DPP to clarify the role and degree of support that healthcare professionals would be allowed to provide. As I write at the end of 2013, this trio of 'right-to-life' test cases has finally arrived at the UK's Supreme Court before a panel of nine judges—an unprecedented number, indicating the hearing's legal significance. The case lasted four days and judgement is expected in early 2014.

We must have the utmost empathy and sympathy for all those who live and suffer on a daily basis. However, the gravity and consequences of changing the law on assisted suicide or murder, whether those concerned are terminally ill or not, whether their diseases are debilitating or not, are too great. The outcome would be too far-reaching, and too devastating for the disadvantaged, the disabled and the dying. The floodgates to euthanasia would be opened—medical practice, legal protection and our regard for human life would never be the same again.

3.12.8 THE CASE OF ANTHONY BLAND

Modern-day euthanasia cannot be fully understood without reference to the landmark legal case of Anthony Bland, a young victim of the Hillsborough football disaster of 15 April 1989. He was crushed in the crowd chaos, suffered severe brain damage and was later diagnosed as being in a persistent vegetative state (PVS). But contrary to popular belief, he was not on a life-support machine. His condition was fairly stable and he was able to breathe on his own, though he was fed by means of a nasogastric tube and he needed constant nursing care. In 1992, his hospital, with the agreement of his parents, began a journey through the court system seeking permission to allow him to die. To cut a long story short, the judgement of the Law Lords on 4 February 1993, in the action of Airedale National Health Service Trust v. Bland, in effect legalized euthanasia by omission.

The Law Lords asserted that it would not be unlawful to withdraw treatment from Anthony Bland, so enabling him to die. The Law Lords said that Anthony Bland's life could be prematurely ended because 'treatment was futile' and 'invasive' and such a death was in 'his best interests' since he was 'a living death' with 'no dignity'. However, what caused, and still causes, the bioethical uproar was that the so-called 'treatment' to be withdrawn was artificial nutrition and hydration, otherwise known as 'food and water'. As Melanie Phillips astutely observed, 'If it [nutrition] is treatment, then what precisely is the ailment for which food is the remedy?'[74] In effect, Anthony Bland was dehydrated and starved to death over a nine-day period until, on 3 March 1993, he became the ninety-sixth Hillsborough victim.

Many were alarmed that the law was apparently abdicating to economic and social pressures. Peter Singer, professor of bioethics at Princeton University—and another man with whom bioethically I continually disagree—saw it, quite rightly, as a truly historic judgement. He wrote perceptively in the Prologue of his book *Rethinking Life and Death*,

> After ruling our thoughts and our decisions about life and death for nearly two thousand years, the traditional western ethic has collapsed. To mark the precise moment when the old ethic gave way, a future historian might choose 4 February 1993, when Britain's highest court ruled that doctors attending a young man named Anthony Bland could lawfully act to end the life of their patient.[75]

It is somewhat ironic that, of all people, it is Peter Singer who sums up my thesis in this book, namely, that the ethics and practice of modern medicine have collapsed because they have departed from their twenty-century-old Hippocratic–Christian roots.

The case of Anthony Bland was a victory for the euthanasia lobby. It was a defeat for the practitioners of Hippocratic–Christian medicine. It was a salutary warning for the rest of us. It opened the door to euthanasia, just a chink. Since then, the courts have sanctioned a steady stream of elderly patients, as well as those considered to be in PVS, being 'allowed to die'. Euthanasia is coming in by the back door. Each permissive court case opens that door just a weeny bit more.

3.12.9 EUTHANASIA AND PALLIATIVE CARE

Palliative care is much of the answer, the antidote, to calls for euthanasia. It was described by the UK's National Institute for Health and Clinical

CHAPTER 3

(now Care) Excellence (NICE) as 'the active holistic care of patients with advanced, progressive illness. Management of pain and other symptoms and provision of psychological, social and spiritual support is paramount'.

One major argument often raised in favour of euthanasia is centred on pain, usually physical pain. Not every dying person experiences pain. Furthermore, the skilled use of analgesics has, by and large, eliminated pain as an issue in dying. For some, the problem of pain undeniably exists, but the answer is not to legislate for euthanasia, but to commit more resources and care towards those who are suffering. Such a strategy is reinforced by a World Health Organization Expert Committee Report, *Cancer Pain Relief and Palliative Care*, which stated that 'with the development of modern methods of palliative care legislation of voluntary euthanasia is unnecessary. Now that a practical alternative to death in pain exists, there should be concentrated efforts to implement programmes of palliative care, rather than a yielding to pressure for legal euthanasia'.[76]

You may have noticed a certain paradox here. How is it that, in the twenty-first century, people should want to be euthanized, when palliative care is making such positive advances, and when it has never been so proficient nor so widely available? Medical treatment should always be provided when it will be beneficial to the dying patient, and palliative care when it will not, as admirably demonstrated by the hospice movement and its wonderful work, particularly in the UK under the pioneering aegis of the late Dame Cicely Saunders. Hers was a fascinating and wonderfully inspiring life. I was privileged to meet her at 'her' hospice, St Christopher's in South London, and there is a chapter about her in my book *The Edge of Life*. She once said, 'I didn't set out to change the world, I set out to do something about pain';[77] now she is esteemed as 'the woman who changed the face of death'. We should all be thankful for palliative care and the fact that it is one of the fastest-growing specialties in medicine.

Palliative care seeks to control not just pain, but all adverse symptoms. It is delivered best in dedicated hospices, of which there are now about 220 for adults and 40 for children in the UK. Many hospitals have also established special palliative care units and there is an emergent out-patient movement delivering such care in patients' homes. By 2010, the specialist palliative care workforce in the UK consisted of approximately 7,700 doctors, nurses and allied health professionals, plus 100,000 volunteers, who together

Some of the primary issues

supported a quarter of a million patients in hospitals, hospices and homes. That is good, very good, though it still falls short of the increasing demand. The provision of palliative care is not perfect—its availability and quality vary from place to place. Without doubt, it needs enhanced and more secure funding—about 60 per cent, or £400 million per year, of UK hospice income is generated by voluntary donations. And, yes, the service needs extending to include more non-cancer patients.

Now of all times, it is so defeatist to be campaigning to legalize euthanasia. The dying need assisted living, not assisted dying. They need better care, not killing. Of course, it is cheaper to kill rather than care—a week of hospice care costs £1,000, while a lethal dose of barbiturates costs £10. Such facts will undoubtedly have been raised, mostly tacitly, in many government departmental offices, hospital-management board meetings and public-house saloon bars.

3.12.10 EUTHANASIA: WHY THE APPARENT CLAMOUR?

Various opinion polls suggest that about 82 per cent of Britons favour the legalization of some form of euthanasia. All such *vox populi* require interpretation. For example, 8 out of 10 Britons say they support organ donation, but only 1 in 3 has bothered to sign the register. We can be so fickle. Moreover, the results of such polls depend upon the question asked; crafty wording can manipulate the reply. Ask a loaded question—Should a terminally ill man in pain be allowed to end his life?—and the knee-jerk response would typically be 80 per cent agreement. Then ask a more nuanced question—Should a terminally ill man in pain be allowed to end his life, or be given access to palliative care?—and people begin to think about the issue, consider the implications, and often become less resolute. And then again, the age group surveyed can distort the answer. Ask thirty-somethings about euthanasia and they tend to be in favour; ask pensioners and they tend to be less supportive. In addition, pollsters claim that appeals to self-interest can transform survey results—it is known as 'nudge politics'. With that in mind, I would like to see the outcome of a poll that asks: would you like to be euthanized?

So who are these apparently ardent supporters of euthanasia? Perhaps somewhat contrary to expectation, they are not among the medical professions; these have shown little interest in the topic. The Royal

Chapter 3

College of Physicians, the British Medical Association, the Association for Palliative Medicine, the British Geriatrics Society, the Royal College of General Practitioners, some 65 per cent of all doctors and over 90 per cent of palliative medicine specialists are opposed to any change in the law. So—and this is particularly significant—are all the main UK disability-rights groups, including Disability Rights UK, Scope, the UK Disabled People's Council and Not Dead Yet UK. The disabled realize that, come any change in the law, they would find themselves shunted to the head of the queue. In addition, politicians, with a few outspoken exceptions, are not keen supporters—so far, every euthanasia-type bill presented at Westminster has been roundly defeated. And while the general public may say they favour legalization, they are not exactly lining up for the proposed 'treatment', are they?

3.12.11 EUTHANASIA AND DOCTORS

If euthanasia were to be legalized, doctors would be forced inescapably into the firing line. The consequences would be hideous. Think about the seven following issues. For a start, doctors would lose their long-established role as dedicated healers and instead become life terminators—that would be a grotesque prospect, a real Dr Jekyll and Mr Hyde affair. Currently, doctors have a leading role in preventing suicide; a change in the law would ask them to facilitate suicide. Second, the historic patient–doctor relationship of respect and trust would end. Lying in a hospital bed and hearing the footsteps of an approaching doctor, you would ask yourself: I wonder what he or she has got in mind for me? Third, because most doctors would certainly not participate in the killing of their patients, a new profession of euthanasiasts would be required. Their job would be as sinister as that of the hangman of old, and they would be the most creepy neighbours—imagine chatting over the garden fence about your respective days' work. Fourth, just as easy abortion and covert infanticide have created career difficulties for Christians as well as for the 'morally sensitive' in obstetrics, gynaecology and paediatrics, so euthanasia would produce severe dilemmas for those practising, or wishing to practise, in geriatrics. These previously estimable specialties have become too entangled with the culture of death. This current intrusion of sub-standard medicine means that we are already losing some of our best healthcare professionals. Lawful euthanasia would serve to escalate the exodus.

Fifth, whenever and wherever medicine is practised in an atmosphere of second-rate end-of-life care, it provokes other unsatisfactory 'manners and customs'. It is a sort of medical 'broken-glass syndrome'. Accepted norms can easily become overlooked and overturned. For example, some hospital patients, without any discussion between them and their doctors or their relatives, and certainly not with their own informed consent, are having the scary acronym DNR (Do Not Resuscitate) written on their medical notes. Then again, the purpose and implementation of living wills and advance directives can be troublesome. They can be too subjective and hedonistic. Such bits of paper containing the patient's earlier intentions can be used to override a doctor's clinical judgement, ignore new treatments and sidestep what is currently in the 'best interests' of the patient. In other words, they can tie the doctor's hands and they can result in less-than-best treatment. Moreover, they send out a subtle signal, readily subject to misinterpretation by staff, that the patient wants little or nothing done; that is only a small step away from patient neglect. Such sub-standard practices are unwelcome, not only because they produce shoddy end-of-life care, but also because they encourage a climate of medically assisted suicide. Think how that attitude would zip through the wards if euthanasia were to be legalized. Are these examples of some sort of 'soft' euthanasia, lexically engineered and tiptoeing into hospitals under assumed names and practices?

Sixth, tiptoeing in or not, some doctors are already being accused of practising 'hard' euthanasia. The most recent indictments have centred on the Liverpool Care Pathway (LCP). This was a scheme developed in the 1990s which aimed to integrate the best medical and palliative support during the last days and hours of a patient's life. Though it was employed in the majority of UK hospitals, it remained contentious and in 2013, it was axed. Critics claimed it was a crude, tick-box approach with the potential for hastening death because it could, for instance, prompt the over-hasty removal of artificial hydration and nutrition; in short, they claimed that the LCP was 'back-door' euthanasia. By contrast, its supporters said it provided a positive, structured, integrated approach to end-of-life care and communication. The truth is that, like all medicine, it depends on the

Chapter 3

skills and bioethical values of those practising it. The LCP was merely a written protocol kept somewhere in a document folder on the ward. It was always its implementation that highlighted the twofold possibility of good v. bad medicine. Now the question is: what will replace the LCP? It is not as though there is a corpus of brilliant and untried remedial alternatives waiting to be put into practice.

And this raises yet another associated thorny issue, that of sedation. Again, this can be helpful when used in the palliative context to relieve distress, agitation and anxiety, but utterly unhelpful when used as continuous and deep terminal sedation to ensure that the patient remains unconscious until death—an increasingly common practice in the euthanasia-friendly Netherlands.

Seventh, and lastly, the euthanasia supporters' lobby and their medical allies are usually appalled, if not fiercely outraged, by comparisons made between them and the perpetrators of the Holocaust in Nazi Germany. For a scholarly yet profoundly unsettling account of the history of the latter, read Michael Burleigh's book *Death and Deliverance: 'Euthanasia' in Germany c. 1900–1945*[78] and judge for yourself. Its reviewer for *The Times* memorably wrote, 'This is a terrible book. Everyone ought to read it.'[79] It was German doctors and other medical professionals who were right there in the midst of the Third Reich's devising, developing and implementing of that euthanasia plan. It was doctors as the patrons, the aficionados, of death. Can you believe that? Surely history could not repeat itself—could it?

3.12.12 EUTHANASIA AND LEGAL CRITERIA

As already noted, the problems associated with defining the eligibility criteria and bolstering the safeguards for any prospective law have been the major reasons why so many legislatures have rejected euthanasia—the difficulties are insurmountable. Those governments and other authorities have concluded that the vulnerable, including the elderly, the senile and the disabled, simply cannot be accurately identified and sufficiently protected by legalese, however grand the words printed on paper might be. Such guidelines, rules, regulations and laws can never be redacted to be wholly benign and watertight.

To appreciate something of the problem, consider the impossibility of these six putative qualifying factors. First, the existence of an incurable disease cannot be an acceptable criterion for euthanasia. Many medical conditions are incurable, such as short-sightedness, asthma, some mental illnesses, arthritis and so on. Second, a fatal diagnosis cannot be adequate. Such a diagnosis is not necessarily indicative of imminent demise—death could be years away. Third, there are misdiagnoses, spontaneous remissions and unexpected recoveries—you probably know of some. But if someone has signed up to a euthanasia plan, would such unanticipated occurrences come too late? I used to think this was a rather theoretical objection until a friend recently told me about his neighbour's mother. She was gravely ill and had consented to a euthanasia scheme in Belgium. She then began to recover, but her son's entreaties on her behalf proved to be too late, and she was 'put down' as planned. Fourth, the degree of pain or other suffering cannot be a reliable criterion. It varies from person to person, and besides, many distressing illnesses are physically painless, including Parkinson's and Alzheimer's.

Fifth, depression and its associated disorders cannot be used as an eligibility criterion. Many sufferers of serious illnesses experience acute depression, especially in the early days after initial diagnosis. In such a frame of mind, euthanasia may seem attractive to them. But often those depressive feelings are overcome and a buoyancy returns, perhaps in a month, six months or longer, and they continue to live with dignity, fulfilment and as an inspiration to others. That is to say, it is common knowledge that depressed people change their minds with time. Sixth, the end of a so-called 'rational existence' cannot be a satisfactory qualifying condition for euthanasia. To whom is this old, bed-ridden man no longer of any value? Have all meaning and worth drained from his life as he approaches his end? Try arguing that proposition with a dedicated palliative-care nurse. It was one of Cicely Saunders's maxims that 'The last days must not be lost days'.

3.12.13 EUTHANASIA AND FAMILY BURDENS

Again, if euthanasia were ever to become lawful, it would create huge predicaments for us all. Here are five such burdens. First, living in a future culture of tolerated euthanasia, many of the frail and the elderly would soon start to feel a lumber to their children and grandchildren. For them, any legal 'right to die' would rapidly become a moral 'duty to die'. Second,

Chapter 3

consider the dutiful daughter who has gladly sacrificed her career and social life to care for Mum; she would feel cheated and dishonoured if euthanasia became the accepted convention. Third, there would be financial quandaries. Think about the young family who would begin to begrudge the cost of long-term care as it whittled away the inheritance. Hints about the 'benefits' of voluntary euthanasia would become uncomfortable table talk. Such pressures might prompt Dad to mull over the question: is it now my time to decide to go? Fourth, legalized euthanasia would drag families into more formalized 'quality of life' assessments—a harsh classifying into groups of 'us' and 'them', the latter being those who have 'lives not worthy to be lived'. These appraisals would eventually become simple mathematical equations, balancing the interests of the State v. the patient. They would degenerate to a scheme with a pass mark of, say, 2.0, so with a score of 2.3, you win, but with 1.7, you lose. Fifth, the vulnerable would be increasingly coerced into making life-changing, life-ending decisions. Yet it is well known that many among the senile and the confused, the very targets of euthanasia, habitually experience acute depressive disorders that can result in bad decisions made quickly, under considerable pressure. None of these burdens would foster happy family relationships or social harmony.

At the same time, we must be entirely realistic and practical in this area. Nobody should underestimate the stresses and strains of caring for the sick, the elderly and the dying. For many people, such situations will create problems that need to be confronted and shared, not ignored and shelved—and these dilemmas are always to be resolved with absolutely never a thought, never a hint, of prematurely and deliberately killing Mum or Dad. Again, raising, thinking and talking about these topics and proactively coming to some bioethically sound, family-agreed conclusions in the very near future is prudent; do not wait until it is too late. And when your loved one is dying, make sure you keep clear communication going, not only between family members, but also between you and the medical staff, and especially between you and the patient. Be a brick, not in that toe-curling, bumptious manner, but as the Lord Jesus would be—gently, genuinely and compassionately. Ask questions. Make sure you understand what is happening; what are the patient's diagnosis, prognosis and proposed treatment? Such actions on your part will contribute not only to your loved

Some of the primary issues

one dying well, but also to the experience and memory of a good death by all the other people involved.

3.12.14 FEARS ASSOCIATED WITH DYING AND DEATH

Here's the thing. The majority of us will escape direct, personal involvement with most of the primary bioethical issues already rehearsed in this book—but not this one. This one is unquestionably, inescapably yours (and mine). So, pay attention!

Fears about dying and death abound. Many of them are quite groundless. Here are six. First, we can fear dying and death because we are unsure what it will entail. It will, of course, be a new experience, and we usually fear the unknown. Dying and death are undeniably momentous events. Yet remember this: nearly all of us, you, me and my best friend, will die simply, quietly and unspectacularly. It will be neither complex nor gruelling. While most of us might prefer to die in our own familiar beds, about 50 per cent of us will die in hospital, 20 per cent in a care home, 10 per cent in a hospice and only 20 per cent at home. Second, you will almost certainty not be hooked up to any life-support equipment, such as a ventilator. You therefore need not fear that you will be a victim of a 'pulling the plug' decision. The proper use of such apparatus is to get through an acute crisis, not merely to extend the duration of breathing and heartbeat. In a very, very few circumstances, difficult decisions have to be made and pointless treatments have to be stopped. Even so, the situation of, say, a fourteen-year-old boy who has accidentally nearly drowned in the local swimming pool is very different from that of an eighty-six-year-old man who has advanced cancer and suffers yet another massive stroke—good medicine would not automatically hook up both patients. Third, you may fear that an unscrupulous transplant team will be hanging around eager to harvest your bodily organs in prime condition, so death may be intentionally hastened. That is an improbable occurrence. Perhaps you watch too many hospital dramas on TV. Or perhaps you are fearful that the practice of organ-donation euthanasia (ODE) will spread from permissive Belgium. That is another good reason to keep euthanasia legislation at bay.

Fourth, there is the fear of 'burdensome' and 'futile' medicine. For example, what should be done in the case of a terminally ill man, close to death, with just a few days to live, who suffers a heart attack? He is,

Chapter 3

in all probability, not a suitable candidate for the trauma of open-heart surgery. Similarly with the close-to-death woman with successive and multiple tumours—there comes a point when she is not to be subjected to even more major surgery. And what about the elderly, dying man with recurrent pneumonia, the so-called 'old man's friend'? There is a time to stop pumping him with huge doses of antibiotics in repeated attempts to keep the inflammation of his lungs at bay. These kinds of 'heroic' treatments for patients 'at death's door' are quite inappropriate. The question to ask is this: would any of these measures produce a meaningful extension to life, or just an unnatural and insensitive prolonging of the process of dying? In other words, are they burdensome to the patient and futile to his or her recovery? In these *in extremis* situations, it is sweet palliative care that is needed, not aggressive conventional medicine. These are unfamiliar territories and difficult concepts for many people, but there does come a time when it is only right to stop a treatment and wrong to persist with it—it is called the time to die. Perhaps we harbour doubts about Ecclesiastes 3:2a; 7:2b; Romans 5:12; and Hebrews 9:27. Fifth, some people fear that doctors might prescribe a lethal overdose of drugs, sedatives or painkillers. This is most unlikely. Doctors will invariably go for pain and adverse-symptom control. They may gradually increase doses from a minimum, and if necessary, to a maximum. But 'maximum' is not equivalent to 'lethal'. For example, with diamorphine, the commonest of analgesics used in end-of-life situations, the lethal dose is about four to eight times that of the 'maximum'. And anyway, deliberate overdoses are unlikely to be administered because of their ease of detection.

Sixth, and most importantly—perhaps the most important message of this whole section, if not of the entire book—there really is 'a time to die' (Eccles. 3:2). Yes indeed, every person, every reader of this book and all of those worldwide 7.5 billion non-readers, currently terminally ill or not yet, will die. We all know that cerebrally, as a rational truth, but few of us have grasped it emotionally, as a future, experiential certainty. And yes, I am fully aware of the reality of the Second Coming (John 14:1–3; Acts 1:10–11; 1 Thes. 4:16–17) and thus the escape of death for some. That notwithstanding, our present thinking about these issues of dying and death is probably insufficiently grounded in Scripture, as well as skewed by our society's mores. Here is part of our problem: all our lives we have gone into hospital and then been discharged, by and large restored to health. We carelessly think that this is the pattern for evermore. But a time is coming when we will not walk out of that hospital, care home or hospice, or get up from our own bed. In truth, there is a deathbed for us all. Have you fully realized that yet? Arguably, there is not a more significant and enduring lesson to learn.

3.12.15 DEATH AND THE BIBLE

Much of our confusion about euthanasia is down to our uncertainty about death. Unlike most of us, the Bible tackles the subject of death head-on and in depth. Indeed, it has been argued that there are only two topics throughout the whole Bible—life and death. These two words occur about 1,000 times in a life–death ratio of approximately 60:40, and that somehow seems to be exactly the right balance. Most of us tend to operate on a ratio more like 95:5 and we would doubtless profit from adopting a more biblical ratio in our thinking and living. It is my contention that, while many of us have a decent practical theology of living, in order to counter the menace of modern-day euthanasia we need to develop a better theology of dying and death so that we not only live well, but also die well. If you have a teaching responsibility or a pastoral role in a church, fellowship or other meeting, here is a pertinent question: what are you teaching your people about dying and death? Anything?

Death is thus a central theme of the Bible; one of its commonest phrases is 'and he died'. Death is awesome for at least three reasons. First, because it is the great inevitability. Our days are numbered (Job 14:5; Ps. 139:16). The clock is ticking and the hands ratchet only one way. Death will come to us all—unless, of course, the Parousia, the Second Coming, intervenes (Matt. 24:30–31; 1 Thes. 4:13–18). Second, death is awesome because of its pervasiveness (Eccles. 7:2; Rom. 5:12; Heb. 9:27). Each year, about 54 million people die worldwide. In England and Wales, about 485,000 people die every year, or 1,330 every day, leaving more than 3 million of us, as close family members, bereaved. Third, it is awesome because of its finality (Gen. 2:17; Isa. 40:6–8; Rom. 6:23). Death finishes a life on earth, it terminates relationships and it halts all mortal prospects.

In order to die well, we need to contemplate the above Bible verses alongside that motif from Amos 4:12: 'prepare to meet your God'. We need to grasp Genesis 1–3 and 1 Corinthians 15:26, 42–44; and we need to

Chapter 3

hope in John 14:2–3; Deuteronomy 31:6; Hebrews 13:5; and Matthew 5:4. Therein is gospel comfort and true Christian assurance. And that is not all, because Christ will be there. He will warm our deathbed, he will be our *amicus mortis*, our friend during dying and then at death. Of course, earthly life is precious, but it must end. Yet 'Precious in the sight of the Lord is the death of his saints' (Ps. 116:15). When Christians die, it is sad and moving, but never tragic; rather, it is the fulfilment of their salvation, the gateway to heaven.

We all need to recapture the essence of that original, true euthanasia—dying well, a good death. We have all begun the biological process of dying. Now we need to develop the spiritual process—we must cultivate that theology of living *and* of dying. Most of our days we defy death, but there will come a day when we must submit rather than resist. In that tremendous day, God will 'free those who all their lives were held in slavery by their fear of death' (Heb. 2:15). Such a biblical perspective will shield and deliver us, and those who care for us, from many of those potentially dreadful end-of-life decisions and practices.

3.12.16 EUTHANASIA AND ASSISTED SUICIDE IN THE FUTURE

At last, the elderly are being seen for what they are, or rather, for who we are—the greatest bioethical challenge of the early twenty-first century. During 2010, the over-eighty-year-olds became the fastest-growing age group in the UK. It is now obvious that their current, and certainly their future, medical and care needs will be eye-wateringly costly. Such a realization could help pave the way for the legalization of euthanasia; it will be regarded in some quarters as a good, even essential, course of action. The signs are all around us. Celebrities, professors, churchmen, cultural trendsetters and notable others are coming out in favour of, at least, assisted suicide. Euthanasia talk is commonplace. The chattering classes are taken up with euthanasia in Swiss facilities, TV dramas and documentaries, advocacy groups, parliamentary debates, letters to newspaper editors, police investigations with no prosecutions, and so forth. The principal principle against euthanasia—that intentionally killing people is never good medicine—has been largely forgotten and, for some, the discourse has moved on to disagreements over the finer points of eligibility, safeguards and methods.

SOME OF THE PRIMARY ISSUES

Of course, any such prospective legalization and public policy will still be unpopular and resisted by many, especially those religious folk and their 'morally sensitive' chums. So we will be constantly cajoled to get real, face facts, lighten up, go with the flow, think progressively and consider the benefits that will accrue from a public-policy change. Consider the high financial and personal costs and the other demands of caring for the elderly, along with those guilty consciences among reluctant relatives and disinclined friends: just think, euthanasia will deal with them all, and so neatly. After that, the debate will progress from assisted suicide to voluntary euthanasia, to non-voluntary euthanasia. And why not? Why not help those poor old incompetent folk by making those difficult decisions for them? After all, is not that what personal autonomy and true compassion are all about—accepting people and doing them good? Tut, you Christians, and tut-tut, you morally sensitive!

Can you see where this is going? Are you ready to stand against the flow? The Suicide Act 1961 is already under attack. Its resolute provisions have already been contested. In 2010, the prosecuting criteria behind it were softly 'adjusted' by the Director of Public Prosecutions. Further challenges are in the wings and the pipelines, ready to come to the courts to chip, chip away at it. The claims of Nicklinson, Martin and Lamb have already been mentioned (Section 3.12.7). And while the circumstances of these challengers are unquestionably tragic, such a small number of individual cases must not be allowed to obscure the fundamental bioethical issues. Before long, Parliament will be forced to decide. Perhaps some form of euthanasia, probably assisted suicide, will be legalized, in only a limited way at first, opening the door just a little wider than at present. After all, the currently approved practice of picking off a few elderly patients and some of those in a persistent vegetative state (PVS), by denying them food and drink or resuscitation, is a pretty powerful indicator of the direction of any likely future policy. Their disingenuous enforcement will be the very antithesis of good medicine.

The UK authorities will then turn a bioethical and administrative blind eye to what is really happening, as has occurred in the Netherlands and other euthanasia-approving jurisdictions for many years. Once any form of euthanasia—clinically killing patients prematurely—is established as a legitimate practice within mainstream medicine, Hippocratic–Christian

Chapter 3

medicine itself will have finally died and, potentially, we will all be at risk. Medicine and human life will have been torn asunder. Of course, such a policy will ease the bed-blocking jam in our hospitals—thousands linger there. Of course, it will ease the economic fix in our hospitals—some 50 per cent of lifetime medical costs typically occur in the last year or two of a person's life. Of course, someone, somewhere in the corridors of Whitehall will have done the sums—euthanasia is remarkably cost effective. Of course, it will be presented as a double whammy—it will not only help hospitals achieve, even exceed, their patient-performance targets, but it will also save huge sums of money. Of course, these are the very remedies we need for a struggling National Health Service and for a straitened economy. Who needs bioethics?

3.12.17 EUTHANASIA AND ASSISTED SUICIDE: IN CONCLUSION

What should we think of modern-day euthanasia? Our biblical, bioethical bedrock is this: we believe that it is God who sovereignly gives (Gen. 1:27; Acts 17:28), sustains (Ps. 66:9; Dan. 5:23; Heb. 1:3) and finally takes human life (Job 1:21; Eccles. 8:8). That is to say, it is God who oversaw our conception, who superintends our continuance and who will ensure our consummation. Therefore, we are vehemently opposed to all modern euthanasia, whether it is carried out on the newborn because of some genetic or physical disorder, whether the patient is elderly and judged to have a 'life not worthy to be lived', or whether it is defined in terms of commission or omission, as active or passive, as death with dignity or assisted dying—it matters not a jot. If the intention is to kill the person, it is euthanasia, and it is wrong. Such practices break the Sixth Commandment (Exod. 20:13) and ridicule the Golden Rule (Matt. 22:39). Such procedures abrogate the historic role of the medical profession by ignoring the Hippocratic directive to 'First, do no harm'. Such actions are callous and unworthy of any decent society. Such modern-day euthanasia cannot be regarded as proper medical treatment. Killing the patient must never be the right answer or action.

How far have we already slipped? How many more bioethical Rubicons are there to be crossed? Euthanasia is undoubtedly a great, if not the greatest, twenty-first-century bioethical issue. How our societies approach it and respond to it will be a measure of our integrity and compassion, and our regard for human life. We do not need modern-day euthanasia.

We need to oppose it whatever clothes it wears and in whatever guise it appears. We need to encourage legislation, resources and actions that will support and cherish human physical, mental and spiritual life, in all its stages, especially as the end approaches.

The Christian gospel is the unique message of truth, forgiveness and hope. It proclaims that all human beings, all those bearers of the *imago Dei*, have the offer, the opportunity—even the duty—to be reconciled to their God (John 3:16; 6:40; Rom. 5:10) and so now live, and then die, in peace and happy assurance (Rom. 5:1; Phil. 1:20–21; Heb. 6:11). Moreover, the people of God are entrusted with this gospel to demonstrate to all people not only how to live well, but also how to die well. Christians must therefore be in the forefront by practising principled compassion towards all those who are lost and suffering—the weary, the wounded and the sad—including, of course, the dying.

3.13 The primary issues: in conclusion

Well, you have reached the end of the chunkiest chapter of this book. Congratulations, especially if you have grasped something of the primary issues and my explanations and arguments. If I have made you think long and hard, my job is almost done. 'Enough is enough,' I hear you cry. Yet these have been only outlines of some—specifically eleven—of the primary bioethical issues. There are other topics, like organ donation, cognitive-enhancing drugs, contraception, nanotechnologies, transgenderism, synthetic biology and quite a few more. But if eleven players are enough to make a fully-fledged team—perhaps for cricket, soccer, hockey or even bandy—then surely eleven issues grasped can make a bioethically informed Christian.

In conclusion, the task now before us will not be easy. Understanding and responding to these bioethical issues will create all sorts of tensions and problems for the Christian. When we read about the need for human embryo research to prevent human suffering and medical tragedies, are we not being hard-hearted to oppose it? When we hear the harrowing stories of the infertile, can you not begin to realize their hopes of IVF or surrogacy? When you see the tensions created by looking after senile parents, can you not understand the attraction of assisted suicide or euthanasia, at least of the voluntary variety? When you learn of problem pregnancies, would not

Chapter 3

some be better dealt with by abortion? Do you not feel yourself to be a bioethical worm to be against all this? Well, we must learn to master our emotions and to handle these pressures. And the best, indeed the only, way forward is to increase our knowledge and understanding of these topics. Otherwise, we will be continually climbing onto an intellectual and emotional rollercoaster—we will be tossed around, like corks on the sea, and our thinking and responses will be habitually uncertain and unhelpful. But, with our robust biblical credenda and agenda, our words and deeds will be both sure and supportive, driven by principled compassion. Our resistance to the culture of death and our promotion of the culture of life must be nothing other than this thoroughgoing head-heart-hand affair.

QUESTIONS FOR PERSONAL REFLECTION AND GROUP DISCUSSION

1. Is abortion really the keystone topic among these primary issues? Why or why not?

2. Disability is a recurring theme among these primary issues. Why is that?

3. How does the culture of death currently impinge upon your life?

4. Have you ever thought realistically about dying and death?

5. Have you resolved the issues surrounding burdensome and futile treatments?

6. Are you now ready to talk with, for example, your workmate, neighbour or cousin about these issues?

7. Which 'new' or 'old' bioethical issues are likely to dominate during the next decade or so?

CHAPTER 4

Some of the secondary issues

By definition, primary issues are paramount, yet secondary issues are not unimportant. There are at least fifteen secondary, or peripheral, issues that can help us grasp these primary bioethical issues more firmly; they will bring them more clearly into focus and context. Additionally, they will help us better understand where other people are 'coming from', and enable us to communicate with them, not only more knowledgeably, but also more cogently.

4.1 The need for ethical integration

This book is all about bioethical issues as they relate to human medicine. But such concerns must never be neatly pigeonholed and segregated from other ethical issues that surround, say, education or economics, family or famine, poverty or politics. We must not become 'single-issue' people. We must strive to be integrated people, head-heart-hand people—never double-minded—with a consistent, coherent and stalwart ethical response to all of life's issues, bioethical and otherwise. Only Christianity delivers all this. This must therefore be the threefold aim of every Christian: to be mature, with the mind of Christ (1 Cor. 2:16); informed by the Word of God (2 Tim. 3:16); and guided by the Holy Spirit (John 16:13).

4.2 A false view of bioethics

There is no doubt that Christians would like to ban, or, at least, severely restrict, many practices within the culture of death. Some people will therefore accuse us of simply wanting to change the law on, say, abortion or destructive human embryo research, and thereby impose a Christian ethic on a pluralistic society. This argument reflects a false view of the relationship between ethics and law. All laws reflect a society's sense of justice and fairness, and they therefore inevitably contain an ethical component; the

Chapter 4

idea of an ethically neutral law is an illusion. The question therefore is not *whether* laws should reflect an ethical worldview, but rather *which* ethical worldview should they reflect? So why should the ethics of historic, orthodox, biblical Christianity be excluded from legal and public-policy debates? If Christians do not stand up and speak up, others certainly will.

Let us be realistic. Any serious alteration to the law on, say, abortion will come not as a surprise, overnight. It will come as the result of a steady transformation of the hearts and minds of the people, the electorate, which will eventually be reflected in Parliament with an amendment to, and ultimately the repeal of, the Abortion Act 1967. This will take—indeed, is taking—considerable time. Remember the long-drawn-out campaign that finally led to the nineteenth-century victory over the wicked practice of slavery.

Furthermore, and this point deserves repeating, we all 'own' bioethics. It is wrong to think that bioethical issues are the exclusive domain of doctors, scientists, lawyers, politicians, academics, media know-alls and other alleged experts. Such men and women do not necessarily have any special bioethical insight—indeed, nor will we unless we work at it. Bioethical issues belong to us all. They affect us all. They sit on our doorstep. That is why we all need to grasp something of these issues, instead of passing the buck and leaving them to others, as if they were none of our business.

4.3 Understanding the times

We are living in times when traditional bioethical foundations are being uprooted, and time-honoured customs and conduct are under attack. Some call it a postmodern, post-Christian, metamodern, even a post-postmodern era. In short, Christianity is on the rack and it seems fashionable to bash a Christian—although perhaps it was ever thus. We shall swiftly pass over the facts, published in 2012, that 59 per cent of people in Britain and 73 per cent in the USA identify themselves as 'Christian'. Despite those seemingly optimistic statistics, there is undoubtedly a revitalized secular humanism and an aggressive and intolerant atheism prowling around out there. Add to these troubles and troublemakers the other diverse supporters of the culture of death and we may fear that we have hardly any legitimate answers, and even fewer true friends. These resurgent ideologies and their adherents can be intimidating because they regard most things Christian as fair game, and when targeted too many Christians appear either dumbstruck or ill-equipped to respond. There is no time like the present to redress these failings and deficiencies. Therefore, get knowledge and take action. And may God 'encourage your hearts and strengthen you in every good deed and word' (2 Thes. 2:17). Now is not the time to faint, or feint.

4.4 Everyone has a worldview

We all have a worldview, a *Weltanschauung* (from the German *Welt*, world, and *Anschauung*, outlook). It determines the way we think and act. Everyone has a moral compass, a private morality. Every secular humanist has an array of personal convictions, every atheist has a canon, every eco-warrior has a mantra, every pantheist has a cosmic consciousness, every animal-rights activist has a creed, every New Age eccentric has a guide, every agnostic has a panoply of uncertainties. As Paul declared to his sophisticated but pagan and idol-worshipping audience at the Areopagus, 'I see that in every way you are very religious' (Acts 17:22). Two thousand years later, that assessment still holds. We are all predisposed to be 'very religious', to believe and to worship, to yearn for something more, to find our place in the big picture. The reason for religion, whether the true or an aberrant version, is because we are bearers of the *imago Dei*, an indissoluble Creator–creature bond exists and we are thus naturally inclined towards God—we are hard-wired that way. As Paul then went on to confirm, 'For in him [God] we live and move and have our being' (Acts 17:28). Christians gladly confess this; unbelievers deny, or even loathe, the very notion. They refuse to acknowledge the triune God and instead they revere and rely upon strange idols, including mainly themselves (Rom. 1:19–23).

The Christian's worldview is therefore God-centred, whereas that of the secularist, the neo-pagan, the humanist and the atheist is man-centred. Contrary to that of the Christian, the unbeliever's worldview is typically informal, non-doctrinal, unwritten, non-monotheistic and non-transcendent. Yet unbelievers also possess a set of beliefs, themes, values, ethics and emotions about 'life, the universe and everything'. By any other name, their worldview is almost a religion, or at the least, a pseudo-religion, and they exhibit a quasi-religious faith.

So when that disparaging voice—be it of some hubristic scientist or your nice next-door neighbour—seeks to dismiss you and your worldview

Chapter 4

because you and your ideas are Christian, evangelical, fundamentalist, old-fashioned or just plain religious, do not take it. Withstand it. Explain that they too express trust, conviction, hope and belief in something—perhaps science, fate, astrology or some -ism—or in someone—perhaps a clairvoyant, a celebrity, their mother or probably themselves—and so they are not as devoutly non-religious as they might either wish or profess. Dictionary definitions of religion as 'the belief in a personal God' as well as 'a thing that one is devoted to' are remarkably broad. Show me a non-religious person and I will show you a cadaver. End of pointless argument; let's move on.

4.5 Science and scientism

The topics of science and scientism are distinct, yet related. Science, in this context, is the stuff we learned at school—chemistry, physics, biology and so on. Such supposedly 'hard' science deals with factual information about the material and living universe, its laws and its phenomena. At its core, science depends upon the scientific method. This is the way in which new scientific knowledge is obtained, and it involves systematic observation, measurement and experimentation, plus the formulation, testing and modification of hypotheses. At a practical level, it means that a scientific experiment conducted in London will give the same results when meticulously repeated in Aberystwyth or Tokyo. Science works because of the basic laws of the universe—a concept that presents no problem for Christians and their Creator God.

On the other hand, scientism is a philosophy. It is an illegitimate extension of true science. It is a worldview which declares that 'all there is' and 'all that can be known' must be forced through the prism of the scientific method. Simply put, scientism says that science is king. It declares that if you cannot measure an entity, if it cannot be verified by the scientific method—be it love, the dignity of human life, justice, Christian experience or the significance of fatherhood—it is merely opinion or fantasy. And the dangerous corollary is that scientists alone have the right to formulate a society's ethics, practices and public policies, merely on the basis of their scientific expertise—it is the coming of out-and-out technocracy.

Science is our ally from which we have nothing to fear. Why should the Christian be afraid of truth? Scientism is our enemy. It believes that science will overcome all the limitations of the human condition. It constructs a deterministic belief system that is devoid of any *imago Dei* attributes. It produces a reductionist and amoral outlook on the world, one which approves of all the activities within the culture of death. It holds that since the bioethical worth of an embryo cannot be quantified, or the moral value of a dying man cannot be computed, such characteristics are meaningless, so what reason can there be for not destroying both? Scientism is becoming a bane of twenty-first-century bioethics.

4.6 The importance of presuppositions

Everyone comes to every bioethical debate with presuppositions; none comes empty-headed. These presuppositions are part of everyone's worldview, that frame of reference and the means by which we decide what is right and what is wrong, what we should and should not do.

These presuppositions are picked up from parents, peers, papers and so forth, and they are expressed in the language people use. We need to be aware and recognize this; presuppositions are everywhere, and they can be very subtle. They often emerge in what I call lexical engineering—bioethical wordplay, distorting language for a purpose. Various examples have already been given, but here are some more. A while ago, I was on the radio pitted against the Director of the Nuffield Council on Bioethics, who was trying to defend the destruction of human embryos for therapeutic cloning on the grounds that they were 'only very early' embryos—as if the addition of two adverbs and an adjective somehow makes their deliberate extermination acceptable. Or again, there was a time when the pre-fourteen-day human embryo was frequently referred to as a 'pre-embryo'. But, in deploring the coining of this new-fangled term, the *New Scientist* forthrightly stated, 'Definitions are as important in science as the truth. Calling things by other names to suit the arguments will fool no-one.'[1] Yet some scientists still persist in demeaningly talking about 'a fertilized egg' instead of a zygote or an early embryo. Others like to lump together adult and embryonic stem-cell technologies, as if there were no bioethical conflicts between the two practices. So is an abortion a termination of a pregnancy, a TOP, the removal of uterine contents, an interruption of a pregnancy, or the taking of the life of an unborn child? Is a human embryo a potential human being,

Chapter 4

or a human being with potential? Does dying with dignity refer to palliative care or assisted suicide? It makes a world of difference.

We should also remember that a person's presuppositions will permeate and spill over into other bioethical issues. For example, a pro-abortionist is unlikely to have many reservations about destructive experimentation on human embryos. Similarly, someone already in favour of voluntary euthanasia will, in all probability, easily be persuaded of the merits of non-voluntary, or perhaps even involuntary, euthanasia.

We should also be able to recognize the presuppositional blind spots of others. For example, I have never understood why, on the one hand, the National Union of Students will campaign against racism and ethnic cleansing, will allow no discrimination against disabled people, and will even spend serious sums of money on wheelchair access and the like; yet, on the other hand, it will blindly give financial support to, for instance, Abortion Rights, an organization that has consistently campaigned for the abortion of the disabled, up to birth.[2] Or why is it that Western, pro-choice feminists raise no objections to the unbridled gender-based abortions occurring in countries such as India and China, when it is unborn girls who are mostly being killed? These are clear cases of bioethical duplicity based on deep-seated, but also deeply-flawed, presuppositions.

4.7 Consequences and principles

The terms 'pro-life' and 'pro-choice' are often employed as bioethical shorthand. They may at times be caricatures, but they are helpful here in denoting those who generally uphold the culture of life and those who support the culture of death.

As previously stated, people's bioethical opinions and options are determined by their worldviews and presuppositions. This leads to the concept of consequences and principles. For example, the arguments and decisions made by pro-choice people are nearly always based upon consequences that tend to emphasize a person's autonomy, that is, 'what is best for me'. Abortion is the great example. Here the typical consequence-based arguments are, 'I don't want it because I couldn't cope'; 'Now is not a good time for me to be having a baby'; 'My parents would throw me out if they knew'. The problem with this type of argument is that we are unable to control or predict the actual consequences, so that any decision resting on consequences alone is inevitably built on incomplete data, on shifting sand. For instance, a student, shocked at being told she is pregnant, requests an abortion because she feels isolated and without help and hope; the immediate consequences of continuing with the pregnancy look too grim. But, in the ensuing days, she may change her mind, especially if her friends, parents, university tutor and father of the child rally round; that is, those predicted grim consequences that formed the basis of her original decision to abort have changed. Her circumstances have shifted.

On the other hand, pro-life arguments and decision-making processes tend to be principle-based. 'It's wrong to deny anyone the right to life.' 'All euthanasia is bad medicine.' 'Remember the Sixth Commandment.' Sometimes, pro-life people can sound so principle-minded that it seems as though they are not interested in the consequences to the woman and child, or to the disabled, or senile, person. Such an approach can be cold and cruel, cerebral and cloistered. Moreover, it is not the authentic Christian response. When formulating arguments and making bioethical decisions, Christians should be concerned about both principles and consequences. Our responses must be rooted in principles that are compassionate, as well as in compassion that regards consequences—in other words, principled compassion.

4.8 Human value and worth

The question of human value and worth should not be a problem for the Christian, but it certainly can be for the non-Christian. Today, men and women are commonly judged by extrinsic factors—how much they earn, what they do for a living, the size of their houses or the extent of their social networks—rather than by intrinsic factors—who they are, what makes them tick, what they enjoy or dislike, and so on, highlighting their own inherent value and worth simply because they are human beings, bearers of the *imago Dei*. Such contemporary, vulgar assessments of people can lead to a serious problem; those who earn or own little, or who make little or no apparent contribution to the community, are then often seen as a drag on society and as a burden to family and friends, and therefore of little or no worth. Historically, people of limited value and worth have been considered to have 'life not worthy to be lived', *lebensunwertes Leben*—the very maxim of the Nazi regime.

Chapter 4

And there is a supplementary, more subtle, aspect to this topic, especially in relation to discrimination against the disabled. People with physical or mental disabilities are usually instantly recognizable, and so we tend to weigh up quickly whether to help, hinder or leave them alone. Because we often fail to engage with the disabled, our judgements based on their intrinsic factors are typically incomplete and therefore inadequate. Instead, we hurriedly appraise them according to extrinsic factors, made on largely assumed and often biased or erroneous information. That is why our assessments of the disabled are frequently mistaken and sometimes malicious. Thus, we can easily become discriminatory and less than kind-hearted people.

4.9 The meaning of autonomy

'Autonomy' (from the Greek *autos*, self, and *nomos*, law) means 'self-government' or 'personal freedom'. When properly applied, this word can rightfully stress the moral responsibility that each of us should exercise. For example, medicine has, in recent times, seen a welcome movement away from some of the awful medical paternalism of the past—'I'm the doctor, and I know what's best for you'—towards a more reasonable patient autonomy—'But I'm the patient, so please explain it to me.' Such an appropriate application of conditional autonomy can only be beneficial to all concerned.

However, like several other decent bioethical words and concepts, autonomy has now taken on a more malevolent meaning. By claiming it to be unconditional, it now carries a connotation of 'lawlessness'. As one of the buzzwords of modern bioethics, 'autonomy' now expresses the idea that we have the right, and even the duty, to do whatever we want with our own lives, that there should be no limits, legal or otherwise, to our individual freedom. Therefore, we can set our own personal rules and our own private standards for morality and behaviour. This, of course, is nonsense. As members of any society, we all accept certain boundaries to our freedom, such as observing speed limits, paying taxes and, where indicated, keeping off the grass.

In the realm of bioethics, misapplied, unconditional, absolute autonomy produces self-centred responses like, 'It's my life, it's my body, and it's my decision' and 'I will choose to die when, where and how I want to'. But what does a person mean when he or she proclaims, for instance, 'It's my life'? If a woman says, 'It's my book', we all understand that she bought it, she read it, she put it on her shelf and so on. But 'my book' is in an entirely different category from 'my life', unless, of course, you hold that everything—human life, society, a book and the entire universe—is just a mechanistic phenomenon, a matter of merely the atomic and the molecular.

Such an overdose of autonomy can be disastrous. It allows the individual to take centre stage, to be the prima donna or the leading man. So, for example, it excludes others from what would best be relational, family-based or even society-centred decisions. It can sideline family, friends, wise counsellors and—perhaps most importantly in, for example, the case of aborting the unborn child—the father.

Autonomy, as a key feature of modern bioethics, puts the individual above all others, and it puts self, rather than God, at the very centre—a defining characteristic of secular humanism. Think of all those unattractive, un-Christian words like self-aggrandizement, self-assertion, self-centred, self-contained, self-indulgent, self-reliant, self-righteous, self-seeking and self-sufficient, and you will begin to understand both the meaning and the end product of unconditional autonomy.

4.10 The problem of rights

This leads to the subject of rights. There are huge difficulties here for the Christian. The idea of rights originated from a European liberal tradition some eight hundred years ago, rather than from the Bible and the Christian worldview. It began to blossom in the seventeenth century so that these days, 'rights talk', 'rights language' and 'rights-based morality' are common parlance in the students' union, the workplace and among all who feel they have a grievance to be aired. Nowadays, everybody everywhere is encouraged to 'claim your rights' and to 'get what is rightly yours'. Ours has indeed become the Age of Entitlement.

On 2 October 2000, the Human Rights Act 1998 came into force as the UK ratified the European Convention on Human Rights 1950 (ECHR). This was the UK's first written statement of people's rights. Sitting at the top of the list of the eighteen is, interestingly in the context of this book, Article 2, which categorically states, 'Everyone's right to life shall be protected by

Chapter 4

law.' However, what this actually means for human embryos, the unborn, the newborn and the elderly has yet to be tested in our courts.

Even so, this human-rights culture has already infiltrated many areas of bioethics, and the outcome has not been good. A woman may talk about insisting upon her rights, but subtly the dynamics of such insistence often conceal the fact that she is actually making claims upon others. She may consider that it is her 'right' to have a child, so she claims this from her doctor—he must arrange IVF treatment for her. Similarly, a doctor must arrange an abortion for another woman, because that is her reproductive health 'right'. Or, because the old man thinks he has a 'right' to die, his doctor must at least arrange, if not actually participate in, his assisted suicide.

All this talk of rights creates additional problems for the thinking Christian. What is the origin of these rights—are they given by God, by society or by self? What are their limits—are they personal and ephemeral, or are they universal and permanent? What is their hierarchy, their pecking order—is the right to work superseded by the right to life, or the right to freedom? Are a mother's rights greater than those of her unborn child? Who decides when there is a conflict of rights—is it the patient, the family, the doctor, the hospital ethics committee or the courts?

The Scriptures take a quite different tack. They stress our responsibilities rather than our rights. The Christian mind has a well-developed sense of gratitude. Christians know that they are debtors, that they are owed nothing, and that all they are and all they possess has been given by the grace of God alone (Ps. 130:3–4; Eph. 2:8). So a Christian will not be constantly 'on the take', but rather 'on the give'. A Christian will major on his or her responsibilities, duties and obligations, not on his or her so-called rights. Was it the robbed and beaten man's right to be helped, or was it the good Samaritan's responsibility to assist him (Luke 10:25–37)? Was it Paul's right to expect the hospitality of Gaius, or was it Gaius's duty to look after the apostle (Rom. 16:23)? I think you know.

4.11 The nature of dependency

Mutual dependency is a Christian characteristic. Yet some people disparage such a notion. For example, proponents of euthanasia consider that dependency on others can be degrading and dehumanizing. 'People', they say, 'should be free to live and to die as they see fit. They should be totally at liberty to decide for themselves. They should be wholly independent and unbothered by others.' But such utter independency is the ugly sister of autonomy. It is like the young rebel who longs to be free, with no limits, no rules, no parents, no nothing—totally independent and totally autonomous. Oh, but he soon discovers that the good life does not work that way. He is obliged to become dependent on other people and society. It is the rules that make the game—laws protect him, parents are valuable, others are supportive, a job is useful, relationships are rewarding and so on. There is nothing degrading or dehumanizing about such reliance; in fact, quite the opposite.

As John Donne famously wrote in his Meditation XVII, 'No man is an Island, entire of itself', and more appositely Paul wrote in Romans 14:7, 'For none of us lives to himself alone and none of us dies to himself alone.' So dependency is a feature of proper living—not only dependency upon God, but also dependency upon others within a community. Christians, above all others, should be living in mutual inter-dependency (Rom. 12:4–5; 1 Peter 2:4–10), and perhaps we need to recover and reaffirm this theme. Such a recovery would counter the sterile individualism, and even the widespread isolation and loneliness, of much of our society, with its overemphasis on personal autonomy and rights. For the Christian, it is the church, the body of Christ, that is the working model (Rom. 12:4–8; 1 Cor. 12:12–31) and it is the Bible, the Word of Christ, that is the instruction manual. It is here that the good life and its in-built dependency are best expounded.

4.12 Changing views of the medical profession

As previously explained (see Chapter 1), massive changes have occurred in medical ethics and practice during the last sixty or so years. Alongside these have been changes in the way we, the general public, perceive the medical profession. Nowadays, doctors are less likely to be those old-fashioned carers and healers who know all about us and our families. Instead, they are more likely to be career-conscious professionals and modern-day resource-allocators, often far removed, in thought and action, from those under the original Hippocratic–Christian type of patient–doctor relationship.

Furthermore, we now tend to regard and treat doctors as 'need-meeters'. We ask, and they provide. You are pregnant and do not want to be, so you

Chapter 4

go along to your doctor and say, 'Please meet my need.' You are infertile and you say, 'Please answer my request.' Your life is miserable and you say, 'Please grant my wish.' This fulfilling of 'my needs' is analogous to that of 'my rights'—it just appears to be a little more courteous.

Sadly, more and more doctors are becoming mere public servants, medical functionaries, doing what other people tell them to do, rather than bravely abiding by the original ideals of their profession. Of course, this new perception of the medical profession is especially unnerving within the culture of death. Here doctors are no longer healers and preservers, but rather takers and dispatchers of human life. They are the social executioners of our time. We approve abortion—they do it. We want infanticide—they carry it out. We legalize euthanasia—they perform it.

At this point, do not misunderstand me, please. None of this is a vendetta against the entire medical profession. While this book steadfastly and uncompromisingly declares that, to a large extent, modern medicine has lost its way, both ethically and practically, because it has departed from its Hippocratic–Christian roots, the condemnation is not universal. Way back in the Preface, I wrote, 'Of course, not all medicine has become so corrupted or tainted.' Out there are some of the finest, most bioethically scrupulous medical practitioners and healthcare workers you could ever wish to meet—I am privileged to know some as good friends. On the other hand, I have also met some medical shysters. I trust there is no ambiguity about this matter.

4.13 Financial resources and medicine

Medicine costs money, and economics influences the practice of medicine. There is always a finite pot of cash and infinite ways to spend it. Not every procedure, operation or drug regimen can be afforded. In a word, there has to be 'rationing', as it used to be called—what is now known as 'resource allocation' and what will, in the near future, probably be termed 'financial sustainability'. Whatever it is called, its implementation should be honest and equitable; the poor, the small and the vulnerable must not be discounted or sidelined.

Our society tends to make more and more judgements based on economic criteria and on people's apparent or imagined value and worth, but such monetary-based thinking and practice must be resisted. To this end, the increasing involvement of Christians in costly caring initiatives—such as homes for the elderly, housing for the disabled, accommodation and practical care for pregnant women and girls, respite services for carers, palliative care and hospice provision—is to be warmly welcomed and encouraged. But more is always needed—the State cannot, or will not, or should not, ever provide enough. Step up, you wealthy, or rather, you generous, do-gooders! And remember, 'God loves a cheerful giver' (2 Cor. 9:7).

4.14 The changing role of the law

Parallel to these changes in medicine have come changes in the law. What has happened with abortion law is very instructive. The UK's abortion law was changed radically by the Abortion Act 1967. The new law gave permission for abortion to be performed under certain quite limited circumstances. But that original *permission* soon became an *expectation*. Any pregnant woman attending an abortion clinic expected a termination. But that expectation has now become a *requirement*. In the current climate of virtually 'abortion on demand' or the 'free supply of abortion', a woman no longer simply expects, but now actually insists upon, an abortion. Can you see the reality of this legal version of the slippery slope? Think how this might affect, for example, euthanasia legislation. The legal boundaries and safeguards in these matters of life and death need to be much more carefully and tightly drawn; loopholes, rather than getting plugged, have a nasty habit of getting stretched, and sometimes they even break.

4.15 The slippery slope

This brings us to what some bioethicists call the 'slippery slope', the 'thin end of the wedge', the 'opening of the door', the 'domino effect', 'mission creep' and other such phrases. Whatever it is called, the idea is simple: once a previously unthinkable practice has been legalized, that practice inevitably grows in public acceptability, and it also grows numerically. There are two main causes of this phenomenon. First, the very bases of many Acts of Parliament, government regulations or quango guidelines are arbitrary. They reflect the lack of any coherent bioethical foundation. They contain vague words like 'substantial' and 'normally'. These cause general confusion, which allows interpretation, which in turn encourages not just a moving, but also a widening, of the goalposts. Second, any

Chapter 4

particular bioethical practice will throw up 'difficult' or 'hard' cases. These go through the courts, which make new case law, expanding the original legal boundaries. Yes, the old saying is true: hard cases make bad law. The legally permitted death of the few, be they embryos, foetuses, unborn children or the elderly, will, without doubt, over the years, become the death of the many. The wedge will penetrate deeper and deeper, the door will slowly be opened wider and wider. The once unthinkable will soon become the acceptable; the once limited will soon become the widespread.

Just three examples, already alluded to in earlier sections, should suffice to demonstrate the reality and diversity of the slippery slope. First, as explained in Section 3.2.1, it is seen numerically with abortion. In 1966, there were 6,100 recorded abortions in NHS hospitals. During 1968, the year the provisions of the infamous 1967 Act came into effect and legalized abortion was getting underway, the slippery slope had begun and there were 23,641 abortions in England and Wales. A mere five years later we were slipping down the slope helter-skelter and there were 167,149 abortions—a sevenfold increase; now, at the start of the twenty-first century, the total hovers around the 200,000 mark. The steepness of, and the speed with which we have hurtled down, this slope have taken even some pro-abortion parliamentarians and others quite by surprise.

Second, it is seen in broken promises, with the misnamed emergency hormonal 'contraception' (EHC), the morning-after pill (MAP). As described in Section 3.2.3, MAPs contain a high dose of progestogen, and since one of its modes of action occurs *after* fertilization, it can function as an abortifacient. MAPs were introduced into the UK in the 1980s, amid protests from many pro-life people, but with reassurances from the Department of Health and Social Security that they would be used only in exceptional circumstances, and that they would remain as prescription-only drugs. At the end of 2000, the government approved them for over-the-counter sales at chemists to girls over sixteen. By the beginning of 2001, they were available for under-age girls from nurses working in State schools. No longer were doctors required to supervise their use and no longer were they regarded as 'emergency-only': street-wise girls began to carry them in their handbags as an 'ever-ready' aid, just in case. The once-tight regulations had been relaxed—we were now well down that slippery slope. What next? Will MAPs be available at all good newsagents and petrol stations? Will

SOME OF THE SECONDARY ISSUES

they be included in pupils' welcome packs on their first day at secondary school?

Third, it is seen in society's thinking with regard to the disabled. The required low-grade political, medical and social mindsets were formulated during the early twentieth century; as outlined in Section 3.8.2, eugenics was modish among many of the so-called intelligentsia, and thus the disabled were repeatedly deemed to have 'lives not worthy to be lived'. Therefore, it was decided that we should do our best to get rid of them, as early as possible, and preferably before they made their presence felt, or seen. In other words, both of society's bioethical feet were firmly planted on the slippery eugenic slope. By the late twentieth century, the 'search and destroy' armoury, namely, the package of screening plus prenatal diagnosis (PND) plus abortion, was well established, as already detailed in Section 3.9.3. Now, during the twenty-first century, the entire spectrum of destructive practices for the disabled is available. It begins with detecting, by preimplantation genetic diagnosis (PGD), and then destroying the disabled as genetically faulty embryos; then it descends to terminating the handicapped unborn (abortion); then there is a rapid descent that brings about the death of the impaired newborn (infanticide); and finally there are procedures for getting rid of the genetically deficient elderly (euthanasia).

But some notable bioethical commentators disagree. They see no slippery slopes, wedges, doors or dominoes. Consider two examples. First, the case of Regina v. Arthur was probably the most famous infanticide trial of the last century. It has already been discussed in Section 3.11.8. In 1980, Dr Leonard Arthur had prescribed dihydrocodeine and 'nursing care only' to John Pearson, a newborn infant with Down's syndrome, who died, poisoned by the drug, three days later. Dr Arthur was charged with attempted murder but was later acquitted. It was, and still is, a controversial verdict. The then doyen of bioethical law, Professor Ian Kennedy of London University, wrote an article in *New Society* entitled 'Reflections on the Arthur Trial'. He concluded, 'I am not persuaded of the inevitability of the wedge argument—that one step down the road towards removing one class of the disabled, the very severely disabled child, from our midst, means that we must inevitably take the next step.'[3] Professor Kennedy does not appear to understand either the flow of bioethical history or human nature. Or maybe both. Second, and similarly, Britain's current doyenne

CHAPTER 4

of all things bioethical, Baroness Warnock, has expressed contempt for the slippery-slope argument. She maintains in her book *An Intelligent Person's Guide to Ethics* that it is 'an illogical argument' which is 'used by people who do not trust doctors or hospital ethics committees'.[4] Well, you are partly right there, Mrs Warnock! Years after making their statements, given the subsequent course taken by most bioethical issues, I wonder whether Professor Sir Ian Kennedy and Baroness Warnock would still hold such sanguine views.

4.16 Secondary issues: in conclusion

Fifteen secondary issues have been outlined here. They lie in ambush, lurking in the background of any discussion of bioethical issues. Understand them and you will be better informed and better equipped to meet the day, the opposition and, perhaps more likely, the just plain undecided. Happy articulation—keep it clear and expressive!

QUESTIONS FOR PERSONAL REFLECTION AND GROUP DISCUSSION

1. *Which of these secondary issues particularly shed light on the primary issues?*

2. *How would you rank these secondary issues in order of importance?*

3. *What other secondary issues can you think of?*

4. *What are the presuppositions you bring to bioethical discussions?*

5. *Are terms like 'pro-life', 'pro-choice' and 'slippery slope' useful or useless? Why?*

6. *Is discussing these secondary issues just a distraction from the primary issues?*

7. *What have been the greatest influences upon the formation of your worldview?*

CHAPTER 5

When does human life begin?

The most commonly asked—and arguably the most inadequately answered—question in the whole of bioethics is this: when does human life begin? It certainly is a big question. The answer you give indicates your views on practically every bioethical issue. It will reveal your thinking on the biological, legal and sociological nature and status of the human embryo, your regard for the human foetus, how you would treat the unborn and newborn child, and even your attitude towards those at the other end of the age spectrum, the elderly. But there is much more at stake here than revealing just your own worldview. This great question also has a collective, societal answer. For with the answer comes the implicit understanding of when 'it' is worthy of some respect, and when 'it' is to be protected by the mores and laws of society. So the question is pointed—it has both a private and a public dimension—and the answer is pivotal—it either opens, or closes, the door on the culture of death.

Some people, quite wrongly, consider that these two aspects of the start and status of human life should be kept separate. They say that the first is a biological issue, whereas the second is an ethical issue. For instance, Peter Singer, renowned professor of bioethics at Princeton University, betrayed this error in his letter to *The New York Times*: 'The crucial moral question is not when human life begins, but when human life reaches the point at which it merits protection. Unless we separate these two questions ... we are unlikely to achieve any clarity about the moral status of embryos.'[1] Such an approach fails to appreciate that it is factual evidence that determines the ethical practice—information decides policy, knowledge predicates deed. It is that credenda–agenda link again. In other words, whenever human life is deemed to begin (the credenda) *is* the point when protection is to be conferred (the agenda). Bioethical questions demand integrated thinking: it is credenda *plus* agenda. The two must be kept inseparable, inextricably bound together, like a horse and cart. Moreover, the two must also be kept

Bioethical Issues **221**

Chapter 5

sequential, one after the other, like the horse and then the cart. They must be kept inseparable because if, for example, we knew that human life did not begin until, say, twenty-four weeks (the credenda), it would follow that abortion of the unborn (the agenda) would be entirely unobjectionable. They must be kept sequential because modern-day bioethicists tend first to approve a particular practice (such as their abortion agenda) and only afterwards search for supporting evidence (such as the idea that life begins at viability, their credenda). They say, 'We agree with abortion; now let's think why.' Similarly, as explained above in Section 3.5.1, the Warnock Committee first endorsed human embryo experimentation (its agenda) and only afterwards concocted the fourteen-day rule (its credenda). It is that erroneous cart-before-the-horse bioethics again. Proper bioethics consists of credenda first, agenda second: truth then action, understanding then responding, principles then regulations; both together, securely integrated, not separated, in series, sequent and consequent. In other words, the start of life *is* the point at which protection is merited. Thus, there are not two questions to answer. There is only one, yet the answer brings with it huge ramifications.

Because of its centrality in bioethical issues, this whole chapter is devoted to a discussion of this big question. True, we have already considered the biblical evidence in Chapter 2. For many, that is sufficient—and quite right too! But that is not the end of the matter. For if we are going to speak out there, in the real world, in the market place or the public square, in a so-called non-Christian, sub-Christian, post-Christian society, we would be wise to be well acquainted with the arguments of its citizens. We should never be afraid to tackle the world and its thinking; the Christian-based, pro-life case is unanswerable. Why should we fear truth, or the frowns of men and women?

In response to this great question, there are basically four schools of thought, and therefore four different answers.

5.1 The lazy school

The answer from the lazy school to the question 'When does human life begin?' is, 'I don't know, and I don't care.' This is rarely encountered, though some of my (and, it must be said, less successful) students have been known to hold this indolent view; I trust no reader does. The other lazy—yet quite droll—answer is, 'When your last child leaves home.'

5.2 The agnostic school

The second answer given is, 'It is unanswerable—the question is too difficult.' Listen again, for example, to the Warnock Report's evasive response: 'when life or personhood begin ... are complex amalgams of factual and moral judgements';[2] or to the grand old man of IVF, Lord Robert Winston, who boldly affirmed, 'I do not consider that we can say with any clarity at all when life begins.'[3] This is bioethical agnosticism. Some from this school will mock anyone who has the audacity even to ask such a question; they will chide the questioner for being simplistic. Others will prefer to shelter behind the semantics of psychobabble, so they will talk somewhat arrogantly, or perhaps mystically, of the importance of 'personhood', 'the divine spark', 'consciousness' and 'ensoulment', none of which they can define adequately. But the question is much more straightforward than any of these four red herrings implies; do not let the blatherskites hide behind their sophistic smokescreens.

Being deliberately vague about the beginning of human life is not a virtue. Being stubbornly agnostic is reprehensible, for at least three reasons. First, practically, it empowers men and women to destroy human life, in particular, unborn human life. Second, psychologically, it allows them to continue in their self-deception that they are acting entirely honourably, both intellectually and bioethically. As one abortionist has put it, 'It's not a baby to me until the mother tells me it's a baby.' Third, societally, it permits them to evade the reality of their actions. They can say to the world, without a twinge of conscience, 'Because human life does not begin until implantation/fourteen days/twenty-four weeks, we can justly prescribe and use abortifacient "contraceptives", experiment, clone, manipulate and finally destroy human embryos, and also sanction permissive abortion laws.' Such men and women knowingly bend the truth, redefine facts and misinform others.

Nevertheless, there are some bioethical agnostics who are genuinely uncertain about an answer. To be consistent and true to themselves, those who hold such a view must take a very conservative stance over this question and provide protection for all human life from the earliest time,

CHAPTER 5

otherwise they run the risk of killing or abusing a fellow human being. If you are not sure, you must be extremely careful; you must err on the side of caution. You apply what is known as the precautionary principle, which evokes that dictum of the Hippocratic Oath, 'First, do no harm', which may be paraphrased and vernacularized as, 'Better safe than sorry'. If there is a suspected risk of harm, you are obliged either to provide protection or to prove the non-existence of that harm.

The famous analogy is that of the mountain-rescue team, which decides not to venture out on a cold and frosty night because there is at least an even chance that the lost climbers will already be dead; no decent rescue team would think and behave like that. So likewise, bioethical agnostics must be extra-circumspect; genuine bioethical agnosticism is therefore incompatible with destructive activities such as human embryo experimentation, abortion and so on.

5.3 The gradualist school

The third answer comes from those who belong to the gradualist school. They use the incrementalist argument. They admit that the developing embryo or foetus is becoming 'one of us', but they maintain that some observable trait, some recognizable feature, has to arrive, or be reached, before the 'it' has truly become 'one of us'. In plain English, they say that 'it' is less than human, yet more than nothing.

Initially, this answer may hold some attraction. All of us know of the greater expectancy as a pregnancy continues and the unborn child develops. Bonding and excitement increase when we see the first ultrasound scan pictures or feel the first prenatal kicks. But can one criterion of recognition, or the appearance of one physical feature, selected from among the myriad of contemporaneously occurring developmental changes, be sufficient to define that momentous watershed, namely, the beginning of human life? And, if that were so, what about one day, or one hour, or one minute *before* that criterion was reached or recognized? Is there really an essential difference between a twenty-four-week-old unborn child and one of twenty-three weeks and six days, or between a fourteen- and a fifteen-day-old human embryo? Moreover, how precise can the timing of these various developmental stages be, especially when they are known to vary from individual to individual? To accept that a particular point in time should be legally 'set in stone' is quite unwarranted. Philosophically and biologically, these would seem to be implacable objections to the gradualist's position.

The gradualist school is a mixed comprehensive school, but its many and diverse classes are united by one common theme: the 'not yet' argument. This is typified by that ancient ruse, that old decoy of personhood 'not yet' attained, now dressed up in twenty-first-century clothes. Its proponents will concede that life in the womb is 'sort of' human life, but, they say, it is 'not yet' *personal* human life. It is 'something', but not yet 'someone'. In other words, personhood has 'not yet' been achieved, meaning that 'it'—embryo, foetus, newborn—is not yet capable of, for example, self-knowledge, self-determination, choosing and so on—characteristics which they insist are indispensable criteria for the existence of distinct, full, personal human life. Of course, insistence upon such criteria means that the little child, the sleeping teenager, the anaesthetized woman, the senile man and many others are immediately excluded from the human race. Moreover, why should human embryos, foetuses and newborns be evaluated according to the characteristics of human adults? Well, of course, because it is the human adults who are making the judgements. When the value of human beings is determined by what we have (capacities and possessions), or what we can do (functions and utilities), rather than by our intrinsic status, worth and dignity, then prejudice, inequality and discrimination are just around the corner, or even nearer.

The corrective premise is this: all of those mentioned in the paragraph above, all of those human beings, have the radical (the root, the fundamental) ability (the active capacity) to know, will and choose from the very beginning, otherwise these attributes could never be expressed later on. These attributes are not added exogenously, like some bolt-on accessories; they are endogenous, already there, waiting to be revealed. Every human zygote possesses these attributes of personal life radically—indisputably rooted in that unique genome. Hence, life in the womb is never a 'sort of' or 'not yet' human life; it is always personal human life, both biological and biographical. We were never human non-persons. You were always fully you—zygotic you, embryonic you, foetal you, childish you, teenage you and so forth.

This philosophical 'personhood' falsehood has a physical counterpart. Show a picture of a twenty-four-week-old unborn child to a group of

Chapter 5

students and they will certainly recognize a human being. Substitute a picture of a two-week-old human embryo and they will be less certain, even though the picture reproduces exactly the features of a complete human being of that age. The students' uncertainty is caused not by a biological disjuncture or a category change, but by their unfamiliarity with and ignorance of the continuity of human development. Yet, once upon a time, they too looked like that embryo, because that is what embryonic human beings of that age look like. Today, those students are able to comprehend, determine and decide as, one day, that two-week-old embryo will. People's ideas about embryonic human life can be so Platonic, too naïve, mostly ill-informed. They say, 'It doesn't look like a human being, therefore it can't be a human being—at least, not yet.' Their understanding is faulty. It should be fashioned, not by hazy assumptions and irrational ideas, but rather by down-to-earth science and clear-cut thinking.

But that is not all. An embryonic human being is not bioethically inferior to an adult human being just because attributes such as knowing, willing and choosing are 'not yet' developed and displayed. It therefore follows that the right to life of the embryo is no less than that of the adult. To take away the embryo's radical ability to live long enough to become an adult and display those mature attributes is plainly wrong and constitutes a grave harm. The gradualist school's 'not yet' presupposition fails because it is false.

Having established that the gradualist school is a failing school, 'in special measures', it is only fitting to inspect some of its teachings in order to expose the precise reasons for its downfall. What is wrong with its curricula? Six of its mainstream teaching modules are examined here.

5.3.1 AFTER BIRTH

The first answer, the opening lesson, features a seemingly outrageous possibility: that human life begins sometime after birth. Its proponents say that the newborn is not really 'one of us' until as much as one year after birth, when the activity of the brain has developed so that the powers of speech and communication have begun. Amazingly, the two Nobel prizewinners who discovered the structure of DNA have broadly supported this view. One was James Watson, who has argued that 'If a child were not declared alive until three days after birth, then all parents could be allowed the choice only a few are given under the present system'.[4] Similarly, his Nobel prize collaborator, Francis Crick, has said that 'no newborn infant should be declared human until it has passed certain tests regarding its genetic endowment and ... if it fails these tests, it forfeits the right to live'.[5] This is frightening stuff from the elite of the biological sciences.

Philosophers can be just as bad. The infamous bioethicists Helga Kuhse and Peter Singer have suggested that 'a period of 28 days after birth might be allowed before an infant is accepted as having the same right to live as others'.[6] That is to say, newborn babies should be destroyed if they cannot demonstrate certain 'normal' human attributes. For Kuhse and Singer, the 'not yet' period is about a month postnatally.

5.3.2 AT BIRTH

This second below-standard teaching is still popular with the great British public as the indicator of the beginning of human life. True, it is a very dramatic step. For the first time in nine months we can properly see, hear, touch, taste and smell the baby. Oh yes, birth is an emotional time—I've been there! Birth also heralds a new independence for the baby, though self-sufficiency is still many years away. Birth is also the beginning of lung breathing and oral feeding—but the objects of breathing and feeding, namely, respiration and nutrient supply, have been occurring since when? Well, every living cell, including that tiny zygote, must respire and receive nutrients. These two biological processes are part and parcel of all life, so at birth they cannot be diagnostic of life's beginning because they have been going on already for the previous nine months. It is simply the mode of breathing and feeding that changes at birth.

Furthermore, it is a false exegesis of Genesis 2:7—'the LORD God ... breathed into his [Adam's] nostrils the breath of life'—to conclude that 'breath' and 'life' are in some way uniquely cause-and-effect and therefore mark the beginning of every human being's existence. The 'breath of life' was common to every living creature (Gen. 6:17), but the creational event recorded in Genesis 2 occurred once only, when God transformed the dust of the ground into a living being. Adam was quite different from us in this respect—he had no conception, no nine-month gestation and no navel. Verses such as Job 33:4 and Acts 17:25 simply emphasize our Adamic lineage and our dependence upon the sustaining power of God.

Chapter 5

They lend no credence to the idea that our first extra-uterine breath marked the beginning of our life.

5.3.3 VIABILITY

The third gradualist school's teaching is that human life begins at viability, when the child can survive outside the womb. The law in England and Wales, in the form of the Infant Life (Preservation) Act 1929, has protected unborn children once they are 'capable of being born alive'. But when is this viability attained? In the UK, at least in 1929 and for some time after, it was understood to occur at twenty-eight weeks. But this has been constantly decreasing with advances in obstetric practice. Nowadays, premature babies of a gestational age of twenty-four, or even twenty-two, weeks are routinely born alive and they often survive. For instance, last year, Rachel was born at just twenty-four weeks and one day to friends at my church and given a 40 to 60 per cent chance of survival; at the time of writing, she has just celebrated her first birthday, rosy-cheeked and full of beans. So viability is a changing definition and therefore unsatisfactory as a criterion either to provide the unborn with that certain status which engenders legal protection or to enable the parents to exclaim, 'Look, our child's life has just begun!' Viability is a moveable feast and, in a word, inadequate.

5.3.4 SOME PHYSIOLOGICAL INDICATOR

The school's fourth curricular answer depends upon the appearance of various indicators. Some say that human life begins after six days; others hold that fourteen days is decisive, or forty-two days, and so forth. This very range of answers, given by various 'authorities' in medicine, philosophy and religion, bears witness to the dubiety and arbitrariness of them all. They cannot all be right. When confronted by these professed experts, you should ask them a supplementary question: OK, you say your answer is fourteen days, but fourteen days *after* what? Their response will contain a certain ring of truth.

Nevertheless, it is important to rehearse, and counter, these wayward opinions. For example, some think that the appearance of blood, at about three weeks into the pregnancy, when the primitive heart begins to beat, is significant. This criterion has even been used with supposedly biblical warrant. Again, this is faulty exegesis, in this case of Genesis 9:4: 'But you must not eat meat that has its lifeblood still in it.' This, and other similar Mosaic passages, are chiefly concerned with God granting his people animal flesh to eat. Moses uses 'blood' metaphorically to expound 'life', in much the same way that the New International Version of the Bible uses the single word 'lifeblood'. Calvin agreed, commenting, 'not because blood is in itself the life but ... a token which represents life'.[7] Put another way, it was a colloquial device. What Moses was doing here was cautioning the people of Israel to view and handle blood with respect and care, since it was, and still is, the means of atonement. This theme of blood finds fruition in John 6:53–56. It has nothing to do with defining the beginning of human life.

Others choose as their criterion the appearance of brainwaves, at about six weeks. Peter Singer and Deane Wells have argued the case in their book *The Reproduction Revolution*: 'We suggest that the embryo be regarded as a thing, rather than a person, until the point at which there is some brain function. Brain function could not occur before the end of the sixth week after conception.'[8] Some opt for twenty weeks and more, the time of the establishment of a criterion often referred to as sentience— that is, when the unborn child reacts with the environment and has the capacity to respond to stimuli and to experience sensations. Others have decided that the onset of foetal pain is crucial, but, because of its lack of objective assessment, the timing is widely disputed and varies from about eleven to twenty-four weeks. Nevertheless, its proponents' argument goes, astonishingly, like this: 'If the pre-sentient cannot feel pain, they cannot be harmed, therefore they can be destroyed.' But brain development and function, like all other such indicators, are simply expressions of processes already going on and proceeding at tremendous rates. In addition, they all depend upon the sensitivity of the technology used to detect them. If we take the 'appearance of blood' as 'the beginning', what is the measure? Is it when blood is first visible with a naked eye, or with a light microscope, or with an electron microscope? Or is it when the blood vessels are being structured, or when the blood proteins are being synthesized? We have here a process, or rather, a series of processes, by which blood appears. Therefore, if this is the answer to the big question, it is unavoidably going to be 'about so many days'. That is, it is going to be non-specific, imprecise, and therefore unsatisfactory.

CHAPTER 5

5.3.5 PRIMITIVE STREAK

Fifth, there is the Warnock Report's propaganda, the appearance of the primitive streak at about day fourteen. The Warnock Report was concerned to produce a recommendation for an upper time limit for experimenting on human embryos. That is to say, the Report set a time limit after which it presumed there was something valuable present, something to be protected by law; before that time limit there was apparently something of lesser value that could be freely experimented upon, and indeed, capriciously destroyed. So, by default, the Warnock Committee was defining the beginning of human life, or, at least, a stage which the Committee members considered to be sufficiently significant, such that after its passing the embryo commanded some respect by experimenters as well as some protection by law.

The Warnock Report decided that the primitive streak was definitive because it is 'a heaping-up of cells at one end of the embryonic disc on the fourteenth or fifteenth day after fertilisation'.[9] By contrast, major scientific authorities, such as Leon W. Browder, consider that the primitive streak is merely 'a passageway through which cells of the embryo pass in order to continue differentiation'.[10] The *American Heritage Medical Dictionary* describes it as 'an ectodermal ridge in the midline at the caudal end of the embryonic disk from which the intraembryonic mesoderm arises'.[11] Nothing very definitive about that, is there?

One question worth asking is, why fourteen days? Why not seven, or twenty-one days? Why not indeed? One French research group suggested twelve weeks, which, as the legal deadline for abortions in France, at least possessed a certain logic: why should the killing of embryos have a different timetable from the killing of foetuses? So why fourteen days? Strangely, and almost incredibly, the Warnock Report states, 'once the process has begun, there is no particular part of the developmental process that is more important than another; all are part of a continuous process.'[12] It continues, 'Thus biologically there is no one single identifiable stage in the development of the embryo beyond which the *in vitro* embryo should not be kept alive.'[13] So, according to the Warnock Report, there is no scientific justification for choosing a cut-off point. You would therefore expect none to be proposed. But the Warnock Report proposes fourteen days. In view of the above, is this not intellectually indefensible?

WHEN DOES HUMAN LIFE BEGIN?

But Warnock says, 'some precise decision must be taken.'[14] 'Why?', you may ask. Warnock answers, 'in order to allay public anxiety.' So, though this is admittedly absurd and arbitrary, fourteen days will keep the British public happy, even though it is pulling the wool over their eyes. Thus, the Warnock Report forgets what has gone before and decides that there really is a stage, a time when something of value is present, beyond which we should not go, namely, when the primitive streak appears.

In an attempt to reinforce this arbitrary significance of the primitive streak, the Warnock Report produces two arguments. First, the Report maintains that it is the earliest recognizable feature of the embryo proper: 'The primitive streak is the first of several identifiable features.'[15] However, it is certainly not the beginning of cellular differentiation, because at the morula stage (about sixteen cells, on day three), cells of the so-called inner mass are distinguishable. Moreover, at the early blastocyst stage (about a hundred cells, on day six), the inner mass cells have separated from those of the trophoblast, the outer layer, from which the placenta and other tissues develop. So this ephemeral appearance of the primitive streak is but one of several 'identifiable features' that come to pass during the early days, certainly prior to fourteen days, of a human life.

The second argument Warnock produces says, 'This is the latest stage at which identical twins can occur.'[16] The Report's idea is that embryo experimentation should not occur after twinning because we would then certainly be dealing with human individuals, beings with real value. So, it is permissible to keep alive and experiment with in vitro embryos until then, but wrong afterwards. This is philosophical bromide, for at least four reasons. First, if this were true, the ban on experimentation should be at the earliest, not the latest, point that twinning could occur: identical, monozygotic twins can arise at the two-cell stage during day one or two. Second, the 'trigger', or the determinant, for twinning may occur at fertilization. Our understanding of the twinning process is poor, so it is more accurate to say that twinning is observable later on, not that it necessarily commences later on. Third, if twinning does occur at some time subsequent to fertilization, what do we conclude? Now there are two individuals, two embryonic human beings. But before that, what was there? There was never none. There was always at least one. Fourth, if experimentation is objectionable on post-fourteen-day-old individuals, and

CHAPTER 5

since it is impossible to spot the minority of potential 'twinners' in advance, should not all embryo experimentation be halted?

The primitive streak fails as a criterion for the beginning of human life, or, for that matter, for anything else of much significance. To suggest that the Warnock Committee, Parliament, the HFEA, Mother Nature or anyone else can draw a bright red bioethical line of demarcation at this time of embryonic development is nonsense. And thus the fourteen-day rule of the Human Fertilisation and Embryology Act 1990 is shown for what it really is: humbug. Yet Dame Mary Warnock herself remains adamant. She has asserted, 'If one put the question, When did I become me, the answer would be 14 days and not before.'[17]

5.3.6 IMPLANTATION

The sixth gradualist answer commonly taught in the school of errors is implantation. This has become popular since the 1980s, when the then Department of Health and Social Security (DHSS) re-wrote basic human biology, as we all once knew it, and invented the 'new biology'. This is yet another example of lexical engineering preceding social engineering— an important, but improper, feature of so much of modern bioethics. For example, mass abortion has already been subsumed under the seemingly respectable pretext of 'termination of pregnancy' or 'a woman's right to choose'. Now a similar verbal cloak is being used to cover up the truth about the beginning of human life. We should not be fooled.

Implantation occurs about six days after fertilization and lasts for between five and twelve days. It is therefore a process that continues for about a week. Of course, implantation is essential for the continuing growth and development of the embryo, but it marks neither the beginning nor the end of anything. It is one of the countless processes that takes place, remarkably rapidly, and in a wonderful sequence, once an ovum has been fertilized. It is simply a stage through which the human embryo must pass during a pregnancy.

To become pregnant is to conceive; fertilization is the start of a pregnancy. Therefore, conception and fertilization are synonyms that describe the events on day one of a pregnancy. 'No they are not,' cry the promoters of the 'new biology'. They claim that conception and fertilization are now *not* the same. This flies in the face of centuries of biological and medical scholarship. Nevertheless, they now say that conception has not taken place until the embryo has implanted in the mother's womb. So a pregnancy does not now last on average forty weeks, but only thirty-nine weeks and one day. *Ipso facto*, human life begins at day six, or thereabouts.

Despite the fact that the embryo is carried by the mother before implantation, they now say that 'carriage' does not begin until implantation. In defiance of common sense, they say that something cannot be carried unless it is actually attached to the person. But what about the pound coin in my pocket? This 'new biology' was a mischievous invention by the DHSS to ensure that the morning-after pill (MAP), known also as emergency hormonal contraception (EHC), was no longer illegal. As discussed earlier (see Section 3.2.3), one of the modes of action of the MAP is abortifacient, that is, it can disrupt the endometrium, the lining of the womb, making it hostile towards the embryo so that implantation cannot happen and the embryo dies. This non-contraceptive activity would have contravened the Offences Against the Person Act 1861, which forbids anyone to use anything 'to procure the miscarriage of any woman'. The term 'miscarriage' here is the equivalent of deliberate abortion, as defined in the 1803 Ellenborough Act (see Section 6.1).

The clear, age-old definition of the word 'contraceptive', from its Latin roots (*contra*, against, and *concipere*, to conceive), is keeping sperm and ova apart, by either physical or chemical means, so that fertilization is prevented, conception cannot occur and day one remains fruitless. This 'new biology' now demands a different definition. Now, contraception is the use of something that works up to six days after fertilization, something that can destroy the human blastocyst prior to implantation. Thus, early abortion has been lexically engineered as 'emergency contraception', and implantation has been upgraded from a transitory process to the very origination, the progeniture, of real human life. Now that is what I call social engineering.

The early development of the human being is astounding, and some of the steps and stages highlighted in the various curricula of the gradualist school are undoubtedly huge. But is any sufficient to count convincingly as the beginning of human life? Do not all of its confused and confusing teachings fail? Can anyone say with conviction, without intellectually blushing, of any of them, 'Before this I was not; now I am'?

5.4 The conception school

The fourth and final school says that human life begins at the earliest time, namely, at conception or fertilization—synonyms for what occurs on day one. Let no one drive a wedge between them. It has been the dogma held by scientific and medical authorities for centuries. This was certainly the view expressed in the life-protecting Declaration of Geneva 1948: 'from the time of conception'. It is still the standard opinion of leading medical textbooks. For example, William J. Larsen states that male and female gametes 'unite at fertilization to initiate the embryonic development of a new individual'.[18] Similarly, Keith L. Moore, T. V. N. Persaud and Mark G. Torchia affirm, 'Human development begins at fertilization when a sperm fuses with an oocyte to form a single cell, a zygote. This highly specialized, totipotent cell marks the beginning of each of us as a unique human being.'[19]

What happens on this action-packed day one? Once a month, a woman normally ovulates, that is, she produces one ovum, approximately 140 μm in diameter. This begins a journey down one of the Fallopian tubes to her uterus. If sexual intercourse occurs, some 250 million sperm, each about 50 μm in length, are deposited in her vagina and begin a journey towards the Fallopian tubes. For conception to occur, one sperm must penetrate the ovum. The head of the successful sperm absorbs fluid from the ovum and forms a spherical nucleus. The two nuclei, containing the paternal and maternal DNA, approach one another and fuse to produce a fertilized ovum. This irreversible event creates a new, genetically unique, single-celled discrete entity, technically known as a zygote. *This is the beginning of human life.*

Some have confusedly thought that if fertilization marks the beginning of human life, why cannot the zygote's precursors, the sperm and ovum, be regarded as the beginning too? After all, they are human. That is incontestable. And they are alive. However, they are unable to replicate, reproduce or genetically express themselves. They will die quickly unless they are kept alive artificially. They will forever be only single cells. But when one fuses with the other, twenty-three chromosomes from the mother's ovum and twenty-three chromosomes from the father's sperm produce a unique, genetically distinct human being. This zygote contains all the hereditary material, the forty-six chromosomes, for the future girl or boy, woman or man. From this zygote, this one cell, will develop all the different organs, tissues and features of the human body. Is there anything more commonplace, yet more amazing? In just the two seconds it took you to read that last sentence, estimates suggest that human fertilization occurred perhaps twenty times around the world. See what I mean? Ordinary, yet extraordinary. Common, yet incomparable.

Once fertilization has occurred, the first cell division (mitosis) takes place after about thirty hours. After about three days, there is an embryo of approximately sixteen cells, a small ball called a morula. After about six days, the embryo, now called a blastocyst and consisting of around a hundred cells, reaches the uterus. It is here that implantation occurs. Enzymes secreted by the embryo produce a small cavity in the receptive uterine wall, or endometrium, and the embryo adheres there. Around day ten, finger-like projections penetrate the wall and the embryo begins absorbing nutrients from the mother's blood supply. Hormonal changes alter her monthly cycle so that the uterine lining is not shed at fourteen days after ovulation. At this stage, the embryo is about 1.5 mm in length and the mother misses her menstrual period and suspects she might be pregnant. From weeks two to four there is a remarkable and rapid cellular division and differentiation into rudimentary, yet real, eyes, brain, spinal cord, lungs, digestive system and heart; the last starts its lifetime of beating at about day twenty-one. And so this in utero growth and development continue for another eight months, until birth.

From all the possible permutations of my father's billions of sperm and my mother's thousands of ova, the uniting of just two produced *me*. That is when I began. We were all once a zygote, a morula, a blastocyst, an embryo. Whenever I give a talk on this topic, I always ask the audience, 'Who of you was never once a zygote? Put your hand up.' To date, nobody has raised their hand! Once fertilization had occurred, all these other events were set in motion; your developmental trajectory had been activated. Given a hospitable environment, adequate nutrition and some time, that zygotic you continued on its pathway to the adult you. But from day one, you were a unified, self-integrated, self-directing, internally communicating, biochemically coordinated, life-encoded, inchoate organism of the species *Homo sapiens*—a thing most wonderful! Whatever you have become today, you were rooted in that original plan, launched by the act of fertilization. Sit back and wonder at it all. Implantation, viability, birth, infancy, teenage years, adulthood—these are simply stages in

Chapter 5

a human life already begun at conception, on day one. For some, this is an inconvenient truth. For me, it is phenomenal.

5.5. When does human life begin? In conclusion

Why have I laboured answering this big question? Because when we read the Warnock Report, scientific research papers or IVF clinic leaflets, hear news and discussions on television and radio, or join in conversations with friends, we are presented with information and opinions about zygotes, blastocysts and human embryos. Similarly, when we discuss abortion, we are confronted with terms like 'foetus', 'the products of conception' and 'the unborn child'. We need to decide what we—and others—are talking about. Are we talking about personal human lives and fellow human beings? Are we dealing with 'one of us', or are we dealing with something else? And, if the latter, what is that something else? We need to know. We need to know intellectually, but also practically, otherwise our own use or recommendation of abortion, MAPs, IVF and so forth may violate our own professed bioethical boundaries.

So when does human life begin? Think very carefully before you give your reply. Your answer to this question is crucial in expressing your views on, and in formulating your responses to, the entire range of bioethical issues. It is the sum and substance of bioethics.

QUESTIONS FOR PERSONAL REFLECTION AND GROUP DISCUSSION

1. Why is the answer to this chapter's big question so important?

2. So, what is your answer to this big question? Can you defend it?

3. Had you thought about all the different answers to this question before?

4. Which of the various 'schools' create the most difficulties for you? Why?

5. Have you come across the 'implantation' answer in everyday life?

6. Why has the Warnock Report had so much influence?

7. If 'fertilization' is your answer to this question, what obligations does that impose upon you?

CHAPTER 6

How did we get the Abortion Act 1967?

Contrary to the schoolboy's paraphrase of Hegel's dictum, history *can* teach us something. Looking back and seeing how these issues developed will help us understand more fully why we are in the bioethical mess, in the culture of death, we are in today. Changes in abortion law provide an excellent vehicle to demonstrate how that potent mix of a nation's ethical decline, the ambitions of an elite few, the communication of some half-truths, a distracted church and some political shenanigans can alter our world, for the worse.

Though the changes described here applied specifically to the case of England, Wales and Scotland (the 1967 Act does not extend to Northern Ireland), the same themes have been repeated in other Western countries and beyond. Furthermore, these changes in British abortion law heralded significant legislative shifts in other issues, ranging from human embryo abuse to euthanasia; they have helped define the political aims and refine the tactics of advocacy groups campaigning on these other bioethical fronts. Such historical perspectives are not only fascinating, they are also instructive—the lessons of bioethical history are there to be learned. And they may help us to avoid making the same mistakes again, *Deo volente*.

6.1 Pre-1967 abortion laws

Abortion has doubtless occurred throughout history and in all cultures. While it is still illegal in almost all countries of the world, it is also now generally permissible, under certain circumstances, in almost all countries of the world.

It seems that from the time of the Saxons, and certainly from the thirteenth century, according to Henry de Bracton, an authoritative writer on English law from that period, it was the accepted legal opinion that to

Chapter 6

kill a foetus which was 'formed or animated' in the womb was murder, or at least manslaughter. However, during those times, the definitions of, and associated punishments for, abortion were often variable and were generally a matter for the ecclesiastical courts. The latter were abolished during the Reformation and the crime of abortion became the province of the common-law courts. In the seventeenth century, Lord Coke and others redefined murder as the unlawful killing of a 'reasonable creature in being', or *in rerum natura*, that is, one living *outside* the womb. Even so, to kill an unborn child, that is, one living *inside* the womb, 'once its presence was made known', though no longer regarded as murder, remained a serious criminal offence.

Significant revision and clarification of the legal prohibition on abortion came with Lord Ellenborough's 1803 Act, which made it a statutory, or, in the Act's own word, a 'heinous', offence. This Act also unambiguously stated that 'in every such case the Person or Persons so offending, their Counsellors, Aiders, and Abettors, knowing of and privy to such Offence ... shall suffer Death'. Thus, Parliament declared in Section 1 of the Act that the abortion of any woman 'being quick with child', that is, one capable of extensive and felt movements, at about sixteen to eighteen weeks onwards, was a capital offence. Section 2 of the Act stated that abortion performed 'where the woman may not be quick with child', that is, before sixteen weeks, was still a criminal offence, though subject to lesser penalties, such as fines, imprisonment, whipping or transportation not exceeding fourteen years. Abortion thus became subject to statute rather than common law. However, although this 1803 Act tightened the law on abortion, it continued to reflect the popularly held belief that the foetus was not truly 'one of us' until quickening, meaning that the pre-sixteen-week-old foetus lacked full human status. This arbitrary division of foetal development was a legacy from the false teaching first proposed by Aristotle regarding the concept of 'animation', namely, that a morally significant distinction exists between the 'unformed' (inanimate, or pre-quick) and the 'formed' (animate, or quick) foetus. This notion, though shown to be entirely erroneous by subsequent advances in our understanding of pregnancy, has proved, over the centuries, to be a stubbornly intractable feature of the general public's thinking about both the beginning of human life and the development of the unborn child. It also persists among unthinking parliamentarians, medical practitioners,

How did we get the Abortion Act 1967?

churchmen, bioethicists, lawyers and other 'experts'. All subdivisions of a pregnancy are biologically artificial and thus bioethically insignificant.

The next relevant statute was Lord Lansdowne's Act 1828, which, among other things, closed a loophole in Section 1 of the 1803 Act to include abortions procured by the use of 'any Instrument'. This was followed by the Offences Against the Person Act 1837, which abolished the death penalty for abortionists, replacing it with life imprisonment. It also abolished that artificial boundary of pre- and post-quickening, so that a pregnancy was now rightly regarded as a continuous process. But it was the wide-ranging Offences Against the Person Act 1861 which brought together assorted aspects of legal protection for the individual (from the making and misuse of gunpowder to the interruption of church services) that was to become the long-standing abortion-law benchmark. Section 58 outlawed abortions and made it a crime for a pregnant woman, or anyone else, to attempt, or assist, by 'any Poison or other noxious Thing ... or ... any Instrument or other Means whatsoever ... to procure the Miscarriage of any Woman, whether she be or not be with Child ...' The offender could therefore be a pregnant woman guilty of attempted self-abortion, or a third party, even if the woman were not pregnant. The penalty continued to be a maximum of life imprisonment. Section 59 created a new offence by which a person would 'unlawfully supply or procure any Poison or other noxious Thing, or any Instrument or Thing whatsoever', knowing that it was intended for the purpose of abortion—a misdemeanour liable to imprisonment not exceeding three years, but later amended to five by the Penal Servitude Act 1891.

The Infant Life (Preservation) Act 1929 then filled a gap in the law by protecting the unborn child who might be killed during the course of actually being born. Anyone convicted of 'the felony of child destruction' was liable to 'penal servitude for life'. The Act stated that a woman who had been 'pregnant for a period of twenty-eight weeks or more shall be *prima facie* proof that she was at that time pregnant of a child capable of being born alive'. The crucial phrase was a child 'capable of being born alive'. The Act did not say that a child of less than twenty-eight weeks is *not* capable of being born alive, nor did it deal with the matter of subsequent survival. This twenty-eight-week cut-off may have been acceptable as the lower time limit of successful childbirth some eighty and more years ago, but it is well known that modern obstetric and neonatal care allows those of twenty-six,

Chapter 6

twenty-four or even twenty-two weeks not only to be born alive, but also to survive. It should also be noted that neither the 1861 nor the 1929 Acts said that an offence had been committed if the pregnancy was terminated 'for the purpose only of preserving the life of the mother'.

This brief review demonstrates that, over the last two centuries, as public condemnation of abortion became more widespread, protection for the unborn and their mothers improved, the law became more restrictive, and the punishments for those involved continued to be severe. So, what were the reasons for the sweeping reform of abortion law during the 1960s? How did England, Wales and Scotland come to acquire just about the most liberal and ruthless abortion law in Europe, the West and even the world? How did we get the Abortion Act 1967? There were at least nine decisive factors.

6.2 The social revolution

The Swinging Sixties was a time of unparalleled social upheaval. It was the time of the coming-of-age of the post-war children, the baby boomers. This was my generation too—in 1963, I saw the Beatles live at the Adelphi Cinema, Slough! Public morality was in a trough. There was a new affluence, emerging feminist and civil-rights movements, freely available illegal drugs and increasing sexual promiscuity. A social revolution was underway and the world would never be the same again. It was also a time when the church was in general disarray and decline. Much of it was becoming an insipid reflection of society—the liberals were in charge and they had hopelessly lost their way. Just think: the most influential Christian book of the 1960s was Bishop John Robinson's *Honest to God*, which was a sceptical diatribe against historic, biblical Christianity. It sold more than a million copies, but, thankfully, no one bothers to read it today.

So, the time was ripe for the liberalizing, secular humanist groups, the radicals, the subversives and some woolly minded clerics to have their heyday. And they did. In Britain, ground-breaking laws were passed. For example, in 1965, there was the Murder (Abolition of Death Penalty) Act. In 1967, the Sexual Offences Act decriminalized homosexuality. Censorship of the theatre was abolished in 1968, and in 1969, the Divorce Reform Act not only widened the basis for marriage annulment, but also weakened the institution of marriage itself. All that occurred within five years. Society was changing, and it was changing fast. Abortion-law reform was in the wind and on the minds of many; soon it would be on the table and before the House.

6.3 The Abortion Law Reform Association

Another of the seeds of the Abortion Act 1967 was sown some thirty years earlier. In 1936, just three women had formed the Abortion Law Reform Association (ALRA). For the next three decades, its membership was to remain small, at between only two and three hundred. Then in 1966, under new leadership, it flourished and grew to about a thousand members. They were mainly well-educated women; several were medically qualified and about a third had already had abortions. Most had come from conventional religious backgrounds, but many now regarded themselves as atheists, agnostics or 'freethinkers'. Thus, they were quite unlike the vast majority of women in the UK; indeed, ALRA members were a distinct elite.

Yet this tiny, tiny group was largely responsible for the massive change in our abortion laws. How did they do it? They exerted their influence by three relatively simple means: by publishing newsletters, by educating women's groups and by writing to the press. They were knowledgeable, they were dedicated and they were persistent. Therein are lessons for us all.

6.4 Children as a disaster

The sinister notion of 'children as a disaster' gained a wider acceptance as the twentieth century rolled on. The idea was expressed that, for some children, it would have been 'better for them if they had not been born'—a Bible phrase inappropriately plucked out of Matthew 26:24. This was an ideological product of the eugenics movement, fashionable from the end of the nineteenth and the beginning of the twentieth centuries. Its ethos was reinforced by the thalidomide tragedy during the early 1960s. This drug had been used as a sedative by pregnant European women in order to overcome morning sickness. But it had an unforeseen teratogenic side effect on the unborn, which resulted in about 400 children in the UK, and 3,000 in Germany, being born with serious deformities, such as stunted, or even no, limbs. Compassion was expressed, but it was largely of the counterfeit and hollow variety because, deep down, much of society decreed that for

Chapter 6

these children it would indeed have been 'better for them if they had not been born'.

Added to this was an emerging perception that children could, quite justifiably, be redefined as unwanted, unloved and uncared for. While much of this was myth and mischief, there was, during the 1960s, an undoubted increase in broken homes, divorce, and career ambitions among women; children were no longer necessarily the centre of traditional family life. Indeed, some were becoming distinctly unwelcome. They were no longer safe. In addition, the 'new causes' of women's liberation, sexual freedom, world population and environmental pollution all helped to formulate and bolster the idea that children could be a nuisance, a tragedy, and yes, even a disaster.

6.5 The lever of hard cases

During the 1960s, some leading medical and legal authorities, such as the Royal Medico-Psychological Association and the American Law Institute, were suggesting a little relaxation of abortion laws on both sides of the Atlantic. In particular, attention was directed at the so-called 'hard' cases, such as incest, rape and genetic defects. At the same time, doctors, and especially psychiatrists, were increasingly using women's mental health as a justification for procuring abortions. What in fact was developing among this academic and medical elite was a 'quality of life' ethic at the expense of human life itself. Although it was common knowledge that 'hard cases make bad law', they were being used as powerful levers to hasten wholesale changes to abortion law.

6.6 The practice of illegal abortion

Illegal abortion was usually, but not always, the so-called 'backstreet' abortion, which could lead to sterility, general ill-health and even death. Pro-abortionists argued that legalizing abortion would clean up the burgeoning backstreet and thus protect women from its dangers. However, there is good evidence that the number of backstreet abortions was actually in decline even before the 1967 Act. How many of these illegal abortions actually occurred each year is still a matter of conjecture. Estimates for the UK vary from 10,000 to 250,000. A 1966 report from the Royal College of Obstetricians and Gynaecologists estimated 14,000. Similarly, the numbers of women who died, or who were severely injured, at the hands of criminal abortionists are contested data. Contrary to much of the propaganda from pro-abortionists, one of their chief exponents, David Paintin, considered that 'that side of abortion has to some extent been exaggerated. Most illegal abortionists in the 1960s were really quite skilful'.[1]

Whatever the true numbers and associated health hazards, the spectre of such activities was employed to scare the general public and to press home the perceived need for a revision of the abortion laws. Half-truths began to acquire the ring of truth, and although people were being largely misled, many were being disturbed.

6.7 Inequalities in medical practice

Today, we might call this 'postcode lottery' medicine. The fact was that, in the early- and mid-twentieth century, some doctors performed abortions and some did not, depending largely on their personal views of medicine, law and religion. The role of the psychiatrist was often pivotal because the only way to obtain a lawful abortion, apart from serious health- and life-threatening medical conditions, was on a psychiatrist's recommendation. The threat of a pregnant woman's suicide was an additional pressure sometimes used to cajole doctors to abort. As one doctor recalled, the advice of the day was, 'Bring your daughter back when you find her with her head in the gas oven. And a suicide note would help!' Also, there was seemingly one law for the rich and another for the poor; having 100 or 200 guineas and knowing the 'right' person were often the best ways to obtain an abortion. Such inequalities incensed members of the Labour Party as well as the 'freethinkers' of ALRA, who exploited them to press for reform.

6.8 The role of contraception

In 1965, Sir Dugald Baird, the eminent gynaecologist and abortionist, coined the phrase 'the tyranny of excessive fertility'. Women in post-war Britain tended to complete their families by the time they were twenty to twenty-five years old. They were then faced with about 80 per cent of their fertile, married lives ahead of them, often without adequate and reliable contraception.

The commonest form of contraception, the condom, put the onus of responsibility upon the man. The introduction of the contraceptive pill, which

CHAPTER 6

appeared in Britain in 1961, shifted this onus onto the woman. For the first time in history, not only was sexual intercourse becoming more consistently separated from procreation, but also women were moving into the sexual 'driving seat' and were beginning to control their own fertility; the cliché of the coming age was 'reproductive choice'. These were changes that were to rock society. Sex was everywhere. Sexual freedom, premarital sex, promiscuity, cohabitation and much more were the revolutionary ingredients of this sexual upheaval. Today, by contrast, these activities are regarded merely as 'normal' or 'alternative lifestyle choices', but in the 1960s, they were social dynamite.

But how could you be one of the 'sexually liberated' without the encumbrance of getting pregnant? Overcoming fertility in an increasingly sexually permissive age was the problem. The old and new contraceptive methods were the generally accepted ways and when they failed, or were misused, or even unused, then abortion became the escape route, the backstop, for many pregnant girls and women. The 1960s' bioethical equation was quite simple: more permissive sexual intercourse = more demand for abortions.

6.9 The case of Rex v. Bourne

Medical practice and abortion law had become disconnected—illegal abortions were taking place, yet no doctors were being prosecuted. Many had thought of challenging, or, at least, clarifying, this tangled situation. One such notable person was Aleck Bourne, an obstetric surgeon at St Mary's Hospital, London. He became the defendant in Rex v. Bourne, a most odd but far-reaching legal case.

In 1938, on Wednesday, 27 April, a fourteen-year-old girl, subsequently referred to in court as Miss H., was walking with friends outside Wellington Barracks in London. Some off-duty officers from the Royal Horse Guards invited her in to come and see a horse with a green tail. Sadly, she did and she was raped by several of the soldiers. A few days later, the distressed girl, along with her mother, was seen by Dr Bourne. She was now presumed to be pregnant. On 6 June, Dr Bourne admitted her to St Mary's Hospital. A pregnancy test proved positive and, on 14 June, he operated illegally to terminate the six-week pregnancy.

Dr Bourne informed the police of his action and was duly arrested. What followed was a historic trial at the Old Bailey which opened on 18 July

How did we get the Abortion Act 1967?

before Mr Justice Macnaghten. Bourne was charged under Section 58 of the Offences Against the Person Act 1861: 'whosoever, with intent to procure the Miscarriage of any Woman ... shall unlawfully use any Instrument ... shall be guilty of felony'. Bourne pleaded not guilty. After a two-day trial, he was acquitted, but it was a most dubious verdict. Nevertheless, it established a case-law precedent—abortions could be performed, no longer solely for the preservation of a mother's life, but also for her physical and mental health: grounds upon which increasing numbers of abortions were performed during the next thirty years.

In his celebrated summing-up, Mr Macnaghten initially questioned the meaning of a word from the 1861 Act under which Bourne was charged, namely, 'unlawfully'. His assessment of Bourne's action was 'A man of the highest skill, openly, in one of our great hospitals, performs the operation ... as an act of charity, without fee or reward'. The judge went on to question whether this could be construed as acting 'unlawfully'; or was the defendant acting 'in good faith for the purpose only of preserving her life?' This led to Mr Macnaghten's second question. It was already established that both the 1861 and the 1929 Acts allowed a pregnancy to be terminated 'for the purpose only of preserving the life of the mother'. But Mr Macnaghten questioned the difference in meaning of the two phrases used by the prosecution counsel throughout the trial: 'danger to life' and 'danger to health' of the mother. He confessed that he could not properly understand the discussion, 'Since', he argued, 'life depends upon health'. Furthermore, he maintained, if a doctor considered that the 'continuance of the pregnancy will ... make the woman a physical or mental wreck', an abortion was justified 'for the purpose of preserving the life of the mother'. In other words, the phrase 'preserving the life of the mother' was interpreted by the judge to be far wider than just saving her from an imminent death; it also meant preserving her long-term physical and mental health, preventing her from becoming 'a physical or mental wreck'. The case thus turned on whether or not Bourne performed the abortion 'in good faith for the purpose of preserving the [physical and mental] health of the girl'. The jury decided he had, and he was judged 'not guilty'. So, Rex v. Bourne extended the legal basis of abortion: one sector of the previously 'criminal abortion' was rebranded as 'therapeutic abortion'. As a result, the door of permission

Chapter 6

was pushed open wider and the deed of illegal abortion was deemed a little less illicit.

However, there is an unexpected addendum to the story of Aleck Bourne. He was once a member of ALRA's medico-legal committee, but later he jumped ship and became a member of the executive committee of the pro-life group the Society for the Protection of Unborn Children (SPUC). He believed that his acquittal in 1938 had had an undesirable effect and he later stated that he was 'strongly opposed to abortion for purely social or trivial indications'.

6.10 The pro-life and medical lobbies

There was no organized pro-life counterpart to ALRA for thirty years, that is, not until the debates on the bill which led to the Abortion Act were well underway. Then, on 11 January 1967, SPUC was formed. It gathered together a 0.5-million-signature petition asking Parliament to set up a Royal Commission to research the abortion issue before the law was amended. But, in reality, it was too little, too late.

The medical fraternity—and interestingly, it was men who were, and still often are, in most Western societies, chiefly involved in the provision of abortion—had mixed feelings and convictions. Psychiatrists declared themselves largely in favour of termination up to twelve weeks—in hindsight, a rather mild demand. But even they were against abortion on the grounds of convenience alone. Much of the medical profession was largely conservative. For example, the Royal College of Obstetricians and Gynaecologists saw no urgent need for a law change. The British Medical Association was somewhat more liberal, but it wanted considerable conditions to be fulfilled before an abortion took place, and then only on the grounds of the health of the mother or serious abnormality of the unborn child. There was yet no mention of any 'social considerations', which were to become the major ground for abortions post-1967.

6.11 The Abortion Act 1967

Pre-1967 statutes and case law permitted abortions only for the preservation of the mother's life and of her health. For some, this was not enough—if the door to abortion was, at that time, ajar, they wanted it ripped off its hinges. Yet no British government had been keen to grasp the political nettle of

How did we get the Abortion Act 1967?

abortion-law reform. Instead, for several years, various private members had introduced reforming bills, but they had all foundered. During 1965 and 1966, Lord Silkin had introduced two abortion bills into the House of Lords. ALRA had provided assistance and the Lords had provided their considerable debating, amending and redrafting skills—the Silkin bills became administrative forerunners, clearing a pathway for the next big step. That came in June 1966, when David Steel MP drew third place in the ballot for private members' bills and brought his Medical Termination of Pregnancy Bill to the House of Commons. The Bill was broadly based on Silkin's proposals in the House of Lords, which he promptly dropped to allow the pro-abortion reformers to concentrate on the coming contest in the Commons.

The Steel Bill, with its first reading on 15 June 1966, was debated long and hard and was significantly amended during its passage through Westminster. Several turgid academic tomes and other bulky books have traced the minutiae of these happenings. Suffice it to say that pro-abortion parliamentarians, medical personnel and members of ALRA spent days and nights arguing, advising, rewording, lobbying and generally manipulating events in both Houses—quite legitimately, they seized their opportunity. Eventually, with parliamentary time being given by the Labour government of the day to ensure its success, the Bill passed its third reading on Friday, 14 July 1967, by a majority of 262 to 181, and it received the Royal Assent on 27 October. Six months later, on 27 April 1968, the Act came into operation—the legalized killing started. One year later, its sponsor, David Steel, speaking at an ALRA meeting, said that the Bill was successful because 'The right men were in the right place at the right time'. By contrast is the dismal fact that the number of evangelical Christian leaders who 'saw the issue' and stood up and spoke out against the Bill can be counted on the fingers of one hand.

The Act was, and still is, regarded by many not only as a compromise, but also as a poorly drafted piece of legislation. This may have suited the purposes of the pro-abortionists, because over the years most of its intended legal boundaries have been ridden over roughshod. Simply put, the Act proved to be a leaky legal bucket that held virtually no water of restraint. During the next two decades, no fewer than fifteen attempts were made to revise the Act, including the best-known private members' bills introduced

Chapter 6

by John Corrie in 1979 and David Alton in 1987. Basically, these measures proposed either a tightening of the criteria for abortion or a lowering of the upper time limit. All failed.

In outline, the Abortion Act 1967 did not legalize abortion *in toto*; it gave no right to a woman to an abortion; it did not provide 'abortion on demand'. Also, it imposed no duty on any doctor to carry out an abortion. However, it did offer a defence against the charge of unlawfully attempting 'to procure the miscarriage of any woman' under the Offences Against the Person Act 1861. Thus it did, according to Section 1, protect from prosecution a 'registered medical practitioner' who performed an abortion, as long as two such doctors certified that, in their opinion, formed in good faith, the continuance of the pregnancy would involve risk, on one or more of the following six grounds, greater than if the pregnancy were terminated:

1. risk to the life of the pregnant woman
2. risk of injury to the physical or mental health of the pregnant woman
3. risk of injury to the physical or mental health of any existing children of her family
4. risk that if the child were born, it would suffer from such physical or mental abnormalities as to be seriously handicapped
5. in an emergency, to save the life of the pregnant woman
6. in an emergency, to prevent grave permanent injury to the physical or mental health of the pregnant woman.

Section 4 of the Act relates to 'conscientious objection to participation in treatment'. This states that 'no person shall be under any duty ... to participate in any treatment authorised by this Act to which he has a conscientious objection'. Put another way, doctors and nurses can opt out of performing, or assisting in, abortions, though they are still obliged to participate in emergency procedures when a woman's life may be in jeopardy. The Act, in effect, created a system of presumed consent where 'the burden of proof of conscientious objection shall rest on the person claiming to rely on it'. Forewarned is forearmed. This Section 4 remains the only commendable feature of the entire wretched statute. Not surprisingly, this entitlement to conscientious objection has been repeatedly challenged by hardline abortionists.

How did we get the Abortion Act 1967?

It was always obvious that the Abortion Act 1967 was set to become a schismatic piece of legislation. It is therefore instructive to return and re-examine four of the most popular arguments raised in favour of liberalizing abortion law. First, during the parliamentary debates, the abortionists said that easier abortion would decrease the illegitimacy rate, then at less than 10 per cent in the UK. In 2012, this was 47.5 per cent and rising. Second, they said it would lessen child battering because 'every child would be a wanted child'. There are now an estimated 400,000 violent crimes against UK children each year. Third, they said it would decrease the number of children in care—currently about 68,000 in the UK. And fourth, they said it would decrease violent sexual crime against children; annually, there are now about 19,000 such sex crimes against children under sixteen in the UK. It is striking that all of those insinuated benefits, from the Act's most enthusiastic devotees, have proved to be quite empty.

Certainly, abortion nowadays is carried out mostly not for those women that the Act's proponents professed to help and protect, namely, the overstressed, sick mother already with a large family, in poor housing and with little financial or social support. Today, abortion clients are mainly young, single, not particularly poor, socially connected, decently housed, healthy women carrying thriving babies. It all seems so, so wrong.

6.12 The Human Fertilisation and Embryology Act 1990

In 1984, the Warnock Report, with its liberal recommendations, was published and presented to Parliament. Bioethical battle was again enjoined at Westminster, this time chiefly to protect the human embryo. Pro-life private members' bills in 1985, 1986 and 1987 were introduced by Enoch Powell, Ken Hargreaves and Alistair Burt, respectively. These would have outlawed any attempts to create, store or use human embryos other than in assisting a woman to become pregnant. They all failed.

As a consequence, most of the recommendations of the Warnock Report became the backbone of the Human Fertilisation and Embryology Act 1990. Although this Act dealt primarily with issues of reproductive technology, human embryo experimentation and the licensing of clinics and research facilities, its Section 37 amended the Abortion Act 1967. The upper time limit of twenty-eight weeks was generally reduced to twenty-four. It also

Chapter 6

altered the old six criteria for abortion to seven new (and here somewhat abbreviated) grounds:
- A: in case of risk to the life of the pregnant woman
- B: to prevent grave permanent injury to the physical or mental health of the pregnant woman
- C: in case of risk of injury to the physical or mental health of the pregnant woman (pregnancy has not exceeded its twenty-fourth week)
- D: in case of risk of injury to the physical or mental health of any existing children of the family of the pregnant woman (pregnancy has not exceeded its twenty-fourth week)
- E: in case of a substantial risk that if the child were born, it would suffer from such physical or mental abnormalities as to be seriously handicapped
- F: in an emergency, to save the life of the woman
- G: in an emergency, to prevent grave permanent injury to the physical or mental health of the pregnant woman.

As can be seen, the 1990 Act inserted a limit of twenty-four weeks for abortion on both grounds C (old ground 2) and D (old 3). It also introduced an additional criterion, ground B, which has no time limit. This 'no time limit' was also extended to grounds A (old ground 1) and E (old 4), so that abortions where there is 'a substantial risk of the child being born seriously handicapped' can now be performed up to birth—yes, up to forty weeks.

According to the Department of Health, the total number of abortions performed in England and Wales during 2012 was 190,972. This figure includes 5,850 for non-residents. The following data show the grounds and their associated numbers:
- A: 62
- B: 130
- C: 185,758
- D: 2,193
- E: 2,829

Abortions performed in emergencies under grounds F and G are now so rare that they often appear as 0 in the official statistics, but in 2012 there was 1.

These shameful figures have already been discussed in Section 3.2, but for completeness, three brief observations will be noted here. First, they demonstrate that the vast majority (97.3 per cent) of abortions were justified under ground C, the 'social clause'. Second, fewer than 1.5 per cent of all abortions were performed under ground E, the 'handicap', or so-called 'foetal anomaly', clause. Third, these may be just figures to a statistician or to an ardent abortionist, but in truth they represent real, unborn children who have had their lives snuffed out—every single datum is a human tragedy.

This 1990 Act also legalized the barbarous practice of the 'selective reduction' of unborn children in multiple pregnancies (see Section 3.2.4 above). Additionally, it paved the way for the use of early medical abortions (EMAs) by abortifacients, like RU-486, mifepristone (see Section 3.2.2). It also, among other things, created the Human Fertilisation and Embryology Authority (HFEA) as the statutory body to oversee, monitor and license all fertility treatments, storage and research in the UK that involve the use of human gametes and embryos. It started work on 1 August 1991—but that is another gloomy story, which has been partly retold in previous sections.

6.13 The Human Fertilisation and Embryology Act 2008

Almost twenty years passed before abortion law was again debated in Parliament. The Human Fertilisation and Embryology Bill (2008) was presented as a supposedly sensible and timely reforming measure, necessary to overhaul and update the 1990 Act; in truth, it was set to dismantle the fundamentals of human dignity, good medicine, family structure and even human life itself.

The Bill dealt mainly with infertility treatments and human embryo research, but there were several proposed amendments affecting the issue of abortion law. The pro-choice lobby was hoping to increase access with 'no questions asked' abortion up to perhaps thirteen weeks, scrapping the two-doctor signature requirement, allowing nurses to supervise early medical abortions (EMAs), extending the 1967 Act to Northern Ireland, and repealing the conscience clause, thereby hunting down pro-life doctors and nurses. These clauses were provocative, even inflammatory—the pro-abortionists were certainly aiming high.

On the other side of the bioethical divide, pro-life MPs were proposing to reduce the abortion upper time limit to twenty, perhaps even eighteen weeks, insisting on proper informed consent, allowing a cooling-off period

Chapter 6

for women prior to abortion, involving parents when under-sixteen-year-olds were considering abortion, and banning eugenic abortions for minor disabilities, including cleft palate, club foot and so forth. These pro-choice and pro-life amendments reveal something of the aspirations of both sides, but in the event, none of them made any procedural progress.

Even so, Monday, 19 and Tuesday, 20 May 2008 were dreadful days. They were the days when the Committee of the Whole House of Commons debated the Bill. They were the days when the United Kingdom of Great Britain and Northern Ireland became less compassionate and more God-dishonouring. The government applied the rarely used time guillotine so that four vast bioethical topics—human-admixed embryos, saviour siblings, the need for a father and abortion—were debated for just three or four hours each. It was a parliamentary debacle.

Concerning the abortion issue, the question before the House was: should the twenty-four-week upper limit be reduced? There was some expectation that a twenty-two-week compromise might win the day. It was not to be; a series of amendments was lost, progressing from twelve weeks (393 Noes v. 71 Ayes), sixteen weeks (387 v. 84), twenty weeks (332 v. 190) through to twenty-two weeks (304 v. 233). The twenty-four-week status quo won the day, and as a consequence, some 3,000 unborn children of between twenty and twenty-four weeks will continue to lose their lives in the UK each year.

Rod Liddle, one of Britain's most polemic journalists, writing in *The Spectator* the day after the parliamentary debate, declared, 'The Commons vote securing the 24-week limit is no more than a craven politician's fudge, designed to postpone the day when the law of the land finally catches up with the indisputable findings of science.' He continued, 'I may be wrong about this, but it strikes me that in a century or so, or maybe even less, we will be appalled that we allowed abortions at all ... we will be mystified as to how such a primitive and brutal procedure could have become state-sanctioned and commonplace.'[2] There is nothing to add to that.

6.14 The US situation

The American abortion story has been somewhat different, mainly because of its several diverse state laws, but the same trends in thinking and practice can be detected and traced out. On 22 January 1973, some five

HOW DID WE GET THE ABORTION ACT 1967?

years after the UK's landmark Abortion Act 1967 was passed, the Supreme Court of the United States decided in the case of Roe v. Wade. The Court announced that the US Constitution contained 'a right to abortion' based upon its concepts of liberty and privacy. Thus, abortion law and practice were revolutionized and harmonized across the entire USA. Whereas the UK's 1967 abortion law was a parliamentary affair, based mainly on the perceived risks to the physical and mental health of the woman, the USA's law was a Court affair, based wholly on rights that are deep-seated in the US Constitution.

The key events begin here. In the summer of 1969, Norma McCorvey, a twenty-one-year-old mother of two, became pregnant again, but this time she wanted an abortion. Texas law prohibited abortion, except to save a woman's life, so McCorvey sought one illegally, but without success. In the meantime, she had met two lawyers, Linda Coffee and Sarah Weddington, who were looking for somebody—anybody—to further their own pro-abortion legal ambitions. McCorvey agreed to become the plaintiff, under the alias of Jane Roe, in a test case alleging that the Texas anti-abortion law of 1859 was unconstitutional. On 3 March 1970, a complaint was filed naming Dallas County District Attorney Henry B. Wade as the defendant.

On 10 October 1972, after a journey through the lower courts, the Roe v. Wade case finally arrived at the Supreme Court. The plaintiffs emphasized the constitutional right to personal privacy, while the state of Texas claimed a compelling interest to protect both prenatal life and the mother's health. Some three months later, Justice Harry Blackmun delivered the 7-to-2 majority decision of the Supreme Court in favour of Roe. The Court decided that the right of personal privacy, including restrictions upon state intrusion, as contained in the Ninth and Fourteenth Amendments of the Constitution, was broad enough to encompass a woman's decision to terminate her pregnancy. Moreover, the word 'person', as used in the Constitution and the Fourteenth Amendment, did not include the unborn. The Court also found that it could not decide on the question of when human life begins. However, it did hold that neither the lack of a right to protection for a foetus by the state, nor a woman's right to privacy, was absolute.

Finally, on 22 January 1973, the Court presented 'its landmark formula to balance these competing interests. During the first trimester of pregnancy,

Chapter 6

'the abortion decision ... must be left to the medical judgement of the pregnant woman's attending physician'. During the second trimester, 'the State ... may ... regulate the abortion procedure in ways that are reasonably related to maternal health'. During 'the stage subsequent to viability, the State ... may ... regulate, and even proscribe, abortion except where necessary, in appropriate medical judgment, for the preservation of the life or health of the mother'. In short, the outcome was the creation of a new liberty, namely, the constitutional right of a woman to obtain an abortion at any time. During the first six months of a pregnancy—the first and second trimesters—a woman would need no particular reason, but in the last three months—the third trimester—she had to have a reason, any reason. This was set to become 'abortion on demand' US-style, and now there are about 1.1 million such abortions performed each year across the country.

On that same day in 1973, the Supreme Court issued another judgement in another abortion case, Doe v. Bolton. It concerned the plaintiff, Sandra Cano, alias Mary Doe, who was pregnant and challenging the state law of Georgia, which had previously refused her request for an abortion. The defendant was Arthur K. Bolton, the Attorney General of Georgia. The Court found the state's existing 'procedural requirements'—which stipulated, for example, that abortions must be performed in certain hospitals and only on residents of Georgia—to be unconstitutional. It also declared that a woman could obtain an abortion after viability, if necessary to protect her health. In effect, Roe v. Wade and Doe v. Bolton together declared abortion to be a constitutional right and transferred abortion from the numerous restrictive laws of individual states into one big, liberal, federal law.

There were two unexpected postscripts to these two judicial verdicts. Both Norma McCorvey and Sandra Cano believed that they had been 'set up' by the pro-choice movement and especially by their women lawyers. Both women came to regret their part in legalizing US abortion. Norma McCorvey subsequently stated, 'I think abortion is wrong ... I just have to take a pro-life position.' Sandra Cano also declared, 'I am against abortion. Abortion is murder.' These sentiments are reminiscent of Aleck Bourne's, who, despite his acquittal in his 1938 trial—a verdict that helped facilitate

How did we get the Abortion Act 1967?

abortion in the UK—went on to oppose the Abortion Act 1967 and predicted that it would lead to 'the greatest holocaust in history'.

There was one more turn in the McCorvey saga. Fearing for her safety, she initially hid her 'Roe' identity. She then went to work in a Dallas abortion clinic. During that time, some evangelical Christians and others picketed her workplace; some screamed at her, while others befriended her. One day, Emily, the seven-year-old daughter of such a pro-life friend, asked her, 'Why do you let them kill the babies at the clinic?' The child's artless question pierced McCorvey's heart and prompted the great change. In 1995, she professed to have found God, left her job at that Texan abortion clinic and turned pro-life. She is still actively involved in the movement that seeks to overturn Roe v. Wade.

The Roe v. Wade decision was certainly controversial; it reshaped US politics and it split the country, and continues to do so. It has been subjected to numerous legal challenges from both the pro-abortion and pro-life camps. Two have been significant. First, in the 1992 case of Planned Parenthood of Southeastern Pennsylvania v. Casey, the Supreme Court upheld the basic provisions of Roe v. Wade, but overturned, by a 5-to-4 decision, its trimester basis and insisted that no law must place an undue burden on a woman's right to an abortion before foetal viability. Second, in 2003, the Partial-Birth Abortion Ban Act became law and prohibited a particularly gruesome type of abortion, usually performed between fifteen and twenty-six weeks and technically known as 'intact dilation and extraction'. It allows a living unborn child to be partially delivered; the head is then crushed, so that eventually a dead baby is extracted. The pro-abortionists were outraged at the ban and immediately challenged the Act's constitutionality. However, in 2007, the Supreme Court finally decided, by a 5-4 decision in the case of Gonzales v. Carhart, that this Act did not violate the constitution. It was the first time that any restriction had been placed on Roe v. Wade.

Though the Supreme Court has subsequently reduced federal spending on abortions, by upholding the so-called Hyde Amendment, it has generally continued to endorse the tenets of Roe v. Wade. Yet in recent years, more and more state legislatures have been busy passing pro-life restrictive laws on abortion time limits, procedures, cooling-off periods, compulsory counselling, embryo protection and much more. In addition, surveys of US young people show them to be markedly more conservative on the abortion

CHAPTER 6

issue than their parents. Perhaps the tide among the more youthful American populace, in contrast to most of its old-guard politicians and judiciary, is beginning to turn. A legal challenge to the Roe v. Wade colossus would, if successful, have enormous bioethical repercussions around the world. It may yet come, and soon. Indeed, one US political commentator, who is herself a supporter of 'abortion on demand', has stated, 'I think we are going to see Roe overturned ... I'm thinking 2015.'[3]

6.15 How did we get the Abortion Act 1967? In conclusion

Here is my quandary. I had assumed that Georg Hegel (1770–1831) was cynical and wrong when he wrote, 'But what experience and history teach is this, that peoples and governments never have learned anything from history.' I had always hoped that history would teach us many valuable lessons. And it undeniably has done in some areas. But, regrettably, so far, Hegel's assessment looks correct. Learning about the depressing chronicle of abortion-law reform has had little effect upon either its numerical diminution or its ingrained policy direction; it has gone from good, to bad, to worse. But that is not the end, nor the future.

During the nineteenth century, the fight against the practice of slavery took many, many years, and much hard work, by the evangelicals of the Clapham Sect and other co-belligerents, before the Slave Trade Act 1807 abolished the trading of slaves—though not slavery itself—in the British Empire. It was not until 1 August 1834, when the Slavery Abolition Act 1833 became law, that slavery was officially ended, and slaves throughout the British Empire were freed. That day was a long time, decades long, coming; William Wilberforce had presented abolition bills every year from 1789 to 1806, only to be defeated every year. Yet his day finally came. Ours will too. The slave was once considered to be a non-person, just like the unborn child is today. What we need is a new generation of abolitionists—abortion abolitionists—to contest current abortion law and practice.

Is a pro-life victory just a pipe dream? No! There is this precedent from slavery emancipation, but think what other dramatic changes have been achieved in other areas of politics and law during the last generation. Fascism has been dealt a severe blow, colonialism has been seriously weakened, democracies have been built, welfare has been strengthened, the Cold War has been won and justice for women has advanced. Of course,

How did we get the Abortion Act 1967?

other global threats and terrors exist, but much has improved. Yet there is this one bioethical black hole—the abortion of our unborn children—that dominates contemporary life. It has become the stubborn blot on human civilization. The post-war promises that we would never kill again on an industrial scale now ring hollow. Another holocaust has come back to haunt our world. The culture of death is still here.

Yet there will be a time when the Abortion Act 1967, and all its epigones, will be seen for what they are—cruel, discriminatory, deadly pieces of legislation. One day, people will look back and ask: how could a seemingly civilized society ever contemplate, let alone approve, such laws and practices? In that happy day, we will marvel at all human life, and we will cherish and protect every one of our offspring. May that day come soon!

Questions for personal reflection and group discussion

1. *What lessons does the history of abortion legalization teach us?*

2. *What patterns of bioethical and legal thinking can you discern in this history?*

3. *How important were individuals, groups and governments in changing abortion law?*

4. *What are the obstacles to the repeal of the Abortion Act 1967 and Roe v. Wade?*

5. *If abortion is to be made rarer, what could you do to help bring this about?*

6. *What do the stories of Bourne, McCorvey and Cano teach us?*

7. *In a general discussion of abortion, what particular aspects would you seek to highlight?*

CHAPTER 7

What of the future?

Past, present and pending—the three ages of time, life and lifetime. We have the God-given ability to contemplate all three, even concurrently—that is a uniquely human attribute, part of bearing the *imago Dei*. Therefore, do not neglect to reflect! While Socrates' declaration that 'The unexamined life is not worth living' is perhaps too harsh, Santayana's assertion that 'Those who cannot remember the past are condemned to repeat it' rings only too true. That is why, in the previous chapter, we looked back specifically to learn some bioethical lessons from the recent past. Other chapters have concentrated on assessing present-day issues, with just a nod to their possible futures. Now we look forward to the pending, in a more concerted manner.

But first, another smidgen of past and present. Scientifically, the nineteenth century is often regarded as the century of chemistry. Likewise, the twentieth century was dominated by physics. Now, the twenty-first century is predicted to become 'the century of biology'. It certainly opened with an auspicious fanfare. On 26 June 2000, President Bill Clinton and Prime Minister Tony Blair hosted a press conference on the White House lawn to herald the completion of the first draft of the human genome—the sequencing of the three billion chemical 'letters' of our DNA. Clinton called it 'the most important, the most wondrous map ever produced by humankind'. Blair declared it to be 'a breakthrough that takes humankind across a frontier and into a new era'. It was unquestionably a scientific, and specifically a biological, landmark—comparable to, according to some, the invention of the wheel or the splitting of the atom.

Surely, then, none can doubt that our twenty-first century world is one of biological science—of biomedical science, of medicine, of genetics, of biologically questioning just what and who we are, and of attempting to improve ourselves by its appliance. There is nothing intrinsically wrong with any of these scientific pursuits, as long as they are bioethically ring-fenced.

What of the future?

But look how it can all go haywire when unbridled science or shameless scientism rules! This book has repeatedly sounded that alarm bell. The culture of death is already here, chronologically and geographically—right now, and on your doorstep. But where might it be, and what shape could it take, in, say, ten years' time?

Thinking about the future is one thing; predicting it is quite another. Impossible or not, that has never stopped the enterprising, as well as the foolish, from attempting to spot emerging challenges, threats, developments and opportunities; in techno-jargon, it is dubbed 'horizon scanning'. Emulating the men of Issachar, who 'understood the times and knew what Israel should do' (1 Chr. 12:32), will help prime us to face our own future. As they say, *praemonitus praemunitus*: forewarned is forearmed. So, with a sort of prospective 2020 vision, here are some on-trend topics that will probably be underlying and overarching most bioethical issues for the next decade or thereabouts. Come, put on your bioethical binoculars.

7.1 The general outlook

Here is an elementary question: will it get any better? The plain answer, at least in the short term, is: no, not yet. The culture of death is now so firmly embedded in our society's thinking and practices that it cannot be uprooted overnight, or, more to the point, perhaps not even within the next decade or two. The truth is that we have seen only the first fruits. There is yet considerable capacity for the culture of death to grow and eventually to produce its full rotten harvest—I am thinking especially of far-reaching genetic abuse and full-scale euthanasia. To put it another way, there is a bioethical omnishambles threatening out there.

Therefore, we must face it: currently, we are in a deep bioethical pit. Furthermore, there is no point in mincing our words—much of the blame for this mess lies at the door, on the doorstep, of the evangelical Christian church. How different it could have been if the estimated one million and more evangelical Christians in the UK had understood the issues and responded with principled compassion, in biblical ways. Instead, during the last fifty or more years, too many evangelicals have been too absorbed by too many secondary issues, such as music groups, big-name events and interdenominational bickering, or even tertiary issues, like—well, you

Chapter 7

name your own trivial pursuits that mean we have had little time or energy to grasp and tackle these bioethical issues.

It is as if we have undergone some sort of bioethical bypass. Ours has been a woeful and regrettable history of let-down, a half-century of lame excuses, a 'shoulda-woulda-coulda' saga. But recognizing, regretting and repenting of such past failure and then moving on is the proper Christian response. This is not some kind of self-indulgent, wishful thinking, or the politics of denial; rather, it is an important precept of living the Christian life. 'But one thing I do: Forgetting what is behind and straining towards what is ahead, I press on towards the goal to win the prize for which God has called me heavenwards in Christ Jesus' (Phil. 3:13–14). In the face of the culture of death, such a biblical strategy will keep us from discouragement, defeatism and dormancy.

Consequently, there is always—and it is a realistic and comforting theme—Christian hope. Thinking and practice can change. A society's mindset, a church's attitude as well as an individual's worldview can be informed, reformed, even transformed. Remember the global influences for good brought about by the New Testament church, the Reformation and the eighteenth-century Evangelical Awakenings? We are still feeling the positive ripples of those movements today. Who, in the eighteenth century, would have thought that the well-ingrained practice of cruel slavery would have ended in the following century? Or who, fifty years ago, would have thought that evangelicals today would be interested in understanding and responding to bioethical issues? After all, you are reading this book!

So all is not lost. Although the culture of death does seem to be in the ascendant, that is not the full story, or the whole picture. More and more people are becoming pro-life. Most established pro-life organizations are reporting increased consolidation, professionalism, membership and activities. At times, progress may be frustratingly, even imperceptibly, slow, but fundamentally there is a one-way flow of intellectually convinced and emotionally moved individuals towards the pro-life position.

Yes, there are glimmers of hope for now and the near future. For example, in the late 1990s, a survey entitled 'Members' Attitudes to Abortion' was conducted by the UK's Christian Medical Fellowship. To the question 'When does human life have full value?', about 70 per cent of the Christian student doctors answered 'At fertilization', whereas fewer than 40 per cent of Christian practising doctors gave that answer. Furthermore, the student doctors were invariably more pro-life in their attitudes towards abortion than their older mentors. Today, those student doctors are fully fledged, and many will be exerting their pro-life influence in a thousand locations. But these positive changes are occurring not just among the Christians in the medical profession; an online survey of UK medical students conducted during 2011 found that 45 per cent thought that conscientious objection was essential to allow them to opt-out of certain procedures, and 44 per cent of them objected to abortion of the disabled after twenty-four weeks. These bioethical shifts are sharper in the USA. A 2011 survey of practising US doctors showed that only 14 per cent were willing to participate in any abortions; in 2008, that figure had been 22 per cent.

This pro-life swing is also evident among the general public. It is gradual, but it has started, and it seems to be gaining traction. For example, opinion polls—with all their caveats—look encouraging. Again, the USA leads the way. A 2012 Gallup poll showed that a new high of 50 per cent of Americans identified themselves as 'pro-life'. The 'pro-choice' camp registered just 41 per cent, its lowest figure since this annual survey began in 1995. Gallup has described this move towards a personal pro-life stance as 'the new normal'. Britain lags behind as more solidly pro-choice, though the trend is otherwise. A 2011 MORI poll showed that although half (53 per cent) of the UK public agreed that abortion should be legally available, this figure had fallen from 65 per cent in 2001 and from 63 per cent in 2006. In addition, a YouGov poll published in 2012 found that half (49 per cent) of all UK women favoured a reduction in the current twenty-four-week abortion upper time limit.

Is there a growing bioethical sensitivity at home and abroad? What could all this mean for the future? Consider just four particulars. First, the UK pro-abortionists are already opining that women's access to abortion services may become more limited. In 2007, the Royal College of Obstetricians and Gynaecologists wrung its collective hands about 'the slow but growing problem of trainees opting out of training in the termination of pregnancy' and expressed concern 'about the abortion service of the future'.[1] Second, could Spain become the first country within the European Union to backtrack on its own liberal law, which currently allows 'abortion on demand' up to fourteen weeks? On 20 December 2013, the Spanish cabinet

Chapter 7

approved a draft bill that would permit abortions only in the case of rape or serious health risks to the mother or her unborn child. The Spanish parliament is expected to vote on this bill in early 2014—pass or fail, the very proposal has sent shockwaves through the pro-abortion community. Third, even post-Soviet Russia has moved to curtail its massive abortion industry, with its estimated 1.2 million terminations each year, by a 2011 ban on most abortions after twelve weeks. The reasons given for this volte-face are a plunging population and a wish to recover traditional moral values. Fourth, in the USA, health regulations and anti-abortion laws in several states are already reining-in access and shutting down facilities. In 1991, there were 2,176 abortion clinics nationwide; by 2013, there were only 582. For example, in 2011, Kansas introduced rules that closed two of the state's three remaining abortion clinics. Since 2012, Mississippi's only remaining abortion clinic has been in a legal battle over its closure. In 2013, Arkansas and North Dakota respectively approved bills to ban most abortions after week twelve of a pregnancy or when a foetal heartbeat is detectable, namely, after about week six. And several states are pressing for the introduction of so-called 'personhood amendments', which insist upon legal status and protection of human life from fertilization. Such changes have not gone unchallenged and the courts will undoubtedly become busy battlegrounds as these moves are contested—consequent lawsuits may even end up in the Supreme Court.

Maybe this is all part of the long process of turning around the big, bad ship *Abortion*. On the other hand, how few bad doctors does a state or a country need to maintain its current abortion quota? Nevertheless, there does seem to be a real sea change out there—perhaps the tide is turning and we are witnessing a genuine and growing international aversion to abortion. Are men and women on both sides of the Atlantic becoming less enamoured of its ethics and practice? Could it be that the generation that grew up with legalized abortion is beginning to reject it? Abortion remains the keystone issue; when its ethics, practice and public approval begin to crack, other bioethical issues, such as human embryo abuse, infanticide and euthanasia, will follow suit.

This world 'belongs' to the current generation of young men and women, medical and otherwise. And those determinedly pro-life doctors and nurses, unfettered by the medical paternalism and bioethical ideology of the past, who refuse to get involved with abortion and the rest of the culture of death will advance the pro-life cause enormously. And so will all those other Millennials, those twenty- and thirty-somethings—the current, reproducing cohort. Their stance against abortion, embryo destruction, eugenic diagnoses and so on, will be essential if we are to see a better bioethical world. Let us pray for them, educate them, and encourage them to stand steadfast and to live by the non-negotiable truths of the Word. Indeed, there is Christian hope.

In summary, yes, the general outlook is currently pretty dire, yet it possibly, seemingly probably, will get better—but not without much ado. Abortion, embryo abuse, surrogacy, assisted suicide and so on remain massive stumbling blocks. Nevertheless, the public is perhaps beginning to sense that these issues are at least abnormal, if not yet entirely wrong. The major snag, for us and for them, is that abortion, IVF and the rest, are mostly legal and readily available, and they can look so very handy and helpful—such simple solutions, such quick fixes—for those pressing personal jams. But despite these cumbersome obstacles, the shoots of a culture of life are becoming more visible. Some of the figures and trends look encouraging. More pro-life people are emerging and pro-life sentiment is swelling. The bioethical understanding and the responses of the next generation will be decisive.

7.2 The PC world

If, in the future, we are going to respond effectively to the culture of death, it will probably be at an increasing personal cost. The world of PC, of political correctness, is fast becoming an enemy of the Christian. We are told that diversity and equality are the essential hallmarks of a twenty-first-century society, yet anyone caught opposing, or operating outside of, its liberal, secular humanist framework will not be tolerated; such supposedly broad-minded tolerance can be so intolerant, so totalitarian. I am mindful of those Christians around the world who have paid great prices, even unto death, for following the Saviour. But back to our own, less harsh doorstep: there is already a growing list of people who have been reprimanded, demoted, or who have even lost their jobs, because they refused to compromise their convictions about sexual behaviours, abortion, marriage, family and so on. This can be the high cost of discipleship.

Chapter 7

And, as if bioethically principled healthcare personnel are not already sufficiently hassled and beleaguered, another battle is looming on the horizon. Will those who conscientiously object to certain medical procedures still be allowed to opt out? Or will they—including student doctors and nurses—be compelled to lend a hand in abortions and assist in suicides, and will pharmacists be forced to fill prescriptions for abortifacient and life-ending drugs? Will many Christians, along with the 'morally sensitive', simply be squeezed out of their chosen careers? If so, the practice of proper medicine will become incalculably worse without them.

For me, this PC confrontation started early. Years ago, I was summoned to appear before the head of my university department. Apparently, an undergraduate student had written a letter complaining about my approach to teaching bioethical issues—it was allegedly biased because I had made reference to the impact of Christianity upon bioethical thinking and practice throughout the ages. 'But how can anyone teach the history of bioethics properly, or, for that matter, almost any other subject, without referring to Christian influences?' I asked. No answer was given. My lecture notes were examined and found to contain less than 3 per cent of what might be construed as Christian content. I was told to remove such material. 'But then that *would* make my lectures biased,' I complained. 'Go!' I was told. Incidentally, though I repeatedly asked to see the complaining letter from the student, it was never produced. Of course it was not—who needs evidence when prejudice is pandemic? How sad that even in our universities, traditionally the last bastions of free speech, the exchange of ideas and the advancement of critical thinking, the PC thought-police have begun to run the show. I fear there is worse to come.

In spite of this, we must never develop a siege mentality, a persecution complex or a victim fixation, but we do need to be aware that for many in our postmodern world, truth is largely irrelevant. For them, truth is not even a consensus, a 51 per cent thing; now it no longer exists in any objective shape or form. And for many, Christianity, with its emphasis on truth, and a truth that prescribes and demands a vigorously ethical lifestyle, has become a foe to be suppressed. Take heed—the honest and the upright will be persecuted. In the coming years, good men and women will be at a premium. The Christian and the 'morally sensitive' will be increasingly targeted and will come under special fire. Even so, the Christian's marching orders are to 'be strong' and 'stand firm' (Eph. 6:10–17).

7.3 Sexual behaviours

Almost all of the issues covered in this book have a strong association with sex. No surprises there. After all, sex, in all its forms and functions, is one of the most powerful drivers of human life, as well as that indispensible component of its reproductive commencement. This procreational compulsion is an attribute of bearing the *imago Dei*—God creates and we too create. If sex is that noble and potent gift from God, it needs harnessing because men and woman have a post-Fall propensity to spoil, or even destroy, whatever is good. For daily proof of that assertion, read a newspaper or look around you. For biblical proof, look at the description of 'your earthly nature' in Colossian 3:5: 'sexual immorality, impurity, lust, evil desires and greed'. Or try the portrayal of society in Ephesians 4:19: 'Having lost all sensitivity, they have given themselves over to sensuality so as to indulge in every kind of impurity, with a continual lust for more.' In other words, human sexual behaviours can be both out of place and out of control—they need defining and confining. And the solutions are found in marriage—it is the double-lock key.

First, defining. Sexual behaviours are defined generally, and explicitly, in terms of sexual intercourse, by the creational arrangement of the marriage covenant, as outlined in Genesis 2:24. This is repeated and expanded, with reference to the sexually distinct Adam and Eve, by the Lord Jesus Christ in Matthew 19:4–5: '"Haven't you read," he replied, "that at the beginning the Creator 'made them male and female', and said, 'For this reason a man will leave his father and mother and be united to his wife, and the two will become one flesh'?"' The biblical view is that sexual behaviours are to be defined by the concept and the model of marriage. And marriage is the lifelong, exclusive bond between one man and one woman. It is heterosexual monogamy that reflects the complementary natures of men and women (Eph. 5:22–33). All else is promiscuous, improper, out-of-place sexual behaviour. Simply put, the nature and meaning of sex are defined by the covenant, the solemn pledge, the promised vows of marriage; marriage is the context, time and place for sexual intercourse.

Second, confining. Expressed sexual behaviours—again, generally, but especially, as sexual intercourse—are confined to within marriage.

Chapter 7

Marriage is therefore the relational framework for the procreation and nurturing of children. So the stringent biblical pattern is sexual chastity before marriage and sexual fidelity within marriage (1 Thes. 4:3–5; Heb. 13:4). All else is sexual behaviour unconfined, out of control, sexual aberration. No fornication, no adultery, no incest, no bestiality, no sodomy, no paedophilia: all are a gross breach of God-approved sexual behaviour. Tellingly, the list of the fruit of the Spirit begins with 'love' and ends with 'self-control' (Gal. 5:22–23), and Christians are called to be 'blameless and pure … in a crooked and depraved generation' (Phil. 2:15). The Bible's sexual behaviour bar is set high, and post-Fall men and women often fall short (Rom. 3:23). None of us is immune and some of us are prone—we all know that. Marriage is therefore a fundamental social good. It defines and confines. It restrains evil and promotes stability. It is much more than an honourable legal and social institution, but it is never less. As a consequence, we tinker with marriage, its definition, its boundaries and its adjuncts at our peril.

No small wonder, then, that Christians, and many others, are disturbed by twenty-first-century sexual behaviours as practised by large sections of the adult and teenage population. We are apprehensive, even alarmed—we know their potential for damage. Indeed, nearly all of the primary bioethical issues, including surrogacy, cloning, abortion, IVF and human embryo research, are rooted in sexual behaviours gone wrong. Sexual intercourse was never meant to lead to death; anything but. The Bible's declaration that men and women can be aberrant in their sexual thoughts and practices is vindicated (Rom. 1–3). Sexual relationships are becoming increasingly shaky, risky, damaging and destructive. Consider just two examples that epitomize these physical and emotional harms: teenage pregnancy and sexually transmitted infections (STIs).

First, teenage pregnancy. The total number of conceptions among under-eighteen-year-olds in England and Wales during the last decade has hovered around 42,000 each year. These have included some 7,500 girls less than sixteen years old and 330 under fourteen—below the legal age of consent. During 2011, total teenage conceptions at 31,051 were at their lowest since records began in 1969. And the rate of teenage conception has decreased during recent years from 43 in 2001 to a 2011 figure of 31 per 1,000 girls aged fifteen to seventeen. Despite these welcome reductions,

WHAT OF THE FUTURE?

these figures still remain among the highest in Western Europe, and with nearly 50 per cent of such pregnancies ending in abortion, they will continue to perplex governments, teachers, parents and even young people themselves. Some riders are in order. First, government 'conception' figures are the sum of registered births plus recorded abortions, and therefore they take no account of, for example, natural miscarriages or early abortions caused by MAPs—so they are invariably underestimates. Second, if the so-called 'teenage' statistics were to include all teenagers, namely, those aged thirteen to nineteen, the annual total for England and Wales zooms up to around 84,000. Third, not all teenage conceptions are problematic; some are intentional and welcomed.

Yet, what to do about those tens of thousands of conceptions deemed unintentional and unwelcomed? In 1999, the then Labour government launched the Teenage Pregnancy Strategy, with its key objective of halving the rate of under-eighteen conceptions by 2010. Did it work? By 2010, the teenage conception rate had fallen by a mere 13.3 per cent, rather than the intended 50 per cent. No wonder this strategy failed. It was based on the expectation that teenagers would have sexual intercourse. It responded to this unfounded and dangerous assumption by relying on the promotion of explicit sex education, free condoms and pills—contraceptive and morning-after. That is to say, it equipped our children with everything they needed to start a disastrous life of multiple sexual relationships, unplanned pregnancies and STIs. There was virtually nothing in the strategy about delay, respect, or, least of all, abstinence. Successive governments have continued to sneer at abstinence, yet, in theory and practice, it must work. While anxious policy makers repeatedly urge us to avoid the health risks of smoking, gorging, boozing, drug-abusing, polluting and even overspending, there is rarely a warning word against premature, promiscuous sexual intercourse, though its psychological and physical harms are self-evident. All that notwithstanding, the subsequent government approach, 'Framework for Sexual Health Improvement in England', announced in 2013, consisted of, almost unbelievably, more of the same failed measures. The same 'open and honest' graphic sexual health education, the same 'rapid and easy access' to abortion and contraception—now including long-acting reversible contraception (LARC) injections and implants—and the same

Chapter 7

amoral 'safer sex' ethos, now with a little more about relationships and STIs. When will legislators and educators learn?

Second, there is the totem of sexually transmitted infections (STIs). These are not exclusively teenage-related; far from it. In fact, people over sixty years old are now the fastest-growing group contracting STIs. For instance, in the decade since 2002, syphilis tripled among the over sixty-fives in the UK. Greater life expectancy, improved health, widespread divorce and Internet dating have all contributed to an older generation that is wantonly and unsafely sexually active.

Even so, it is across the entire adult age range that new cases of STIs are spiralling. Approximately 14,000 were reported in England in 1990, 20,000 in 1998 and a massive 426,867 in 2011. *Chlamydia trachomatis* is the most common and most rapidly spreading STI, with over 186,000 new cases detected in England during 2011; this is followed by genital warts, with just over 76,000 cases, and almost 21,000 cases of gonorrhoea. The last figure represented an annual increase of 25 per cent, and the infectious bacterium is showing disturbing signs of becoming resistant to conventional antibiotics. These figures are causing consternation in all genitourinary medicine (GUM) clinics, as well as at the Department of Health.

Of course, easier access to STI testing and better methods of detection account for a share of these increases, but the greater proportion is a reflection of more people leading more promiscuous sex lives, among both the heterosexual and homosexual populations. And STIs are not just embarrassing—they can be medically serious because some of them will cause infertility as well as life-threatening complications, especially among women during pregnancy.

Can you picture the bioethical, self-sustaining chain reaction of the future? It will segue from more sexually active people to more unwanted pregnancies, to more abortions, to more STIs, to more infertility, to more IVF. Until one of these links in the chain is uncoupled, this cheerless course of people's lives, characterized by more physical damage and more emotional heartache, will continue. For young people, especially those shackled to popular culture, this will be the depressing prospect of living their teenage years within the culture of death.

Our youngsters are especially vulnerable—we should fear for them. They are being misled about the meaning and purpose of sex. According to 2011

WHAT OF THE FUTURE?

UK figures, more girls (27 per cent) than boys (23 per cent) are now having their first experience of sexual intercourse before the age of sixteen. They may be sexually experienced, but they are still emotionally immature. Most parents are quite unaware of the depths to which some aspects of youth culture have sunk. Have you watched TV recently? Have you any idea what teenagers come across on the Internet? Have you an inkling about what is revealed on Facebook? Have you heard them chattering in Starbucks? For many teenagers, sexual intercourse has become a recreational distraction, a sporting pastime. And if parents and churches make no effort to tell the truth and redress the balance, the next decade will give rise to a new crowd of life-jaded, sexually tired, genitally diseased, emotionally damaged, celebrity aping, unrestrained youngsters. Is that really an overstatement?

Nowadays, our society too often sees a girl's fertility as a curse of nature that only contraception, backed up by abortion, can control. This is not sex education—this is anti-natal education, a policy of avoidance of pregnancy at all costs, as if that is the sum total of sexual health and well-being. The positives of virtue, responsibility, chastity, restraint, marriage and fidelity are due—long overdue—for a comeback in the classroom and elsewhere. Alongside these moral affirmatives, we need to recapture something of the wonders and joys of fertility, motherhood and fatherhood. Being pregnant is not a disease. We have allowed Christian teaching and Christian values to be squeezed out of our schools and to be replaced by this 'sex education', or, as it is sometimes referred to in the contrived language of government, 'teenage fertility management'. So why should Christian ideals not be taught confidently in our schools, and, yes, certainly in our churches? Are you planning to change the future?

7.4 Genomic medicine

We were told that the spin-offs from the Human Genome Project would bring about a medical revolution—genomic medicine would be the fresh flavour of twenty-first-century medicine. Has this promised age dawned, of bespoke medicine wherein healthcare is transformed, diagnoses are fine-tuned and drugs are tailor-made to fit the individual's genetic profile? In a word, no. That initial sizzle of eager expectation has become more of a fizzle of dull disappointment. In all the excitement, we forgot that it typically takes two or more decades for novel medical technologies to reach

Chapter 7

the patient. As a consequence, the promised age of personalized, genomic medicine has been somewhat delayed, but, make no mistake, it will be coming.

One token of that future is the plummeting cost and increasing speed of DNA sequencing—your personal genome analysis will soon become such a smart Christmas present. However, what you would do with it is another matter. The advent of this cheap, rapid genome sequencing, generating oodles of genetic data, is no longer the bottleneck; skilful interpretation of its raw results, so-called data mining, in terms of biological function and failure, and the likely predisposition of the patient to particular diseases, is. This hiatus between the supply of genetic raw information and its medical meaning is very real. In 2013, the USA Food and Drug Administration (FDA) halted the sale of the $99 personal DNA-testing service—which claims to discover the user's predisposition to 250 different genetic diseases—of the pioneering Californian-based company 23andMe, until proof of that fine line of biological–clinical accuracy is mutually resolved. And, while the medical geneticists are poring over your DNA data, they might, perchance, also be able to tell you about the disease from which you will likely die—it could all be so informative!

However, eventually, genomic medicine will bring about striking benefits. Currently, doctors typically treat the *effects* rather than the *causes* of diseases—Prozac for depression, statins for high cholesterol and so on. Genomic medicine will allow doctors to begin to understand the biological mechanisms of the causes and the development, the pathogenesis, of diseases. Perhaps within the next decade or two, the majority of the genetic factors involved in some of the more common human diseases will be defined and this information used to advance new treatments.

But at the very start of this innovative genomic journey, it has become obvious that the road from laboratory bench to chemist's counter and hospital bedside is long, tortuous, expensive, hazardous and largely uncharted. At least three types of challenges exist. First, there are the severe technological challenges of converting those basic genetic findings into the design and synthesis of putative drugs, their evaluation by laboratory and animal testing, and the setting up and completion of human clinical trials to confirm their safety and effectiveness—a pathway of progression known as translational medicine. And then the additional technical

What of the future?

problems of producing the required medications by the pharmaceutical and biotechnology industries and their commercial upscaling, in sufficient quantity and of satisfactory quality, to treat thousands of patients, will have to be overcome.

Second, numerous bureaucratic challenges have already arisen. These concern issues such as data privacy, informed consent, genetic discrimination, patent assignments, public–private partnerships, and legislative and administrative regulation. Perhaps the lawyers are to blame. Furthermore, convincing financial investors of the viability of the entire enterprise will be no small matter. None of these issues is insuperable, but the resolution of them all will require ingenuity and considerable time.

Third, formidable conceptual challenges have emerged. Although scores of disease-causing genes have been identified, their medical impact remains mostly minimal. For instance, consider the discovery of the BRCA-1 and BRCA-2 genes back in the mid-1990s. These genes function naturally as tumour suppressors, but when mutated they have been linked to the onset of hereditary ovarian and breast cancers. This knowledge has had a significant impact on the healthcare of those women who have inherited these deleterious genetic mutations and developed, for instance, breast cancer, but they are only a minority; it has been of no consequence for the other 95 per cent of UK women diagnosed with different types of breast cancers caused by mutations in other genes.

The question therefore arises: what about those everyday genetic diseases that affect millions of people, like the big four—common cancers, diabetes, heart diseases and mental illnesses? For these multifactorial disorders, the outlook is more complex and less optimistic. The existence of hundreds, sometimes thousands, of genetic variants has proved to be daunting. New variants are being reported almost weekly, but because they tend to be widespread, their influence on the aetiology, the cause, of a particular disease remains low. In other words, while many of us may have a particular faulty gene, its bearing, by itself, on a disease is typically minimal. Add to this almost unimaginable complexity the newish discipline of epigenetics—the study of heritable changes in gene expression caused, not by the DNA sequence, but by a host of other subtle modifiers that can turn genes on and off, sometimes at inappropriate times—and the whole genomic medicine conundrum is ratcheted up to an extraordinarily

Chapter 7

convoluted state. Understanding these multifarious gene interactions, plus the virtually unknown roles of environmental influences, is the next key needed to unlock the causes and future therapies of many common diseases. Only when these complexities are better understood will we be prescribed the required personalized therapeutic drugs.

Despite the delays, the future long-term goal is clear: your partial or complete genome will be sequenced and stored in your medical records to serve as a resource to manage your disease-prevention strategies and to aid selection of your appropriate drug treatments. This future genomic medicine has already coined a new language: epigenetics, pharmacogenomics, data mining, copy-number variations, genome-wide association studies and bioinformatics. You may need to learn to speak it when you visit your doctor in a few years' time.

But a word of caution: medical and scientific researchers have a habit of promising more than they can ever deliver. Genomic medicine is indeed coming, it will assist you and yours, but not yet. In the meantime, be patient and keep a cool head. And to stay entirely level-headed, always remember this sobering fact: most illnesses that affect human beings throughout the whole world are not genetic in origin but are caused by other agents, predominantly malnutrition and microorganisms. Their management and treatment require an entirely different, non-genetic medical approach.

7.5 Population and demography

The fear of global overpopulation was popularized during the nineteenth century by none other than a clergyman, the Reverend Thomas Robert Malthus FRS. In 1798, he published his famous *Essay on the Principle of Population*, in which he forecast that population growth would outstrip the world's food supply. Then, in 1968, came Paul Ehrlich's alarmist book *The Population Bomb*, predicting that the early years of the twenty-first century would be faced with mass global famine. The following year, at a meeting in London organized by the Institute of Biology, this same professor of biology from Stanford University declared that 'by the year 2000 the United Kingdom will simply be a small group of impoverished islands, inhabited by some 70 million hungry people'.[2] Ehrlich was so, so wrong, on so many fronts. For instance, he did not foresee the coming of the Green Revolution, which transformed and boosted global food production

WHAT OF THE FUTURE?

by the use of genetically improved seeds, synthetic fertilizers and pesticides. Nor did he foresee the tumbling of global fertility rates. And, according to my informants, most UK residents are both well-off and well-fed, often overfed.

Neo-Malthusians have often invoked widespread sterilization and abortion as solutions to their perceived problem: prevent or slaughter the hungry-mouthed before they can start to eat. But their predictions and crass proposals have now been invalidated by a curious demographic twist—in fact, a U-turn. In more and more countries of the developed world the problem has become quite the reverse of overpopulation; they are experiencing zero, or even negative, growth rates. They are simply not producing enough babies to maintain a stable population—numerically, they are declining. They are facing a 'birth dearth'.

The world fertility rate in 1960 was 4.9 children per woman aged between fifteen and forty-four, assumed to be her child-bearing years. At the turn of this century, it was down to 2.6, and by 2040, it is predicted to be something like 1.8. The necessary replacement rate for any country to maintain a steady population—that is, neither growing nor declining—is reckoned to be 2.1 children per woman. According to UN data published in 2010, below-replacement growth rates are already serious problems in countries as diverse as Italy (1.38), Russia (1.51), Singapore (1.25), Japan (1.32), Czech Republic (1.41), Canada (1.65), the UK (1.83), the USA (2.07) and many others. This means, for instance, that Italy will face a projected 23 per cent reduction in its population, equivalent to fourteen million fewer people, by 2050. To reverse these declines, some countries have implemented measures such as financial birth bonuses, subsidized childcare, tax incentives and paid parental leave. Russia is so concerned about its falling birthrate that from 2011 it barred most abortions after twelve weeks, introduced a minimum forty-eight-hour cooling-off period and, in 2013, banned abortion advertising. Singapore has even introduced a government-sponsored dating service.

Low fertility and high abortion rates are the two principal reasons for this modern phenomenon. Low fertility has many social and medical causes—economic choices, financial constraints and community strictures mean smaller families; increasing employment opportunities for women mean that couples are postponing starting their families, so that infertility

Chapter 7

is often diagnosed too late to treat. In addition, the growing numbers of single, unattached adults—by preference and by circumstance—also make a childless contribution to this population milieu. And, obviously, rampant abortion remains the other principal means by which population numbers are directly cut. In the UK alone, almost a quarter of all pregnancies end in abortion. The negative consequences of such child reductions upon the health and welfare of future ageing populations, such as economic growth, affordable pensions, adoptions, medical resources and so on, will be profound. Some call it the 'demographic cliff'.

So much for the developed world; what about the developing world? The ranks of the supporters of population control have recently been joined by the eco-pessimists. Already, Population Matters, formerly the UK's Optimum Population Trust, is urging us to offset our global carbon footprint by funding Third World 'reproductive and sexual health' (also known as sterilization and abortion) programmes; cutting the number of babies born by physical, chemical or surgical means are the favoured tools of such organizations. Some are now even praising the barbaric, abortion-based one-child policy of China as a model appropriate for the whole world. Yet that sort of brutal demographic strategy is beginning to implode as, for example, news of covert forced and late abortions becomes public knowledge and sex-selective abortions continue to upset the gender balance in China, India and elsewhere; governments are beginning to be embarrassed by their own cruel schemes. While there is no doubt that these kinds of aggressive administrative and cultural policies, once entrenched, are difficult to retract, there are signs that, within the next decade, they will be revised and toned down—perhaps driven by external political pressure, but also by internal necessity. For example, during 2012, China's labour pool shrank for the first time in fifty years, and in 2013, it announced a substantial relaxation of its one-child policy, so that, for instance, couples can have two children if either parent is an only child.

In fact, the future of the entire global population looks demographically stable, if not necessarily bioethically bright. Several recent studies have predicted that the human population will peak mid-century at between nine and ten billion, plateau and then slowly decline, a pattern of development known as demographic transition. But is this altogether good news? How much of this 'progress' will depend upon future policies of voluntary or enforced abortion, sterilization, laissez-faire infanticide and legalized euthanasia? That is the pending unknown. The culture of death is the present known. As for the past, it does appear that those population time bombs of Malthus and Ehrlich have now been safely defused.

7.6 The ageing population

Global demography is a fluid entity that quietly ebbs and flows with time. Whatever its tidal flux, any country's healthy social and economic demographic pattern always looks like a pyramid—lots of young at the base and fewer elderly citizens at the apex. Today, many countries have stood this configuration on its head; their demographic pattern is like an inverted pyramid. This means that the needs, economic and otherwise, of an increasingly elderly, non-working population are having to be supplied by a shrinking population of young workers. Some call it the 'demographic storm'.

The elderly are growing both in numbers and in age—more people are getting older. It has become known as the silver tsunami. One in six Britons alive today, about ten million people in total, are expected to reach their hundredth birthday and beyond. Some think that figure could even be pushed up to 120 years. In 2010, Queen Elizabeth II sent out 11,610 birthday messages to British centenarians, compared with only 255 in 1952. I have just completed an online life-expectancy questionnaire and I am predicted to live to only ninety-seven, thereby just missing out on those royal felicitations—what a pity!

This increased longevity is mainly a result of medical advances, better nutrition, enhanced hygiene and improvements in social facilities. Allowing substantial immigration and increasing the retirement age are the suggested quick-fix solutions to this problem. Indeed, the UK has already done both. During 2010, net UK immigration rose to almost 240,000; in the mid-1990s, it was just 50,000 a year. Also in 2010, the UK government announced that the State pension qualifying age would rise from the current sixty-five to sixty-six for men, and from sixty to sixty-six for women by 2020, and then to sixty-seven for both by 2028.

Of course, abortion has only exacerbated this demographic dilemma. In the UK, for example, legalized abortion has 'taken away' some seven million of our youngsters; a substantial chunk of the base of our pyramid

Chapter 7

has been lost; some 10 per cent of our population has vanished. This has occurred within less than fifty years; they are like 'a missing generation, within two generations', a posterity nowhere to be found.

Social, economic and population stability are such a delicate balance of bioethical issues. Too many aborted children have upset our population pattern, and now too many surviving elderly are skewing it still further. And the pro-life solution? Less abortion and more care for the elderly. Simple—though it will take a generation to put right. And the non-pro-life solution? Neo-eugenicists, together with some demographers, politicians, economists and doomsters, are telling us that what we need—just like those old-time eugenicists told us—is the appliance of science, the machinery of macabre medicine. What we need, they say, is a managed number of healthy offspring, who can work, raise a healthy family and pay their way and their taxes. What we do not need, they say, are the unfit, whether young or old, who are economically unproductive, reproductively irresponsible and costly. Hence, to engineer their Utopia, or at least a seemingly stable society, we need, they say, resolute public policies of fertility control, abortion, infanticide and euthanasia. That is to say, we need scientific and medical control of human life at every stage—in vitro, in utero, ex utero and in senio (meaning, old age or dotage). Within the next twenty years or so, if all goes very badly wrong, we should just about be there: welcome to Dystopia.

7.7 Miscellaneous futures

There are people who make a good living from prognosticating. They include weather forecasters, astrologers, horserace tipsters, science-fiction writers and investment bankers. Some are sensible; others are spooky. Some deal in fact; others deal in fiction. But as time goes by, there is occasionally an uncanny merging of these two categories; it is like the blurring of actuality and illusion, as life imitates art, and as the past becomes the present and then the future. Think in the bioethical context of, for example, genetic engineering—from the fantasy of old-fashioned Frankenstein to the reality of modern-day gene therapy, and to the future prospect of non-human humans. It can all seem a little odd.

Consider, then, the oddity that is transhumanism. In the past, it was decidedly the stuff of storybooks. At the present time, it exists as a rather abstruse, 'academic', utopian movement. In the future, it may impact subtly on our thinking and doing, on our brains and on our bodies. Its enthusiasts believe that, in the future, the human condition, with all its frailties, can be transformed and extended by the use of emerging technologies. They talk about overcoming ageing and enhancing human intellectual and physical capabilities. They are fascinated by biotechnology, cognitive and brain studies, nanotechnology and computers. They expect that death, disease and other human weaknesses will all be overcome one day. They discuss whether future humans will be born or assembled. They look forward to space travel, brain–computer interfaces, humanoid robots, cryopreservation and immortality.

Weird? Yes, but hold on. For here is the slightly unsettling aspect of it all. If transhumanists have been predicting that our future will consist of people choosing reconstructive surgery, reproductive technologies, ubiquitous atheism, novel family configurations, impersonal computer communication and eugenics, then perhaps we are further down their track than we might suppose. Maybe it is time to read again Aldous Huxley's *Brave New World* and C. S. Lewis's *The Abolition of Man*.

Indeed, could our future be one in which our humanness is overtaken by a post-human, super-human, non-human, something-other-than-human existence? Will future humans be re-engineered into cybernetic organisms? Are humans really nothing more than information? Will the future be technologic and anti-human? Are the transhumanists genuine soothsayers, accurate forecasters? Such issues are, thankfully, beyond the remit of this present book. You may wish to discuss these sorts of currently hypothetical bioethical questions with your friends—but do not spend too much time on such flights of fancy. The future is important, but today is already here. And this very day, we have more than enough bioethical troubles to sort out. Remember, the culture of death is right here, right now—at this moment, on your doorstep.

7.8 The past good, present good and future good

This chapter is ending on a somewhat dismal note. Let me redress that. A good place to start any reassessment of the past, the present and the pending is Hebrews 13:8: 'Jesus Christ is the same yesterday and today and for ever.' Therein is transcendent constancy and comfort. Indeed, the future

Chapter 7

is not necessarily gloomy or comfortless. This longed-for culture of life is not some castle in the air—it already exists, often only barely emergent, yet constantly growing. There is a continuing good out there. It includes pro-life educational programmes in schools and elsewhere—telling the truth and helping people, young and old, to understand the issues of life and death. It includes political work and lobbying efforts inside and outside Parliament—upholding righteous laws and seeking to amend ignoble statutes. It includes the caring initiatives established by pro-life people—including crisis pregnancy care centres, hospices for babies, children and adults, practical care and support for the vulnerable and disadvantaged, and homes for the mentally and physically disabled and the aged. These, and a thousand other good works, are shining examples of the culture of life in operation. Bravo! Long may they blossom!

Furthermore, perhaps in the near future, additional, more complex facilities, like fertility care clinics and, as the culture of death threatens to spread, health centres, and perhaps even hospitals, practising and providing comprehensive, pro-life medical care, will be needed. In the meantime, these present-day projects are no small achievements; they are courageous and commendable, and such pro-life activities deserve our whole-hearted support—in terms of finance, prayer, time and so on.

7.9 What of the future? In conclusion

While we must not ignore this chapter's overcast forecast, neither must we run away with the idea that things will only, always, get worse—that is unbiblical defeatism, non-Christian pessimism (1 John 5:4–5), which can lead to spiritual depression. Nor must we resign ourselves to the false notion that because everything is in God's hands, we need do nothing—that is hyper-Calvinism, which can lead to a sterile indifference (Matt. 22:29). Nor must we think that our efforts alone will be sufficient—that is mere humanism, which can lead to a disregard of the true nature of our struggle and the assistance available (Eph. 6:12–13). All such views betray faulty theology. We need to grapple with the antinomy of the sovereignty of God *and* the responsibility of man, and act upon them both. The future bioethical landscape depends upon God *and* upon us—me and you.

So, what will *you* be doing, during the next ten years, to bring about something different, something good, something for the culture of life?

WHAT OF THE FUTURE?

Will you and I be sufficient to rise to the current, and future, challenges from the culture of death? Dare we fail? You should be asking, 'So what can I do—no, what *must* I do?' I am glad you raised that question. The next chapter answers it.

QUESTIONS FOR PERSONAL REFLECTION AND GROUP DISCUSSION

1. What other bioethical issues are likely to become important during the next decade?

2. Is human life becoming too controlled by science and medicine?

3. What are the future challenges to being human, to bearing the imago Dei?

4. How in particular can we help our children and our elderly to face the bioethical future?

5. Are future doctors and the practice of medicine really a threat? If so, in what ways?

6. What positive aspects of bioethical issues are likely to occur in the near future?

7. Are you now prepared to tackle the demands of the agenda, the next chapter, of this book?

Chapter 8

So what must we do?

> When the foundations are being destroyed, what can the righteous do?
> Ps. 11:3

This book has a plan. It develops, and then depends upon, this simple thesis: credenda + agenda = principled compassion. This basic equation undergirds and summarizes the entire book. Now, at last, we have arrived at the second part of this credenda–agenda couplet, initially encountered back in the Introduction, in Section 1.4. Having rehearsed the biblical approach to tackling bioethical issues and constructed a robust framework as the basis for what we should believe about them—our credenda—it is now time to consider how to respond to them—our agenda. It may seem that this credenda–agenda arrangement implies two distinct, disparate components. Nothing could be more mistaken. The two must always be inextricably linked, like peaches and cream, or love and marriage. As John R. W. Stott wrote in his *Issues Facing Christians Today*, 'Truth is powerful when it is argued; it is even more powerful when it is exhibited. For people need not only to understand the arguments, but to see its benefits displayed.'[1] There it is: credenda (truth argued) plus agenda (truth exhibited).

Let me put it another way. Because credenda and agenda ineluctably belong together, we must strive to be integrated, well-rounded, joined-up, truth-believing, actively responding individuals. And what are the principal characteristics of such professing, responsive Christian men and women? Quintessentially, they are the indebted bearers of the *imago Dei*, fully human and three dimensional; in short, they are head-heart-hand people.

8.1 Responding is a head-heart-hand affair

First, Christians are head people. They must never say to preachers and teachers, 'Don't give us that doctrinal, cerebral stuff—just give us a warm feeling, an emotional tingle.' Such statements betray a dreadful misunderstanding of true religion. The only reason to become, and stay, a Christian is because

So what must we do?

Christianity is true; it communicates this truth using words in statements, claims and arguments that are explicable. Christianity therefore consists of propositional truths. Without such a corpus of 'knowable' knowledge, the Word and the world will make no sense, and Christianity would be mere religious gobbledegook and mumbo-jumbo. Therefore, we are to use our heads, apply our brains, regenerate our thinking and 'be transformed by the renewing of your mind' (Rom. 12:2). That is the 'head' part.

Second, Christians are heart people. When that objective, 'knowable' knowledge is transformed into subjective, 'understood' knowledge, it becomes the stirrer, the mover, of our hearts—it drops that vital 450 mm down from the grey matter to the great muscle, from head to heart, from intellect to affection. We can be touched emotionally by all sorts of events and phenomena—music, conversations, pictures, thoughts and much more—but their effects are usually ephemeral. The stuff that sticks and changes our affections permanently is 'heart truth', and the biblical sort is the best sort. 'Give me understanding, and I will keep your law and obey it with all my heart' (Ps. 119:34). That is the 'heart' part.

Third, Christians are hand people. Truth in our head leads to a stirred heart, which leads to a moved hand. This book is ultimately seeking the practical response of a moved hand—doing something for others, for the pro-life cause, for the culture of life, for the Lord Jesus Christ. Head alone will be sterile, lacking the warmth of compassion and deed. Heart alone will be emotional, lacking the anchors of truth and endeavour. Hand alone will be undirected, lacking the guidance of thought and enthusiasm. What we all need is that sequential translation from head to heart to hand. 'Whatever your hand finds to do, do it with all your might' (Eccles. 9:10). That is the 'hand' part.

Therefore, responding to the culture of death must be a head-heart-hand affair. It is a fully integrated venture. Christians are not unfamiliar with this kind of comprehensive, multifaceted, personal paradigm. After all, we know that the greatest commandment is nothing if not all-inclusive and wide-ranging, namely, to 'Love the Lord your God with all your heart and with all your soul and with all your strength [and with all your mind]'. This was first set out in Deuteronomy 6:5 and subsequently reiterated in all three of the synoptic Gospels—Matthew 22:37; Mark 12:30; Luke 10:27. If that is the foremost rule, what comes next? 'And the second is like it: "Love your

Chapter 8

neighbour as yourself"'(Matt. 22:39; Mark 12:31; Luke 10:27). Or again, look what I read the day before writing this chapter: 'I the LORD search the heart and examine the mind, to reward a man according to his conduct, according to what his deeds deserve' (Jer. 17:10). Can you see the head-heart-hand paradigm here and elsewhere? There is no need for intricate exegesis. Scripture overflows with this theme of personal comprehensiveness and all-or-nothing Christianity. It is the Bible's most basic call to Christian living. It therefore needs to be the pattern, the blueprint, for our bioethical understanding and responding, for our principled compassion.

Over the years, I have read many, and formally reviewed several, Christian books on bioethical issues. Almost without exception, they have had one signal weakness. Though they have usually expounded the Scriptures decently, and often described the issues adequately, they have largely ignored the next step, namely, to provide answers to the question: so what must we do? That is not going to be a deficiency of this current primer. Here is the denouement of this book. There are at least five responses to this chapter's great question.

8.2 We must pray

King David once began to pray using these words: 'Hear, O LORD, and answer me, for I am poor and needy' (Ps. 86:1). That is a tender expression of the link, the transcendent connection, between the created and the Creator, the needy and the provider. No wonder it can be said that 'The prayer of a righteous man is powerful and effective' (James 5:16). This is Christian life support—God does hear *and* he does answer. He can, and he does, sovereignly transform situations, individuals and communities. So prayer must be the precondition, the starting point, for real change. Therefore, these bioethical issues ought to be a regular part of our prayer lives, both personal and corporate.

We start with ourselves. And first of all, never, ever, forget to be thankful for 'the few days of life God has given' (Eccles. 5:18) and for 'the gracious gift of life' (1 Peter 3:7). Never be an ingrate. Then, remember head-heart-hand. We must pray for our own minds—that they might be biblically informed; for our own affections—that they might be biblically motivated; and for our own responses—that they might be biblically fragrant. In other words, we should pray that we might be informed, kind-hearted and productive.

We must pray for those personally caught up, and sometimes trapped, in the awfulness of the culture of death—the pregnant, the disabled, the senile, the infertile and so on. We must also pray for their carers, advisers, families and churches. And we should pray for our own particular friends and acquaintances who are bewildered, struggling, hurting, even sinking under the weight of these issues. Rescue, refresh, revisit, renew, restore, revive them, Lord.

We must pray for those in the forefront of the battles—for doctors, hospital administrators, and especially for nurses. We must pray for Christians and others engaged in these particular occupations, that they would resist the culture of death and stand up for the culture of life. 'Pray for us. We are sure that we have a clear conscience and desire to live honourably in every way' (Heb. 13:18).

We must also pray for our leaders and decision makers (1 Tim. 2:1–3). So, we must pray for members of the government and those in opposition, for the police, trade-union leaders, parents, schoolteachers, employers, magistrates, 'for kings and all those in authority'. The list is almost endless. 'From everyone who has been given much, much will be demanded' (Luke 12:48).

And what else must we pray for? In more general terms, we plead for righteousness, justice, compassion and forgiveness—they are all good Bible words, and our nation and its people need all four. And there is Proverbs 14:34; 29:2, and so much more.

8.3 We must educate

Next comes education. Alas, some people have seemingly given up on thinking and learning. They dislike the idea that acquiring knowledge and understanding are worthy, lifelong activities; perhaps they did badly at school and quit education years ago. A few have even complained that the first edition of this book was too difficult—I am naturally drawn to such critics! God has gifted you with a brain, so you have an obligation to exercise it. And some knowledge and understanding are the prerequisites to becoming bioethically savvy and useful.

Again, we start this education process with ourselves. Learn all you

Chapter 8

can while you can. There are no shortcuts here—it will demand a certain discipline, a little sacrifice and some practised application. From now on, it is articles, booklets and books—read, mark and learn from them. The task may seem overwhelming, but it is not. Keep in mind that practical axiom from Isaiah 28:10: 'a little here, a little there'. You are not aiming to become a professional bioethicist, but rather an informed, kind-hearted and productive person who can respond with principled compassion.

Forty years ago, there was virtually no decent Christian literature that dealt with these issues. Just about the only book on abortion was R. F. R. Gardner's *Abortion: The Personal Dilemma*.[2] It was an influential but a confused, and confusing, volume, partly because, under certain circumstances, such as disability, it advocated 'doing all we can to prevent the birth of deformed children';[3] and, for 'the half-caste child', it considered that abortion 'may well be the wisest management for the sake of the fetus'.[4] Nowadays, there are many excellent, thoroughly pro-life leaflets, magazines, booklets, books, audio/video media and websites—see the list of resources at the end of this book in Chapter 10. Today, there are no excuses for not getting an educational grip on these bioethical topics.

We need to grasp a little history and some current trends so that we gain a decent perspective; previous chapters have already described some relevant aspects. We need to learn a few facts. For example, did you know that there were as many as 780 abortions performed every weekday in Great Britain? Or were you aware that tens of thousands of human embryos are being wilfully destroyed each year? And we need to root out some myths. Abortion is not 'simple, progressive and enlightened', as it is so often portrayed. Infanticide is still occurring here, there and everywhere. Eugenics is not something that disappeared with the Nazis in the 1940s. Modern-day euthanasia must never be regarded as either proper medical treatment or a 'good death'.

We may need to change our attitude towards the physically and mentally disabled, the unborn, the elderly, the senile, and human embryos—all those made in the image of God, the bearers of the *imago Dei*. That alone can be a difficult task which will require some conscious severance from this world's thinking.

After educating ourselves, we turn to our families—parents, brothers, sisters, grandparents, aunts, uncles and cousins. And, especially, we must

So what must we do?

educate our children. If we are parents, then, in the economy of God, we are responsible for instructing our children in truth and righteousness. As Proverbs 22:6 reminds us, 'Train a child in the way he should go, and when he is old he will not turn from it.' If we ignore our responsibilities at this point, our children will certainly pick up myths, claptrap and anti-Christian ideas in the playground, classroom and elsewhere, just as they pick up measles. Parents must not abrogate their duties and somehow hope that schoolteachers and others will do their work for them.

Again, if we are parents, we can also check on our schools' sex-education curricula. Did you know, for example, that abortion is now a topic within the syllabuses of GCSE religious studies, as well as Personal, Social, Health and Economic (PSHE) education? How is this taught? Is abortion being implicitly recommended to our children? What about IVF, euthanasia, human embryo experimentation, cloning, surrogacy, genetic engineering and all the other bioethical issues? Without doubt, some of these are being discussed in the classroom. It would be grievous if our children first heard about such topics from a confused teacher, rather than from informed parents. And, do not forget: there are always new opportunities to become school governors who can influence the bioethical ethos of a school; if you volunteer, you will almost certainly be accepted.

We all need to understand the times. We must not be naïve. The British Pregnancy Advisory Service (bpas) may sound like an admirable organization, but it is the largest supplier of abortion in the UK. What about Progress? It is a public-relations operation, sponsored by pharmaceutical giants and others, which promotes genetic manipulation and destructive research on human embryos. Dignity in Dying—nice name, bad aim—is the old Voluntary Euthanasia Society.

We must watch the media and learn to judge its bias. We may fondly think that the UK has fair and balanced broadcasting and news reporting. Wrong. It is too often anti-Christian and pro-choice in its personnel, outlook and output. Even those seemingly wholesome women's magazines, such as *Woman* and *Woman's Own*, can be similar in their editorial stance and feature articles to the more outrageously pro-choice ones, such as *Cosmopolitan* and *Glamour*. I know because, from time to time, I stand in a local newsagent's shop and flick through them. And when we hear on the radio, see on the TV or read in newspapers and periodicals comments from

Chapter 8

spokespeople from pro-choice and other organizations, beware: they can seem so attractive, articulate and convincing. All such hearing, viewing and reading should be done with 'the mind of Christ' (1 Cor. 2:16).

We can help educate our friends and neighbours by talking about these issues; now and again the opportunities arise, perhaps while waiting at the school gate, at the bus stop, in the supermarket car park or at a funeral. Something a little more formal would be to invite a few friends to your home for coffee and cakes and show one of the many good, short DVDs available from the various pro-life organizations—they can be effective conversation starters. And sometimes you will be surprised, and usually pleasantly so, by the reactions of friends and others to these life-and-death issues. Remember, 'be prepared in season and out of season' (2 Tim. 4:2). And do not forget my wife's often timely rebuke to me: 'A gentle answer turns away wrath, but a harsh word stirs up anger' (Prov. 15:1).

We need to educate our churches. Evangelical Christians have been slow off the mark—some are still dawdling around the starting line. Where were the warning voices of the evangelical leaders in 1966, when the Abortion Bill was going through Parliament? The few who did speak up were mostly unheard and mainly ignored. It is only in the last thirty or so years that evangelicals have started to understand these issues and have been prepared to stand up and be counted. In the past, large numbers pleaded some sort of neutrality, which perjured the truth. And churches must never be so small-minded as to make the unmarried pregnant woman or girl so fearful of scandal that she seeks an abortion. These days, thankfully, such episodes occur less and less frequently; Christians must never ostracize or turn away these women.

Ministers and church leaders have a key role and responsibility here. We must not continue to blight the lives of our young people, and the rest of our congregations, by failing to teach them the Bible's foundations and responses to these issues—the biblical credenda and agenda. Too many are still confused about the bioethics of, for example, abortion or IVF treatments, and too few have developed a decent theology of living and of dying so that euthanasia and assisted suicide remain issues of incertitude. How do you expect your people to cope in a Christian way with these issues, which they encounter day in, day out, if you never raise them didactically? No excuses now—my Bible is full of sex, death, forgiveness, rape, families,

So what must we do?

love, conception, weakness, suicide, dignity, fatherhood, hate, surrogacy, disability, infanticide, failure, life, childbirth ... Your congregation needs educating, but ahead of that, perhaps you do too.

Some churches have organized, either alone, or, better still, with other churches in their area, successful day or half-day conferences, or simple evening meetings, on various bioethical issues. What about planning one for your church, your locality, your women's group or your fraternal? There are well-informed, first-rate speakers who would be delighted to be invited—my personal motto has always been, 'Have invitation, will travel!' Such gatherings, as well as being excellent educational exercises, can also be times of constructive fellowship with like-minded others. The outcomes of such ventures can be better-educated Christians and the formulation of local strategies for future collaborative pro-life efforts.

We must never forget that Christians are not immune to abortion, infertility and so on. Some of the estimated 1 in 4 UK women who have had an abortion, and the 1 in 7 couples who are infertile, as well as parents and relatives of the disabled, the senile and the dying, will be sitting in our congregations. And, of course, none of us is exempt from old age—we are the next, or the next but one, generation of the elderly and infirm. The Christian flock always deserves the best instruction and the finest pastoral care.

When it comes to bioethical education, Christians can be quite lazy, untaught, even unteachable, students. It pains me to write it. We think that we can somehow absorb knowledge effortlessly, passively. Books on a shelf can be a great resource, but they do need to be taken down, opened up and read, studiously. Staring at the medicine in a bottle has never cured anyone. To read a worthwhile book properly I have to make notes, even underline the text and add jottings in the margin (but only if it is my own copy), and at its end, I ask myself: what lessons have I learned? Try telling someone else what benefits you have gained—it is a sobering exercise. Attendance at church conferences and other events can be similarly ineffectual—we can easily be slightly entertained rather than seriously educated. Consider the enthusiast, the sportsman, the supporter or the stamp collector: such a person reads, talks, spends time and money on the hobby and is actively taken up by it. So why do we fool ourselves that we will ever attain any decent understanding of these bioethical issues—or, for that matter, a

CHAPTER 8

grasp of any other topic under the sun—if we make no passable effort? Remember the 1997 Labour government's three priorities for the nation: 'Education, education, education.' Go to it!

8.4 We must engage

During the Sermon on the Mount, just after presenting the Beatitudes, the Lord Jesus Christ declared that his people, his disciples, are salt and light (Matt. 5:13–16). Note the two key words 'you are'. Verses 13 and 14 do not say 'you will be' or 'you ought to be'. All Christians *are* salt and light. What remarkable metaphors to illustrate the Christian's effect upon neighbours and culture. But the Lord also warned, in the same verses, that we can become pretty insipid and rather dull: that is to say, we can be poor ambassadors of the King and his kingdom.

So how salty are you? Salt has a wonderful dual property. First, it stops decay and rottenness, and therefore it preserves and safeguards what is good. Second, it seasons, enhances and brings out the best, whenever and wherever it is applied. But to be of any use, it has to get out of the salt cellar—it needs to be sprinkled on, or even better, rubbed in. There is no room here for Christian isolationism. To stop the rot, to sting the evil, to improve our world, to challenge the culture of death, Christians need to be kneaded into society, to rub shoulders with people.

Then again, how bright is your light? It too has a twofold property. First, light chases away darkness and gloom, it exposes untruths and grubby activities and it reveals wicked deeds. Second, it highlights the truth and illuminates closed minds, enabling those around us to see themselves and their world more clearly, the way ahead, the direction to walk in and how to live. And to be of any use, a light must not be hidden under a bucket; Christians must therefore be open and visible, seen by men and women.

Being salt and light mean that we are to combat decay and shine for Jesus. This world needs salt and light, and Christians are the suppliers of both commodities—but how can we ever supply the goods if we fail to engage with potential customers? Then we would be 'no longer good for anything' (Matt. 5:13) and people will walk all over us. Then we might as well ditch our goods, turn out the lights and find a hermitage. No, don't do that.

Do this instead. As card-carrying members of the salt-and-light brigade, we are called to resist evil and to struggle for Christian values (Exod.

So what must we do?

20:1–17; Matt. 5:2–12). And what happens when we stop struggling? Not nothing: non-Christian values win the day. Christians are therefore, by their thinking and responding, to make this world less spoiled, more palatable, warmer and brighter. When Christians disengage from society, when they remain silent and hidden, the world becomes a worse place. If we are insipid and dull, we get the bioethical climate we deserve. And that is precisely where we are today in so many areas of society, particularly in terms of the culture of death. Of course, we bemoan it. Christians have too often become moaners par excellence. But are we prepared to labour to bring about the necessary changes that we long for? If we are to see the regeneration and reformation of our society, we must be those well-seasoned and bright-lit Christian disciples. Stay salty, stay bright.

The civic and political arenas are foreign places for most Christians. Yet we have the franchise and, as good citizens, we should use it, carefully. So often we disenfranchise ourselves and fail to engage with the general public, policy makers, social practitioners and politicians. The early church had little, if any, political power and therefore never really had to face the question of what to do with it; it is quite different for us. We do have political clout. Of course, we should not give our vote automatically to the pro-life candidate; he or she may be dreadful in other matters. But, at least, we should raise some of the great bioethical issues with aspiring politicians as they speak at the hustings or stand canvassing at our front doors. I well remember a parliamentary candidate and his wife having a good old intra-marital ding-dong about human embryo experimentation when I raised the topic after he rang my doorbell—it was obvious that they had never discussed it before. He lost the election, but I like to think he gained some bioethical insight.

We can meet with and write to our MPs, AMs, MSPs, MLAs, MEPs, TDs, congressmen, senators and so on. Have you ever met yours? Resolve to do so before you die, or better still, within the next year or even sooner—it can be such an eye-opener! The timid can form a small delegation. All our representatives hold regular 'surgeries' and your local library and newspapers will have the details of dates, times and places. They cannot be well informed about all subjects, and many will actually welcome some reasoned input. Several years ago, my wife and I visited our MP to discuss human embryo experimentation. However, at the meeting he was more

Chapter 8

interested in the euthanasia issue, so we deftly switched topics and handed him some appropriate literature (always go prepared!). Such visits can do much good. You can at least disabuse our politicians of the idea that to be bioethically concerned and pro-life is to be cranky. After all, who else will speak up for the unborn, the disabled, the weak and the senile?

When writing, or speaking, to those in authority, there are some basic rules to bear in mind. Be polite. Be ready. Be winsome. Remember, the key is communication. If you want to avoid the dreary, standard, photocopied answer, make sure you ask a pertinent question, perhaps requesting some local information or a precise future voting intention. And there is little point in starting a letter as I once saw one written to a former MP: 'Do you not know what the Bible says in Genesis 1:27 ...?' The MP probably did not know, and was unlikely to be persuaded to care much either. Such ripsnorting letters will almost certainly end up in that little filing receptacle in the corner of every MP's office in the House of Commons. Such 'hot' letters may salve the consciences of Christians, but they communicate little, and they advance the cause of Christ and the culture of life even less. Instead, we should be courteous and gentle, yet straightforward and appealing—no trickery, no threats, no browbeating. We are not point-scoring; rather, we are trying to persuade a man or woman that the Bible's teaching on a certain issue, and the ensuing Christian response, is both entirely reasonable and eminently workable, and that if followed, the outcome would be for the betterment of all. Think how true that is, for example, regarding marriage, sexuality, family life and so on.

I have for many years sought to engage with the various MPs representing my constituency. It has not always been easy or successful, but whenever a particular bioethical topic has emerged at Westminster, I have written to or met with them. With my current MP it is going rather well. We email regularly, we occasionally meet in the street, and sometimes he even buys me lunch in the House of Commons. He asks for my opinion on some issues, though he does not always vote the 'right' way. There is mutual respect. But—and this is my point—I had to initiate this contact. And you will too.

Of course, it may be that your MP is pro-life, and even a Christian. If so, make the most of it and support and encourage your MP in the stand he or she is taking. Do not forget that letters of appreciation and cheerful

So what must we do?

support are a pleasure to write and presumably to receive. We are not only men and women with grievances: Christians can be a jolly lot too—and those who have stood up and espoused our bioethical stance, sometimes at considerable personal cost to themselves, deserve our admiration and our thanks, whatever their politics, religion or failings.

Our Christian proclamation always needs to be set alongside an appeal to the hearts and minds of those in our secular society. Evangelical Christians are, by and large, not very good at this. That is not surprising—we lack the practice. We are living in the twenty-first century and most parliamentarians, together with the vast majority of the population, have virtually no Christian knowledge or comprehension—we must remember this. Yet the stakes are sky-high—we are dealing with the specialness of the human race. Christians have an onerous task here. We have been entrusted with both the diagnosis and the cure. Our underlying strength and comfort is that the Christian worldview does possess the correct diagnosis, followed by rugged answers to difficult questions. Therefore, we do, or, at least, we should, have a first-class understanding of bioethical issues. Because we have come to know God, we also know ourselves, and the issues of life and death have become our daily bread. There is so much confusion and heartache within our society, but if we believe that God has a better way for human beings to live and to die, we must present our arguments as attractively and as cogently as possible. We need not fear men or women. And remember, a lisping, stammering tongue is not a sign of the weakness or the falsity of our cause—it is certainly far more honourable than a silent tongue. Recall the directive of Proverbs 31:8: 'Speak up for those who cannot speak for themselves.'

We can check on the activities of the National Health Service and our clinical commissioning groups (CCGs), local health boards and so on. How do you know that an abortion clinic is not planned for your area, or even next to your church building? Shock of shocks, the latter did happen to one pastor I know, though the proposal was eventually vetoed. Does your local hospital perform abortions or IVF? Does it have a policy on resuscitation of the elderly and infirm? Does your nearby university experiment with human embryos? This is not a call for Christians to become a band of snoopers and whistle-blowers, but we all have an obligation to exercise responsible citizenship.

Chapter 8

From time to time, the government and its agencies, such as the Human Fertilisation and Embryology Authority (HFEA), ask for comment on particular bioethical practices, such as preimplantation genetic diagnosis (PGD) or human cloning. Responding to these consultations can be an invaluable exercise, not only in clarifying your own thinking, but also because it is imperative to convey something of the culture of life to those in authority. However, it must be said that responding to such questionnaires has become more problematic in recent years, for two main reasons. First, several once-questionable practices have now become unquestionably acceptable; and, second, ours is a tick-box age. In other words, it is sometimes impossible to object to primary issues in any meaningful fashion. For example, a recent HFEA consultation concerned what were reasonable expenses for surrogates and gamete donors. Because such activities are now lawful, there was no provision to disapprove of them as such—the questions simply moved on to ask about various rates of remuneration. But none of these drawbacks should deter you. It is Proverbs 31:8 again: 'Speak up for those who cannot speak for themselves.'

If you are a trade-union member, do you know your union's policies on these bioethical issues? They may be deliberately ambiguous and non-committal, but they may not be. Some trade unions have become dominated by pro-choice officials and delegates. Check them out. If you oppose their views, stand for election against them.

We can write letters to local and national newspapers. Letters' pages are some of the most popular parts of news media and short, pithy letters are among the most read. You can meet with the editor of your local newspaper, give him or her some literature and talk about pro-life action in your area—a short write-up, accompanied by a good photograph, will usually be gratefully received. You can also contact national and local radio and television stations. Local stations often welcome pro-life comment on news stories and phone-ins, and once you have proved yourself, they will contact you again, and again—sometimes quite early in the morning. Of course, such activities are not for everyone, but I have no doubt that some reading this book could become serious media commentators. It is always refreshing to read letters or hear contributions from the culture-of-life perspective. We all regret that the authentic Christian voice is so rarely heard in the media these days—but do not just complain about it: change

So what must we do?

it! And the digital age has removed all our previous excuses, such as, 'I'm not near a phone', 'I can't find an envelope' or 'I've run out of postage stamps'.

Now, though, some words of restraint. It is possible to overdo this engagement. Some pro-life people—including a noticeably disproportionate number of men—have become so frustrated with seeking to change, for example, abortion policy by democratic means, that they now consider civil, and occasionally violent, disobedience to be the only way forward. A few, in the USA, have even murdered doctors connected with the abortion industry. Such behaviour is to be utterly abhorred and rejected—it requires no further comment.

But what is to be our proper relationship to government and law with regard to these issues? Romans 13:1–7 and 1 Peter 2:13–17 are among the decisive passages of Scripture from which three principles can be drawn. First, God has commanded us to obey the State. Second, God has not set up authority and law in the State that is separate from himself. Both civil government and its laws stand under the law and judgement of God. Third, the State is the agent of justice, to restrain evil and the evil-doer.

Are we then to obey the State no matter what? Matthew 22:21 says, 'No!' The bottom line is that, at a certain point, there is a Christian duty to disobey the State. For example, Shadrach, Meshach and Abednego refused to bow down and worship a golden statue erected by King Nebuchadnezzar (Dan. 3:13–37), and Daniel refused to stop praying to God even though the same king had banned such activity (Dan. 6:10). The early Christians similarly disobeyed when the State of Rome insisted that they worship Caesar (Matt. 22:21; Acts 17:7) and stop preaching (Acts 4:18–20). As the apostles summarily declared, 'We must obey God rather than men!' (Acts 5:29). Therefore, civil governments and their laws are to be resisted only when, first, they command something forbidden by God, such as idol-worship; and, second, when they forbid something commanded by God, such as praying or preaching. Thus, the Bible commands civil law-breaking when the State requires us to sin. But the State has not required, or commanded, us to kill the unborn. Yet abortion is contrary to the law of God. Do we then have a mandate to act against, say, abortion clinics and their staff? No. Our duty is to encourage, not force, others to do what is morally right. So, can we break into and disrupt an abortion clinic?

Chapter 8

No. The violation of a proper law, such as that of trespass, as a means of protesting against a rotten law, such as that of allowing abortion, is unworthy of Christian behaviour. It is the logic of terrorism. But does not, for example, the mass killing of the unborn demand exceptional tactics? Cannot we simply enter abortion clinics and rescue those being led away to slaughter, based on Proverbs 24:11? No. This passage of Scripture outlines an awesome responsibility, not a method. The legitimate methods before us are legion: we can pray, discuss, counsel, debate, entreat, leaflet, visit, broadcast, petition, educate and write. They are enough; so far, we have not done even these adequately.

And always remember this sequence of Scripture: Romans 13 is preceded by Romans 12. Our Romans-13 uneasy, bitter-sweet relationship with government, its officers and all those responsible for shaping and upholding the law of the land is to be controlled by Romans 12. We may regard these men and women as not pleasant and as our adversaries, but we are never to curse them, repay them with malevolence or take revenge against them (Rom. 12:14–19). They may well be our enemies, but our biblical mandate is to treat them kindly—we are to 'overcome evil with good' (Rom. 12:21).

Here is a relevant question: are pro-life and pro-choice supporters destined to be perpetually poles apart, constantly unengaged? Will they continue just to shout at one another, or is some measured communication possible? The answer to the last has to be, 'Yes'. And I want to make the case, even plea, for some engagement, some dialogue. It will not be easy—it never has been—but then most worthwhile ventures are neither uncomplicated nor undemanding. The answer is 'Yes' because common ground does exist. In the realm of bioethics, such basic commonality is rooted in the concept of 'natural law', as expressed in Acts 17, Romans 1–2 and elsewhere, which applies to all men and women: it is 'written on their hearts' (Rom. 2:15). This concord is not exactly obvious because 'of men who suppress the truth' (Rom. 1:18), so clearly there is no current consensus across all bioethical issues. More dialogue, discussion, debate and dialectic would help. Yes, of course, we should engage and talk, and some people will finally make up their minds and others will change their minds. Once, long ago, I did exactly that myself. And, interestingly, I have only ever known people switch from a pro-choice to a pro-life position, never the other way round. I hope this book can foster more of that bioethical transition.

So what must we do?

Finally, we need to settle this issue of co-belligerency, co-labouring and co-engagement. This frightens some evangelical Christians. Out there are many, many people who agree with us that, for example, abortion and euthanasia are wrong. They are the 'morally sensitive', and scores of them are among the nicest folk you will ever meet. There is no compromise in working with them as co-belligerents. I have been a volunteer in the LIFE organization, with its mix of religious people, atheists and agnostics, for more than thirty years and never have I once had to compromise my allegiance to Christ. We are fighting the same bioethical battles. Of course, we may come to them from quite different worldviews. Ecclesiastically, we may be miles apart; we may never agree on the primary doctrines of Christianity. But apart from some of these people, the pro-life flame would have been snuffed out in Britain long ago. We, as rather sluggish, disengaged evangelicals, need to come to these issues with a certain amount of shame and humility; we should have been in the vanguard, but instead we have been a reluctant rearguard. And anyway, working as co-belligerents can be a most refreshing opportunity to get out of our evangelical ghettos and meet some real unbelievers. Try it.

Now you can see that there is no room for apathy. There is plenty to do. You can engage. You can be daring. You can act creatively, thoughtfully and effectively. You must bring your salt and light to these bioethical problems. May we yet prove that 'Righteousness exalts a nation, but sin is a disgrace to any people' (Prov. 14:34).

8.5 We must care

The people of the watching world, despite their own inconsistencies and deficiencies, will readily tell us that there is no credibility to anything we say, do or object to, unless we are prepared to care. We can say that abortion is wrong, but no one will listen if we are not willing to support those with crisis pregnancies. Protesting at 'search and destroy' strategies is good, but it will never be enough unless we are willing to help the disabled. We may declare that infanticide is wicked, but that alone is insufficient. We forfeit all entitlements to condemn euthanasia if we will not assist the elderly and the dying. Words—written, spoken or heard—are never enough. For the Christian, it is an uncomfortable reminder of James 1:22: 'Do not merely listen to the word, and so deceive yourselves. Do what it says.' Or, as the

Chapter 8

King James Version of the Bible punchily puts it, 'But be ye doers of the word, and not hearers only, deceiving your own selves.'

Caring must permeate all our doing. The Golden Rule, spoken from the very lips of the Lord Jesus Christ, is recorded in Matthew 7:12 as 'in everything, do to others what you would have them do to you'. It was deemed to be such important teaching that it was paraphrased to appear in both the Old and the New Testaments, in Leviticus 19:18 and in Matthew 22:39, as 'Love your neighbour as yourself'. This, according to Paul in Romans 13:9, is the summation, the acme and the zenith, of the law. And this Golden Rule is *our* rule. Christians are caring do-gooders.

You cannot read the Scriptures without being struck by the number of times we are pressed to care, to 'do good'. Evangelical Christians have often been guilty of discounting, or at least, demoting, such injunctions. Historically, we have majored on personal salvation by faith alone and dismissed 'works' as having no part in that salvation. And, theologically, quite right too. But, to our discredit, we have gone too far, and minored on the place of 'good works' in our sanctification, which is where they belong, and centrally so.

A few passages of Scripture can help rectify the imbalance in our thinking. For example, Titus 2:14 states that the Lord Jesus Christ wants 'a people that are his very own, eager to do what is good'. Paul, when he bade farewell to the Ephesian elders, reminded them of his labours: 'In everything I did, I showed you that by this kind of hard work we must help the weak, remembering the words the Lord Jesus himself said: "It is more blessed to give than to receive"' (Acts 20:35). Or reflect on Ephesians 2:10: 'For we are God's workmanship, created in Christ Jesus to do good works, which God prepared in advance for us to do.' And Philippians 2:4 reminds us that 'Each of you should look not only to your own interests, but also to the interests of others'.

These can be awkward items on our agenda. Nevertheless, we are to be 'full of good works'. It is simply wrong-headed spirituality to think that the Christian life consists of nothing more than witnessing and evangelism, and that it is for others, the less competent, somewhere in the background, to do the caring thing. A look at the life of Christ will show us how false a notion that is.

Let me give a concrete and very telling example of what I mean. In the UK, an examination of data published by the Department of Health shows

So what must we do?

that the average client undergoing an abortion is a white, single, twenty-two-year-old woman, with no previous children, living with a partner. She goes to an independent-sector clinic with her unborn child of seven weeks' gestation and has a surgical abortion by means of vacuum aspiration, funded by NHS contract, under statutory ground C, the so-called 'social clause'—that is, because of 'risk of injury to the physical or mental health of the pregnant woman'. But when you look at the actual medical conditions that produce the risk to her 'physical or mental health', you do not see multiple sclerosis of the mother, pelvic deformation, diabetes, haemorrhaging, chromosomal abnormality or rubella contact. In truth, 99.94 per cent of all abortions performed under ground C are done ostensibly for neurotic and depressive disorders. No doubt, a few of these are women who need expert medical care. But I suggest—no, I know—that the majority want, crave and need friendship, support, love, and just someone to talk to. These are not women who are manic-depressives or neurotics. These are women—and there are tens of thousands of them—who need some affection and practical care. And maybe you, with some appropriate training, could give that, couldn't you? Yes, you could.

Yet caring is an assorted activity. It need not be heroic or on the frontline—after all, we are very ordinary, not extra-ordinary, people. So, how about doing some shopping or baby-sitting for the mother of four with number five on the way? Or how about visiting, reading and talking with an elderly man or woman? Or how about helping the parents of a disabled child, teenager or adult? Or how about befriending the weak and the vulnerable? And if you can think of nothing you can do, give the smallest, cheapest, simplest gift—perhaps a cup of cold water (Matt. 10:42). Such down-to-earth 'good works' are the fruit of recognizing the inherent preciousness of these people, acknowledging that they too bear the *imago Dei*.

Whenever we care for others with personal problems and difficulties, we do so as those who have ourselves failed. There is no bioethical high ground for us here. It is not our native wit or cleverness that has rescued and delivered us from the culture of death; it is God's grace. Yet there is too often a gaping chasm between our Christian declaration and our Christian doing. I feel that, and I suspect that you do too. One of my family's aphorisms is 'It's easy to say, harder to do'. We may know what the right response is, but have we done it—once, twice, or at least seventy

CHAPTER 8

times seven? It is salutary to remember that some of the Lord Jesus Christ's harshest words were against unfruitfulness, or Christian indolence—check out the parable of the talents (Matt. 25:14–30) and the fate of that lazy, one-talent man.

So the call is loud and clear: we must care. And more Christians are doing just that; they are responding. There are growing numbers of believers taking on leadership roles in pro-life organizations, at both the national and local level, as chairpersons, treasurers, educators, fundraisers, secretaries, counsellors and general helpers. The call, and the need, is not for detached clichés and half-hearted sympathies, but rather for staunch, straightforward Christian orthodoxy and orthopraxy, which is nothing other than that principled compassion—the real PC.

8.6 We must support

There are already pro-life groups in almost every city and town. And if there is not one near you, you know what to do—start one! Remember, once upon a time, every such group began with just two or three founding members. Somebody had to make the first move. There are also superb national organizations. I have been particularly associated with the LIFE charity, as well as with the Christian Institute, but there are numerous others. And none will turn away a subscribing member, a willing volunteer, a positive can-do person, an enthusiastic supporter. Support one—join one.

Support means joining, and support also means giving. We give of ourselves, our time, our energy as well as our money. But my intention is not to rub raw the consciences of men and women. I know that some are already hard-pressed, but I also know that if many of us could cut out, say, just one hour of television per week, we could write that letter, make that visit, phone that person, do that good work. Why not stop now and zip off that overdue letter, put on your coat and make a visit, give a financial gift to a pro-life group, send flowers or a good book, pray, pick up the phone … and make someone's day. And would I urge anyone to do something that I am not prepared to do myself? No, of course not! Accordingly, as I write this, I have just telephoned an elderly friend and I have also sent a donation to a pro-life charity—just three clicks on the Internet. See, it is not that difficult, is it?

So what must we do?

Of course, many people are not wealthy. Nevertheless, it is every charity's experience that it is the poor who are so often the most generous. We are all gifted; there is not one of us who cannot do something to advance the culture of life. And such involvement can be so refreshing and life-enhancing. There are latent talents to be discovered—you may be surprised at how good you can be at producing a poster, organizing a coffee morning, responding to a government consultation, stuffing two hundred envelopes, writing a letter to your local newspaper, and much more.

Women are especially good at being directly involved, for example, in counselling at pregnancy care centres or visiting the elderly. Men can decorate old people's homes, plan pro-life activities, and fetch and carry for fundraising events. Every organization needs extra people for phoning, counting, driving, reading, speaking, cleaning, opening and shutting, selling and buying, serving and clearing, and so forth. And we need not fear about committing ourselves for a lifetime—why not help to begin with for, say, just a year or two? Our circumstances may change, our prospects may alter, but there are always some good works to be done somewhere, and our supporting, joining and giving can become an integral part of our Christian service.

We really must join the struggle. How can we experience being 'more than conquerors' (Rom. 8:37) if we only ever loiter on the sidelines and merely watch the battle? We can do little on our own. Over the years, some individuals and some churches have tried. But they have generally failed, mainly because they lacked the expertise, good literature, proper advice, and so on, that well-known organizations have developed over many years—so why bother to try to reinvent the wheel? Support the already organized, coordinated struggle by throwing in your lot with one of the established pro-life groups.

8.7 So what must we do? In conclusion

These have been five answers to the question 'So what must we do?' They are the Christian's agenda—the things to be done—and they are rooted in the Christian's credenda—the things to be believed. This twofold paradigm expounds the Christian's duty of principled compassion. This dual configuration is where this book began and where it ends—we have now come full circle. From now on, we are to shun the culture of death

Chapter 8

and embrace the culture of life. From now on, we are to develop an ethic of avoidance and an ethic of engagement. From now on, we are to exercise principled compassion.

And when we understand and respond in principled compassion, what will be the outcome? It will be little communities of people who still maintain the dignity and worth of all human life, whether pre-born, born or approaching its natural end. We will be those life-affirming people who cherish the young and the old, who respect the big and the small, who care for all those who bear the *imago Dei*.

May God grant us the wisdom and energy to accomplish all this. In our striving to be head-heart-hand, bioethically principled, compassionately responding Christians, may we be 'as shrewd as snakes and as innocent as doves' (Matt. 10:16).

> This day I call heaven and earth as witnesses against you that I have set before you life and death, blessings and curses. Now choose life, so that you and your children may live and that you may love the LORD your God, listen to his voice, and hold fast to him.
>
> Deut. 30:19–20

Questions for Personal Reflection and Group Discussion

1. What will you now do to further the culture of life?

2. Why do so many Christians respond so poorly to the culture of death?

3. How can you encourage others—family, friends and churches—to join the struggle?

4. When do you plan to meet your MP or representative? What will you say to him or her?

5. How can the Christian begin to discuss these issues with the secular humanist?

6. If there is one thing that would help you respond more effectively, what would it be?

7. What, for you, has been the take-home message of this book?

CHAPTER 9

Resources

The following resources are but a minuscule fraction of those available. The selection is entirely mine—they are my particular favourites, the ones that have helped, and continue to help, me the most. They are certainly sufficient to get you stuck into some further study of bioethical issues. Warning: they do not all come from a pro-life perspective because we should also be acquainted with what the 'enemy' is thinking. Happy hunting!

9.1 Books

I have read all of the books listed here, and many more besides; these are among the best available.
- Burleigh, Michael, *Death and Deliverance: 'Euthanasia' in Germany 1900–1945* (Cambridge: Cambridge University Press, 2002)
- Grudem, Wayne, *Politics According to the Bible: A Comprehensive Resource for Understanding Modern Political Issues in Light of Scripture* (Grand Rapids: Zondervan, 2010)
- Jones, David A., *The Soul of the Embryo: An Enquiry into the Status of the Human Embryo in the Christian Tradition* (London: Continuum, 2004)
- Keown, John, *Euthanasia, Ethics and Public Policy: An Argument Against Legalisation* (Cambridge: University of Cambridge, 2002)
- Ling, John R., *The Edge of Life: Dying, Death and Euthanasia* (Leominster: Day One, 2002)
- Nilsson, Lennart, *A Child Is Born* (London: Jonathan Cape, 2010)
- Schaeffer, Francis A., and Koop, C. Everett, *Whatever Happened to the Human Race?* (British edn: London: Marshall, Morgan & Scott, 1983; revised US edn: Wheaton, IL: Crossway, 1979)
- Warnock, Mary, *An Intelligent Person's Guide to Ethics* (London: Duckworth, 2006)
- Winston, Robert, *A Child Against the Odds* (London: Bantam, 2006)
- Wyatt, John, *Matters of Life and Death* (Nottingham: IVP, 2009)

CHAPTER 9

9.2 Journals and magazines

I scan several scientific and medical journals regularly. *Nature*, *New Scientist* and *Science* (all weekly) and *Scientific American* (monthly) are available in the current publications section of most public libraries. In addition, the medical journals I read weekly are the *British Medical Journal*, *The Lancet* and *The New England Journal of Medicine*. Daily newspapers and various periodicals, from *Woman's Own* to *Time* magazine, can also be useful.

9.3 Worldwide websites

The Web is a source of billions of articles and comments, but it must be said that the vast majority of them are pretty poor, unreliable and unsuitable. The following is an abridged list of the sites I search frequently, as well as some I refer to infrequently. They are all excellent providers of reliable, but not necessarily pro-life, information.

GENERAL BIOETHICS

- American Medical Association, the official site for US medical thinking and practice: www.ama-assn.org/ama/home.page
- British Medical Journal, one of the best searchable, weekly sites available: www.bmj.com
- *Nature*, the weekly, prestigious science journal: www.nature.com
- Nuffield Council on Bioethics, a useful site for seeing general trends in bioethical thinking: www.nuffieldbioethics.org

PRO-LIFE ORGANIZATIONS

- Center for Bioethics & Human Dignity, a daily updated US site with some good essays on key issues: www.cbhd.org
- Christian Action, Research and Education (CARE), Christian perspective on bioethical issues and much, much more: www.carenotkilling.org.uk
- The Christian Institute, bioethical campaigning and educating information, plus many useful links: www.christian.org.uk
- Christian Medical Fellowship, bioethical issues for doctors, nurses and others: www.cmf.org.uk

RESOURCES

- LIFE, the UK's foremost pro-life organization with press releases, facts and figures, some especially designed for students: www.lifecharity.org.uk
- National Right to Life Committee, the USA's major pro-life organization, with news, facts and articles: www.nrlc.org

ABORTION

- Abortion statistics for England and Wales: www.gov.uk/government/collections/abortion-statistics-for-england-and-wales
- Abortion statistics for Scotland: www.isdscotland.org/Health-Topics/Sexual-Health/Abortions
- Guttmacher Institute, the USA pro-choice organization with facts about reproductive-health research, policy analysis, etc: www.guttmacher.org/sections/abortion.php

ASSISTED-REPRODUCTIVE TECHNOLOGIES

- Human Fertilisation & Embryology Authority (HFEA), information from the statutory body on IVF and human embryo research: www.hfea.gov.uk
- LIFE FertilityCare Programme, a pro-life, pro-woman, pro-child alternative to IVF: www.lifefertilitycare.co.uk

EUTHANASIA AND ASSISTED SUICIDE

- Care Not Killing, a UK-based alliance of individuals and organizations promoting palliative care, opposing killing: www.carenotkilling.org.uk
- Dignity in Dying—this used to be the Voluntary Euthanasia Society. Read what 'the enemy' is thinking and saying: www.dignityindying.org.uk
- Patients Rights Council, mainly US updates on euthanasia, assisted suicide, advance directives, and much more: www.patientsrightscouncil.org

9.4 Film library

The Scottish Council on Human Bioethics keeps a list of documentary and drama films with bioethical themes: www.schb.org.uk/films

ENDNOTES

Chapter 1
1 *British Medical Journal*, 27 June 1947.

Chapter 2
1 Francis A. Schaeffer and C. Everett Koop, *Whatever Happened to the Human Race?* (Old Tappan, NJ: Fleming H. Revell, 1979), p. 152.
2 John Calvin, *Genesis* (Edinburgh: Banner of Truth, 1965), p. 91.
3 Ibid., p. 92.
4 *The New Republic*, 16 October 1995.
5 The Warnock Report 1984, section 11.9; available at http://www.hfea.gov.uk/docs/Warnock_Report_of_the_Committee_of_Inquiry_into_Human_Fertilisation_and_Embryology_1984.pdf.
6 'Let Earth and Heaven Combine'.

Chapter 3
1 Francis A. Schaeffer and C. Everett Koop, *Whatever Happened to the Human Race?* (Old Tappan, NJ: Fleming H. Revell, 1979), p. 31.
2 *British Journal of Psychiatry*, 199 (2011), 180–186.
3 *The Care of Women Requesting Induced Abortion*, 2001, p. 45; available at http://www.rcog.org.uk/womens-health/clinical-guidance/care-women-requesting-induced-abortion.
4 *Induced Abortion and Mental Health: A Systematic Review of the Mental Health Outcomes of Induced Abortion, Including Their Prevalence and Associated Factors*, 2011, p. 8; available at http://www.nccmh.org.uk/reports/ABORTION_REPORT_WEB%20FINAL.pdf.
5 Y. Huang, X. Zhang, W. Li, F. Song, H. Dai, J. Wang, Y. Gao, X. Liu, C. Chen, Y. Yan, Y. Wang, K. Chen, 'A Meta-Analysis of the Association between Induced Abortion and Breast Cancer Risk among Chinese Females', at http://www.ncbi.nlm.nih.gov/pubmed/24272196.
6 Westminster Shorter Catechism, reply to Q4: 'What Is God?'
7 *The Times*, 26 May 2012.
8 The Warnock Report 1984, section 11.17.
9 Ibid., section 11.2.
10 Ibid., sections 11.3 and 11.6.
11 Ibid., section 11.9.
12 Ibid., section 2.11.
13 Snowflakes Embryo Adoption and Donation, at http://www.nightlight.org/snowflakes-embryo-donation-adoption/.
14 J. B. Stanford, T. A. Parnell, P. C. Boyle, 'Outcomes from Treatment of Infertility with Natural Procreative Technology in An Irish General Practice', at http://www.ncbi.nlm.nih.gov/pubmed/18772291.
15 Ibid., section 8.1.
16 Ibid.
17 Ibid., section 2.11.
18 'British Woman in International Surrogacy Row', at http://www.bionews.org.uk/page_10738.asp.
19 Ibid., pp. 87–89.
20 Ibid., section 8.17.
21 Ibid.
22 Ibid.
23 Ibid., section 11.13.
24 Ibid., pp. 90–94.
25 Ibid., section 11.15.
26 Ibid.
27 Ibid., section 11.18.
28 Ibid., section 11.15.
29 Ibid., section 11.19.

ENDNOTES

30 Ibid.
31 Ibid., pp. 84–85.
32 Ibid., sections 11.2 and 11.3.
33 *The New York Times*, 22 November 2007.
34 *Nature*, 7 June 2007.
35 *The New York Times*, 11 December 2007.
36 *The Daily Telegraph*, 16 November 2007.
37 *Nature Reports Stem Cells*, 14 August 2008.
38 *The New York Times*, 22 November 2007.
39 *The Daily Telegraph*, 29 September 2010.
40 'Human Cell Systems', at http://www.millipore.com/stemcell/flx4/human-cell-systems#tab1=3.
41 *The Lancet,* 372 (2008), 2023–2030.
42 *New England Journal of Medicine*, 363 (2010) 147–155.
43 'Geron to Focus on Its Novel Cancer Programs: Company Plans to Partner All Stem Cell Programs', at http://ir.geron.com/phoenix.zhtml?c=67323&p=irol-newsArticle&ID=1635764.
44 Fergus Walsh, 'UK Medics Lead Europe's First Embryonic Stem Cell Trial', 22 September 2011; at http://www.bbc.co.uk/news/mobile/health-15017664.
45 'Advanced Cell Technology Achieves Clinical Milestone,' 8 January 2013; at http://www.advancedcell.com/news-and-media/press-releases/advanced-cell-technology-achieves-clinical-milestone/index.asp.
46 *Science,* 338 (2012), 971-975.
47 *Nature*, 505 (2014), 641–647.
48 *Nature*, 374 (1995), 302–304.
49 *Nature*, 368 (1994), 572.
50 Mary Warnock, *An Intelligent Person's Guide to Ethics* (London: Duckworth, 1998), p. 108.
51 M. Spriggs, 'Lesbian Couple Create a Child Who Is Deaf Like Them', *Journal of Medical Ethics,* 2002; at http://jme.bmj.com/content/28/5/283.full.
52 'Baby Created to Save Older Sister', BBC News, 4 October 2000; at http://news.bbc.co.uk/1/hi/health/954408.stm.
53 'Go-Ahead for Designer Baby', BBC News, 22 February 2002; at http://news.bbc.co.uk/1/hi/health/1836523.stm.
54 'Couple Hope "Designer Baby" Helps Others', BBC News, 4 May 2006; at http://news.bbc.co.uk/1/hi/england/leicestershire/4973028.stm.
55 Counsyl, at https://www.counsyl.com.
56 *The Irish Times*, 17 October 2013.
57 *Histories*, 5.5.
58 Jonathan Glover, *Causing Death and Saving Lives* (Harmondsworth: Pelican, 1977).
59 Ibid., p. 156.
60 Helga Kuhse and Peter Singer, *Should the Baby Live? The Problem of Handicapped Infants* (Oxford: Oxford University Press, 1985).
61 Ibid., p. 196.
62 Alberto Giubilini and Francesca Minerva, 'After-Birth Abortion: Why Should the Baby Live?' in *Journal of Medical Ethics*, 2012; available at http://jme.bmj.com/content/early/2012/03/01/medethics-2011-100411.full.
63 *New England Journal of Medicine*, 289 (1973), 885–894.
64 Ibid., 352 (2005), 959–962.
65 'Chinese Officials Held over Baby Death', BBC News, 22 September 2000; at http://news.bbc.co.uk/1/hi/world/asia-pacific/937991.stm.
66 *Canadian Medical Association Journal,* 183 (2011), 1374–1377.
67 Neil M. Gorsuch, *The Future of Assisted Suicide and Euthanasia* (Princeton: Princeton University Press, 2006), p. 195.

Endnotes

68 John R. Ling, *The Edge of Life: Dying, Death and Euthanasia* (Leominster: Day One, 2002).
69 *New England Journal of Medicine*, 342 (2000), 551–556.
70 At http://knmg.artsennet.nl/Publicaties/KNMGpublicatie/Position-paper-The-role-of-the-physician-in-the-voluntary-termination-of-life-2011.htm.
71 'Debbie Purdy Wins House of Lords Victory to Have Assisted Suicide Law Clarified', *The Daily Telegraph*, 31 July 2009; at http://www.telegraph.co.uk/news/uknews/law-and-order/5942603/Debbie-Purdy-wins-House-of-Lords-victory-to-have-assisted-suicide-law-clarified.html.
72 At http://www.cps.gov.uk/publications/prosecution/assisted_suicide_policy.html.
73 Available under 'Assisted Suicide: Responding to Patient Requests: Guidance for Doctors in England, Wales and Northern Ireland (PDF)', at http://bma.org.uk/search?query=assisted%20suicide.
74 *The Guardian*, 5 February 1993.
75 Peter Singer, *Rethinking Life and Death: The Collapse of Our Traditional Ethics* (New York: St Martin's, 1995), p. 1.
76 *Cancer Pain Relief and Palliative Care*, 1990, p. 55.
77 *The Daily Telegraph*, 5 September 2002.
78 Cambridge: Cambridge University Press, 1994.
79 Anthony Storr, *The Times*, 24 November 1994.

Chapter 4

1 *New Scientist*, 108 (1985), 17.
2 http://www.abortionrights.org.uk/index.php/about-us.
3 *New Society*, 7 January 1982, 13–15.
4 Mary Warnock, *An Intelligent Person's Guide to Ethics* (London: Duckworth, 1998), p. 37.

Chapter 5

1 *The New York Times*, 20 June 2005.
2 The Warnock Report 1984, section 11.9.
3 Robert Winston, *A Child Against All Odds* (London: Bantam Press, 2006), p. 76.
4 Prism, 1 (1973), 13.
5 Quoted by the *Pacific News Service*, January 1978.
6 Helga Kuhse and Peter Singer, *Should the Baby Live? The Problem of Handicapped Infants* (Oxford: Oxford University Press, 1985), p. 195.
7 John Calvin, *Genesis* (Edinburgh: Banner of Truth, 1965), p. 293.
8 Peter Singer and Deane Wells, *The Reproduction Revolution: New Ways of Making Babies* (Oxford: Oxford University Press, 1984), p. 98.
9 The Warnock Report 1984, section 11.5.
10 Leon W. Browder, *Developmental Biology* (New York: Saunders College, 1984), pp. 609, 615.
11 *American Heritage Medical Dictionary* (Boston: Houghton Mifflin Co., 2007).
12 The Warnock Report 1984, section 11.19.
13 Ibid.
14 Ibid.
15 Ibid., section 11.5.
16 Ibid.
17 Mary Warnock, *The Spectator*, 27 July 1984.
18 William J. Larsen, *Human Embryology* (Philadelphia: Elsevier/Churchill Livingstone, 2001), p. 4.
19 Keith L. Moore, T. V. N. Persaud and Mark G. Torchia, *The Developing Human: Clinically Oriented Embryology* (Philadelphia: Saunders, 2013), p. 13.

ENDNOTES

Chapter 6

1 David Paintin, *Abortion Law Reformers: Pioneers of Change* (Stratford-upon-Avon: bpas, 2007), p. 35.
2 *The Spectator,* 21 May 2008.
3 Abby D. Phillip, 'A Supreme Court Abortion Fight Could Come in Time for 2016 Elections', 26 July 2013, ABC News; at http://abcnews.go.com/Politics/wins-supreme-court-abortion-fight/story?id=19777200.

Chapter 7

1 'RCOG Statement on Article "Abortion Crisis as Doctors Refuse to Perform Surgery" (Independent, 16 April 2007)', at http://www.rcog.org.uk/printpdf/1430.
2 Quoted in *New Scientist and Science Journal,* 16 September 1971.

Chapter 8

1 John R. W. Stott, *Issues Facing Christians Today* (London: Marshall Pickering, 1990), p. 75.
2 R. F. R. Gardner, *Abortion: The Personal Dilemma* (Exeter: Paternoster, 1972).
3 Ibid., p. 200.
4 Ibid., p. 192.

INDEX

Abortion, 58, 237
—Abortion Act 1967, 58, 217, 237, 246
—abortion–breast cancer (ABC) link, 71
—Abortion Law Reform Association (ALRA), 241
—'after-birth abortion', 163
—backstreet abortion, 76, 242
—disabilities and ground E abortion, 61, 67, 74, 144, 250
—early medical abortion (EMA), 62, 76, 79, 251
—grounds, 61, 248
—'hard cases', 50, 74, 218, 242
—in USA, 252, 261
—mental health, 61, 69, 242, 245, 248, 297
—post-abortion syndrome (PAS), 69
—statistics, 59, 61, 79, 250
Abstinence, 80, 267
Adoption, 73, 96, 104
Advance directives, 193
Advanced Cell Technology (ACT), 128
'After-birth abortion'—see under *Abortion*
Ageing, 275
Agenda, 29, 221, 280
Alzheimer's disease, 28, 112, 122, 140
Amniocentesis, 145, 149, 167
Arthur, Leonard, 171, 219
Assisted-reproductive technologies (ARTs), 82, 107
Assisted suicide, 174
Austin, Claire, 102
Autonomy, 45, 175, 212

Backstreet abortion—see under *Abortion*
Beginning of human life, 36, 221

Belgian Euthanasia Act 2002, 178, 182, 195
'Best interests', 26, 105, 153, 169, 176, 189, 193
Bland, Anthony, 188
Blastocyst, 43, 84, 117, 231, 235
Bourne, Aleck, 244, 254
BRCA genes, 148, 271
British Medical Association (BMA), 24, 186, 192, 236
Brown, Louise, 82, 87
Burdensome medicine, 164, 197
Burleigh, Michael, 194

Calvin, John, 15, 33, 229
Cano, Sandra (Mary Doe), 254
Castillo, Claudia, 126
Cell nuclear replacement (CNR), 115
Chalcedonian formula, 40
Chlamydia trachomatis, 28, 82, 268
Chorionic villus sampling (CVS), 145, 149, 167
Christian Medical Fellowship, 260
Chromosomes, 43, 132, 143, 234
Clapham Sect, 16, 256
Cloning, 115
—reproductive, 98, 118, 130
—therapeutic, 116, 118, 124
Co-belligerency, 55, 256, 295
Conception, 24, 36, 63, 144, 232, 234, 266
Conscientious objection, 182, 248, 261, 264
Consequences and principles, 210
Contraception, 63, 110, 233, 243, 267
Credenda, 29, 31, 54, 221, 280
Crick, Francis, 132, 167, 227
Culture of death, 24, 57, 259, 281, 299
Culture of life, 23, 33, 263, 278, 300
Cystic fibrosis, 140, 143, 150

308 Bioethical Issues

Index

Death and dying, 29, 46, 178, 197
Declaration of Geneva 1948, 24, 234
Declaration of Helsinki 2008, 120
Demography, 272
Deoxyribonucleic acid (DNA), 112, 132, 258, 270
Department of Health, 59, 67, 218, 250
Designer baby, 135, 149, 157
Dignitas 'clinic', 179, 185
Dignity in Dying, 175, 184, 187, 285
Disabilities and ground E abortion—see under *Abortion*
Doe v. Bolton, 254
Dolly the clone, 115
Donaldson Committee Report (2000), 118
Down's syndrome, 66, 134, 140, 145, 149, 171
Duchenne muscular dystrophy, 140, 145, 150
Dutch Euthanasia Act 2001, 180

Early medical abortion (EMA)—see under *Abortion*
Ehrlich, Paul, 272
Elective single-embryo transfer (eSET), 92
Ellenborough Act 1803, 233, 238
Embryo, 26, 36, 43, 83, 115, 121, 209, 221, 234
 —adoption, 94
 —experimentation, 107, 135
 —fates, 89
Embryonic stem-cell treatments, 127
Emergency hormonal 'contraception' (EHC), 63, 218, 233
ENCODE project, 133
Epigenetics, 133, 271
Eugenics, 26, 67, 108, 133, 151, 162, 219, 241, 276
European Convention on Human Rights (ECHR) 1950, 213
Euthanasia, 23, 26, 47, 174

Evangelical churches, 19, 55, 247, 259, 286, 295
Exodus 21, 49

Falconer, Charles, 185
Families, 29, 92, 101, 107, 195, 213, 242, 251
Farquharson, Mr Justice, 171
Fatherhood, 83, 86, 92, 101, 252
Fertility rate, 273
Fertilization, 36, 43, 232, 234
Fourteen-day rule, 84, 110, 114, 222, 228, 230
Futile medicine, 164, 197

Galton, Francis, 134
Gamete intra-fallopian transfer (GIFT), 85
Gardner, Rex F. R., 284
Gene therapy, 110, 113, 158
Genetic defects, 28, 91, 147
Genetic engineering, 132, 158, 278
Genetic screening, 135, 141, 158
Genomic medicine, 269
Germline gene therapy, 113, 137, 159, 162
Geron Corporation, 128
Gestation, 144
Glover, James, 168
Golden Rule, 23, 202, 296
Good works, 296
Gradualism, 41, 224
Groningen Protocol, 26, 169, 173

Handicap and disability, 50, 62, 67, 74, 135, 139, 144, 151, 167
'Hard cases', 50, 74, 218, 242
Hardy–Weinberg principle, 135
Hawking, Stephen, 35
Head-heart-hand affair, 30, 204, 205, 280, 300

Bioethical Issues   **309**

Index

Hegel, Georg, 237, 256
Hippocratic Oath, 23, 73, 139, 165, 189, 201, 216, 224
Hitchens, Christopher, 16
Hospices, 190, 217, 278
Human-admixed embryos, 112, 129, 252
Human cloning, 110, 115
Human embryo, 26, 36, 83, 89, 99, 107, 121, 209, 221
Human embryo 'spares', 84, 88, 107
Human embryo experimentation, 107, 135, 222
Human Fertilisation and Embryology Act 1990, 61, 84, 93, 104, 107, 110, 111, 118, 167, 232, 249
Human Fertilisation and Embryology Act 2008, 93, 111, 113, 251
Human Fertilisation and Embryology Authority (HFEA), 84, 112, 147, 153, 157, 251
Human genetic experimentation, 132, 158, 276
Human genetics, 132, 156
Human Genome Project, 132, 158, 258, 269
Human life, 24, 32, 99, 221, 300
Human Reproductive Cloning Act 2001, 117
Human Rights Act 1998, 213
Hwang, Woo Suk, 118

Illegitimacy, 29, 249
Imago Dei, 33, 136, 203, 207, 211, 258, 287, 300
Implantation, 232, 235
In vitro fertilization (IVF), 65, 82, 100, 107, 110, 124, 147, 151
Induced pluripotent stem (iPS) cells, 117, 123
Infant Life (Preservation) Act 1929, 228, 239, 245
Infanticide, 26, 48, 74, 163

Infertility, 27, 82, 102, 155
'Inside-out' science, 99, 108
Intracytoplasmic sperm injection (ICSI), 85, 91

Joffe, Joel, 184
Johnston, Raymond, 16
Judaeo-Christian doctrines, 23, 29, 37, 43, 73, 165, 280

Kennedy, Ian, 219
Koop, C. Everett, 14, 32, 58, 81
Kuhse, Helga, 168, 227

Law, 24, 54, 64, 93, 104, 186, 205, 217, 237, 293
Lexical engineering, 67, 120, 126, 134, 175, 209, 232
Liddle, Rod, 252
LIFE FertilityCare, 96
LIFE organization, 14, 18, 298
Liverpool Care Pathway (LCP), 193
Living wills, 175, 193
Lloyd-Jones, Martyn, 16

Macnaghten, Mr Justice, 245
Malthus, Thomas, 272
Marriage, 29, 73, 94, 101, 107, 265
Marriage (Same Sex Couples) Act 2013, 101
McCorvey, Norma (Jane Roe), 253
Medical ethics, 23, 60, 73, 114, 173, 215
Medical profession, 23, 73, 191, 194, 202, 215, 246, 261
Mendel, Gregor, 132
Mitochondrial diseases, 112
Monod, Jacques, 34
'Morally sensitive' people, 53, 73, 150, 173, 201, 295

INDEX

Morning-after pill (MAP), 63, 76, 78, 218, 233, 267

National Institute for Health and Care Excellence (NICE), 97, 189
Natural-cycle IVF, 93
Natural Procreative Technology (NPT), 95
Nature and nurture, 138
Nazi Holocaust, 135, 176, 194
'New biology', 232
Nicklinson, Tony, 187, 201
Nilsson, Lennart, 18

Offences Against the Person Act 1861, 61, 68, 233, 239, 245, 248
Oocyte cryopreservation, 94
Oregon Death with Dignity Act 1997, 178, 182, 184
Organ transplantation, 126, 130, 197
Ovarian hyperstimulation syndrome (OHSS), 90

Pain, 175, 190, 195, 198, 229
Paintin, David, 243
Palliative care, 164, 189, 193, 198, 210
Partial-Birth Abortion Ban Act 2003, 255
Pearson, John, 171
Pellegrini, Graziella, 127
Persistent vegetative state (PVS), 188, 201
Personhood, 37, 90, 223, 225, 262
Phillips, Melanie, 189
Piper, John, 17
Politics, 191, 237, 252, 255, 263, 278, 289
Population and demography, 170, 272, 275
Post-abortion syndrome (PAS)—see under *Abortion*
Predisposition, 141, 270

Pre-embryo, 209
Pregnancy, 16, 39, 70, 75, 91, 104, 144, 155, 224, 232, 248, 266
Preimplantation genetic diagnosis (PGD), 97, 113, 147, 152, 219
Preimplantation tissue typing (PTT), 152
Prenatal diagnosis (PND), 26, 67, 74, 134, 144, 149, 219
Prenatal screening, 26, 74, 135, 141, 144, 155
Presuppositions, , 209
Primitive streak, 110, 230
Principled compassion (PC), 30, 53, 203, 211, 259, 280, 299
Principles, 24, 29, 210, 224, 293
Pro-life and pro-choice, 210, 251, 259, 294
Protagoras, 25
Purdy, Debbie, 185

Rape, 75
Regenerative medicine, 121
Regina v. Arthur, 219
Remmelink Report (1991), 180
ReNeuron, 126
Rex v. Bourne, 244
Rights, 24, 36, 45, 54, 75, 175, 187, 213, 253
Roe v. Wade, 253
Royal College of Obstetricians and Gynaecologists (RCOG), 70, 242, 246, 261
Royal College of Psychiatrists, 70
RU-486, 62, 76, 78, 251

Salt and light, 288, 295
Sartre, Jean-Paul, 34
Saunders, Cicely, 190, 195
Saviour siblings, 151, 252
Schaeffer, Francis, 14, 32, 58, 81
Science and scientism, 137, 208, 259

Bioethical Issues   **311**

INDEX

Screening, 139
Scripture, 31, 37, 198, 214, 282, 293, 296
'Search and destroy', 74, 146, 162, 219, 295
Secular humanism, 19, 25, 31, 47, 206, 213, 240, 263
Selective reduction, 65, 91, 251
Sentience, 36, 229
Severe combined immunodeficiency (SCID), 143, 160
Sex education, 80, 267, 285
Sexual behaviours, 265
Sexually transmitted infections (STIs), 28, 82, 266
Singer, Peter, 168, 189, 221, 227, 229
Sixth Commandment, 23, 48, 50, 177, 202, 211
Slavery Abolition Act 1833, 256
Slippery slope, 105, 112, 148, 163, 180, 217
Somatic cell nuclear transfer (SCNT), 98, 112, 115, 124
Somatic gene therapy, 110, 138, 159
Spina bifida, 67, 145, 164
Statistics, 27, 58
Steel, David, 247
Stem-cell technologies, 121
'Stimulus-triggered acquisition of pluripotency' (STAP) cells, 131
Stott, John R. W., 15, 280
Suicide, 176, 243
—Suicide Act 1961, 176, 184, 201
Superovulation, 87, 90
Surrogacy, 82, 95, 100
—Surrogacy Arrangements Act 1985, 104

Teenage pregnancy, 28, 80, 98, 266
Thalidomide, 241
Therapeutic cloning, 113, 116, 119
Thomson, James, 122, 124

'Three-parent' IVF, 112, 163
Transhumanism, 137, 276
Twinning, 231

USA abortion—see under *Abortion*

Viability, 36, 77, 222, 228, 254
Voluntary Euthanasia Society (VES), 175, 184, 285

Warnock, Mary, 83, 138, 220, 232
Warnock Report (1984), 37, 83, 100, 108, 116, 223, 230, 249
Watson, James, 132, 167, 226
Wilberforce, William, 256
Wilmut, Ian, 116, 124
Winston, Robert, 184, 223
Wolf, Naomi, 36
Worldviews, 25, 34, 55, 175, 207, 213, 221, 260, 295
Worth, identity and purpose, 33, 39, 43, 136

Yamanaka, Shinya, 123

Zeitgeist, 31, 77, 137
Zygote, 39, 43, 90, 113, 115, 121, 209, 225, 234

Also available

The Edge of Life
Dying, Death and Euthanasia

JOHN R LING

288PP, PAPERBACK

ISBN 978-1-903087-30-9

From the author of the highly-acclaimed *Responding to the Culture of Death* comes this timely book. *The Edge of Life—Dying, Death and Euthanasia* tackles big issues.

- First, there is the inevitability of dying and death—you are going to die.
- Second, there is that fundamental question—are you ready to die?
- Third, there is the 'hot' topic of euthanasia—always a gruesome practice.

And there is also infanticide, bereavement, eugenics, ageing, suicide, doubleeffect, slippery slopes, hospices, autonomy, living wills, and much more.

Dr Ling analyses these issues within the rugged ethical framework of the Judaeo-Christian doctrines and the Hippocratic oath. The conclusion is that modern medicine has lost its way because it has departed from its historic foundations. Its ethics have crumbled and many of its practices have become corrupted, creating a culture of death. To counter this, the author calls for a return to the culture of life and the exercise of 'principled compassion'.

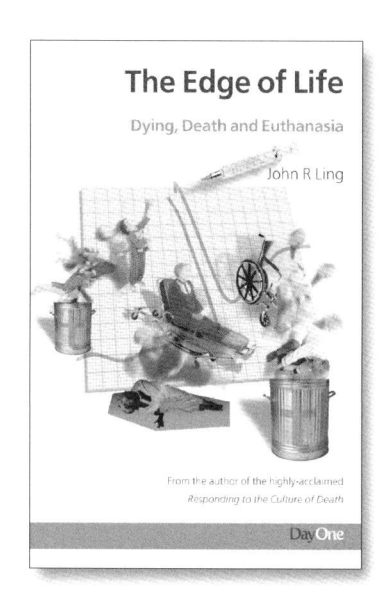

This intensely practical book will help the reader get to grips with these edge-of-life issues. Understanding them enables us to confront and respond to them. Above all, *The Edge of Life* encourages us to think about, and to prepare for, our own dying and death. It is a book to help everyone achieve that last and greatest of all human aspirations—how to die well.

About Day One:

Day One's threefold commitment:
- To be faithful to the Bible, God's inerrant, infallible Word;
- To be relevant to our modern generation;
- To be excellent in our publication standards.

I continue to be thankful for the publications of Day One. They are biblical; they have sound theology; and they are relevant to the issues at hand. The material is condensed and manageable while, at the same time, being complete—a challenging balance to find. We are happy in our ministry to make use of these excellent publications.
JOHN MACARTHUR, PASTOR-TEACHER, GRACE COMMUNITY CHURCH, CALIFORNIA

It is a great encouragement to see Day One making such excellent progress. Their publications are always biblical, accessible and attractively produced, with no compromise on quality. Long may their progress continue and increase!
JOHN BLANCHARD, AUTHOR, EVANGELIST AND APOLOGIST

Visit our web site for more information and
to request a free catalogue of our books.
www.dayone.co.uk